"In my opinion, *Beyond Opinion* is the best book of its kind in print. It was put together by the world's best-known, most widely traveled apologist, Ravi Zacharias, and the world's best global apologetic staff. Characteristic of the Zacharias ministry, it combines intellectual penetration with cross-cultural evangelistic know-how in a comprehensive, complete, and practical way."

DR. NORMAN L. GEISLER
Long-time Dean of Southern Evangelical Seminary
Charlotte, NC (ses.edu)

"Ravi Zacharias is one of the most winsome and persuasive witnesses for the Christian faith today. In this book he brings together a veritable encyclopedia of responses to the deepest questions and challenges believers face in today's world. A wonderful resource for Christ-followers, and a provocative read for all who want to know more about why Christians believe the things they do."

TIMOTHY GEORGE
Dean of Beeson Divinity School, Samford University
and a Senior Editor of Christianity Today

"When I was asked to review *Beyond Opinion,* I feared it would be just another in a long line of multi-authored books in apologetics. Nothing—and I mean *nothing*—could be further from the truth! This book is unique and stands in a class by itself. It doesn't just state problems and list arguments and evidence relevant to solving them (though it does do that); no, the book reads like a conversation. It is a deep, open, honest look into the hearts and souls of the writers as they share their own journeys with all the attendant ups and downs one would expect from authentic people living in a fallen world. And I was surprised and happy to find that the authors all write in the same style so that the book reads like a single-authored volume. *Beyond Opinion* also addresses the topics one seldom finds in a book in apologetics (for example, challenges from youth culture) to include the emotional, spiritual, and social aspects of doubt and struggle. This is a book about spiritual growth and maturity. Apologetic topics are conversationally woven into the broader task of growing as a vibrant, stable disciple of the Lord Jesus. In this way, *Beyond Opinion* will bring apologetical reasoning into the broader Christian culture that is often uninterested in such activity. Once again Ravi Zacharias is to be thanked for providing help to all who are open and honest seekers of the truth."

J. P. MORELAND
Distinguished Professor of Philosophy, Talbot School of Theology,
and author of Kingdom Triangle

"I welcome, applaud, and commend this excellent volume. It is clear in an age that is muddled, savvy in a time that is adrift, and truthful when so many have lost any belief in truth. For all of these reasons it is a most effective contribution."

DAVID F. WELLS
Andrew Mutch Distinguished Professor of Historical and Systematic Theology,
Gordon-Conwell Theological Seminary

"For Ravi Zacharias, Christian apologetics is not just a theoretical discipline, but an intensely personal and engaging way of reaching out to people in the midst of their hurt, perplexity, and anxiety that meets both the demands of their intellects as well as the cries of their hearts. We are to appeal to the whole person: drawing upon the resources of philosophy, science, literature, art, and so on; communicating truth in a dynamic and persuasive manner; looking beneath the surface questions to discern the deeper issues underlying them. In this new book, Ravi and his team admirably model for us this "relational-reality" approach to Christian apologetics."

WILLIAM LANE CRAIG
Research Professor, Talbot School of Theology

"In a world where 'everyone does what is right in his own eyes,' it is incredibly refreshing to read such a commanding treatise on absolute truth. I thank Ravi and his friends for writing with authority on the importance of a biblical world view."

JONI EARECKSON TADA
Founder and CEO of the Joni and Friends International Disability Center

BEYOND OPINION

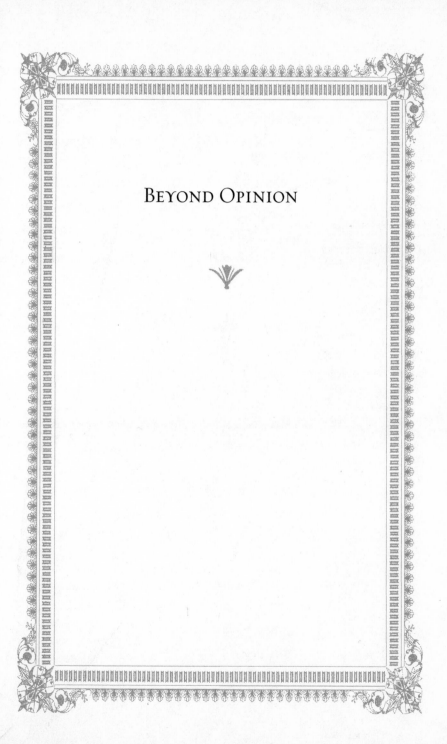

BEYOND OPINION

Living the Faith That We Defend

RAVI ZACHARIAS
Author and General Editor

DANIELLE DURANT
Managing Editor

THOMAS NELSON
Since 1798

NASHVILLE   DALLAS   MEXICO CITY   RIO DE JANEIRO

Published in Nashville, Tennessee, by Thomas Nelson. Thomas Nelson is a registered trademark of Thomas Nelson, Inc.

Published in association with the literary agency of Wolgemuth & Associates, Inc.

Thomas Nelson, Inc., titles may be purchased in bulk for educational, business, fund-raising, or sales promotional use. For information, please e-mail SpecialMarkets@ThomasNelson.com.

ISBN 978-0-8499-4653-0 (trade paper)

Library of Congress Cataloging-in-Publication Data

Zacharias, Ravi K.
    Beyond opinion : living the faith that we defend / Ravi Zacharias, author and general editor
        p. cm.
    Includes bibliographical references.
    ISBN 978-0-8499-1968-8 (hardcover)
1. Apologetics. 2. Christianity and other religions. I. Title.
BT1102.Z33   2008
239—dc22   2007036194

Printed in the United States of America

15 16 17 RRD 12 11 10

To all our colleagues at RZIM worldwide.
Your commitment has been deep; your reach has been wide.
May God be honored in this effort to bring convictions
based on his truth that go beyond mere opinion.

CONTENTS

Contents

INTRODUCTION

AN APOLOGETIC FOR APOLOGETICS

Ravi Zacharias

The word *apologetics* often creates immediate discussion. To the uninitiated in the discipline, the common line is "What are you apologizing for?" To the one who knows and understands the discipline, simply raising the topic evokes debate.

I remember the first time I laid my hands on a text discussing the role and place of apologetics; I could not put it down. It is hard to pinpoint the exact reason I was engrossed in the subject. Was it because I was the product of my culture? I knew that Christians were in the minority, and on every corner I was asked to defend the "why" of my newfound faith. Was it because I was debating these issues within myself? Was it because God himself planned a path for me that I was to undertake in the years that followed? All of these questions had a place along the lines that converged in my personal makeup and calling.

What I did not anticipate was having to give a defense of why I was defending the faith. "You can't argue anybody into the kingdom." "Apologetics only caters to pride, you know." "Conversion is not about the intellect; it is all about the heart." As the litany of questions runs for why we should study apologetics, so the reasons run as to why we should stay out of it.

Apologetics is a subject that ends up defending itself. The one who argues against apologetics ends up using argument to denounce argument. The one who says apologetics is a matter of pride ends up proudly defending one's own impoverishment. The one who says conversion is a matter of the heart and not the intellect ends up presenting intellectual arguments to convince others of this position. So goes the process of self-contradiction.

I am convinced, in the words of C. S. Lewis—who in my estimation is probably the greatest Christian apologist in recent memory—that the question of being an apologist is not so much whether you use an apologetic in answering someone's question, but whether the apologetic you already use is a good one.

When the publisher contacted me to write on this subject, I spent many months thinking about how best to approach something as vast as this. Does any one person really have all the answers to the questions that surface? Some time ago, I recall looking for my gate at an airport. When I arrived there, I rechecked my boarding pass and noticed that the flight number on the marquee at the gate did not match the flight number or the destination that my pass indicated. So I looked at the lady sitting closest to the waiting area and said, "Excuse me, ma'am, but is this the gate for the flight to Atlanta?" She assured me that indeed it was and that they just had not posted the right information yet. I thanked her and started to walk away to find a quiet place to sit. I heard some hurried footsteps behind me and turned to see who it was. It was the lady of whom I had asked the question. She rather shyly asked, "Excuse me, but are you Ravi Zacharias?" "I am," I answered with a smile. "Oh my!" she gasped. "I hear you on the radio all the time, and I didn't know you had questions too." We both chuckled.

I thanked her for the compliment and added, "I have a lot of questions, especially when I'm heading home. I simply cannot afford to miss my flight back to where I belong."

That answer, though tongue-in-cheek, incidentally buttressed how my life has been encapsulated in this calling as an apologist. We are all longing to not miss a turn on our journey home. And on that journey we are often at the mercy of conflicting indications. How do we get to the right destination and not wander afield in some far-off territories?

WHERE WE ARE HEADING

The ultimate calling upon the follower of Christ is to live a life reflecting who he is, and in this book we will highlight three components of discipleship. In part 1, we will look at skeptics'—and believers'—difficult questions. We will suggest that we cannot begin to understand these questions until we ourselves have also wrestled with them intellectually and personally. In part 2, we see that our answers must then be internalized—the essential, lifelong process of spiritual transformation—such that, as seen in part 3, these answers may be lived out with compassion for the lost and a passion for the gospel. These are critical issues, for as I have said many times, I have little doubt that the single greatest obstacle to the impact of the gospel has not been its inability to provide answers, but the failure on our part to live it out.

Ravi Zacharias International Ministries (RZIM) is dedicated to responding to the questions of our time. Malcolm Muggeridge once said that all new news is old news happening to new people. He was right; even as Solomon said, "There is nothing new under the sun" (Eccl.1:9). All that has happened before so often happens again. But in quoting that verse, we forget something very important. The people to whom it is happening are new, and the answers, however old, must never sound stale.

Those two key realities sum up an effective apologetic: how to relate to the questioner and how to make sure that the answers are couched in a relevant context. If we miss those two converging lines, we miss the moment of opportunity. At the peak of my ministry's call, I reflected long and hard on how best to combine these two elements in apologetics. The blueprint was not easy to imagine, and the even greater challenge was building according to the vision. For some people, the hard questions never surface. Life is complicated enough—why complicate it in the questioning? But then there are others for whom every issue has to be carefully deliberated.

Years ago, there was a popular book intriguingly titled *Zen and the Art of Motorcycle Maintenance*.[1] Without going into the details of the story line, the backdrop to the narrative is two different types of riders: the classicist for whom the nuts and bolts of the motorcycle mattered as he journeyed, and the romanticist for whom the enchantment of the journey was all-engrossing—never mind how the motorcycle worked, so long as it did. Ah! But there was the rub. Journeying together, the two could have a wonderful complementariness. Life has both sides. When the machine broke down, the romance of the ride didn't fix the machine. How to put it back together was critical if one were to move on. At the same time, life is not just a how-to manual; there is an instinct and intuitiveness to living.

We at RZIM have found this to be true as we have journeyed across the globe. Not everything is argued. Some realities are felt deeply in a "soulish" sense. Apologetics should therefore respect those elements without violating the absoluteness of God's person and his revealed Word in the Holy Scriptures, and consummately in his Son, Jesus Christ.

There is no greater example in apologetics than the apostle Paul speaking at Mars Hill. The irony of the talk Paul gave is in the difference in reaction the Easterner has when reading Paul's address to that of a Westerner. The Easterner is thrilled at how the apostle wove the message starting from where the listeners were to bring them to where he was in his thinking. The average Westerner is quick to point out that few of his hearers responded. Such an attitude says volumes about why the church in the West has been so intellectually weak. To those in the West, the bigger the number of respondents, the more replicated the technique. The bigger the statistic, the greater the success. Westerners are enamored by size, largesse, number of hands raised, and so on. When the sun has set on these reports, we seem rather dismayed when statistics show the quality of the life of the believer is no different from that of the unbeliever.

As harsh as it sounds, I doubt Jesus' method of apologetics would have appealed to many of us living in the West. I mean, just think of the opportunity Jesus lost when he was asked, "What good thing must I do to get eternal life?" (Matt. 19:16). Is there an evangelist we know of who would have questioned the question, rather than sit down to the task of "closing the deal" with the questioner? We are so eager to pull in the net that we have failed to understand why we are pulling it and for *whom!*

Sometime in the 1980s, Christians in the West began to label evangelistic techniques and reconfigure church services to reduce the message to the lowest level of cognition in the audience. As nobly intentioned as that was, the end result was the lowest level of writing and gospel preaching one could imagine. Mass media was brought to aid this purpose, and before long evangelicals were seen to be masters in entertainment and minimalists in thought. As this was happening, the intellectual arenas were being plundered and young minds gradually driven away from their "faith" in the gospel message. Christians are paying our dues today and likely will pay for an entire generation.

My intention in describing this is not to be critical, because many of us were enamored by huge churches and left the ranks of our youth unprepared for what rabid intellectualism and hedonism were doing at the same time, harnessing the same media for their own purposes.

Let's be candid. In terms of the imagination, the spiritual world cannot match the sensual world because gratification in the sensual is immediate; in the spiritual, it is delayed. A Christian who takes the intellectual track is often rebuked with this verse in 1 Corinthians: "My message and my preaching were not with wise and persuasive words, but with a demonstration of the Spirit's power" (2:4). Some people take that to infer that Paul made a mistake in coming to the Athenians in Acts 17 with a philosophical bent. However, this verse to the church at Corinth implies nothing of the kind. In fact, Paul reminds us to become all things to all people (1 Cor. 9:22), meaning that you start with where the audience is. If there is an intellectual barrier, you start there. If there is a sensory barrier, you start there. If anything, Paul had to spend so much time writing an apologetic to the Corinthian church, arguing about all the problems that had arisen, because they had mindless commitments that harnessed their senses without harnessing their rationality.

Is it not amazing to us that two of the chief defenders of the faith in the Old Testament and in the New—Moses and Paul—were both well-versed in the language, the thinking, and the philosophy of their cultures? Is it at all accidental that when the king of Babylon, Nebuchadnezzar, wanted to reshape the thinking of the Jewish exiles, he selected the best of their young men to educate in the language, the literature, and the philosophy of the Babylonians, and then used them to reach their own? He knew what it would take to reach the foreigners in his midst.

We are fashioned by God to be thinking and emotional creatures. The emotions should follow reason, and not the other way around.

APOLOGETICS IS ABOUT SEEING THINGS GOD'S WAY

The apologetic approach we present to you in this book pays very close attention not just to the question but to the questioner. That, in turn, leads to the relevance of the answer. I take Jesus' walk on the Emmaus road as the classic example of his apologetic approach to the times. His disciples have absolutely no idea that they are walking with the Lord himself. The disciples state rather ironically to their traveling companion that he must be the only one who was not aware of all that had happened in the last few days, when, in fact, he was the only one who did.

To the Jewish mind, then and now, history formed a key component of understanding. They saw in history the unfolding drama of redemption. Granted, they misconstrued it in terms of the immediate breaking off from Rome. In that light, the most important deliverance to the Jews was political. Their hopes of political deliverance were dashed when they saw Jesus' rather ignominious death. To this day, the crucifixion is a stumbling block to the Jew, even as it is to the Muslim.

What is Jesus' response to their mood and their question? Follow the story carefully. These two men are very sincere, I presume, and their hopes are dashed. Why? Was it for the lack of miracle or the lack of presence? Not at all. In fact, they described Jesus to their traveling companion, not knowing it was he: "He was a prophet, powerful in word and deed before God and all the people. The chief priests and our rulers handed him over to be sentenced to death, and they crucified him; but we had hoped that he was the one who was going to redeem Israel. And what is more, it is the third day since all this took place. In addition, some of our women amazed us. They went to the tomb early this morning but didn't find his body. They came and told us that they had seen a vision of angels, who said he was alive. Then some of our companions went to the tomb and found it just as the women had said, but him they did not see" (Luke 24:19–24).

The irony of this passage is immense. The disciples were actually telling this story to the one whom, they assert, his disciples went to the tomb and "did not see"—while they themselves were not seeing who it was they were talking to! To make this even more incredible, the Scriptures tell us that the disciples on the Emmaus Road "were kept from recognizing him" (v. 16).

In this shrouded mystery, Jesus said to them, "'How foolish you are, and how slow of heart to believe all that the prophets have spoken! Did not the Christ have to suffer these things and then enter his glory?' And beginning with Moses and all the Prophets, he explained to them what was said in all the Scriptures concerning himself" (vv. 25–27).

Those of us who like quick-fix, romantic answers find this response a bit extreme. Would it not have been simpler for Jesus to just extend his arms and say, "It is I"? Jesus did that at other times and at appropriate moments (see, for example, John 4:26). But this was not one of them. Instead, Jesus did what was needed in this moment: he pointed out to these two disciples a vast context of fifteen hundred years to show why the event on Calvary had to take place. You see, the gospel is a story, a story that needs to be argued. Sometimes the very presence of God is barred by our presuppositions and our intense and constant desire for triumph. We think if we can only see, all will be well. God even allowed Job all the perils and pitfalls of argument before he could "see."

Apologetics is all about seeing. But it is seeing things God's way. So as you enter into this study, you will at times be journeying through the struggles of our culture. At other times you will be in the intense interaction between Islam and Christianity. You will be refreshed by the thrill of why God has revealed himself as a Holy Trinity: one essence in three persons. You will be introduced to the struggles of responding to the hard question of explaining God's power and sovereignty when life is immersed in grief and pain. You will hear God's voice in understanding the power and reliability of his Word. You will be blessed by seeing his handiwork in the sciences and recognize the continuity of his revelation. You will be exposed to some of the brightest minds presenting a defense of the faith and to articulate voices who have taken on the greatest challenges of our time.

APOLOGETICS IS NOT JUST FOR EXPERTS

As we begin, I say this to you as a reader: *do not underestimate the role you may play in clearing the obstacles in someone's spiritual journey.* A seed sown here, a light shone there may be all that is needed to move someone one step further. The truth is that sometimes the more sophisticated we get in our study and understanding of apologetics, the more often we miss the moment and the impact.

I present two illustrations of my own failings, one in the early days of my ministry and the other when I should have known better. I was asked to come and answer the hard questions of a very successful businessman in Dallas, Texas. The gentleman who flew me in said, "I don't know how to answer this employer of mine, but I believe he is very sincere. Please give me an afternoon, and we will cover the cost." So I undertook the journey and anticipated all the hardball attacks that would be empowered further by the fame and success of this nationally known figure in the business world.

We were into the dialogue but a few minutes when he went into a tirade on all the injustices and evils in the world. I could tell that his passion would intensify whenever that became the point of his question. I carefully answered as best as I could from the self-defeating nature of the question to the classical approaches used in responding to the problem, and even the experiential side of it. I shared logic, Scriptures, personal stories, poetry, yes, to use the metaphor—the whole nine yards.

My friend who had brought us together sat quietly and watched for a couple of hours as we went at the issues back and forth. When there was an obvious moment of silence, as the questioner was sort of replenishing his arsenal, this common friend said in a soft voice, calling his boss by his first name, "As I have listened and watched, I have one question for you. Evidently all the aggregate of human evil in this world is very disturbing to you. Yet are you as disturbed by the evil that you see inside of you?"

There was a deafening silence. We could all sense it was a "checkmate" move done with perfect timing and genuineness. The businessman sat back in his chair. He was speechless for a few obviously convicting moments, and all but asked, "How do I get out of this one?" In a sense, the apologetic reasoning had only drawn the man's pride more and more into the foreground. Yet his colleague's simple, self-indicting question prepared the way for the gospel. I learned early that sometimes the arguments can be a long road to setting up the question, but if they fail to bring it home, they can only serve to evade the proximity of the problem.

The second instance was at the Lenin Military Academy in Moscow, where I was speaking to officers and leaders. I was asked to speak on the existence of God. I used all the approaches that I felt I could connect with through an interpreter. Throughout my talk the audience wore a visibly hostile expression. In fact, one man kept giving me the choke sign through my talk. I kept going because I had been invited to speak by the general and so felt secure in my platform. No sooner had I finished than the man giving me the choke sign stood to his feet and rather rudely sputtered out a series of sentences. I could wait to get the interpretation, but the interpreter interrupted him to give him a chance to catch up. Basically his outrage boiled down to one question: "You've been using the word *God* repeatedly. What on earth are you talking about?"

Was I ever in a state of shock! I had made the fallacious assumption that the idea of a first cause automatically meant a "creator" to the audience. In my defense, I was not able to bring an overtly Christian message, but then again I had missed something very basic. Of course, the obvious answer to cause the questioner to stumble was to ask him, "Are you an atheist?" which, of course, he was. So I asked him, "What, then, are you denying?" Fascinating isn't it, how we all define our own terms but wish to deny the other the privilege of questioning those definitions.

These two illustrations clearly point out that if apologetics is to be done effectively, we do not necessarily need the experts doing it; rather, we need to connect with the questioner at a personal level. Jesus consistently drove this home. His one-on-one conversations were remarkably personal and left the other looking into his or her own heart and spiritual condition.

That is what we hope we have accomplished in this volume. We would be in error if we think this will make for a sophisticated apologetics handbook. It is not intended to be that. It is intended to encourage and challenge the nonexpert to feel comfortable talking about the gospel without feeling the burden of needing a high level of philosophical training.

APOLOGETICS GOES BEYOND OPINION TO CONVICTION

May I add one final word? Our team at RZIM functions at multiple levels. Sometimes we are in overtly hostile environments of intellectual resistance, other times in the deeply suspicious world of interreligious dialogue. Sometimes we are in arenas where the very idea of God is in need of explanation. We function as a team and with numerous adjunct and affiliated faculty brought in from around the globe. Every contributor to this volume is either a full-time apologist with RZIM or an adjunct member of our team. Frankly, I am humbled to be working with such a team. I have learned much from them. Some are veterans who have covered this globe for decades. Others were not even born when some of us began. Yes, we have a few team members still in their twenties, who have amazing depth at such an early age with a deep passion for God's truth and calling.

My prayer is that you will be blessed and equipped as you study these pages. This may not be a "read-through" book that can be absorbed in a single sitting. But I suggest to you that it is a "must-read" book for our times. I say this at the risk of being audacious. The world is in some very precarious times. The volatility of the issues that divide us has reached a crisis point. Young men and women are willing to throw their lives away for ideologies. At the same time, a seeking mind wants desperately to find answers. We in this ministry are committed to being present in such settings, and we have addressed these themes in numerous ways. If we don't come to terms with the crisis times in which we live by presenting the beauty and the distinctive message of Jesus Christ, we will fail our time.

The title is well stated: *Beyond Opinion.* Opinions are preferences amid options. Convictions are woven into one's conscience. This book responds to the opinions of people with the convictions that the gospel and its imperatives commend. May God be pleased with this effort and every reader blessed by its message.

PART ONE
Giving an Answer

SECTION ONE
Addressing the Difficult Questions

I

POSTMODERN CHALLENGES TO THE BIBLE

Amy Orr-Ewing

The Bible is a controversial book that evokes both devotion and derision. It has inspired some of the greatest thinkers this world has ever known and attracted the hostility of others. It takes a central role in any study of Western civilization and touches the most unlikely of souls.

The Bible has also been the subject of wild predictions. In the eighteenth century, the French atheistic philosopher Voltaire predicted, "Another century and there will not be a Bible on earth!" What irony, then, that Voltaire's house later became the headquarters of the Bible Society, printing and distributing many thousands of Bibles.

In this chapter we will examine some of the current challenges to the Bible, and in particular, three challenges from the postmodern worldview. By its very nature the postmodern worldview is difficult to define, and some would resist calling it such. It is an eclectic movement, originating in aesthetics, architecture, and philosophy. A postmodern perspective is skeptical of any grounded theoretical perspectives. It rejects the certainties of modernism and approaches art, science, literature, and philosophy with a pessimistic, disillusioned outlook. Questioning the possibility of clear meaning or truth, this worldview is about discontinuity, suspicion of motive, and an acceptance of logical incoherence. As one scholar notes,

The postmodernist critique of science (for example) consists of two interrelated arguments, epistemological and ideological. Both are based on subjectivity. First, because of the subjectivity of the human object, anthropology, according to the epistemological argument cannot be a science; and in any event the subjectivity of the human subject precludes the possibility of science discovering objective truth. Second, since objectivity is an illusion, science according to the ideological argument, subverts oppressed groups, females, ethnics, third-world peoples.[1]

In my experience as a Christian apologist, the postmodern skeptic raises numerous challenges to the Christian worldview and to the Bible in particular. These questions often focus on ideas of power and authority and fall into three basic categories:

1. Theoretical questions about textual authority
2. Historical questions about textual authority
3. Existential questions about textual authority

In this chapter, we will examine each of these three postmodern challenges to the Bible in more detail.

THEORETICAL QUESTIONS ABOUT TEXTUAL AUTHORITY

The postmodern suspicion of any claim to meaning or truth has a dramatic affect on the status of the word in both written and spoken form. We all remember President Clinton's now infamous statement, "It depends on what the meaning of the word *is* is."[2] This statement caused global shockwaves because the most powerful man in the world appeared to be questioning the very nature of language. Sadly, this example has not proved to be an aberration but rather an illustration of the tendency of our age.

In fact, the idea that there is no ultimate meaning in any text has become extremely powerful in a postmodern context, and it has enormous implications for any communication about the gospel. One literary theorist writes, "Literature . . . by refusing to assign a 'secret,' an ultimate meaning, to the text (and to the world as text), liberates what may be called an anti-theological activity, an activity that is truly revolutionary since to refuse to fix meaning is, in the end, to refuse God."[3]

Suspicion of Any Claim to Authority

The postmodern questioner is likely to operate from a base of suspicion and skepticism when presented with a text such as the Bible, which makes a clear claim to authoritative truth. This is not because the individual is particularly hostile toward the Christian or even the church, but rather because he or she has developed within a cultural context that suspects authority and rejects metanarrative (an overarching or transcendent view of the world). For instance, the French philosopher Jean-François Lyotard argues that a postmodern outlook demands a "war on totality"— a fight against any claim to universal meaning.[4] He does this most powerfully in *The Postmodern Condition: A Report on Knowledge*, where he argues that this perspective is marked by an "incredulity towards meta-narratives."[5]

Again, a metanarrative is a large-scale theory that seeks to make sense of the world, such as the onward and upward progress of the human race throughout history, the confidence that everything is explicable by science, or the possibility of absolute freedom. Lyotard argues that postmoderns have ceased to believe that narratives of this kind are useful for understanding reality. Instead, humans have become alert to difference and diversity, so that postmodernity is characterized by a plethora of micronarratives. Here Lyotard draws heavily on the philosopher Ludwig Wittgenstein and his idea that meaning is possible only within language games. In other words, different communities have different rules and principles that govern their discourse, and these do not necessarily translate across different groups. Thus meaning is possible only within a *particular* context or community, and truth should not be understood as transcending these barriers of diversity. When applied by the postmodern as a challenge to the Bible, this may express itself as a rejection that one truth (such as "Christ died for our sins") can be communicated, understood, and believed by all the diverse groups in the world.

Lyotard's suspicion of authority and denial of metanarrative in practice means that any worldview or framework of meaning that provides an overarching explanation of reality—like the Christian belief in the Bible as revealed truth—is attacked and rejected. As we have seen, this rejection applies equally to the modern myth of progress, the Enlightenment myth of rational beings discovering truth, as well as the Christian myth that God made human beings and reveals himself to them. So the postmodern perspective rejects the idea of the biblical text as revealed truth, as a book to be read and understood that communicates truth directly to us and provides us with a worldview from which to interpret reality.

The fundamental problem with this challenge to the Bible—this suspicion of authority and rejection of metanarrative—is that it is essentially inconsistent. That is, we soon discover when probing this denial of overarching stories that an exception is made for the overarching idea that there are no overarching ideas! Postmodern skeptics critique all worldviews except their own.

Authority as Power Play

After hearing a powerful preacher speaking to seven hundred people in a packed Oxford church, a student demanded to speak privately with him. In the preacher's study the young man tore into his host, shouting and swearing in anger at what he had heard. The main objection that the student raised was the fact that anyone would dare speak powerfully and persuasively about an idea. As a postmodern, he saw this kind of speaking as a malevolent force—an imposition of a truth claim on another person, an assault on the individual's autonomy, and something dangerous that ought to be resisted.

This classic postmodern challenge is often specifically directed at the Bible. The Bible is seen as a text that is used to take power over people's lives; its authority is seen as a power play exerted over the weak. The French thinker Michel Foucault spoke of an essential interplay between knowledge and power. Echoing Nietzsche's phrase "will to power," Foucault called any pursuit of truth a "will to knowledge" that arbitrarily establishes its own "truth." This "truth" is then imposed on others, thereby handing over power to the speaker or writer. So the human quest for knowledge is written off as the pursuit of power, and this power for Foucault and other postmoderns is embodied and expressed in institutionalized languages. He wrote, "Power produces knowledge. . . . There is no power relation without the correlative constitution of a field of knowledge, nor any knowledge that does not presuppose and constitute at the same time power relations."[6]

When applied to the Bible this challenge is a powerful one, for is not this religious text simply a tool in the hands of power-hungry individuals who use it to assert authority and strengthen their own hands? Of course the problem with this idea is that it falls into the same trap as many other postmodern challenges: it lacks self-awareness and self-consistency. After all, if Foucault really believed that language and the quest for knowledge through words can be reduced to a power play in the end, how could he communicate such ideas without using words and attempting to persuade us as well? Was he not simply exerting his authority and his considerable power over us? Didn't he become as power hungry as his opponents? Shouldn't Foucault's critique of Christian thought and the Bible be applied to his own ideas as well? When all is said and done, if he really believed his own philosophy, why didn't he remain silent?

Authority and the Question of Interpretation

These postmodern challenges to the authority of a text culminate in the ultimate relativist statement: "Isn't it all a matter of interpretation?" This statement sounds like a question, but in fact, when we examine it carefully, it is a truth claim. It is a claim that there is no one truth, no one clear message. Thus, even when we come to a so-called revealed or inspired text like the Bible, the claim is that there are many valid interpretations of a given text, hence absolute truth eludes us again.

The postmodern challenge I have heard on numerous occasions goes something like this: "You don't mean to say that you take the Bible *literally,* do you?" I love to answer with the words of a great Christian who was asked this question and reportedly replied, "The Bible says that Herod is a fox, but we don't think that means he had pointy ears and a bushy tail. It also mentions that Jesus is a door—which does not mean that he is flat, wooden, and swings on hinges."

This question of interpretation is raised by the postmodern in order to cast doubt on the possibility that real meaning is possible at all. The idea of the non-possibility of clear meaning in a text was most powerfully argued by the postmodern thinker Jacques Derrida. Following Nietzsche, Derrida asserted that if God does not exist, then there is no foundation for language and words are not able to signify or present any given reality. He attacked the view that human statements are representations of the world as it actually is and denied that language could have fixed meaning connected to a fixed reality or that it has the capacity to convey definitive truth. If language has meaning, it causes people to search for "the transcendental signified" (some ultimate word or essence—such as God—truth or reality).[7] Derrida argued that such ultimate things do not exist, yet when turned on its head, what his argument reveals is that in order for postmoderns to reject God, they have to undermine language itself.

After all, if no such "transcendental signified" exists, the meanings of words must arise purely out of their relationship with an immediate context. That is, words have no actual meaning—a word on a page or a word being heard only has the meaning that a reader or a hearer gives it. It does not itself carry any ultimate meaning because there is no God ("transcendental signified") to give ultimate meaning to words. Thus language becomes completely self-referential. Any written document is meaningless because if words cannot be carriers of meaning, and they have no ontological referent, they must derive their meaning solely from the hearer or the reader.

At a popular level, this is often expressed in a simple phrase like "It's all just a matter of interpretation." This is a clever challenge to the Bible and a serious objection to the very possibility of words as carriers of meaning. However, let us remember that this is only a problem if God does not exist. But surely if this were the case, we would not be able to assert his nonexistence using words!

Once again we find a postmodern challenge to the Bible that is not rigorous enough to stand up to its own scrutiny. This idea falls at the first hurdle since it is unable to be communicated or argued without the use of words. How can Derrida tell us that a transcendental signified does not exist and that words only have the meaning a particular reader or cultural context gives them—since he used words to tell us this and expected us to understand them, no matter our culture?

How Christians practice hermeneutics with real integrity is a question for a different book. How we interpret the Bible and uphold the word of truth in our generation is a challenge for any serious student of the Word of God. But before we get there, we must recognize these postmodern challenges to the theoretical possibility of meaning in any text and deal with them if we are to give a reason for the hope within to a postmodern skeptic.

HISTORICAL QUESTIONS ABOUT TEXTUAL AUTHORITY

Having examined some of the theoretical questions about textual authority that form part of the postmodern challenge to the Bible, we will now look at the growing number of historical questions about the text of the Bible. The increasing number of books being produced that claim to rival the Bible—whether they be treatises on little known gnostic gospels or rehashes of medieval forgeries—have caught the imagination of a skeptical public interested in conspiracy theories and the like. As we have noted, the postmodern attitude toward truth makes it increasingly difficult to challenge these rival books and reveal them for what they are. Furthermore, a central plank of postmodern thought with regard to history is that we cannot be certain about what happened in the past. As New

Testament scholar E. P. Sanders puts it, "Historical events could not be verified even if we had a video recording."[8]

This rejection of certainty with regard to history is part of a larger movement characterized by disillusionment with any kind of certainty. The philosopher Foucault argued that just like any other form of ideas, historical research can make no claim to be free of the perspectives and values of the historian and therefore to be neutral. He concluded that since the desire to know the past cannot come from a disinterested quest for truth, it must arise from a desire to control the past for some purpose or other.[9] His conception of the will to power through knowledge emerges again, but now with regard to historical narratives. Again this logic failed to meet up to its own standard since Foucault did not subject his own thinking to this idea. Thus, we are left asking ourselves why he tried to dominate and control us with all of these words.

Alternatives to the Bible

Postmodern ideas about history challenge any authoritative version of the past given by the Bible as suspicious and founded in power play. Yet interestingly, the Bible is then compared to flimsy challenges of whacky alternative theories. For instance, the *Gospel of Judas* has been heralded by the Western media as a serious challenge to the Bible. Upon reading it, the archbishop of Canterbury, Rowan Williams, noted, "It's actually a fairly conventional book of its kind—and there were dozens like it around in the early centuries of the Church. People who weren't satisfied with the sort of thing the New Testament had to say spent quite a lot of energy trying to produce something which suited them better. They wanted Christian teaching to be a matter of exotic and mystical information, shared only with an in-group."[10]

According to *The Da Vinci Code*, the church suppressed the real version of events that can be found in so-called gnostic gospels like the *Gospel of Mary* and the *Gospel of Thomas*.[11] These are, in fact, not gospels at all but rather collections of random sayings and stories put together to form a challenge to the first-century Christian gospels. Nevertheless, these sources were compiled and written much later than the canonical gospels, only exist in fragmentary form, and were rejected as specious at the time. Oddly, such facts do not dampen the zeal of theorists intent on casting suspicion on the authoritative versions attested by historical evidence and the witness of the church. This is all a part of the postmodern challenge that can be answered with historical data and a scholarly account of fourth-century Gnosticism.[12] This challenge itself, though, should first be understood as being a product of the postmodern culture.

But How Did the Canon Come to Be?

A further development of the postmodern suspicion of the Bible's claim to historical authority is found in the increasing questions regarding the process of the compilation of the New Testament. Some assert that the emperor Constantine wanted to control his chosen religion for his empire and so insisted on a group of men gathering to determine the content of the Christian Holy Book in AD 325 at the Council of Nicaea. In fact, this was not the purpose of the council at all, and it was much later that a council of the church first met to discuss the canon.

The sources are clear that Constantine called the Council of Nicaea to deal with two specific issues causing disagreement within the church: the heresy of Arianism (which questioned the deity of Christ) and the date of Easter. It was not until AD 393 that a council of church leaders met in Hippo and then again in 397 in Carthage to confirm the canon and counteract early heresies and persecution. It would be a misreading of history to deduce from this that the content of the New Testament was "decided" upon by a group of men in AD 397. As F. F. Bruce writes, "When at last a Church Council—the Synod of Hippo in AD 393—listed the twenty-seven books of the New Testament, it did not confer upon them any authority which they did not already possess, but simply recorded their previously established canonicity."[13]

In fact, the development of the canon was an overwhelmingly organic process. What we discover is that during the lifetime of the apostles, the church grew at a phenomenal rate throughout the Roman Empire. Europe, Asia Minor, and North Africa all boasted growing churches during the first four centuries of Christianity. The books of the New Testament as we have them today were copied and reproduced throughout the spread of the church. This was encouraged by the writers of the New Testament. Indeed, Paul tells the Colossians to make sure the Laodicean church reads his letter (Col. 4:16), and he encourages the Thessalonians to "have this letter read to all the brothers" (1 Thess. 5:27).

The early records show that everywhere the church spread, the contents of the New Testament were known and reproduced. Thus, a Christian could travel anywhere and be welcomed in a distant church as a brother or sister in Christ. Such letters were clearly the means of communication between the distant churches. (Additionally, as noted below, there are many examples of such letters from Clement of Rome writing to the church in Corinth, and of Ignatius writing to various churches on the eve of his martyrdom.) The degree of publicity of the New Testament and the sheer numbers of churches involved in reading and propagating it acted as a protection against forgery and fraud, as any interloper would have had to convince large numbers of people across a vast geographical area. The communion of the different parts of the church with one another across these boundaries meant that mistakes and frauds could be recognized and guarded against.

This means that the manuscript tradition of the New Testament is preserved in a great number of texts from different places around the globe. There are versions in Latin, Greek, Syriac, Coptic, Sahidic, Arabic, Ethiopic, Armenian, and many other languages. This wealth of manuscript material, existing in different parts of the world in different languages, forms an independent witness for a common, original text.

Not only do we have this early, widespread witness to the text of the New Testament in many languages, but we also have clear evidence that by the end of the first century, the books of the New Testament were already regarded as being the Word of God. They did not gain this status as a result of a church council; the New Testament was always recognized as being authoritative. Even at the end of the first century AD, Clement, Bishop of Rome, writes to the church in Corinth and quotes from Paul's letter to the Corinthians as though it had binding authority similar to that of the Old Testament. Justin Martyr quotes from the Gospels and begins his citations with the important formula "it is written"—equating the authority of Paul's letters to that of the Old Testament.

The Greek father Origen, born in AD 185, less than ninety years after the death of the apostle John, refers to the books of the New Testament in a way that exactly corresponds with our present canon.[14] The church father Eusebius, who was born in AD 270, also mentions the various books of the New Testament. He does have some questions about the authorship of the book of James, but they seem to be resolved by the inclusion of this book in the Syriac translation of the New Testament, since Syria bordered Palestine, where James had been the bishop.

Eusebius specifically denounces some heretical literature in his works, naming writings such as *Shepherd by Hermas* and the *Epistle of Barnabas*. One scholar commented, "The recognition of the books of the New Testament as scriptural was overwhelmingly a natural process, not a matter of ecclesiastical regulation. The core of the New Testament was accepted so early that subsequent rulings do no more than recognize the obvious."[15]

Where there were question marks, these were dealt with openly. When questions were raised about the authorship of the Epistle to the Hebrews, again it was in the Syriac canon and mentioned by many of the church fathers and councils. The book of Hebrews was, of course, finally included in the canon. On the whole, the New Testament books made their way into the church naturally and were accepted from the time they were written by the apostles and evangelists by the church across the world. Moreover, those books that were questioned did not come to final acceptance or rejection by fiat or by a group of powerful men. Rather, a consensus emerged in the church either recognizing their authority or rejecting it.

So in conclusion, it is significant to note that the councils of the church that met to confirm the canon and counteract the increasing number of fourth-century forgeries and heresies were a representative group of the geographical breadth of the church. They came to agree officially on what had organically emerged as the original, truthful, untampered writings of the apostles.

EXISTENTIAL QUESTIONS ABOUT TEXTUAL AUTHORITY

Having examined the theoretical and historical questions that form part of a postmodern challenge to the Bible and its authority, we come now to look at the heart of the matter for many people. This is where the true impact of the message of the Bible emerges as a reality that will genuinely mean something in the personal or moral sphere. The postmodern who holds to relativist morality is stunned by the prospect of a book claiming to have authority to speak into the realm of human feelings, choices, and ethics. And so the question comes: "Can I really let a book determine my ethics? Isn't this dangerous?"

The rise of militant Islam in the world scene, and in particular in Western consciousness, has made the question of textual authority more complex to the postmodern mind. Any discussion of a text having moral authority tends to conjure up images of Islamic terrorists citing the Qur'an as their authority for committing outrageous crimes.

A few months ago, I was speaking to a gathering of West Wing staff at the White House. This was an incredible privilege and quite a nerve-wracking opportunity. At the end of my talk, we opened the platform for questions, and they came thick and fast. One question I will never forget came toward the end of the meeting, and as a British visitor to the White House, it was difficult for me to answer. The question was, "The president recently described Islam as a peaceful religion. Do you agree with his assessment?"

Mustering all of my diplomatic energy, I answered that politicians find themselves in the unenviable position of needing to make statements that will build peaceful community relations both in their own countries and abroad. And while I agreed with the American president that many Muslims were peaceful people, I could not agree that *peaceful* was a good adjective to describe the religion as a whole either historically or in the present day. In fact the Qur'an lends itself to a spectrum of interpretation and is used by moderate Muslims to uphold peace and by other Muslims to incite violence.

The globalized situation we find ourselves in means that postmodern questions of textual authority may well be asked interchangeably of the Bible and the Qur'an. For the evangelical Christian, it may be surprising to hear one's devotion to the Bible being equated with a fundamentalist Muslim's reverence for the Qur'an. But this is precisely what has happened. Rather than exposing the pluralist dream for what it is, 9/11 and other terrorist activities have simply confirmed in the minds of many postmoderns that any serious commitment to a holy book is a dangerous thing. It is not Islam in particular that should be reforming itself, they say, but rather any passionate belief in a holy book. And so it is "fundamentalism" that is considered the enemy, and evangelicals are equated with Al Qaeda.

Of course, any serious critique of this view reveals that belief in a book ought not to be dangerous per se. It is only if that book incites violence that we have a problem. When scrutinized, we find that the Bible stands on very different footing than the Qur'an. But this is disputed by some and brings us on to the heart of the matter. Is the Bible a book by which to live? If we take a moral question like that of war, does the Bible have a meaningful, authoritative voice in our postmodern world?

War in the Old Testament

I have frequently been asked by skeptical friends or audiences how I can believe in God when so many wars have been caused by religion. The implication of this question is that if only people would leave behind their convictions about the existence of God, then the world would be a better and more peaceful place. Of course, very few questioners ever reflect on the fact that the exact reverse of this was demonstrated in the twentieth century. Indeed, in this last century, the atheistic communist and Nazi ideologies gave rise to more killing than the previous nineteen centuries put together. However, this is not to say that war and violence are not real questions with regard to the Bible. For the postmodern, one of the most potent arguments against the authority of the Bible as a guide containing moral absolutes is the fact that killing is sanctioned by God in the Old Testament.

So how does one respond? The first important point to make here is that when examining the Old Testament, we need to remember that not everything recorded in the Bible is approved by the Bible. For example, the Bible records in Abraham's era that various kings went to war against each other. This action is neither condemned nor praised; it is simply relayed to us in Genesis 14. Some of the acts of violence recorded in the Bible would fall into this category. We need to be careful, then, how we read the different accounts of war in the Old Testament. It is true to say that some wars are commanded by God, particularly with regard to the historic nation of Israel taking possession of the land that God gives to them after they are rescued from slavery in Egypt. Nevertheless, Christians have deliberated for many generations how to understand these passages as well as how to build a Christian response to war in their own contemporary contexts.

Second, the question one might pose to the postmodern skeptic who wonders whether war can ever be a good thing is "Would it be a demonstration of goodness to show no opposition to evil?" Can we approve of a government that offers no resistance to the criminal, whether burglar, rapist, murderer, or child abuser? This is an important question because both the Old and New Testaments present a portrait of a moral God who judges evil. One of the means of God's judgment in the pages of the Old Testament is war. It is extremely important to note at this point that God's chosen people, the Israelites, are not always the ones who bring about God's will on the battlefield. In fact, they are often on the receiving end of his judgment, finding themselves massacred and enslaved just as at other times they are militarily victorious over other powers.

The Rules of Warfare

The rules of war for God's people are laid down in Deuteronomy 20, and they represent a control of justice, fairness, and kindness in the use of the sword. Special hardship conditions were defined as a ground for excusing individual soldiers from military duty until those conditions were cleared (Deut. 20:5–7). Even those who had no such excuse but were simply afraid and reluctant to fight were likewise allowed to go home (v. 8). Unlike the contemporary armies of other nations, who might attack a city without giving it an opportunity to surrender on terms (1 Sam. 11:2–3), the armies of Israel were required to grant a city an opportunity to surrender without bloodshed before moving on to mount a full-scale siege and destruction of the city. In this context, the women and children were to be spared from death and cared for by their captors (Deut. 20:14). Only in the case of the particularly depraved inhabitants of Canaan itself was there to be total destruction (v. 16). The reason given to God-sanctioned war and destruction of the inhabitants of Canaan was the likely corruption of the moral and spiritual standards of Israelite society, in areas such as child sacrifice: "Otherwise, they will teach you to follow all the detestable things they do in worshiping their gods, and you will sin against the LORD your God" (v. 18).

Consider two historic examples from Joshua and 1 Samuel. In the case of the destruction of Jericho (Joshua 6), God had given the people more than four hundred years to turn from abominable practices such as child sacrifice—while Israel endured slavery in Egypt. The killing of the inhabitants of Jericho by the Israelite army is a means of God's judgment. Incidentally, those who did repent and show favor to Joshua were spared, namely the prostitute Rahab, who appears in Matthew's genealogy of Christ.

The second example is from 1 Samuel 15, where Saul is commanded to wipe out the Amalekites. Saul displeases God by only killing that which is weak and despised and keeping the rest of the plunder for himself. This example and the destruction of Jericho are exceptions to the rules for war laid out in Deuteronomy 20, which offer a chance to surrender and other constraints on the best possible way to conduct war.[16] It is important to note here that Israel is most often on the receiving end of God's judgment rather than doling it out to others. In these two cases where intensive killing is done by Israel with the approval of God, the particular immorality of their enemies is cited as the reason. There is no sense of a carte blanche for Israel to kill and maim, but rather a period of struggle for this people to get established in a land that is conquered and reconquered by many groups.

What this means for the character of the God of the Bible is that he is revealed as the One who judges evil. Until I moved to London, I found this idea quite hard to understand. But in the community I live in, we are surrounded by the everyday reality of evil—from child prostitution to domestic violence, from drug dealers preying on the vulnerable to fatal shootings. We have stood with a mother in our congregation who buried her son, who had been stabbed in a contract killing. These painful incidents cause one to cry out for justice and to stand up for the victims. When the Bible talks about God judging evil, this is what it means. He will not allow perpetrators to go unpunished; even if they evade human justice, divine justice will stand.

Some postmoderns equate these biblical examples of violence with the acts of violence committed by Muhammad, the early Muslims, and subsequent followers of Islam to the present day. One of the clear distinctions between the wars in the Old Testament and the acts of violence committed and encouraged by Muhammad is that the biblical accounts occur in the context of a nation-state going to war against other nations. They occur within a limited time period that comes to a clear end rather than existing as generic examples that could be taken up by individuals or groups. The reader of the Old Testament is certainly not encouraged to take up arms, a view clearly seconded by reading the New Testament. The same cannot be said of the Qur'an.

How Does the God Who Orders War Relate to the God of the New Testament?
Many people pit the picture of a violent God who destroys his enemies on the battlefield in the Old Testament against the New Testament understanding of God as a God of love who sends his Son to the cross to die for evil people.[17] In fact, Jesus actually tells his disciple Peter to "put your sword back in its place" (Matt. 26:52). However, we do see the awesome, judging, powerful God who destroys evil in the New Testament in such places as Revelation 20:11–15:

> Then I saw a great white throne and him who was seated on it. Earth and sky fled from his presence, and there was no place for them. And I saw the dead, great and small, standing before the throne, and books were opened. Another book was opened, which is the book of life. The dead were judged according to what they had done as recorded in the books. The sea gave up the dead that were in it, and death and Hades gave up the dead that were in them, and each person was judged according to what he had done. Then death and Hades were thrown into the lake of fire. The lake of fire is the second death. If anyone's name was not found written in the book of life, he was thrown into the lake of fire.

The Bible is the story of a cosmic struggle between good and evil from beginning to end. A Christian reading of the Old Testament interprets the battles depicted in the context of this cosmic struggle. Thus the battle of Jericho, the wars against the southern coalition of Canaanite kings, and the wars against the northern coalition in Canaan are historical examples of this larger struggle. God fought on behalf of many of the judges in the Old Testament as well as for faithful kings such as David and Jehoshaphat. At times God even used foreign nations to fight against Israel's enemies in ways that helped his people. For example, the prophet Nahum announced the appearance of the divine warrior who would fight (in this instance through the Babylonians) against Israel's longtime oppressor Assyria (Nah. 2:1–4).

When Israel disobeyed God, they too faced his judgment: "The LORD will cause you to be defeated before your enemies. You will come at them from one direction but flee from them in seven, and you will become a thing of horror to all the kingdoms on earth" (Deut. 28:25). Further, there is an entire book of the Bible devoted to giving an emotional and theological response to the fall of Jerusalem, the book of Lamentations. This book paints a picture of God as a warrior. But in this case the warrior was not protecting his people; he was acting as their enemy: "The Lord is like an enemy; he has swallowed up Israel. He has swallowed up all her palaces and destroyed her strongholds. He has multiplied mourning and lamentation for the Daughter of Judah" (Lam. 2:5). There is no sense, then, of Israel being used to judge others while remaining immune from God's judgment.

Commands from God to go into battle and kill people may seem to contradict the idea of a God of love, but the Christian interprets these passages in the context of the overall story of the Bible that introduces us to a God who is just and good, who fights against evil and judges those who fight against him. The coming of Christ and the beginning of the New Testament institute a new era in a biblical understanding of battle. Jesus appears as the divine warrior, but he has intensified and heightened the battle. No longer is the battle a physical battle against flesh-and-blood enemies over a piece of land. Now it is directed toward spiritual powers and authorities.

The exorcisms of the New Testament point toward this. Here we see the violent nature of the conflict. Jesus has authority over all the powers in the universe, even though they assert themselves against him. It is ultimately in his death on the cross that he demonstrates his supremacy over that which would oppose him. Jesus' ascension into heaven is described in military language when Psalm 68 is referred to in Ephesians 4:7–8: "But to each one of us grace has been given as Christ apportioned it. This is why it says: 'When he ascended on high, he led captives in his train and gave gifts to men.'"

Jesus defeated the powers and authorities, not by killing people but by dying for them. This transition from the prior way of warfare in terms of historic physical battles over land to the new era of spiritual warfare was dramatically demonstrated when Jesus was arrested in the Garden of Gethsemane. The Gospels describe how Jesus' disciple Peter grabbed a sword and chopped off the ear of the high priest's servant (Matt. 26:47–56; Mark 14:43–52; Luke 22:47–53; John 18:1–11). Jesus responded by healing the man's ear and saying, "Put your sword back in its place . . . for all who draw the sword will die by the sword. Do you think I cannot call on my Father, and he will at once put at my disposal more than twelve legions of angels? But how then would the Scriptures be fulfilled that say it must happen in this way?" (Matt. 26:52–54).

The object of Christ's warfare focuses on spiritual realities, and the weapons used are spiritual, not physical. This becomes one of the most important metaphors for living the Christian life. Ephesians 6:10–18 is the famous passage that employs military metaphors for the spiritual task of following Christ and living a prayerful, godly life. Paul writes, "Put on the full armor of God so that you can take your stand against the devil's schemes. For our struggle is not against flesh and blood, but against the rulers, against the authorities, against the powers of this dark world and against the spiritual forces of evil in the heavenly realms" (vv. 11–12).

Jesus has shown that it is now a betrayal of the gospel to take up physical arms explicitly to promote the interests of Christ. Thus there is some discontinuity between the Old and New Testaments when it comes to warfare, yet this discontinuity is not absolute.[18] We also see continuity, especially in light of the New Testament's picture of the final judgment, and its form of warfare that uses spiritual weapons to demolish spiritual strongholds.

Does the Bible Have Moral Authority on the Question of War?

Whereas postmoderns argue that no text can have absolute authority and that the Bible's morality is questionable due to killing in the Old Testament, I believe that we can answer these charges. We have seen that war in the Old Testament occurs in a limited context, in a particular historical era that very definitely comes to an end. The fact that Jesus resists reestablishing an independent Israel but rather fulfils the promises and purposes of the Old Testament in himself and establishes a global church demonstrates that it is in the New Testament era that we are now to live and reason when it comes to war.

We have seen that the New Testament talks of the cosmic struggle between good and evil in spiritual terms since the revelation of God through the physical nation of Israel has found ultimate fulfillment in the person of Christ. So what does this mean for Christians living around the world for the last two thousand years in terms of a biblical view of war? On the one hand, the New Testament itself does not condemn the vocation of a soldier if the work is carried out in a responsible and lawful fashion (Luke 3:14; Acts 10:1–6). Yet on the other hand, passages such as "Blessed are the peacemakers for they will be called sons of God" (Matt 5:9) seem to point toward pacifism.

There are broadly four historical Christian positions when it comes to seeking a biblical understanding of just war:[19]

1. *Thoroughgoing militarism*: Any war, anytime, anyplace, and for any cause is just. Christians could work as mercenaries.
2. *Selective militarism*: Only war that the state declares is just. Christians could serve as soldiers in their nation's armed forces.
3. *Selective pacifism*: Only war with which the individual agrees is just. Christians could volunteer to serve in their nation's armed forces for a particular conflict.
4. *Thoroughgoing pacifism*: No war anytime, anyplace, or for any cause is just. No Christian should ever serve in the armed forces.[20]

The early church's response to war was initially a pacifism that allowed for the possibility of Christian converts staying in the army. Before Constantine, theologians and church leaders such as Tertullian took the rebuke of Peter as an absolutist position that totally spiritualized the battles in the Old Testament and did not allow for any Christian approval of war. The church father Origen was very concerned to show that Christians were not bad citizens by virtue of refusing to fight or kill. He developed an argument that Christian prayers would be of more use to the king than any number of soldiers.

It is Augustine who introduced "just war" theory into Christian thinking.

This theory originated in classical thinking, but Augustine built upon it borrowing also from the work of the fourth-century theologian Ambrose.[21] Augustine begins by justifying some wars by the fact that God orders wars in the Old Testament. He frames (as does Aquinas) a deontological argument: if God allows and orders war in the Old Testament, then the nature of God as just determines that there must be such a thing as a just war, since God cannot order what is immoral. This is then the starting place for laying down principles by which a Christian can deduce whether or not a particular war is a just war.[22]

When we come to this question of war and ask ourselves whether the Bible has real existential moral authority, we discover that individual Christians are given responsibility to think for themselves. Christian moral reasoning is not simplistic and is not dictated. An astronaut floating in space without the pull of gravity may seem to be free, but this would be a depressing, aimless existence. True freedom must have parameters. For the Christian, the Bible offers a free framework for life and thought—a framework that we believe is revealed by God but appeals for our consent rather than imposing a terrorizing force of authority.

CONCLUSION

Of course, it is not possible to conduct a comprehensive defense of the Bible from a postmodern critique in one short chapter. But we have seen that postmodern challenges to the Bible can be usefully divided into theoretical, historical, and existential questions about textual authority. At each of these levels the Bible withstands the scrutiny of the skeptic, encouraging the thinker to appreciate that the Scriptures contain and uphold theoretical meaning, historical integrity, and moral authority that connect with our existential reality. The Bible is a book that is worthy of the interest and passion it inspires around the world. Even in the midst of the shadows of disillusionment and doubt cast by postmodernism, the Bible has the power to speak, connect with, and guide those who will open and read it.

2

CHALLENGES FROM ATHEISM

Alister McGrath

Atheism remains an important challenge to faith throughout the Western world, especially in the United States. Many of its critics believe that the movement has lost its way and that its intellectual credentials and cultural appeal have dwindled in recent years. In this chapter, we shall explore this godless worldview and assess its importance for Christian apologetics. We will do this by exploring atheism's recent history and asking why it came to be of such importance in the last two centuries, examining its core arguments and offering rebuttals, and by considering how best to engage with atheists in public debate and private conversation.

Apologetics has two major components—one negative, one positive. Negatively, apologetics identifies and responds to objections that are raised against faith. Positively, it works out how best to communicate and commend the gospel to each audience it engages. It is therefore vitally important to determine the leading objections raised by atheists against faith and to consider how to deal with these—and also how best to engage atheism as we try to explore and explain the truth and relevance of the gospel.

BY WAY OF INTRODUCTION

Before we explore atheism's recent history, I should tell you why I have a personal interest in this matter: *I used to be an atheist myself.*[1] Religious tensions exploded into violence in Northern Ireland while I was living in Belfast during my final years at school. It seemed obvious to me that religion was the cause of violence, just as it seemed equally clear that the elimination of religion would lead to peace. Like many who grew up during the late 1960s, I was intrigued by Marxism and found its predictions of the triumph of socialism and the demise of religion intellectually compelling. And more than that, I was studying the natural sciences, which seemed to me to leave no conceptual space for God. God was a redundancy, a relic from the past that appeared to have no place in the future.

There are, of course, different kinds of atheists. There are the rather gracious types, who personally don't believe in God but are happy if other people find the idea meaningful. And then there are the rather aggressive, intolerant sorts of atheists, who regard people who believe in God as fools, knaves, and liars and want to rid the world of them. I regret to tell you that I fell into the second category.

Part of the reasoning that led me to this conclusion was based on the natural sciences. I specialized in mathematics and science during high school, in preparation for going to Oxford University to study chemistry. While my primary motivation for studying the sciences was gaining fascinating insights into the wonderful world of nature, I also found them to be a highly convenient ally in my critique of religion. Atheism and the natural sciences seemed to be coupled together by the most rigorous of intellectual bonds. Science disproved God! I admit it was a very facile and simplistic viewpoint, but it was one found in popular atheist works of the time—and, indeed, even today. And there things rested, until I arrived at Oxford in October 1971.

Studying chemistry and then doing advanced research in molecular biophysics proved to be intellectually exhilarating. At times, I found myself overwhelmed with enthusiasm as more and more of the complexities of the natural world seemed to fall into place. Yet alongside this growing delight in the natural sciences, which exceeded anything I could have hoped for, I found myself rethinking my atheism. It is not easy for anyone to subject his core beliefs to criticism; my reason for doing so was the growing realization that things were not quite as straightforward as I had once thought. A number of factors had converged to bring about what could reasonably be described as a crisis of faith.

Atheism, I began to realize, rested on a less-than-satisfactory evidential basis. The arguments that had once seemed bold, decisive, and conclusive increasingly turned out to be circular, tentative, and uncertain. They had to be talked up; their intellectual cracks had to be papered over; a veil had to be drawn over their logical flaws. The opportunity to talk to Christians about their faith revealed to me that I actually understood relatively little about Christianity, which I had come to know chiefly through the not-always-accurate descriptions of its leading critics, such as Bertrand Russell and Karl Marx. Perhaps more importantly, I began to realize that my assumption of the inexorable link between the natural sciences and atheism was rather naive and uninformed.

My doubts about the intellectual foundations of atheism began to coalesce into a realization that atheism was actually a belief system, whereas I had assumed it to be a factual statement about reality (a matter we will return to later in this chapter). I also discovered that I knew far less about Christianity than I had assumed. As I began to read Christian books and listen to Christian friends explain what they actually believed, it gradually became clear to me that what I had rejected was merely a religious stereotype. I had some major rethinking to do. After checking out Christianity's credentials and discovering its immense spiritual vitality and intellectual potency, I came to faith in the God whom I had once regarded as little more than an obsolete curiosity. So in the end, I turned my back on one faith and embraced another. Although I am no longer an atheist, I retain my respect for atheism and continue to be interested in it as a major belief system that deserves careful, respectful, yet critical attention.

My own journey to the Christian faith has had a major impact on how I approach apologetics. I was an atheist partly because I had misunderstood Christianity. My objections were often directed against a caricature, a straw man. I have found that *one of the best ways of defending Christianity is simply to explain what Christianity actually is.* Before I get into arguments or deep discussions with my opponents, I offer them a brief résumé of the main themes of my faith. This disarms many of the traditional atheist stereotypes of faith.

I remember one particular argument with a leading atheist, who said to me in a public debate, "I could never believe in a vicious, violent God!" I responded, "And neither could I. Shall I tell you a little bit about the God I *do* believe in?"

God suffered in Christ. He knows what it is like to experience pain. God is not a hero with feet of clay, who demands that others suffer while he remains aloof from the world of pain. The God in whom Christians believe and trust is a God who himself suffered and, by so doing, transfigures the sufferings of his people. After I had finished talking about the love of God seen in the atoning death of Christ (John 3:16; 1 John 4:9–10), my opponent was somewhat deflated.

In this chapter, we shall consider the challenges posed to Christian faith by atheism and how we can respond. The first thing we need to do is appreciate why atheism became such an important element of modern Western culture and what can be learned from this.

The Rise of Atheism in the West

What can we learn from the growth of atheism in the last two centuries? Why did this movement achieve such significance in the Western world? For the apologist, one of the most important questions to ask about non-Christian worldviews is this: why would anyone *want* to believe this? What is it that makes this view attractive? Understanding the reasons people respond to the intellectual and spiritual rivals of Christianity helps us identify weaknesses in the way Christian apologists have responded to challenges and thus equips us better for handling them today.

Sometimes these spiritual alternatives may seem weird or even slightly creepy—for example, those who believe in the power of crystals to protect or guide them. We can, of course, challenge these views, and this can sometimes lead to some helpful discussions and outcomes. But we can also ask a deeper question: what lies behind this belief? For example, the belief in crystals often reflects a deep longing for security and meaning—two vital points of contact for the Christian gospel. Having met someone with an interest in crystals, I explained to her how I knew God to be my protector and guide, and I explored with her the image of God as shepherd (Ps. 23:1). She was fascinated by the idea of a personal God, as opposed to the impersonal forces she associated with her crystals. What was particularly worrisome was that this way of thinking about God was *new* to her. We have a lot of explaining to do, don't we?

So why has atheism been so potent? Atheism had its origins in the classical world. One of the most powerful factors in triggering its emergence was a belief that the gods of Mount Olympus were fickle, jealous, degenerate beings who could not be taken seriously by intellectually sophisticated people. Homer's *Iliad*, one of the greatest pieces of classical literature, portrayed the gods as getting involved in petty and vindictive squabbles. *Surely,* many began to wonder, *the gods were meant to be better than this.*[2] One of the fundamental factors leading to the rise of atheism is a perception that belief in the divine does not lead to a morality that is clearly superior to that offered by secular culture. We must bear this point in mind, as this theme recurs throughout history.

Historically, the real growth of atheism is to be dated from the eighteenth century. The French Revolution propelled atheism to center stage.[3] Why were revolutionaries so hostile to Christianity? While there were many factors involved in bringing about this revolution, one of the fundamental causes was that the French church was seen as being on the side of the establishment. The church seemed to be more interested in its own status and power than in the welfare of the people. As a result of this negative assessment, atheism began to be seen in a positive light. For many in early modern Europe, the conclusion was obvious: *religion is an oppressor; atheism is a liberator.* There is an important point to be learned here. Where the church is seen to be on the side of ordinary people, atheism has relatively little appeal.

The importance of this point can be seen by comparing the French Revolution of 1789 with the American Revolution of 1776. Revolutions do not need to be atheistic! Most American revolutionaries saw themselves as called to throw off British rule: political, social, economic, and religious. The original idea behind the separation of church and state was not to exclude religion from public life, but to prevent any specific Christian denomination from being or becoming the establishment.

Yet, there is another important point to make: atheism was certainly seen as a liberator in France in 1789, but what happened when atheism gained power and became the establishment itself? How would a movement that was such a powerful critic of the religious establishment behave when it *became* that religious establishment? This is precisely what happened as a result of the Russian Revolution of 1917, and subsequently through the establishment of the Soviet Bloc in Eastern Europe after the Second World War. In the German Democratic Republic, atheism was enforced without any significant popular support.[4] As the popular euphoria at the fall of the Berlin Wall in 1989 made clear: atheist states end up oppressing people. The same set of ideas that were seen as "liberating" by some back in 1789 were seen as oppressive in 1989. Unsurprisingly, we have seen a resurgence of religion in many parts of the Soviet empire, and especially in Russia.[5]

As the archives of the former Soviet Union and its allies were opened up to scholarly inspection after the end of the Cold War, detailed documentation of all kinds of human rights abuses emerged. Atheists regularly pointed to the poor human rights records of allegedly "Christian" states in the past, such as Spain in the sixteenth century. Yet here were states whose official ideology or "established nonreligion" was atheism committing serious acts of violence, abuse, and oppression in the twentieth century—an age of supposed progress and enlightenment. The publication of the famous *Black Book of Communism* documented these abuses with unprecedented rigor, causing a public relations crisis at the political level for Western communism and at the religious level for the atheism that undergirded it.[6]

Still, the cultural appeal of atheism often seems to be determined by its social context, rather than by anything intrinsic to its ideas. Where religion is said to oppress, confine, deprive, and limit, atheism is lauded for offering humanity a larger vision of freedom. In the past, atheism offered a vision that captured the imagination of Western Europe. We all need to dream, to imagine a better existence—and atheism empowered some people in the eighteenth century to overthrow the past and create a brave new world. But that was then; what about now?

The appeal of atheism as a public philosophy in the West largely came to an end in 1989 with the collapse of the Berlin Wall. Atheism, once hailed as a liberator, was now cordially loathed as an oppressor. The beliefs of atheism were pretty much the same as before; their appeal, however, was very different. As the Soviet Empire crumbled at a dizzying rate in the 1990s, those who had once been "liberated" from God rushed to embrace him once more. Islam is resurgent in central Soviet Asia, and Eastern Orthodoxy in Russia itself. Harsh and bitter memories of state-enforced atheism linger throughout Eastern Europe, with major implications for the religious and cultural future of the European Union as former Soviet bloc nations achieve membership.

Where people enjoy their religion, seeing it as something life enhancing and identity giving, they are going to find atheism unattractive. The recent surge of evidence-based studies demonstrating the positive impact of religion on human well-being has yet to be assimilated by atheist writers.[7] It is only where religion is cast as the enemy that atheism's demands for its elimination will be taken seriously. Atheism's problem is that its own baleful legacy in the former Soviet Union has led many to view it as the enemy, with religion as its antidote.

Interestingly, *atheism has very limited influence outside Western culture.* The only African nation in which it has any significant presence is South Africa, predominantly among the white population. This is a telling indicator of its Western roots, and therefore its predominantly Western appeal. But there is more to this observation than at first seems to be the case. It is not simply that atheism is a Western product. It is actually a product of one specific era in Western culture: the Enlightenment, or "modernity,"[8] which is now coming to an end.[9] We shall return to this point later.

This very brief exploration of some aspects of the history of atheism has raised some important issues, and we shall return to these later in this chapter. We must now turn to consider some of the atheist arguments that make their appearance in the media and in personal conversations. It is important to appreciate the way recent terrorist events have given a new plausibility to the traditional atheist argument that religion leads to violence. So then, let us reflect on the events of 9/11 and consider their importance for contemporary atheism.

THE IMPACT OF 9/11

There is little doubt that the suicide attacks of September 11, 2001, on New York and Washington DC, now universally known as 9/11, led to a surge of atheist criticism of religion. At least three major best-selling books by atheists were published as a direct response to this event: Sam Harris's *The End of Faith*, Daniel Dennett's *Breaking the Spell*, and Richard Dawkins's *The God Delusion*.[10] These three works have had a significant impact in many sections of the American media, reinforcing a perception that religion has become such a major force in modern public life that it poses a serious threat. At the hands of these atheists, an important public debate about the causes of such events has been hijacked into a piece of crude antireligious polemic. The take-home message of Dawkins's recent book *The God Delusion* can be summarized very simply: religion causes bombings! Get rid of religion, and the greatest threat to global peace and security will be eliminated.

Such fiery, passionate rhetoric has struck a chord within the hitherto demoralized American secularist movement.[11] Might the public outrage at these terrorist actions become a weapon in the fight against the resurgence of religion? Yet serious scholarly examination of the phenomenon of suicide bombers reveals a much more complex pattern of motivations that does not fit well with the simplistic sloganeering of recent atheist propagandists.[12] Religion turns out to be neither a necessary nor a sufficient condition for causing such outrages. If there is any common factor, it is a sense of total helplessness in the face of perceived oppression, coupled with a lack of conventional military capacity. Both of these factors lead individuals to decide to use themselves as weapons and to take out as many of their enemies as possible by doing so. It doesn't make for the neat antireligious slogans that some would like, but it is much more accurate in its analysis.

A real effect of 9/11 has been to force a discussion about religious violence into the forefront of popular debate. The 9/11 tragedy created the impression that religion has a propensity to violence, thus making it all the more important for a Christian apologist to address this issue. We shall explore this point in the following section, when we turn to consider the main criticisms leveled by contemporary atheists.

The Fundamental Atheist Challenges and Responses

So what are the intellectual challenges that atheism poses for Christian faith? What are the main atheist arguments against God, and how can we respond? In what follows, I shall set out the main lines of criticism that atheists direct against Christians, based partly on my own analysis of works of atheist polemics and partly on my debates in Oxford and elsewhere with prominent atheists. The main atheist challenges seem to be the following:

1. Christianity, like all religions, leads to violence.
2. God is just an invention designed to console losers.
3. Christian faith is a leap in the dark without any reliable basis.
4. The natural sciences have disproved God.

Each of these challenges recurs in debates and discussions with atheists, and it is therefore important to explore each of them.

Challenge #1: Christianity Causes Violence
When I was growing up in Northern Ireland during the 1960s, one of the things that distressed me was religious violence. For many, religion is perceived to be

something that creates conflict and incites violence. Wouldn't the world be a better place without it? I certainly thought so as a young man. I could easily empathize with John Lennon's song *Imagine*, which asks us to imagine a world without religion. Get rid of religion and the world would be safer and kinder. It's an argument that you still find in some older atheist writings, and one that is recycled in some more recent works of this nature.[13]

Once, it was possible to argue that religion alone was the source of the world's evils. Look at the record of violence of the Spanish Inquisition, or at the oppression of the French people in the 1780s under the Roman Catholic Church and the Bourbon monarchy. The list could be extended endlessly to make the same powerful moral point: wherever religion exercises power, it oppresses and corrupts, using violence to enforce its own beliefs and agendas. Religion can indeed lead people to do some very bad things—I doubt if anyone would disagree. But that is not the real issue.

Atheism argued that it abolished violence and tyranny by getting rid of what ultimately caused it: faith in God. It was a credible claim in the nineteenth century precisely because atheism had not yet enjoyed the power and influence once exercised by religion. But all that has changed. Atheism's innocence has now evaporated. In the twentieth century, atheism managed to grasp the power that had hitherto eluded it. But then atheism proved just as fallible, just as corrupt, and just as oppressive as any belief system that had gone before it.[14] Stalin's death squads were just as murderous as their religious antecedents. Those who dreamed of freedom in the new atheist paradise often found themselves counting trees in Siberia or confined to the Gulag—and they were the lucky ones.

Like many back in the late 1960s, I was unaware of the darker side of atheism, as practiced in the Soviet Union. I assumed that religion would die away naturally in the face of the compelling intellectual arguments and moral vision offered by atheism. I failed to ask what might happen if people did not want to have their faith eliminated. After all, a desire to eliminate belief in God at the *intellectual* or *cultural* level has the most unfortunate tendency to encourage others to do this at the *physical* level. Lenin, frustrated after the Russian Revolution by the Russian people's obstinate refusal to espouse atheism voluntarily and naturally, enforced it, arguing in a famous letter of March 1922 that the "protracted use of brutality" was the necessary means of achieving this goal.[15]

Some of the greatest atrocities of the twentieth century were committed by regimes that espoused atheism, often with a fanaticism that some naive Western atheists seem to think is reserved only for religious people. Now we know what really happened under Stalin, even if it was unfashionable to talk about this in progressive circles in the West until the 1990s. We all know that extremism results from a number of sources, but the firing squads Stalin sent to liquidate the Buddhist monks of Mongolia gained at least something of their fanaticism and hatred of religion from those who told them that religion generates fanaticism and hatred.

Atheists often attack religion by presenting the pathological as if it is the normal, relying on flagrant misrepresentation and a lack of basic religious awareness on the part of their audiences to score points. The real truth is that there is something about human nature that makes it capable of being inspired by what it believes to be right to do both wonderful and appalling things. Neither atheism nor religion may be at fault—it might be some deeply troubling flaw in human nature itself. It is an uncomfortable thought, but one that demands careful reflection. The real problem is *extremism*, whether religious, antireligious, or political.

But what of the argument that religion, through its appeal to God, gives a new motivation for violence? Does not an appeal to the transcendent trump ordinary human arguments? This is an important point. To explore it, let's ask what happens when a society rejects the idea of God. Does this mean there is no longer any transcendent set of values? When a society rejects God, it tends to transcendentalize alternatives, such as the ideals of liberty or equality. These now become quasi-divine authorities that are not regarded as being open to challenge.

Perhaps the most familiar example of this dates from the French Revolution, at a time when traditional notions of God were discarded as obsolete or repressive, and replaced by transcendentalized human values. One of these was the idea of liberty, which rapidly assumed the status of a quasi-divine entity, a transcendent reality in its own right. In this markedly antireligious phase of its history, the French Revolution appealed to the pursuit of liberty as the justification of violence and oppression. The end of liberty was held to justify the means of terror.

In one famous episode, Marie-Jeanne Roland de la Platière—better known to history as Madame Roland—was brought to the guillotine to face execution on trumped-up charges in 1793. She had been highly active in revolutionary politics in the early 1780s, but had now fallen out of favor with the revolutionary elite. As she prepared to die, she bowed mockingly toward the statue of Liberty in the Place de la Révolution and uttered the words for which she is remembered: "Oh Liberty, what crimes are committed in thy name." The point is simple. All ideals—divine, transcendent, human, or invented—are capable of being abused. That's just the way human nature is. And that happens to religion, as well. Belief in God can be abused, and we need to be very clear, in the first place, that this abuse happens, and in the second, that we need to confront and oppose this. But abuse of an ideal does not negate its validity. Indeed, it often points to its vital importance for many people.

Challenge #2: God Is Invented by People to Console Themselves

A second argument that often emerges in debate or conversation runs like this: God is just an invention, corresponding to a human desire. A phrase from Karl Marx is often cited here: "Religion is the opium of the people."[16] The basic idea is that God is some kind of spiritual narcotic that dulls our senses to the pain of the world and helps us cope with it. We want there to be a God to console us and so we invent him. In this view, religion offers succor for suckers and losers, but not for serious and sophisticated people.

This argument has its roots in the works of the left-wing German philosopher Ludwig Feuerbach, who argued that the idea of God arises understandably, but mistakenly, from human experience. Religion in general is simply the projection of human nature onto an illusory transcendent plane. Human beings mistakenly objectify their own feelings. They interpret their experience as an awareness of God, whereas it is in fact nothing other than an experience of themselves. God is the longing of the human soul personified. This idea was developed by Karl Marx, who argued that belief in God arose from sociological factors, and by Sigmund Freud, who argued that it arose from psychological pressures.[17] (Neither, I must add, had any scientific warrant for doing so!)

So what might we say in response? First, it is reasonable to ask whether all human beings do indeed long for the existence of God. For example, consider a serial murderer who took delight in the pain and trauma of his victims. Would there not be excellent reasons for supposing that he might hope that God does *not* exist, given what might await him on the Day of Judgment? And might not his atheism itself be a wish fulfillment? The history of Western thought makes it clear that one fundamental motivation for atheism is the fear of accountability and retribution in the sight of God.

Second, Feuerbach's critique of religion is just as effective a criticism of atheism.

He argues that the wish is father to the thought. People invent their religious ideas to suit their longings and aspirations. In that human beings wish for God, their longing is satisfied by their invention of that God by a process of projection. On the basis of Feuerbach's analysis, it is not simply Christianity but also atheism that can be regarded as a projection of human hopes. This resonates with much sociological and historical analysis of the rise of atheism in the late eighteenth and early nineteenth centuries, which emphasize how so many longed for a godless world and chose to create one in which reality was adapted to their longings.

The Polish poet Czeslaw Milosz, who won the Nobel Prize in Literature in 1980, has an interesting point to make here. Having found himself intellectually bullied and politically silenced, first under Nazism and then under Stalinism, Milosz had no doubt as to the ultimate source of despair and tyranny in the twentieth century. In a remarkable essay entitled "The Discreet Charm of Nihilism," he pointed out that it was not religion, but its denial—above all, the denial of accountability in the sight of God—that lay at the root of the century's oppressive totalitarianisms. Here are some wise words from that article:

> Religion, opium for the people! To those suffering pain, humiliation, illness, and serfdom, it promised a reward in afterlife. And now we are witnessing a transformation. A true opium of the people is a belief in nothingness after death, the huge solace of thinking that for our betrayals, greed, cowardice, murders we are not going to be judged. The Marxist creed has now been inverted. The true opium of modernity is the belief that there is *no* God, so that humans are free to do precisely as they please.[18]

There is also a third point of concern about this approach, which is perhaps more serious. There is a fatal logical error in Feuerbach's analysis. Let me explain. It is certainly true that nothing actually exists because I wish it to. But does this mean that because I want something to be true, it cannot be? Imagine the man who longs for a drink of water on a long, hot, dusty day. Does water not exist because he wants some? Hardly![19]

Challenge #3: Christian Faith Is a Leap in the Dark
Recent atheist critiques of Christianity have been severely critical of the idea of faith. The prominent atheist Richard Dawkins has famously argued that faith is

a "process of non-thinking."[20] Other influential misrepresentations of faith from Dawkins include "blind trust, in the absence of evidence, even in the teeth of evidence."[21] These definitions have, quite simply, been invented to discredit belief in God. They are straw men set up to ridicule the ideas in question. There is no attempt to engage what Christians actually mean by faith.

Dawkins has made some frankly ludicrous statements, such as "Faith is not allowed to justify itself by argument."[22] Has he not read, or even heard of writers such as C. S. Lewis, Richard Swinburne, Nicholas Wolterstorff, or Alvin Plantinga—to mention four very obvious twentieth-century writers—who regard the establishment of a core intellectual foundation to faith as essential? And who, in the judgment of many, have done precisely that?[23]

The apologetic ministry of Ravi Zacharias is itself a powerful witness to the robust intellectual case that can be made for God. And even the subtitle of a recent book by Francis S. Collins, director of the Human Genome Project, ought to give Dawkins pause for thought: *A Scientist Presents Evidence for Belief!*[24] Now I do not expect Dawkins to agree with these people, but at least he ought to acknowledge and interact with their arguments. His ludicrous misrepresentation of faith does little to create confidence in his counterarguments, which are often as weak and unsatisfactory as the way he characterizes his opponents. Dawkins seems to be guilty of precisely the evasion of serious thought that he believes is characteristic of his opponents.

Faith is infantile, Dawkins tells us. It can only survive by being crammed into the minds of impressionable young children. We've grown up now, and we need to move on. Why should we believe things that can't be scientifically proved? Faith in God, Dawkins argues, is just like believing in Santa Claus and the Tooth Fairy. When you grow up, you grow out of it.

This is actually a rather childish argument that seems to have found its way into what is meant to be an adult discussion. It is amateurish and unconvincing. There is no serious empirical evidence that people regard God, Santa Claus, and the Tooth Fairy as being in the same category. I stopped believing in Santa Claus and the Tooth Fairy when I was about six years old. After being an atheist for some years, I discovered God when I was eighteen and have never regarded this as some kind of infantile regression. As I noticed while researching my book *The Twilight of Atheism*, a large number of people come to believe in God in later life—when they are grown up. I have yet to meet anyone who came to believe in Santa Claus or the Tooth Fairy late in life.

If Dawkins's rather simplistic argument has any plausibility, it requires a real analogy between God and Santa Claus to exist—which it clearly does not. Everyone knows that people do not regard belief in God as belonging to the same category as these childish beliefs. Dawkins, of course, argues that they both represent belief in nonexistent entities. But this represents a very elementary confusion over which is the conclusion and which the presupposition of an argument.

Undeterred, Dawkins introduces yet another pseudoscientific idea into the debate about God. God, he announces, is a highly contagious virus of the mind that infects people in much the same way as a malignant virus infects a computer and corrupts its capacity to work properly.[25] There is, of course, no experimental evidence that belief in God—or any other belief for that matter, including atheism—is a "virus of the mind." Nobody has ever seen one, and nobody expects to. It is yet another dogmatic belief that Dawkins tries to pass off as scientific. In the end, Dawkins makes his own subjective judgment the criterion of which ideas count as imaginary mental viruses and which are legitimate, trustworthy ideas. It is not a serious argument, so I will give it no more space here, but one encounters it occasionally in debate.

Challenge #4: Science Has Disproved God

The most aggressive forms of atheism in modern Western culture come from the pens of scientists such as Dawkins (especially influential in the United Kingdom and Australasia) and Daniel Dennett (especially influential in North America). Both argue that the natural sciences are an intellectual superhighway to disbelief in God. Now this is actually a very puzzling assertion, as the best surveys suggest that at least 40 percent of active scientists, and probably more, believe in God.

The point that needs to be made here is that the scientific method is incapable of delivering a decisive adjudication of the God question, one way or the other. Those who believe that science proves or disproves the existence of God press that method beyond its legitimate limits and run the risk of abusing or discrediting it. Some distinguished biologists argue that the natural sciences create a positive presumption of faith; others claim they have negative implications for theistic belief. But they prove nothing, either way. If the God question is to be settled, it must be settled on other grounds.

This is not a new idea. Indeed, the recognition of the religious limits of the scientific method was well understood around the time of Charles Darwin himself. As Stephen Jay Gould, America's foremost evolutionary biologist until his recent death from cancer, pointed out, "Science simply cannot [by its legitimate methods] adjudicate the issue of God's possible superintendence of nature. We neither affirm nor deny it; we simply can't comment on it as scientists."[26]

The basic point that Gould is making is not controversial: there are limits to the sciences beyond which they cannot be pressed. The calibration of the field of competency of any discipline is immensely important, and Dawkins appears to adopt a naive and utterly simplistic attitude to this question. A very different approach is found with Sir Peter Medawar, who won the Nobel Prize in Medicine in 1960. Medawar pointed out that the existence of a limit to science is obvious from its inability to answer "childlike elementary questions," such as "What are we all here for?" or "What is the point of living?" The simplistic exaggeration of the scope of the sciences, he argued, only generates incredulity and skepticism within the intellectual community.[27]

There is, of course, a deeper philosophical point here, which is raised by many philosophers of science but strongly resisted by those wanting to peddle a simplistic atheism rather than deal with the important intellectual questions associated with the limits of science. It is this: *the sciences are, by their very nature, incapable of answering big-picture questions.* As philosopher Gilbert Harman pointed out some years ago, the sciences are not capable of the kind of proof these questions demand. How can you prove what the point of life is on the basis of the sciences? Instead, we must use techniques such as "inference to the best explanation" that simply cannot offer any degree of certainty—only probability.[28] The alleged certainty of scientific atheism is simply an illusion that cannot be defended on scientific grounds.

This is not the sort of argument that atheist apologists like. They want to argue that the sciences disprove God. And yet they find themselves unable to justify this by argument, by experiment, or even by an appeal to the scientific community as a whole. It reminds us that atheism itself is a *belief system*, a set of ideas that cannot actually be proved. We will have more to say about this in the next section.

ENGAGING WITH ATHEISM

So how can we engage in a productive dialogue with the belief system of atheism? How can we begin to find ways of opening up the big questions of life with an atheist audience? Although this sounds challenging, it is actually easier than many believe. One reason is this: atheists believe you can commit yourself to a world-view—in this case, that there is no God. There is none of the vague agnosticism that is such a feature of many sections of modern Western culture. Atheists, like Christians, believe we can commit ourselves to a belief system that informs our lives. A senior British scientist wrote to me a year ago, "After reading your book [*Dawkins' God*], I realize that I am now an atheist who has lost his faith."[29]

But already I have made an assertion that many atheists will find irritating, even disconcerting. Atheism, they might respond, is most emphatically not a belief system! It is factually true! Christianity is about faith; atheism is about fact! Now that response is a very good starting point for an apologetic conversation.[30] Let's see how it might go.

> *Atheist:* There is no God!
>
> *Christian:* Are you sure about that? Can you prove that?
>
> *Atheist:* I don't need to! It's obvious.
>
> *Christian:* Well, humor me. Prove it!
>
> *Atheist:* Well, I can't prove it with total certainty. But it's the best option.
>
> *Christian:* I see. So what you are saying is that you can't prove that there is no God—but that you believe the nonexistence of God is the most likely option.
>
> *Atheist:* That's right.
>
> *Christian:* So atheism is a belief, then.

This is just the skeleton of a conversation, as I am sure you understand. But you see the point. All atheist philosophers concede that the nonexistence of God cannot be proved. Kai Nielsen, in my view one of the best atheist philosophers, made this point with perfect clarity: "All the proofs of God's existence may fail, but it still may be the case that God exists."[31] Once you have got that point established, the conversation turns to some very different questions: given that both atheism and Christianity are belief systems, which is better? And how might we go about judging this?

This allows us to use an approach to apologetics that involves inviting someone to step into our worldview, seeing things from our perspective. We find this approach used at several points in the writings of C. S. Lewis, as here: "I believe in Christianity as I believe that the Sun has risen, not only because I see it, but because by it I see everything else."[32] We invite people to see the world and themselves from a Christian perspective, noting how much sense the Christian faith makes of the ordering of the world, the puzzles of human experience, and the new dignity and significance Christianity brings to an understanding of human nature and destiny.

As Blaise Pascal pointed out in the seventeenth century, the best apologetic strategy is to make people wish that something were true—and then show them that it is. Once people get a vision of the difference that the gospel makes to the way they see and understand the world, they will have a new interest in asking whether this really is true. And at this point, we can begin to develop the many arguments that C. S. Lewis, Ravi Zacharias, and others have given us for showing the reasonableness of faith.[33]

A second area of conversation might be to ask what seems to have happened to the appeal of atheism recently on account of the rise of postmodernity, especially among younger people. The point is that postmodernism has raised a new challenge to atheism within the West that atheist writers have been slow to recognize and reluctant to engage. Let me explain.

Historians of ideas often note that atheism is the ideal religion of modernity—the cultural period ushered in by the Enlightenment.[34] But modernity is in the process of being displaced by postmodernity, which rejects precisely those aspects of modernity that made atheism the obvious choice as the preferred modern religion. Postmodernity has thus spawned *post-atheism*.[35] Yet atheism seems to be turning a blind eye to this massive cultural shift and its implications for the future of its faith.

In marked contrast, gallons of ink have been spilled and immense intellectual energy expended by Christian writers in identifying and meeting the challenges of postmodernism.[36] Two are of particular relevance here. First, in general terms, postmodernism is intensely suspicious of worldviews that claim to offer a total view of reality. Christian apologists have realized this; since Christianity claims to be *right* where others are wrong, it has to make this credible to a culture that is strongly resistant to any claim to be telling the whole truth in the first place.[37]

Second (again in general terms), postmodernism regards purely materialist approaches to reality as inadequate and has a genuine interest in recovering a spiritual dimension to life. Now, this new interest in spirituality has no necessary connection with organized religion of any kind, let alone Christianity. So churches need to work out how they can connect with such aspirations, which often seem to lead away from conventional church life rather than toward faith. Yet this can certainly be done, and be done well. As Ravi Zacharias and others have shown, the new interest in issues of spirituality can be addressed and redirected in order to reconnect with the gospel.

Atheism has been slow, even reluctant, to engage with either of these developments, tending to dismiss them as irrational and superstitious. (Richard Dawkins is a case in point.) Yet it is easy to see why the rise of postmodernity poses a significantly greater threat to atheism than to Christianity. Atheism offers precisely the kind of metanarrative, or big picture, that postmodern thinkers believe leads to intolerance and oppression. Its uncompromising and definitive denial of God today sounds arrogant and repressive rather than as principled and moral.[38]

For intellectual historians, atheism is a superb example of a modern metanarrative: a "totalizing" view of things locked into the worldview of the Enlightenment. Many now argue that the Enlightenment encouraged oppression and violence and colluded with totalitarianism. Fundamental to the Enlightenment worldview is the idea that there is only one way of looking at things, and that those who disagree are either mad or bad. The simple truth is that the cultural pressures that once made atheism seem attractive are being displaced by others that make it seem intolerant, unimaginative, and disconnected from spiritual realities. It is an interesting question, and one I don't see many atheists rushing in to engage with.

So what about the surge of interest in spirituality? The burgeoning postmodern fascination with spirituality is much more troubling for atheism than for Christianity. For the Christian, the problem is how to relate or convert an interest in spirituality to the church or to Jesus Christ. For the atheist, it represents a quasi-superstitious reintroduction of spiritual ideas, leading postmodernity backward into religious beliefs that atheism thought it had exorcised.

Atheism seems curiously disconnected from this shift in cultural mood. Atheists appear to be graying intellectually, recycling the same old stale arguments and inhabiting a dying modern world, while around them a new interest in the forbidden fruit of the spiritual realm is gaining the upper hand, above all among young people. What might the implications of such developments be for the future of atheism in the West—and for those of us who engage it in public debate?

Conclusion

In this chapter we have explored some of the themes that arise in encountering modern Western atheism—for example, in public debates, personal conversations, or newspaper or other media correspondence. Yes, there is much more that needs to be said and explored. It is, however, hoped that this brief introduction will give you an idea of the challenges of atheism, and how we, as thinking and reflective Christians, can engage with them.

Remember, the very action of giving a well-informed, thoughtful response to an atheist, especially in public, undermines one of modern atheism's most basic claims: that faith is a "process of non-thinking"!

3

CHALLENGES FROM YOUTH

Alison Thomas

In this chapter, I hope to offer you a fresh perspective on the struggles within youth culture, since I myself am in the very midst of it. This chapter will explore some of the challenges to Christianity from youth in North America. We will do this in two parts. First, we will examine why apologetics is not only necessary for adults but vital for youth as well. Second, we will explore how to best equip young people at school, church, and home.

CHRISTOPHOBIA ON CAMPUS

When Christian college freshmen arrive on a typical secular campus, their faith will be ridiculed on all sides by their very own friends and teachers. They will hear that the Bible is unreliable, that Christ was no different than any other religious teacher, and that any Christian who thinks otherwise has been seriously misguided. Professor J. Budziszewski notes, "Modern institutions of higher learning have changed dramatically in the last half-century, and from the moment students set foot on the contemporary campus, their Christian convictions and discipline are assaulted."[1]

As a recent college graduate, I affirm that this was exactly my experience. From the moment I entered my university campus, my faith was attacked from every direction. My professors scoffed at the idea that I considered the Bible to be historically trustworthy. My classmates declared Christianity to be the cause of all the problems in the world, including violence, racism, and sexism. Members of my community reveled in the public disgrace of prominent evangelicals. There were also lifestyle challenges that presented themselves to me daily: parties, sex, alcohol, drugs. Combine this with sleep deprivation, poor nutrition, lack of exercise, fickle relationships, and the absence of mentors and accountability partners, and it is the perfect recipe for disaster. The combination of all of these factors makes spiritual growth in college a unique challenge. My fresh memory of this experience heavily influences the way I do youth apologetics today.

It is the difficult classroom discussions that I most clearly remember. I still get knots in my stomach when I recall the probing questions that were thrown at me day after day. One such encounter took place on my very first day of college. It was a conversation with another student that left me quite jolted. Sitting next to me in class was a handsome Indian student. He introduced himself, and after talking for a little while, he invited me to go to a Hindu festival of sorts with him, since I am also of Indian descent. When I sheepishly declined, he asked if I was a Christian. He was convinced that Christianity was the explanation for my being so closed-minded to ethnic festivities and celebrations of harmonious religious inclusion. To make matters worse, he was appalled that I would deny my own heritage and Indian roots. To him, being an Indian and a Christian were mutually exclusive. He proceeded to tell me a story that shook the foundations of my belief. He told me that the only reason I followed the Christian faith is because years ago missionaries went to India and brainwashed my ancestors.

Of course, behind his simple question "Are you a Christian?" were layers of other questions: "Do you accept me even though I am different from you?" "Do you think your way is the only way?" "Are you going to try to convert me to your view?" He challenged me to give him one good reason for being a Christian besides the fact that my parents, grandparents, great-grandparents, and so forth were. I didn't have any good reasons. In fact, I didn't have any reasons period! I was speechless. It was at that moment that I realized I was just clinging to the coattails of my parents' beliefs; my faith had never truly become my own. I was not prepared to give him an answer.

Another difficult classroom discussion concerned an odd homework assignment I was given early one semester. My class was instructed to walk to the main library at the heart of the campus. Once there, we were to carefully observe all of the walkways that led to the main entrance of the library and draw a detailed picture of them. We were all quite confused as to why our first assignment in a class that was supposed to be focused on reading and writing was to draw a picture—and a picture of the ground at that!

We drew our pictures and brought them to class. The professor told us that if we were observant, we would have drawn not just the main pavements made of concrete, but also the other walkways made of brick and stone. And if we were extremely observant, we would have included the most interesting type of walkway, the unique paths that people have created for themselves by wearing out the grass with their own footsteps. The purpose of this assignment, he said, was to show that even though there were a variety of different paths, they all led to the same place—the main entrance—just as all the world's religions lead to God. This pluralism was to be our framework for the rest of the semester as we read the sacred texts of the world: all religions lead to God and are essentially all the same.

I wish I had known at the time that to accept pluralism is not to embrace openness but to reject one's own tradition for another, the pluralist's. Pluralism renders vacuous the notion of being in a given religious tradition. How is this preserving the uniqueness of individual religions? Alister McGrath ironically notes that this crude homogenizing of world religions implies that only the Western liberal academic can truly understand the world's religions.[2] Pluralists distort the claims of world religions by imposing their views upon them. If I had been aware of this counterperspective, I would have had an answer ready. But instead, I sat in class silenced.

My view of my college professors has been summarized well by one atheist writer: "They will see me as just another liberal professor trying to cajole them out of some of their convictions, and they are dead right about that—that's what I am, and that's exactly what I am trying to do."[3]

When professors do not prohibit or openly insult Christian expression, they often use the more subtle approach of patronizing it. For example, in a sociology class the professor described Jesus as "a really nice guy" who "was just all about love and peace." She would never use such sweeping generalizations to describe a leader of another religion. But to her, it was perfectly acceptable to describe Jesus in that manner. Basic conversation etiquette in the classroom did not apply when discussing Jesus. In an advertising class, I had a professor who summarized Jesus as a brilliant advertising executive who was "going about his father's business" selling redemption. He was no Lamb of God but a full-fledged salesman out hustling with his little band of entrepreneurs. Although university professors tout tolerance, many show no tolerance toward Christianity.

Therefore, "Parents should try to make sure that their children are grounded in apologetics before sending them off," says Christian apologist Dr. Richard Howe. He continues, "This does not mean that the students would have to have all the answers before they go. But it does mean that, if the need arises for an answer, they will know where to go and with whom to consult when the intellectual battle starts to rage. And it most certainly will rage."[4] Howe concludes, "Students may not sign up for it as a class, but Leftist Indoctrination 101 is now part of the core curriculum being taught on college and university campuses nationwide."[5]

KICKING GOD OUT OF GRADE SCHOOL

Anti-Christian sentiment is pervasive not only on today's college campuses, but in elementary and high schools as well. Biology teachers argue that life is merely time plus matter plus chance, devoid of meaning and purpose. History teachers emphasize the subjectivity of historians to undermine the possibility of knowing objective historical fact. Physics teachers say that the material world is all there is, was, and ever will be. Art teachers describe how beauty is ultimately rooted in the eye of the beholder. English teachers claim that all interpretations of texts are equally valid because words do not carry any ultimate meaning. Religion teachers describe how Christianity is no different than any other major world religion.

We would do well to remember that the first schools in the most prosperous nation in the history of the world were rooted in Christian instruction. Acknowledging the Christian roots of American education is not meant to promote Christian teaching in public schools. It is meant to encourage freedom of religious expression for all religions, including Christianity. In early colonial America, ministers commonly doubled as schoolteachers, and classes were often held in churches.[6] The chief textbooks were explicitly Christian and included the Bible, the *New England Primer*, and the *Bay Psalm Book*.[7] The *Primer* contained explicitly Christian material including the names of all the books in the Bible, the Lord's Prayer, the Apostles' Creed, the Ten Commandments, the Westminster Catechism, and *Spiritual Milk for American Babes, Drawn out of the Breasts of Both*

Testaments for their Soul's Nourishment, by Reverend John Cotton.[8] It was often said that the *Primer* taught millions to read and not one to sin. This is in sharp contrast to today, where there is much intolerance in grade school toward voluntary Christian activity even without government sponsorship. Many are moving to destroy religious freedom for Christian students today, and there are numerous examples of this discrimination.[9]

After the 1999 Columbine High School shootings, school officials gave students and families the opportunity to paint tiles above lockers in order to mourn the dead. School officials removed some ninety tiles because they contained "objectionable" phrases such as "God is Love" and "4/20/99 Jesus Wept." The families sued, and the federal district court ruled that the tiles were to be returned to the walls.[10] At Pattison Elementary School in Katy, Texas, school officials not only banned the singing of Christmas songs but threatened grade reductions for students who refused to participate in the singing of songs of other faiths.[11] In Louisville, Colorado, Monarch High School prohibited a group of students from forming a Bible club because it did not "directly relate to the regular curriculum and the educational goals of the school district." However, it allowed other groups to form, including the Gay/Straight Alliance Club, the Multicultural Club, Peace Jam, and Amnesty International.[12] At Northwest Elementary School in Massachusetts, second-grade student Laura Greska brought the book *The First Christmas* to fulfill an assignment about her family's Christmas traditions. Laura was forbidden to share it with the class because it was "religious."[13]

When most Christian students hear statements that challenge the credibility of their faith for the first time, they are often caught off guard and left speechless. In fact, it is estimated that up to 51 percent of Christian college freshmen will renounce their faith before they graduate from college.[14] They have no clue how to defend the biblical worldview because they were never trained to do so. No wonder so many turn their backs on their beliefs! Indeed, I almost abandoned my faith in college because I was not sure if the difficult questions people asked me about Christianity had satisfying answers. I was continually made aware of my inability to respond quickly, thoroughly, and confidently, and I found myself plagued with cynicism and doubt. Nancy Pearcey notes, "It's a familiar but tragic story that devout young people, raised in Christian homes, head off to college and abandon their faith. Why is this pattern so common? Largely because young believers have not been taught how to develop a Biblical worldview. Instead, Christianity has been restricted to a specialized area of religious belief and personal devotion."[15]

The good news is that, with proper training, Christian students can find their college years to be a time of God's blessing instead of a time of spiritual bankruptcy. It is in school that many students rededicate their lives to Christ or genuinely encounter him for the first time. In my collegiate years, I was tempted to ignore the difficult questions that plagued my mind and heart, but it was by facing them head-on and wrestling with them one by one that my faith was strengthened and my life transformed.

Answering Objections to Doing Youth Apologetics

I find it very strange, but I have actually met some parents and youth ministers who are opposed to doing youth apologetics. I've heard them say, "We are afraid to teach our kids apologetics because we don't want them to become arrogant." Can you imagine if they said to those same kids, "You know what, don't study too hard trying to get a good grade on that science test because you might learn too much and become arrogant"? Or, "Don't work too hard at football practice tonight preparing for your game because you might become overly skilled and way too confident"? It is interesting that we are not afraid to demand excellence from students when it comes to grades, sports, and music; but when it comes to teaching them how to articulate matters of faith, there is sometimes incredible fear and unwillingness. We should not be shy or insecure about teaching young people to defend their faith in thought, word, and deed.

Naysayers also argue that if we do not allow teens to make mistakes, then they cannot learn from them and grow into wise adults. Further, we often have no godly sorrow for the sins of our college years. We sometimes reminisce fondly about the struggles that God brought us out of and proclaim that if we did not participate in those sins, we would not be the strong, wise people we are today. This is a dangerous witness to present to the young people who look to us for guidance. I know it is difficult to admit the embarrassing and incriminating sins of our youth. I cringe when teens ask me for personal details of my college years. So when we talk about our past, we often glorify the more humorous and daring aspects to make the experience more palatable for everyone. We are afraid of being seen as uncool by teenagers because they so often intimidate us. Yet it is important to acknowledge that there is godly grief and painful consequences that exist even today because of foolish choices we made in the past, and that it is possible to admit these things without dwelling in the past. It is true that God uses our failures to bring about good, but that doesn't mean that we ought to encourage teens to sin frequently so they can learn the most. That teens will sin is inevitable. They don't need our help. Passively refusing to prepare them to make wise choices is, in fact, actively arranging for them to sin.

Another objection raised to youth apologetics is that training the mind to think critically about core issues of the faith undermines true faith. Dallas Willard describes how "in doing so, they are not honoring to God, but simply yielding to the deeply anti-intellectualist currents of Western egalitarianism, rooted, in turn, in the romantic idealization of impulse and blinded feeling found in David Hume, Jean-Jacques Rousseau, and their nineteenth- and twentieth-century followers. They do not realize that they are operating on the same satanic principle that produced the killing fields of Cambodia, where those with any sign of education—even the wearing of glasses—were killed on the spot or condemned to starvation and murderous labor."[16]

I recently walked through the Cambodian killing fields and saw the remnants of that horror myself. I remember looking down at my sandals to see what had been caught between my toes as I was walking through the grass—it was a human tooth. There are teeth, tattered clothing, bones, and other remains of the tortured still scattered throughout the fields today. One of the taunting slogans of the regime was: "To keep you is no benefit. To destroy you is no loss." While attending a church service in Cambodia, I was served Communion by a former member of the Khmer Rouge whose life was completely transformed by the love of Christ. Many other former regime members have also dedicated their lives to Christ and are active in the church today. If Pol Pot's soldiers can change, then there is hope for even a rebellious teenager.

THE NEED IS GREAT

It is alarming to see the number of Christian young people who reject important aspects of biblical truth. George Barna reports that only 4 percent of born-again teenagers believe in "the accuracy of the Bible, personal responsibility to evangelize, believe in salvation by grace alone, and possess orthodox biblical views on God,

Jesus, and Satan."[17] Many best-selling teen books focus on purpose, romance, and adventure, but few focus on helping youth think critically about their core theology.

I wish I had been prepared for the attack on my faith that took place in college, for I am absolutely convinced that I would have been spared from much doubt, sin, and heartache. This is why I work with teens just before they go to college. Looking back now, I can see how much I would have benefited from such training.

Many teens I talk to about faith issues say it is the first time an adult has asked them why they believe what they believe. Yet make no mistake: *they are learning about God from somewhere.* The question is, who are we allowing to teach them?

EQUIPPING YOUTH AT SCHOOL, CHURCH, AND HOME

Teens need to learn how to engage their faith and talk about it in a mature manner. Young people are remarkably articulate when you drill them on subjects they have been trained in, such as preparing for the SAT or preventing STDs. But when you ask them about God, they often do not have very systematic or coherent answers. Many young people have a difficult time explaining the basics of what they believe, let alone why they believe or the implications of these beliefs for their lives.

Philosopher Charles Taylor argues that inarticulacy undermines the possibilities of reality. Faith and commitment cannot be more than vaguely real when you are unable to have a simple conversation about them. Articulacy fosters the reality of faith. Researchers advise that teens are "to be taught to practice their faith in the sense of consistently working on skills, habits, and virtues in the direction of excellence in faith, analogous to scholars, athletes, and musicians practicing their skills."[18]

We can teach teens to practice and defend their faith by helping them develop their conversation skills. Teens need to practice out loud how to use biblical terminology and imagery winsomely in a conversation without sounding churchy, obnoxious, or offensive. This can be done in a variety of ways and in many different settings.

One important setting in which we must do youth apologetics is in Christian schools. Many Christian parents find that sending their children to solid

Christian schools is a valuable investment and especially important in the tender, formative years of elementary school, where they can be grounded in biblical teaching early on. For teachers, incorporating an apologetic perspective in every subject from English to science is crucial, especially in high school classrooms. Charles F. Potter, author of *Humanism: A New Religion*, writes, "Education is thus a most powerful ally of Humanism, and every American public school is a school of Humanism. What can the theistic Sunday-schools, meeting for an hour once a week, and teaching only a fraction of the children, do to stem the tide of a five-day program of humanistic teaching?"[19] Potter is right. Christian high school teachers can make a world of a difference in the life of future college students in their classroom by anticipating the tough questions their future college professors will ask and by daily equipping the students with sound answers.

How can students share their faith if they don't even know what they believe and why they believe it? Children need to be taught the essentials of their faith before they are sent out to evangelize the world. I am not saying Christian schools guarantee Christian kids—far from it! I am simply saying that for many families, putting children in a school environment grounded in biblical teaching and prayer is a good thing. When I speak at Christian schools, I meet many students who are sent there by non-Christian parents. Not only are these parents not Christian, but they are devout followers of other religions, including Hindus, Muslims, and Buddhists. I remember these students because they are the ones who ask the fiercest questions. If even nonbelievers see the value in sending their children to Christian schools, teaching them biblical morals and deliberately placing them in a Christian environment, we ought also to value this choice.

Parents who choose to send their children to public schools often ask for ways to teach their children apologetics. This is where youth ministers come in. My prayer for weekly youth group gatherings is that they will go from being an entertainment show full of feel-good games to an intense forum that invites tough questions and provides satisfying answers. My prayer is the same for youth retreats, mission trips, small groups, Sunday school, and all other church-related activities. Indeed, says Nancy Pearcey,

> As Christian parents, pastors, teachers, and youth group leaders, we constantly
> see young people pulled down by the undertow of powerful cultural trends. If all

we give them is a "heart" religion, it will not be strong enough to counter the lure of attractive but dangerous ideas. Young believers also need a "brain" religion—training in worldview and apologetics—to equip them to analyze and critique the competing worldviews they will encounter when they will leave home. If forewarned and forearmed, young people at least have a fighting chance when they find themselves a minority of one among their classmates or work colleagues. Training young people to develop a Christian mind is no longer an option; it is part of their necessary survival equipment.[20]

We cannot provide children with a "brain religion" unless youth ministers are required to undergo formal training in theology. Sadly, many people view youth ministers as glorified babysitters and therefore do not expect them to prioritize biblical education. When I was a teen and asked my own youth pastor intellectual questions, he brushed them aside as mere smokescreens to distract from confronting moral sins. I did not receive help from the campus ministries either; they offered me similar patronizing responses and suggested as a solution to my worries that I do-si-do at the barn dance they were hosting that weekend. (I wish I were kidding, but that is the type of thing my university's campus ministries invested in at that time.)

I cannot emphasize enough how dangerous such anti-intellectualism is to spiritual growth. The effect of it is devastating, as we've observed teens abandoning the church in droves. Youngsters do have honest questions, and we must take them seriously and take the time to answer them. Am I glad that I met a man named Norman Geisler who took my questions seriously and was prepared to address them one by one (with delightful candor and no-nonsense directness, I might add). The main reason many kids are encouraged to go to youth group is not to learn but to see their friends and to participate in the fun activities that are provided for them there. In fear of sounding overly dry for emphasizing the importance of worldview studies in youth group, let me assure you that I am not anti-fun. I scuba dive and salsa dance and do invest time in enjoying life and having a good time. I am in no way interested in cultivating nerdy teens. I want to help mentor teens who are diligent in biblical worldview studies but who are also full of joy in their relationships with others and full of wonder at the world around them. It takes extra effort, but it is possible to have both—and hopefully we adults exhibit attractive, overflowing lives as evidence of this.

Preparing Ourselves

You do not have to be a parent, schoolteacher, or ordained pastor to minister to youth. I am none of those things. No matter what your vocation or life situation, you have a profound influence on young people. We often have more of a connection with young people than we think. Whether we are aware of it or not, all of us contribute to shaping youth culture. Teens serve as an accurate barometer of the condition of adults; they reflect back to us the very best and worst conditions of our adult culture. Most problems and issues that we typically label as teenage problems are in fact inextricably linked to problems of the adult world. We adults are just more sophisticated than young people in how we mask our problems. Research shows that "compared to teenagers, adults consume more alcohol, cigarettes, and drugs, commit more crimes and violence, contract more STDs, have more abortions, and more often become obese, drive drunk, commit suicide, and engage in a host of other problems that worry adults about youth."[21]

Few teen problems are invented or promoted by teens; they are created, marketed, and modeled by the adult world. Who markets and profits from selling sex, alcohol, cigarettes, and drugs? Where do teen girls learn to starve themselves? Where do teen boys learn that they are defined by their income? We tell young people to be financially responsible, but we drown ourselves in debt. We say that character is more important than good looks, but we abuse our bodies to appear in shape. We suggest that teens should not view pornography and label it "adult," implying that it is a perfectly legitimate activity for adults to take pleasure in.

Thankfully, of course, many Christians object to such distortions, but my point is that giving an apologetic answer consists of more than concocting witty verbal responses to tough skeptical questions; the character of the adult uttering the verbal argument is often what makes or breaks it.

One afternoon I was having lunch with some friends whose eyes were glued to the television screens in the café. They were watching news reports on multiple school shootings that had taken place that week. I had been on a long trip, so they asked me to lunch so that we could catch up and reconnect. I was trying to share my heart and tell stories about my trip, but they were too distracted by their surroundings to pay any attention to what I was saying. While one friend was simultaneously eating a sandwich, watching TV, talking on his cell phone, text messaging on his BlackBerry, and pretending to listen to me talk, he attributed the embarrassing state of American youth to their short attention span, obsession with technology, and lack of interpersonal skills! The media broadcasts crimes committed by teens, and we should pay special attention to them. But to talk about it as though it is strictly a teenage problem instead of an adult one is self-deceiving.

When *The Times* of London asked Britain's leading intellectuals what they thought was the problem with the world, G. K. Chesterton sent back a postcard response saying, "I am." *We* are what is wrong with the world. The same goes for what is wrong with the teenage world; you and I as adults are the problem. Is it surprising that most born-again adults do not have a Christian worldview (only 9 percent do)?[22] We cannot give to young people what we adults do not possess. In order to equip them, we ourselves have to be prepared in word and deed.

Answering with Gentleness and Respect

Recently I was speaking on pluralism at a chapel service at a boarding school in New York. This private Christian school accepts students from all religious backgrounds from countries all over the world; no faith declaration is necessary. Students are not forced to participate in spiritual activities, but they are aware that the faculty desires to lovingly persuade them to devote their lives to Christ.

I remember having meals with the students in the cafeteria. I would go from table to table during each meal to see if students had any questions or comments about what they heard. I wasn't able to get one bite of food in my mouth, as students were firing question after question at me. I was thrilled to see teenagers so interested in such matters, and their enthusiasm inspired me. At one table at this multireligious and multicultural school, there was a student from Thailand with a Buddhist background, another from India with a Hindu background, one from Egypt with a Muslim background, and another from New York City with an atheistic background. They all were great friends; they sat in class together, lived together, and played sports together.

The Muslim student asked me a question about Jesus that I will never forget. She was a petite, soft-spoken girl who asked if Christ really died on the cross. She said her parents taught her otherwise. When I heard this question, a flood of emotions overwhelmed me. First of all, I was surprised to hear such a specific question about Christ from a young person and nonbeliever. (I am always surprised by this even though it happens so often.) Second, I was overjoyed that I was prepared to answer her question and thankful for the exhaustive work on this topic by Dr. Gary Habermas and others who made my preparation possible.[23] But in addition to my overflowing feelings of joy and gratitude, I confess I was also angry, for her question not only challenged what I believed to be true but also what I held dear: Christ's death on the cross for me. But when I saw her gentle spirit, my anger subsided. She seemed nervous about asking the question, in case it might offend me or hurt my feelings in some way. I could also see that she felt guilty for questioning her parents, whom she seemed to greatly love.

I answered her by taking her hand in mine, looking her straight in the eyes, and saying, "First of all, I want to assure you that it is okay that you are asking this question. You are not offending me at all. And God is not upset that you are asking this question. The Christian faith is one that is open to scrutiny. You can ask me questions about anything in the whole world that you want—I promise! I also want to make it clear that I am not trying to cause division within your family. I don't want you to keep your questions a secret from them or use it to start arguments with them. I want you to tell them what I am about to tell you, and I want you to do it in a respectful and loving way."

I then gave her reasons for believing in the bodily death and resurrection of Christ, and I presented and countered the arguments of some of the popular antideath and antiresurrection theories. She listened quite attentively. She had never heard anything like this before. It was amazing to be able to present something new for her to consider for the first time! She resumed this conversation with her friends, and I smiled as I watched them talk about such things.

But a part of me was still frightened that I would be perceived as trying to cause division among them. I remembered sitting in a university classroom on September 12, 2001, hearing from professor after professor how the tragedy that occurred the day before was the result of religion. I felt incredibly guilty upon hearing this. I wanted to stand up in front of the class and apologize for the atrocities committed in the name of religion. At the root of this belief, however, is an unexamined prejudice that recognizes only the worst contributions of faith instead of the best, such as the abolition of slavery, the promotion of human rights, the rise of universities, and the development of modern science. It is a widely held and unquestioned belief that religion is the main cause of oppression and violence in our world, and that we would be wise to exclude it altogether. Only faiths that are relativistic (true for their believers rather than true independently) are safe and acceptable because they allegedly do not make any exclusivist truth claims.

If this were the case, what then of the atrocities committed by secularist regimes? And why wasn't anyone apologizing for them? Os Guinness reminds us that we must never lose sight of the undeniable fact that more people in the twentieth century were killed by secularist regimes, led by secularist intellectuals and supported by secularist ideologies, than in all the religious persecutions in Western history.[24]

LIFESTYLE APOLOGETICS

As Ravi Zacharias has said, "The greatest obstacle to the impact of the gospel has not been its inability to provide answers, but the failure on our part to live it out."[25] If teens do not see us exhibiting godly moral character in our daily lives, the apologetic arguments we provide them are invalidated, no matter how compelling our words are.

Recent surveys show that Christians are no different from the rest of the world when it comes to issues such as materialism and the poor, physical abuse in marriage, divorce, pornography, and racism.[26] It is not surprising the world has a very negative view of Christians. Though we do not claim that Christian conversion guarantees perfect behavior, we do need to pay close attention to the scandalous disobedience among us. We insist that miracles are central to Christianity, from creation *ex nihilo* and the resurrection of Christ to the moral transformation of sinners. However, when living in disobedience, our own lifestyles can contribute to destroying the credibility of the miraculous. After all, since we profess that conversion to Christianity is a miraculous, supernatural occurrence led by the power of the Holy Spirit, there should be evidence of this miracle illustrated through our extraordinary characters.

When I was in college, anytime I heard about a church scandal in the news, my blood would boil. "Those hypocrites," I would mutter under my breath. It uninspired me in my journey of faith and encouraged me to abandon it. *What's the point if I'm likely to end up like that?* I would think. But now when the latest scandal is exposed, I react with more compassion, especially since now I know what it's like to stand behind the pulpit. Please do not misunderstand me; I am in no way condoning immoral behavior committed by preachers. What I am saying is that the very ability we have to identify frauds and the intense anger we harbor toward them implies that there is actually something authentic from which they depart. Reminding myself of that simple fact over and over again makes all the difference in fueling my desire to seek after God.

Teens often point to the sins of Christians to disprove Christianity. When I ask about difficulties students have with Christianity at high schools I visit, they often tell me stories about their professing Christian classmates. "During the week I see them singing and praying at chapel. On the weekend I see them getting drunk and doing drugs." These non-Christian students do not necessarily have a problem with those behaviors in general, but they become angry when Christians publicly denounce certain behaviors and then participate in them themselves. "At least I'm honest," the non-Christians will say. "I drink and smoke, but the difference is that I am up-front about it. That is what matters."

Since they value consistency, I often ask, "Well, what if I said that doing good deeds as a Christian doesn't matter to me because I don't take the transformation stuff literally. Would it still bother you if I participated in immoral behavior, and would it still disprove Christianity?" It shouldn't. But the moral law continues to churn in their hearts, and their demand for goodness from Christians still persists. One might also ask, if bad behavior is enough to disprove Christianity, then could good behavior verify it? A religion is not automatically proven true because of a devotee's upright behavior.

It is important to point out that research shows that when nominal Christians are distinguished from committed Christians with a biblical worldview, the committed Christians exhibit much better moral behavior: they are twice as likely to volunteer time to help the needy, they are five times less likely to report that their careers come first, they are nine times more likely to avoid Internet pornography.[27] The set of criteria used to identify people with a biblical worldview includes the beliefs that absolute moral truths exist, and that they are conveyed through the Bible. Committed Christians also agreed with all of the following beliefs: God is the all-knowing, all-powerful Creator who still rules the universe; Jesus Christ lived a sinless life; Satan is a real, living entity; salvation is a free gift, not something we can earn; every Christian has a personal responsibility to evangelize; and the Bible is totally accurate in all that it teaches. People with a biblical worldview who adhere to these beliefs actually demonstrate genuinely different behavior.

Young people do find this reassuring and encouraging, especially in a time when evangelicals are under so much public scrutiny. It is clear that biblical orthodoxy matters. Christian apologetics is sometimes seen as focusing on irrelevant, abstract principles "out there," but it ought also to affect us "in here," in our very hearts, which are profoundly shaped by the practical behavioral decisions we make on a daily basis. An objection students express when we respond to hypocrisy by explaining that there actually are morally upright Christians in the world is that the Christians we list are famous ones like Billy Graham whom they do not know personally. There is a disconnect for them. How much more convincing would it be if we lived out our Christian faith before them in our daily lives? Nancy Pearcey says, "In a world of spin and hype, the postmodern generation is searching desperately for something real and authentic. They will not take Christians seriously unless our churches and parachurch organizations demonstrate an authentic way of life—unless they are communities that exhibit the character of God in their relationships and mode of living."[28]

After college, I enrolled in a graduate program in apologetics to learn how to better answer the difficult questions people were constantly asking me. My motives were actually quite self-centered—I wanted to have all the answers so I would not look stupid when I was challenged. Little did I know that I would leave with more questions than answers.

I was stretched more during my time at seminary than at any time in my entire life. I was mentored by an incredible hero of the faith, Dr. Norman Geisler. He constantly challenged me to boldness in every area of my life. I used to be quite timid and insecure. I did not feel I fit in at seminary. I did not look, act, or think like the other students, who were predominantly white, southern males. Yet Dr. Geisler went out of his way to make me feel welcome, constantly involving me in school and church activities. His office door was always open, and I frequently popped in with questions about spirituality, philosophy, even dating. He always listened carefully, never rushing me out the door. He provided candid feedback, prayer, and encouragement. He invited me to his home to spend time with his wife and grandchildren. He showed me how to mentor.

When his assistant connected me with ten teenagers to disciple for a year, I was a little nervous at first, but Dr. Geisler assured me that I could do it. I just did for them what he did for me. I met with them, taught them theology, prayed with them, laughed with them. They watched me closely. They watched how I lived my life: whom I spent time with, what I ate, what I wore, how I spoke, how

I handled stress. The very areas in which I instructed them most fiercely were the areas I struggled with the most—patience, purity, time management—and the areas in which they watched me the closest. Their constant eyes were a challenge and an intense blessing in my life. I believe I learned more from them than they did from me.

God showed me his love by surrounding me with people who loved me in a way that I did not deserve to be loved, a love that I did not reciprocate adequately. I had a teacher who believed in me. I had parents who supported me. I had teenage students who looked up to me. I had families in the community who reached out to me. I had a prospective employer take a risk on me. Receiving sound teaching while witnessing the extraordinary character of Christians around me was truly life changing. If you take the time to mentor a young person, it could be the most compelling argument for the existence of God's love that he or she ever sees.

Faith of the Fatherless

The single most important social influence on the spiritual lives of teens is their parents. Fathers in particular have a vital role to play in the spiritual development of their children. In his fascinating book *Faith of the Fatherless,* social scientist Paul Vitz writes that in his study of the world's most influential atheists (including Friedrich Nietzsche, David Hume, Bertrand Russell, John-Paul Sartre, Albert Camus, and H. G. Wells), all had one thing in common: defective relationships with their fathers. Moreover, when Vitz studied the lives of influential theists (such as Blaise Pascal, Edmund Burke, Moses Mendelssohn, Søren Kierkegaard, G. K. Chesterton, and Dietrich Bonhoeffer) during those same historical time periods, he found they enjoyed a strong, loving relationship with a father figure. Vitz notes that H. G. Wells was contemptuous of both his father and God, writing in his autobiography, "My father was always at cricket, and I think [Mum] realised more and more acutely as the years dragged on without material alleviation, that Our Father and Our Lord, on whom to begin with she had perhaps counted unduly, were also away—playing perhaps at their own sort of cricket in some remote quarter of the starry universe."[29]

Vitz's study challenges the widespread assumption throughout much of the intellectual community that belief in God is based on irrational, immature needs and wishful thinking, whereas skepticism is derived from a rational, no-nonsense appraisal of the way things really are. Since psychology is a weapon that skeptics have chosen to wield against God, it is not unfair for us to ask the same questions of them. With that said, however, as many vehement skeptics have painful memories of negligent fathers underlying their rejection of God, such interior wounds need to be addressed graciously by believers.

Many Asian and Asian-American young people in particular have fathers who model emotional restraint, affirming them sparingly while criticizing generously. Displaying a cold and distant temperament in this cultural context is seen as virtuous; it is the way a respectable father shows that he is stable and in control of his emotions. Children often try to earn such a father's love with certain achievements, yet their works never seem to satisfy. The story of a heavenly Father who offers unconditional love characterized by grace and the theme of reconciliation between estranged parent and child absolutely captivates these young people.

While ministering to teen girls at a shelter in Cambodia, I asked if there were any passages of the Bible that they had a hard time believing. I expected them to ask about Noah and the ark or Jonah and the whale—the stories that most people I meet find whimsical and have problems taking seriously. Yet the only question of the day was: "Why in Romans 8:15 are we described as being 'adopted' rather than God's 'real' children?" The girls who were asking this question were living in a shelter because their birth parents had abandoned them. Many of them had been routinely beaten and raped by their fathers from an early age. They could not comprehend what it meant to be adopted into a family by the grace of a loving father.

Some of these girls were rescued out of brothels and the sex-trafficking business by the founder of the shelter, Reverend Setan Lee. Lee was a former prisoner of the killing fields who once dreamed of becoming a doctor but now does healing of another kind. What can be fittingly described as his "healing fields" include a women's shelter, a trade school, and an orphanage. I asked Setan how one went about rescuing children out of a brothel. He explained that a ransom needed to be paid to redeem the girls since they were in bondage to the brothel boss; everything they owned came from their boss. No matter how much work these girls did, they would never be able to earn enough on their own to repay their debt and buy their freedom. In one sense, these children have already received adoption, as Setan paid the necessary penalty to rescue them and place them in a community together. At the same time, they still anticipate their adoption in its completeness, when they will individually commune with a personal father face to face. This story so beautifully illustrates God's plan of salvation for each of us.

Many young people in the US also have a hard time comprehending adoption into God's family, but for entirely different reasons than the young people in Cambodia. Their confusion does not spring from the problem of pain, but from the problem of pleasure. They have never felt the need to be rescued from torture and poverty and thus have no urgent longing for a savior. "What do we need to be saved from?" they often ask. "We don't do drugs or have sex; we don't need to be saved. We are fine on our own." Biblical terminology is a foreign language to them—words like *atonement* and *sanctification* do not convey meaning to their minds or influence their actions. They often ask why "some guy dying for our sins two thousand years ago" matters today. "Sin" has lost its meaning. If the concept of sin doesn't make sense, then someone dying for our sins is even more confusing and considered downright ridiculous by many.

One thing parents can do in teaching their children is to deeply discuss these significant biblical terms in the home during family devotions. My parents would often have to drag me kicking and screaming as a child to our evening devotions, but looking back now, I am so thankful they did. Much has been written on the problems associated with absentee parents—especially fathers—in American families. While defective fathering increases skeptical attitudes toward God, it may also help generate what Vitz describes as a "widespread father hunger."[30] Parents should be reminded and encouraged that they are without a doubt the most important influence in the spiritual formation of their children.

Conclusion

As George Washington once said, "The future of this nation depends on the Christian training of our youth."[31] It is surprising to see how incredibly teachable teens are when it comes to matters of faith, even though we may assume they are the most rebellious life-form in existence. In my and my colleagues' experience, teens actually enjoy and deeply desire to be trained by us; they are open to being influenced by our love and example. This does not require a PhD in apologetics.

We ordinary adults can make a profound difference in the lives of young people simply by asking them meaningful questions and by providing a safe place where they can respond. The most persuasive apologetic we can offer our children is not a series of carefully constructed verbal arguments, but a life beautifully lived close beside them.

4

CHALLENGES FROM ISLAM

Sam Soloman

Islam poses a huge challenge to the whole world generally and particularly so to the biblical church of Jesus Christ—notwithstanding the firm assurance of the ultimate victory of Christ and his church.[1] Some of us would like to ignore the magnitude of the challenge based on our sure hope as the elect.[2] Others, who may want to realistically face the signs of the times in a more sober and objective way,[3] are often all too prone to narrow it down a bit to something more digestible and state that the threat is posed only by radical political Islam.

Political Islam, radical Islam, moderate Islam, peaceful Islam, mystical Islam, folk Islam, and many other forms and permutations of Islam—all these titles lead us to the first major error of looking at Islam through non-Islamic filters or glasses, and thus interpreting it and measuring it subjectively. We view Islam this way to our peril, overlooking the fact that the challenge is not only political or of a terrorist nature. Rather, as Islam advances in our society, it takes on new faces and new challenges not yet in view.

The primary aim of this chapter is to give Christians some perspective on how Islam views the Christian gospel. Apologetically speaking, it is important to understand that many nonbiblical philosophies or ideologies tend to use biblical terminologies but mean something very different by each term. Islam is a prime example of that, as almost all of its terminology is borrowed from the

Bible—yet its concepts and definitions are fundamentally, dramatically, and totally different.

Many today, even Christians, have the following opinion: "The Qur'an speaks of many Old Testament prophets and Jesus, and it refers favorably to Christians. Furthermore, the two faiths are very similar with similar teaching and only very minor differences." This is a prevalent view, even in evangelical circles. But is it true?

There are increasing social pressures that urge us to focus exclusively on similarities when assessing differing lifestyles and belief systems in our politically correct culture, but such similarity is an illusion at best, especially when it comes to assessing the nature of Islam. A reasonable person knows to examine the differences as well. Therefore, in order to reveal the differences between Islam and Christianity, we must first scrutinize the whole body of thought and faith that is Islam.

Hence, the first section of this chapter will provide a definition of Islam and its constitutional components, the Qur'an and the Sunnah, while providing some pertinent details by defining key terms. I will introduce only those doctrines needed prior to the assessment of the challenges. At that point we will be in the position to examine four key challenges from Islam to the church and society at large, and then the final section concludes with the challenge to Islam from Christianity, documenting the apologetic arguments necessary for interacting evangelically within the system of Islam. I will also relate issues to my personal perspective and experiences. Prior to my encounter of being found by the Lord Jesus through the reading of the New Testament, I had gone through rigorous Islamic training at a very high level. So my argument is not subjective opinion; rather, it is based on a thorough understanding of Islamic sources, manuals, and juristic interpretations.

DEFINITION OF ISLAM

The popular Western view of the word *Islam* meaning "peace" is neither accurate nor Qur'anic. Qur'anically speaking, *Islam* means "submission" or "surrender," but certainly not "peace" by any definition. Sura 49:14 states, "The Bedouins say: 'We believe.' Say: 'You believe not but you only say, We have surrendered [in Islam], for Faith has not yet entered your hearts.'"

Islam cannot be defined as a religion in the Western sense of the word; neither can it be termed as a faith. Muslim scholars state that Islam is an *all-encompassing system*—a sociopolitical, socioreligious system, as well as socioeconomic, socioeducational, legislative, judiciary, and military system governing every aspect of the lives of its adherents, their relationships among themselves, and with those who are non-Muslims.[4]

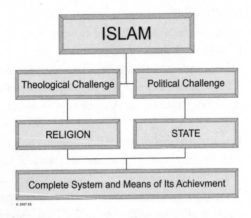

Figure 1: The integration of religion and state leads to a complete system and the development of means for its achievement.

ISLAM'S CONSTITUTIONAL COMPONENTS: THE QUR'AN AND THE SUNNAH

The constitutional components of Islam, the Qur'an and Sunnah, comprise even today in some Muslim countries (such as Saudi Arabia, Iran, and the former Taliban regime) the equivalent of the national constitution. In all Muslim-majority countries (such as Egypt, Jordan, Malaysia, and Indonesia), family law for Muslim communities is based on Sharia law, which is derived from these constitutional components. Even with the participation of the US government, the national constitutions of Iraq and Afghanistan are based on these components, in the sense that these constitutions cannot contradict Islamic law. So let us now briefly examine the basic constitutional ingredients of Islam and their makeup: the Qur'an and the Sunnah (see Figure 2).

Islam claims the book known as the Qur'an to be the final revelation of Allah to mankind through his last and final messenger Muhammad, the seal of all the prophets. This revelation was given to Muhammad piecemeal over a period of twenty-three years through the angel Gabriel. These revelations came to Muhammad mostly in the form of dictated recitations by Gabriel.

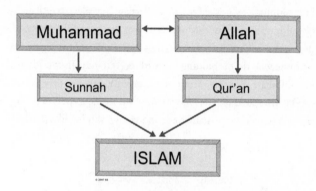

Figure 2: Islam derives its ultimate authority from Allah and Muhammad.

A Reflection on the Author of the Qur'an

Unlike the Bible, the Qur'an has no historical authentic document that can witness to its literary reliability or to its historical authenticity. Its followers claim divine origin from the eternal tablet (see Figure 3).[5] They also claim that the Qur'an has come to perfect the Bible by adding to it. Yet the Qur'an's teachings contradict the very biblical teaching it claims to have come to complete. It does not teach anywhere the Ten Commandments, remains inconsistent with its own teaching, and at best portrays a totally different nature.

And there is the character of its author: Allah. As described in the Qur'an, Allah is not a covenant-making god, for if he were to do that it would diminish his absolute authority and might find him subject to his creatures due to such a covenant. As portrayed, he is master of deception.[6] He contradicts himself and justifies that by calling it *abrogation*, meaning the replacement of earlier revelations with latter ones as they were out of date and no longer applicable—all within a period of twenty-three years. *Tawhid*, the oneness or unity of Allah, is emphasized by repeated denials that Allah has no son, but it is not explained logically or philosophically in the Qur'an. All non-Muslims are Allah's enemies,[7] with specific emphasis on Jews and Christians.[8] He commands the followers of his prophet, whom he calls Muslims, to kill them and regard all non-Muslims as profane.[9] He does not consider the Golden Rule. He never reveals himself, as he is ultratranscendent and unknowable.

All the terminology in the Qur'an is allegedly "revealed" by Allah,[10] whereby he has broken his treaty with non-Muslims forever and has made the shedding of their blood legitimate.[11] There are no absolutes with him.[12] He has prepared a desired place for those who do his bidding but with no certainty. In this place, they would have their full share of sexual pleasures, including alternative lifestyles and beautiful virgins specially created for the enjoyment of his slaves, as well as young handsome boys who will remain perpetually fresh and young, shining like pearls.[13]

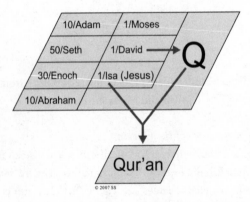

Figure 3: The revelation of the Qur'an as the ultimate, final one from Allah, which replaces all previous revelations, although it allegedly derives its original authority from the same earlier Scriptures (Torah, Psalms, and the Gospels).

In Islam, the highest sacrifice is not that of self-denial for the good of others but of self-sacrifice for the sake of Allah in killing his enemies.[14] The benchmark of true believers is not their ability to love their enemies but how much they can hate them, even if they are their own parents, children, brothers, or kinsmen. Allah has declared his enmity with them forever and ever if they resist him and Muhammad, his apostle.

The Book of the Qur'an

Having introduced the alleged author of the Qur'an, let us consider the book itself. It is composed of 114 chapters known as Suras. They are not chronologically organized. The Arabic language is intrinsically part of the revelation. Therefore, all its translations are regarded as commentaries and not text. Strange as it may sound, the Qur'an has no coherent message, lacks clarity, and is historically inaccurate and internally inconsistent.

Apologetically speaking, the Qur'an has serious fear of biblical teachings and so it distorts them through allusions and by falsification of the biblical truths. Its revelation through inspiration and its methodology are shrouded in secrecy. The original version of the Qur'an, having been preserved in the eternal tablet, was brought down to the atmospheric realm of our earth. Muslims believe that the whole of the Qur'an is an inspired word, with no human influence whatsoever. It has never been subjected to the acid tests that the Bible has been.

The Sunnah of Muhammad: The Exemplar

Sunnah is an Arabic word that means "to form, to shape, to mold, to set, a path a track." In this case, it means "the example of the prophet Muhammad," with the intent of establishing a new community and unifying it away from its tribal and ethnic backgrounds.

Muhammad claimed to be the perfect man and the ultimate example.[15] The implication of the Sunnah is that all Muslims are to model their lives on Muhammad's life. Thus, the Qur'an is like a framework, but at least 80 percent of a Muslim's life is shaped by the Sunnah.

Islamic law declares that insulting the prophet Muhammad is equivalent to insulting Allah. Allah and Muhammad are paired throughout the Qur'an. If one believes in Allah without a belief in Muhammad and his status as the final prophet, he or she is regarded as an infidel and an enemy of Islam. Though denied outwardly, this belief is firmly established and central to the very survival of Islam.

Furthermore, according to the most respected scholars of Islam, Muhammad's spirit was created before Allah created Adam, and the Islamic creed is inscribed on the throne of Allah. As taught in the Qur'an, Muhammad was a lawgiver.[16] Hence, regarding any issue in Islam, the only definitive answer in any given category is what the jurisprudence states, based on these twofold foundations, the Qur'an and the Sunnah, and disseminated by the mosque.

Having outlined the basic constitutional components of Islam, we now need to consider a few of its many challenges—namely, the theological, political, administrative, and pragmatic challenges.

THE THEOLOGICAL CHALLENGE OF ISLAM

Unlike any other religion or ideology, Islam bases its authenticity and legitimacy firmly upon the prior revelations contained in the whole of the Judeo-Christian Scriptures. Let us examine a few of the key Qur'anic declarations as they refer to, and thus draw authenticity from, the Bible.

Jesus Proclaimed the Coming of Muhammad

The Qur'an declares that the sole mission of Jesus was to affirm the Torah and proclaim the coming of Muhammad: "And when Iesa (Jesus), son of Mary, said: 'O Children of Israel! I am the Messenger of Allah unto you confirming the Tauât [(Torah) which came] before me, and giving glad tidings of a Messenger to come after me, whose name shall be Ahmed: But when he [Ahmed i.e. Muhammad] came to them with clear proofs, they said: 'This is plain magic'" (Sura 61:6).

According to the Qur'an, this above-mentioned prophecy by Jesus was one of many within the biblical text that are said to make a clear reference to the coming of Muhammad. And in fact, Muslims say that the whole of Scripture speaks of Muhammad, so that the "Jews and Christians know him well," as referenced in Sura 7:157: "Those who follow the messenger, the unlettered Prophet, whom they find mentioned in their own [scriptures],—in the law and the Gospel."

All Biblical Prophets Were Muslims

The Qur'an regards all biblical prophets as having been Muslims, because Islam, being the religion of Allah, means that all his prophets are Muslims by definition.[17] Further, the Qur'an states that the Old Testament prophets all preached Islam and bowed their will to Allah in Islam, as in Sura 3:67: "Ibrahim (Abraham) was neither a Jew nor a Christian, but he was a true Muslim Hanifa and he bowed his will to Allah in Islam."

One of many other references for this concept is Sura 2:136, in which all the patriarchs and Moses are said to have also been Muslims. "We believe in Allah and that which has been sent down to us and that which has been sent down to Ibrahim (Abraham), Ismail (Ishmael), Ishaque (Isaac), Ya'cub (Jacob), and to Al-Asbat [the twelve sons of Ya'qub (Jacob)], and that which has been given to Musa (Moses) and Iesa (Jesus), and that which has been given to the Prophets from their Lord. We make no distinction between any of them, and to Him we have submitted (in Islam)."

All Mankind Is Created Muslim

Based on this and many other verses, Islam has an even more specific doctrine called *fitrah*, as referenced in Sura 30:30: "So set you (O Muhammad) your face towards the religion of pure Islamic Monotheism Hanifa Allah's Fitrah, with which He has created mankind. No change let there be in Khalq-illâh (i.e., the Religion of Allah Islamic Monotheism), that is the straight religion, but most of men know not." This doctrine teaches that not only were Jesus and the Major Prophets created as Muslims, but that *all* mankind—without exception—is created Muslim. It is only one's parents, community, environment, or other influences that make one a non-Muslim. As such, people who are of another faith—such as a Christian, Jew, pagan, or other belief system—are in a state of rebellion against Allah.

That is why when non-Muslims convert to Islam, the term *reversion* is applied rather than *conversion* because they are "reverting" back to their birth status as Muslims. Therefore, when a Christian or a Jew says the Islamic statement of faith to become a Muslim, they are not "converts"; they are "reverts"—and they are welcomed "home" with great rejoicing by the Muslim community. They are given assistance, training, community, and they have all of their needs met because they have "returned to the religion of Allah."

Muhammad Is the Final Prophet

These disputes, counteraccusations, and the Islamizing of the biblical prophets and their scriptures and revelations promoted the revelations in Muhammad's defense that he was supremely unique, the final prophet, the only means of salvation, and the absolute authority within Islam and thus to all mankind.

Naturally these views were challenged by the Christians and the Jews of Muhammad's day, and these challenges led him to claim that they were both in error and lying. He further accused them of tampering with their own scriptures in order to remove the prophecies that predicted him. This accusation resulted in the Qur'anic doctrine of biblical corruption as explained in more detail in the section on the pragmatic challenge of Islam.

The result of the aforementioned doctrine led to the falsification of all biblical revelations, teachings, values, laws, covenants, doctrines, and thus the rejection of the uniqueness of Christ, his person, and his atoning work. Muhammad then moved on to declare that he represents the perfect model to be followed and imitated by all, calling himself master of the entire human race and claiming to the headship over all the prophets as the only intercessor with Allah.[18]

THE POLITICAL CHALLENGES OF ISLAM

The political challenge is traced to its original roots in the evolution of early Islam under the direction and administration of Muhammad. The full implementation of his political program by his followers for the past fourteen hundred years reveals hardly any change in the doctrines of political Islam, as coded in the Qur'an and the Sunnah. Two important doctrines by Muhammad need to be considered in this regard.

The Doctrine of the Universality of Muhammad's Message and Mission

First is the doctrine of the universality of Muhammad's message and mission. Sura 7:158—"Say O mankind I am an apostle of Allah unto all of you"—means that, since all people need to be brought back to Islam, then Muslims are obligated to implement this goal by *every means necessary*. The resulting political implication divides the world into two territories: the land of Islam and the land of war. The land of Islam is to be fully governed by the Islamic state armed with the Sharia law, and the land of war is to be subdued by every means necessary.

The Doctrine of Jihad

Second is the doctrine of jihad, which evolved to apply to both the land of Islam and the land of war. In the land of Islam, the state is still vulnerable to attacks by Islam's enemies and other religious and political groups. Hence, the means of population control and subjugation of opposition needed to be put in place.

In the land of war, wars were fought by Muhammad and his followers; the so-called enemies of Allah were fought against and were subdued. Some of the pagans were spared on recitation of the creed and upon acceptance of the political and religious hegemony of Islam, or killed if they failed to do so. Only the Jews and Christians were given the choice to convert (revert) or to live a life of servitude and humiliation under strict Islamic regulations with their religious freedom stifled (Sura 9:29).

I am sad to say that not only were millions and millions of people killed in those early Islamic conquests, but jihad in real terms has virtually never stopped. Today persecution is rife, and non-Muslims have at best a token freedom for religious survival with severe penalties if they ever attempt to preach overtly or attempt to convert Muslims.

The Crime of Conversion

Because of this climate of fear regarding charges for converting Muslims, when I asked one of my Christian friends to get me a copy of the New Testament, there was much hesitancy on his part. He refused at first and required a lot of pushing and pleading before he did it. When I got it, I had to hide it. Finally when I could read it, I had to do so in utter secrecy. This is why when it became known that I had embraced the Christian faith, I was arrested and went through a considerably hard time, finally being forced into exile by being deported from my country of birth.

To discard Islam for another faith, or for no faith, is a serious crime no less severe than treason. In some Muslim countries the punishment for embracing Christ is death by public execution, while in other countries it could mean a life of isolation and ostracism, hardship on all fronts, and continuous harassment from the family to the state.

Overall, the supremacy of Islam is prevalent even in the so-called moderate Muslim countries and regions such as Egypt, Jordan, Morocco, Turkey, and the Gulf. This magnifies an already difficult task of evangelism among Muslims.

Sadly, even in the Western world comparatively few Christians are engaged in evangelizing Muslim friends. This may be due to fear or lack of knowledge regarding how to go about it. And when they do, they are at a loss because the lines of distinction are blurred with seeming similarities. Yet the Christian faith and Islam are as far away from each other as the East is from the West.

The Administrative Challenges of Islam

Muhammad stated that Islam is a religion and a state, and he intertwined both, making them inseparable. Muhammad himself claimed authority from top to bottom in the budding Islamic entity, including prophetic office, supreme legislator, judge, commander-in-chief of the armies, and finally as the head of the Muslim community. He established a state, sent armies, conquered his enemies, and collected taxes. He regulated the conduct of his followers by legislating their behaviors in almost every aspect of their public and private lives—both in relation to one another and in relation to non-Muslims. So as stated before, Islam is neither a religion in the Western sense of the word, nor is it a faith; it is an all-encompassing system.

The Islamic View of Life and Religion

When considering the comprehensiveness of the Islamic system, we must note that the relationship between life and religion in a Muslim society is foundationally different from that in other societies. In non-Muslim societies, there is a lot more to life than just religion. Furthermore, the freedom to choose one's religion is in principle a personal matter, respected by others, and protected by law.

In Islam, the very idea of a "choice" is not only an anathema but is also regarded as an anti-Islamic concept. Freedom of choice does not exist in Islam; neither is religion a private or personal matter. All decisions have already been made by Allah and his prophet Muhammad, so Muslims have no choice but to follow these divine regulations, as we see prescribed in Sura 33:36: "It is not for a believer, man or woman, when Allah and His Messenger have decreed a matter that they should have any option in their decision. And whoever disobeys Allah and His Messenger, he has indeed strayed in a plain error."

By way of illustration, consider carefully the following two illustrations as given in Figure 4, which demonstrate visually that in the non-Islamic view religion plays only a part of life. In contrast, in the Islamic view, Islam is basically all of life, with only a small fraction left for personal choice.

The first rectangle (Figure 4a) is entitled "Life," in which religion appears to be a tiny part of that life, indicating it to be private, no matter how ardent one may be in one's beliefs, with the full choice of conscience of when and where to worship, in setting personal prayer times, direction of prayer, kinds of food, what to wear, who to associate with, and so on.

Now consider Figure 4b and compare. The Islamic view is the whole rectangle, whereby it is a religious system and life is a miniscule part of it. According to the Islamic worldview, religion is everything. All that is in life emanates from religion, from the most basic personal hygiene regulations to the most major issues in the community, and in relation to the outside world.

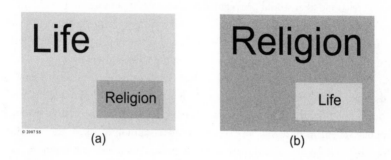

Figure 4: Life vs. Religion in the Non-Islamic and Islamic Worldviews

In Islam, life and religion are so deeply intertwined and inseparable that if a Muslim discards his religion for another, it is regarded as the highest treason and punishable by death in Islamic law. This is the driving principle behind what I have termed the *administrative challenge*: the ability to control the Islamic population within the Islamic state and to prevent Muslims from being liberated from the resulting physical and spiritual oppression.

The Myth of "No Compulsion in Religion"

When engaging Muslims in religious discussion, one usually hears that Islam is a religion of peace and there is "no compulsion in religion." This phrase, often quoted by Muslims when freedom of religion is discussed, is a convenient phrase but not the final word in the Qur'an by any means. The phrase "no compulsion in religion" comes from Sura 2:256, which gives the impression of complete freedom of choice for individuals within an Islamic state or community. Note that "no compulsion" in religion is even at first glance a negative form of freedom, meaning at its best that it tolerates but does not grant the right of freedom for an individual to choose his or her own religion.

If "no compulsion in religion" were to be practiced, then the preaching of the gospel would not be criminalized in Islamic states. Yet people are regularly deported from Islamic countries for giving a Bible to a Muslim, for discussing Christianity with an individual, or in some cases even for possessing a Bible of their own.

Even if one were to make a simple statement with no intention to offend, such as "Muhammad the prophet of Islam was not holy" or "Islam is not the final religion," that would be regarded as blasphemous almost everywhere in the Islamic world. In Pakistan, for instance, one would be charged with blasphemy under Pakistan's penal code of 295A, B, and C with the penalty varying from a minimum ten years to life imprisonment, or even a death sentence.

If the "no compulsion in religion" of Sura 2:256 were to be practiced, then why does the Saudi penal code prescribe a death penalty to any Muslim within Saudi Arabia were he to change his religion? Almost anywhere in the Islamic world, a public statement of a Muslim's conversion or discarding of Islam bears a heavy penalty of isolation, official persecution, imprisonment, and even death. As discussed elsewhere in this chapter, since conversion to a religion other than Islam is considered treason against an Islamic state, the execution is often done in public.

Consequently, depending on the "no compulsion" reference is wishful thinking at best and is in reality a moot point. This is because Sura 2:256, along with other similar verses Muhammad stated earlier in his preaching that proclaim flexibility, has been abrogated and replaced by later revelations, according to Islamic jurisprudence and revered authoritative Qur'anic expositors.[19] This replacement became termed in the Qur'an as the doctrine of abrogation.[20] The definitive references are Sura 16:101 and Sura 2:106:

And when We change a Verse [of the Qur'an, i.e. cancel (abrogate) its order] in place of another, and Allah knows the best of what He sends down, they (the disbelievers) say: "You (O Muhammad) are but a Muftari! (forger, liar)." Nay, but most of them know not.

Whatever a Verse (revelation) do We abrogate or cause to be forgotten, We bring a better one or similar to it. Know you not that Allah is able to do all things?

Furthermore, according to Islamic jurisprudence and Sharia, with the unanimous agreement of all scholars, "no compulsion in religion" simply means that all

Arabs, Jews, Christians, nonbelievers, and pagans have the freedom to convert to Islam, but not the other way around. In other words, it is a one-way freedom.

The Doctrine of Allegiance and Immunity

Muhammad's authority evolved as well. Alongside revelations of Islam being "the religion of Allah," Muhammad claimed his own supremacy as the apostle of Allah, and he consequently taught that all prophets, apostles, or messengers who came before him were simply forerunners who were now replaced. Since he was now the sole authority, all other systems politically were invalid, based on the divine doctrines as expressed in the Qur'an and the Sunnah. This religious-political doctrine is known as doctrine of *Al Wallaa' wa al Baraa* (allegiance and immunity), which is, in short: enmity.[21]

To understand how the administrative challenge works, we need to consider the pragmatic challenge.

THE PRAGMATIC CHALLENGES OF ISLAM

Here we need to consider at least four of the most important ingredients of the pragmatic challenge: doctrine of the Takkiya (cover-up), doctrine of abrogation, doctrine of biblical corruption, and doctrine of living obedience.

The Doctrine of Takkiya (Cover-Up)

Takkiya literally means "caution," "fear," or "disguise." It sanctions lying to or deceiving others to advance the cause of Islam or to preserve its good name. As such, "It permits the suspension, as the need arises, of almost any or all religious requirements, or its doctrines—including a total denial of faith—when fearing threat, injury, or compulsion of any kind in a non-Muslim society, or even in a Muslim society." The Qur'anic injunction for Takkiya is Sura 16:106: "Anyone who after accepting faith in Allah utters Unbelief *(kuffur)* except under compulsion, his heart remaining firm in faith but such as open their breast to unbelief, on them is wrath from Allah."[22]

The wiles used in connection with Takkiya, especially in taking oaths with a complete mental blockage by the user, continue to do incalculable damage and injury to all of its victims.

The Takkiya is very effectively used in apologetics,[23] so a Muslim debater will hide or deny certain parts of the Qur'an to justify and advance the cause of Islam. Always outmaneuvering his Christian opponents, the debater does this with no guilt as this is divinely sanctioned. I personally practiced this prior to coming to the Lord. It is displayed in words, actions, or attitudes.

The Doctrine of Abrogation

The doctrine of abrogation was to Muhammad a doctrine of convenience. So when he claimed a revelation to be no longer suitable, he claimed that it was replaced by some new revelation. For example, initially in his mission Christians were friends and called the nearest and closest to Muslims, but later they were the enemies and the worst of Allah's creatures.

The difficulty with this doctrine is that it is scattered all over the Qur'an, and one phrase or verse may abrogate or replace either one or many. So, for instance, Sura 9:5 abrogates some 124 verses of the Qur'an! Interestingly, the abrogated (nullified) verses are quoted to non-Muslims all the time, causing obfuscation and taking a Christian apologist by surprise. But this practice is justified via the Takkiya doctrine explained above.

The Doctrine of Biblical Corruption

The doctrine of the corruption of the Bible is constantly preached in the mosques and Islamic outlets, deploying all mental and spiritual skills, and in debates. In the initial stages of Muhammad's mission, the early Suras validated the biblical Scriptures, only to be abrogated by later ones. It is not unusual for Muslim speakers to impress their Western audiences with these earlier "friendly" verses and to proclaim that there is hardly any difference between Islam and Christianity![24]

Again, in borrowing biblical terminologies and giving them different interpretations, Islam has taken on the triune God of the universe and his church and, according to Scripture, is bound to fail.

The Doctrine of Living Obedience

Islam declares that Allah has created man and *jinn* (unseen beings) to worship him. Islam, being a religion and a state, obligates a Muslim to such "worship" at both levels. These duties are known as *ibada*. So fasting is worship (Sura 2:183, 185), as is *salat* (ritual prayer) and *zakat* (almsgiving) (Sura 9:60), and so is the *hijab* (women's head covering) and wearing of beards for men (because Muhammad had a beard). But *ibada* also includes killing and slaying Allah's enemies (Sura 2:216).[25]

Hence, every Muslim is a soldier in the state of Islam. As a Muslim soldier, he or she is required to obey and fulfill not only the religious obligations of fasting and praying but also the duties of the state, including fighting and dying for the way of Allah. This is codified in the Qur'an as the "doctrine of living obedience," based, for example, in Sura 61:11: "That you believe in Allah and His Messenger, and that you strive (your utmost) in the Cause of Allah, with your property and your persons: That will be best for you, if you but knew!"

From a pragmatic perspective, the doctrine of living obedience gives the Islamic authorities (combined religious/political/military) full rights to demand any services from the Muslims, including sacrifice of property and even life. In fact, this doctrine is the basis of the current suicide phenomenon observed now on a daily basis.

A Christian Response to the Challenges of Islam

Apologetics generally requires a thinking mind. But Christian apologetics demands more: a thinking head as well as a compassionate heart. This is more easily said than done. Jesus commanded his followers to love their enemies and to pray for them (Matt. 5:44). He knew and said that he was sending them (his disciples) as lambs in the midst of wolves (Matt. 10:16). Muslim evangelism requires a life of prayer, self-denial, and even great risk in some circumstances.

Realizing that Islam fills the minds of its citizens with a different Jesus—and that even to imagine Jesus as the second person of the triune Godhead is a combination of high treason and blasphemy—one begins to understand the desperate state into which Muslims are born through no choice of their own.

A Distorted View of Jesus

Islam is the lens through which Muslims see the Qur'anic version of Christ and even the Trinity. So what they see in Jesus, within their book, is really what apologists call a straw man; in the case of the Trinity, they see an extreme and truly blasphemous case of idolatry. Through this distorted lens they see a Jesus who is a prophet only to the Jews, who came for the purpose of confirming the law of the Torah and to announce the coming of one greater than he—one named Ahmad (another name for Muhammad). To Muslims, Jesus' mission is not universal, as Muhammad's is said to be, and he is alleged to be a Muslim himself; even Jesus is said to bow the knee to Allah in Islam.

To realize this is to develop a compassionate outlook and to begin to comprehend even the most heinous permutation of the Islamic faith we are witnessing today—the growing number of suicide bombers. Contrary to what we hear, these young men and women are often handpicked from among the most moderate of the Muslim population. They are then pressured within a short period of time into taking an action they are assured is necessary to please Allah and at the same time to bring honor to their families.

In spite of this, Muslims yearn for the true God, and many are crying out in search of the truth. In an increasing number of cases, Christ is coming to them and is answering them directly. However, this does not leave us free to abandon the pursuit of reaching Muslims. It just means that our pursuit must be more intentional and that we must realize certain realities make reaching Muslims totally different from any of the other false religions in existence.

A Little Bit of Truth, but Not the Whole Picture

As we have discussed briefly, Islam gains its authenticity from claiming to be the furtherance of the Torah and the Gospels of the New Testament, while at the same time protecting itself from comparison—and thus exposure—through a convenient doctrine of "biblical corruption." This doctrine claims that the Scriptures were altered by the Jews and Christians in order to remove the alleged predictions of the coming prophet of Islam, Muhammad.

So one can see that Muslims have been methodically inoculated on all points by having been given heavy doses of what appears to be true, so that the actual truth looks like the lie. Through their lens, they get a little bit of Jesus, but not the real Jesus, the second person of our triune God, our savior, priest, and king—but a Muslim Jesus, with no cross, no deity, no universal mission as savior of mankind.

Through their lens, they also get a little bit of the patriarchs, the Trinity, and all other key personalities and doctrines—just enough to give the appearance of confirming and extending the Torah and Gospels. They add a little here, omit a little there—so only the appearance remains intact; but the gospel they tell is a "different gospel" that fits the warnings in the Bible against adding or subtracting from the Scriptures (Gal. 1:8; Rev. 22:18–19).

Principles for Reaching Muslims

This is just a brief overview of the challenges of Islam, but we are encouraged greatly by what the Lord is doing in recent days among Muslims, and by the assurances we have that he indeed will go with us when we go in his name and for his purposes.

Below are some principles that apply for those who are moved to take on this formidable challenge to dedicate themselves to reaching Muslims. At first glance, they may seem simplistic, but each principle is distilled from experience on the front lines of Muslim evangelism.

Muslim evangelism is labor intensive. This will not come as a surprise, but it must be intentionally taken into account or one can burn out after feelings of failure set in when coming up against the substantial defenses that Islam has erected in the Muslim mind. Keep in mind always that results are not the issue, but rather perseverance, diligence, and accountability.

Have a backup team of intercessors. These people care about these concerns and can also be a sounding board when you hit obstacles or have theological questions about certain issues. Muslims are drawn to Christians and often share personal issues and request prayer—amazingly enough. Also, you yourself will need backup prayer because of the increasing spiritual pressures you will experience the more successful you are.

Muslim evangelism requires an ongoing commitment to the study of Christian doctrines. In our witness to Muslims, the Bible and its teachings will be severely tested, accused, and refuted—but it is the inspired Word of God that embodies the truth.

Know your enemy and know your spiritual limits. Studying the Qur'an and Islamic sources and issues is essential, but it is also spiritually draining and unhealthy without a constant dose of God's truth. As a general rule, I recommend a four-to-one ratio of praise, worship, and immersion in the Word for every one hour in the Qur'an or other sources. This caution must not be overlooked. You may be able to get by in the beginning, but it will catch up with you, and many have been so seriously wounded that they have become ineffective. We must take heed.

Before engaging in Qur'anic studies, be sure that this is a calling of the Lord. Everyone can witness their faith to Muslims by coming alongside them as friends and through many activities short of studying the Qur'an. However, those who want to go into studies of Islamic sources should be sure of their calling to apologetics or polemics and should approach it with sobriety.

Be careful in your relationships with Muslims. When you converse with Muslims, you need to watch your temper because the lies and refutations will not always be limited to the issues of the Bible, but will spill over into your culture, your country, and all you hold dear. Remember that this is to put you to the test by provoking you. Stay calm and seek the Lord's help under fire. Once you lose your temper, you have lost a lot.

Demonstrate the love of Christ in your relationships with Muslims. Muslims are drawn to the love of Christ, and this is a big responsibility as well as a blessing. When I read the New Testament, what amazed and astounded me the most was the teaching on love, not only toward one's kin and kindred, but even toward one's enemies. It was so different from my training in Islam that it actually made me angry that someone could suggest something so obviously impossible. But as I continued reading, the reality of it entered my heart and changed my life.

And finally, *do not ignore the supernatural in Muslim evangelism,* or take it as an excuse to avoid evangelism, depending on the Lord to come to your Muslim friend in a vision or dream. We have been commanded to proclaim in love—in season and out (2 Tim. 4:2)—so we commend you to obey the Lord even if it means some hardship. After all, we have been called to deny ourselves and carry the cross of Christ for his glory.

5

CHALLENGES FROM EASTERN RELIGIONS

L. T. Jeyachandran

To say the least, the title for this chapter is rather forbidding! One of the ways to defang the title is to recognize that apart from Judaism, Christianity, and Islam, all the other major world religions have been conceived geographically in countries from India and eastward. While all religions are Asian in geographical origin, it is the West that has been more influenced by the gospel of Christ, presumably because the gospel moved westward first in its influence rather than eastward. Christianity has thus come to be spoken of as a Western religion. It is also a fact that Hinduism and Buddhism were born in India;[1] Buddhism moved eastward and has taken various forms in China and Japan as it has combined with certain local beliefs.

In this chapter, I will address Hinduism and Buddhism and some of their modern-day New Age manifestations. I will be careful to point out that New Age beliefs do not naturally flow from the scriptures of Hinduism and Buddhism; rather, some sections of the scriptures of these religions have been speculated upon by philosophers to reach conclusions that provide support to present-day New Age movements.

It will be helpful for us not to see the challenge of Eastern religions in an adversarial or combative way, but rather in a Christlike, sensitive spirit that would help communicate the gospel to the adherents of these faiths. I have made a sincere attempt in this chapter to identify the real longings of Hindus,

Buddhists, and New Agers and to point out how these aspirations can be met in Christ and Christ alone.

How do we understand and critique these religions and their New Age offshoots? We should consciously avoid the danger of assuming that religions have come down to us in terms of philosophical universals. The study of philosophical apologetics encourages such thinking, which, though very useful in addressing the logical contradictions inherent, for example, in much of atheistic thinking, can be somewhat misleading in understanding the beliefs and practices in ancient civilizations. These cannot always be analyzed in terms of purely logical parameters.

In this context, it is important to recognize that of the two religions of Hinduism and Buddhism, the former has come through stories and not creeds. The latter, while originating in the teachings of its founder, Gautama, has evolved in a particularly interesting way to seek a relationship with him as the Buddha. But even in Buddhism, the beliefs have come about through discourses between persons, such as the belief that the individual disintegrates at death, which is found in a conversation between a king and a Buddhist elder.[2]

We will do well to remind ourselves that the Christian faith has come to us as a narrative. N. T. Wright[3] and Kevin Vanhoozer[4] have emphasized this fact—the former as story and the latter as drama. It will therefore be helpful to consider all religions, especially the two that we encounter in this chapter, as stories. We need to enter these stories and begin to retell them from a Christian perspective.[5]

It is significant that James Sire, well known for his book *The Universe Next Door,*[6] rightly raises the following question in his more recent book, *Naming the Elephant:* "Is a worldview an intellectual system, a way of life or a story?"[7] We want to make a serious effort to look out for the stories in which these religions are encapsulated and then seek to identify with the existential struggles that are portrayed in those stories. We can confidently say that the apostle Paul adopts the same method in addressing the Athenians at the Areopagus: though he is himself distressed at the idol worship of the nation, he is willing to identify with their desire for worship. He then goes on to point out how the Creator of the universe does not need anything from us but calls us to repentance in Christ (Acts 17:16–31).

At the end of this chapter, I have applied philosophical analysis to the critique of New Age simply because it has come about by such speculation. Care should be taken not to caricature Hinduism and Buddhism as part of New Age just because some philosophical schools belonging to these religions have contributed to the present New Age movement. As we will see, the tendency for a New Age monism is obvious in many of the ancient philosophies, both Eastern and Western.

UNDERSTANDING HINDUISM

At the outset, it will be important to note a few facts about Hinduism. First, because this religion is not creedal, your Hindu friend or acquaintance may not actually believe what you read in a book on Hinduism—or for that matter, in this chapter! Hinduism is always in a state of flux and is able to absorb aspects of other religions and philosophies without much trouble. It is always important to find out what a Hindu actually believes by carefully listening to him or her before we are able to present the gospel in a relevant way.

Second, Hinduism can be comprised of several contradictory beliefs in the purely analytical sense. At an existential level, the Hindu would be quite comfortable in moving from one position to another that would seem to be mutually exclusive. For example, he could insist in his conversation with you that we are all one with the divine—a favorite New Age approach—and yet will not give a second thought to accompany his wife to the local temple to bow before a deity and ask for favors.

There are eight hundred million Hindus in the world, comprising 13 percent of the world's population. This number could be closer to 1 billion, particularly in terms of converts to hinduized New Age. The word *Hindu* has been historically a reference to the river Indus that now is part of Pakistan. The term is geographical rather than religious in origin.

When studying Hinduism, a Christian is likely to be tempted to simplify it so as to bring it within manageable proportions. Christians are accused (somewhat rightly) of misunderstanding and unfairly criticizing Hinduism. We should therefore take pains to take in as much of the complexities of the religion before we attempt to critique it.

It is best to visualize Hinduism as a spectrum. This model will also help us to picture the complex and sometimes contradictory ingredients that make up this religion.

Popular Hinduism (Polytheism)
If you imagine the systems of belief that comprise Hinduism as a straight line, at one end of the line is the belief in a number of finite personal gods. This aspect of Hinduism can arguably be called *popular Hinduism* and involves worship of and

devotion to one or more of 330 million gods and goddesses. This number is not an agreed figure even among Hindu scholars, but what is relevant to Christians is that this belief expresses genuine love and a desire for relationship with personal deities.

This belief in a multiplicity of gods is called *polytheism* (derived from *polus* = many, *theos* = god).

Philosophical Hinduism (Pantheism)

At the other end of the spectrum is the increasingly marketed belief in the One Infinite, Impersonal Reality (*Brahman*—not to be confused with the Hindu personal god of creation, Brahma, or the Brahmin caste). This view can be called *philosophical Hinduism* as this seeks to explain (or explain away) the multiple and diverse entities in light of the supposed One Entity.

This philosophy of undifferentiated oneness is called *pantheism* (derived from *pan* = all; *theos* = god) and is the Indian contribution to the New Age movement. The proponents of this position would have us believe that there is only one reality—*Brahman*—and the diverse things that we observe in the world are illusory or at best, lower-level manifestations of that one reality. This aspect of Indian philosophy is not separately dealt with in this chapter, but its salient features are covered under New Age.

POPULAR HINDUISM

The earliest available Sanskrit writings on which Hinduism is based can be dated to 150 BC. The Vedas (Words of Knowledge) were orally transmitted from about 1000 BC but were committed to writing much later. Although there are four Vedas, the oldest (the *Rig Veda*) is the original. The *Yajur* and *Sama* are different arrangements of the Vedic hymns for different purposes, and the *Atharva Veda* comprises magical formulas.

The *Rig Veda* consists of a collection of 1,028 hymns of praise to a group of largely male deities who seem to personify various powers of nature, such as the sun, fire, sky, and rain. In this aspect, popular Hinduism is similar to Greek and Roman polytheisms. The chief attribute of the Vedic gods was their power over the lives of human beings. In addition to these *devas* (gods), there are many lesser gods and spirits. The *maruts* were storm deities that rode with Indra in their chariots, singing martial songs. Ribhus are faithful craftsmen spirits (somewhat like gnomes) who worked with metal in the depths of the earth. The Vedas also speak of the lovely *Apsaras*, similar to the nymphs of Greek mythology, who might become the mistresses of gods and men.

The Vedas help us to piece together some picture of the centuries of Aryan immigration into the Indian subcontinent. The historical evidence and interpretation of this immigration is still a matter of much discussion in scholarly circles. It is also important to note that the Vedas are not historical documents in the same sense as the Old Testament. Even at that time, there appear to have been the first indications of class distinction (castes) within their society with priests, rulers, and tribespeople. The initial distinctions were between Aryan and non-Aryan people on the basis of color (*varna*), which later became the order of caste hierarchy. The social classes of the Aryan people—priest, warrior, merchant—assumed the position of the three twice-born castes of Brahmin, Kshatriya, and Vaishya respectively. The term *dasa* (slave) was ascribed to the natives of the subcontinent. These and those born of mixed parentage became the once-born Shudra peasant caste. These indigenous people had to flee into the forest and hills and were later to become the untouchables mainly to be employed in lowly, menial labor.

Worship

All polytheisms—and popular Hinduism is no exception—could have begun as worship of the powerful forces of nature. Eventually, the forces of nature were personified into the earliest deities of Hindu polytheism. It is the later accretion of mythologies that introduced many other gods and goddesses who were not directly related to nature. From a Christian perspective, it must be appreciated that belief in personal gods is symptomatic of a basic human need for relationship with a supernatural personal being. In fact, the *bhakti* (devotion) movement of Hinduism encourages devotion to gods that would put Christians to shame.

At various stages of its development, Hinduism has produced individuals and groups of devotees who composed songs of worship that clearly portray the intense longing of the human heart for linking with the transcendent. Very often these reformers depicted a society in which class distinctions were not exploited to oppress people. Unfortunately, such movements eventually deteriorated into a situation where the groups themselves became castes; in other cases, the caste system eventually found its way into the groups.

Avatars (Incarnations)

The two great Hindu epics, *Ramayana* and *Mahabharata*, are woven around quasi-historical princes and their consorts and are powerful depictions of the struggle between good and evil. The most famous Hindu Scripture popularized in the Western world, the *Bhagavad-Gita*, is part of Mahabharata; it is the purported record of the conversation between Krishna and Arjuna, a warrior who is engaged at that moment in fighting his cousins in a war for justice. Both these epics can be said to contribute to *bhakti* toward the respective heroes, Rama and Krishna, considered to be incarnations of the god of preservation, Vishnu.[8]

Nine of these incarnations are believed to have taken place, and the tenth and the most perfect is still awaited. Each incarnation of Vishnu is for the purpose of destroying evil in a particular aeon of time. Four of the incarnations are animal forms, one is half-human and half-leonine, and the remaining four are human. It is not clear what happens to the incarnation once his job is done.

Soul

The Hindu believes in the eternality of the soul. This is to be clearly distinguished from the Christian teaching of the possibility that a human soul can attain immortality.

Reincarnation

The Hindu believes that the soul (*jivatman*) of the deceased returns to be born into another form—human, animal, vegetable, or mineral—depending upon the good works (*karma*) in the earlier birth. The identity of the soul is preserved. (This is different from the Buddhist idea of reincarnation, which holds that the "soul" at death disintegrates into its constitutive elements only to be reassembled at reincarnation.)

Salvation

The concept of sin is not well developed in Hinduism, and thus the idea of salvation is correspondingly affected. Three ways are suggested according to the capacity and preference of the seeker:

1. *Way of Knowledge* (*Gyana Marga*): Salvation is attained by knowledge that is intuitive and spontaneous of oneness with the divine.

2. *Way of Devotion* (*Bhakti Marga*): Salvation is gained by devotion; concepts like grace are mentioned by Krishna in the *Bhagavad-Gita*.

3. *Way of Good Works* (*Karma Marga*): Salvation is earned by good works; these can contribute toward a better/higher birth in the next cycle of reincarnation or eternal communion with god, not very different from what Christians aspire for.

In ancient Hinduism, *bhakti* movements show a striking similarity to Christian devotion to a personal, relational God.

Sharing the Gospel with Hindus

From the above survey of popular Hinduism, it will be seen that the truths of the gospel can be applied simply but relevantly in presenting the Christian message to adherents of this faith. In fact, the epics of *Ramayana* and *Mahabharata* can be retold within the framework of the Christian narrative that reveals the triune God in action in human history. Some of the salient features of the gospel message are given below.

The Ultimate Reality with whom we interact is the infinite, triune God, who is holy and loving. This God has manifested himself in human history in the person of Jesus Christ, who lived, died, and rose again. The claims of all other rivals have to be evaluated against the person of Christ. This God, who is relational in his own being, invites his human creation into relationship with himself.

The Hindu looks up to gods to help in his or her life of moral purity. Christ, as the Sanctifier, is the answer that satisfies all aspirants to a truly holy life. The impeccable life of Christ has never ceased to fascinate great Hindus of the past like Mahatma Gandhi.

Christ, as the ultimate conqueror of evil and the sovereign ruler over all creation, is the antithesis of a host of capricious gods and goddesses who hold the fate of human beings. The ascended Lord is the One who will eventually bring all things under his benevolent kingship. Through the matrix of a fatalistic world of impersonal cosmic forces pictured in some forms of Hinduism, Satan delights to manipulate individuals and nations to serve him through witchcraft, sorcery, astrology, palmistry, and other devious and demonic techniques.

Christ procures salvation only because humans are incapable of saving themselves. This comes through clearly in the Christian message, but Hindus find it difficult to accept this claim. This is sometimes because their standard for moral perfection is inadequate. The God of the Bible, on the other hand, comes across as a consuming fire of holiness, against which backdrop all our righteous acts are like filthy rags (Isa. 64:6).

Hindus are less prone to feel personal guilt than guilt for acts that bring shame to the community. This should not be seen as a weakness to be overcome; rather, it is an issue that is addressed by Christ as he treats us with honor and does not delight in exacerbating our sense of shame. It is significant that the first symptom after the disobedience of our first parents was shame; fear and guilt followed later (Gen. 3:7–10).

The gospel makes it clear that by our own good works we cannot be saved (Rom. 3:20) because the standard expected by God can never be achieved by any human being, moral or immoral. Thus God in his mercy has to intervene and offer his son, Jesus Christ, as the sacrifice for human wickedness (Rom. 5:8). Moreover, the significant fact that all ancient religions including Hinduism have practiced systems of animal sacrifices lends strong credence to the necessity of this belief. Christ has paid for our *karmic* debt, so to speak!

As part of the gospel message, it should be emphasized that the death of Christ on the cross was not that of a martyr for a good cause. It was predicted seven centuries earlier (Isa. 53) and was part of the divine plan for salvation. Christ's death and its supernatural dimensions stand attested by his resurrection from the dead, a historic fact that is the foundation of the Christian faith. History is therefore not a meaningless, endless cycle of events but is poised for its climax in the coming of Christ.

The three ways of salvation offered by the various forms of Hinduism—*Jnana Marga* (way of knowledge), *Bhakti Marga* (way of devotion) and *Karma Marga* (way of good works)—find their true fulfillment in Jesus Christ. Knowledge (*jnana*) cannot be self-realization but the recognition of the character of God and the work of Christ in our relationship to God through Christ (John 17:3). Devotion (*bhakti*) has to be offered to the One who is thoroughly deserving of it and not to anyone who shares the same frailties as other humans (Matt. 22:37–38). In this context, it is pertinent to point out that Jesus is the true image of the invisible God (Col.1:15), and worship of Jesus should be contrasted with worship of images that do not reflect God truly. Good works (*karma*) issue from that salvation provided by Christ (Eph. 2:10) but can never contribute to salvation.

The Hindu perceives the typical Christian presentation of the gospel as thoroughly Western. A humorous instance from the life of Dayanand Bharati may be in order. He was watching a Tamil Christmas program on one of the cable channels along with his parents, who had not yet come to Christ. They could not understand the language (although they were Tamil speakers) nor could they appreciate the music. The songs were sung in Western style. His mother finally asked him, "Today being Jesus' *jayanti* ('Birthday of Jesus,' a phrase she herself had coined), why don't we sing some *bhajans* (Hindu songs of worship) to him?"[9]

A Note on Idolatry

It must be recognized that indulgence in the despicable sin of idolatry substitutes worship of creatures for the worship of the Creator. Christians should beware that we do not treat image worship as a worse case of idolatry than other substitutes of the true God such as materialism and pursuit of pleasure. It should also be kept in view that in the Bible, God's strongest words of condemnation of idolatry were directed at God's people, who ought to have known better, and not at other nations, such as Nineveh (Jonah 4:10–11).

All idolatries lead invariably to repercussions in the moral (Rom. 1:26–27), mental (Rom. 1:28), and spiritual (1 Cor. 10:20–21) realms. Satan uses these departures from the truth to erect strongholds for himself that resist the gospel of Jesus Christ. However, we need to see that the Second Commandment is against images we make for ourselves (Ex. 20:4).

Yet Jesus is described as the image of the invisible God (Col. 1:15), which is why Jesus could say to Philip, "Anyone who has seen me has seen the Father" (John 14:9). The human longing for a visual representation of God should not be discouraged but rather directed to the person of Jesus Christ. Your Hindu friend can be enabled to "see" Jesus as he reads the Gospels, which give a simple description of Jesus' life.

I give below extracts of a review by Rev. A. J. Appasamy, who was a pastor in the Church of South India:

> The growth of the *bhakti* movement in India has taken place in close association
> with image worship. Most of the *bhakti* saints have worshipped the images in the
> Hindu temples. Some of them have lived in the precincts of the temples and have

spent much time in the service of idols. Many of the beautiful *bhakti* hymns are in praise of the deities represented by the images. They contain many references to the miracles and wonders believed to be wrought by the local gods. The philosophical systems of *bhakti* take idol worship for granted. The problem for the Christian student is to find out what importance may be attached to the *bhakti* experience that has grown out of image worship.

On a question of this nature the light, which is shed by the modern historical and literary criticism of the Bible, is very helpful. Thanks to the patient research and industry of modern scholars, we have come to realize that the growth of Old Testament religion was constantly impeded by lapses into idolatry. In spite of the frequent exhortations of the prophets, the children of Israel continually succumbed to the idolatrous practices and beliefs of the people in whose midst they lived. Gradually they were weaned away from idolatry. This spiritual education of the children of Israel was a long and painful one. Again and again they had to be brought back to the worship of the one true God in spirit and in truth by the great prophets who received the revelation of God and sought to make the people give up idolatry. In course of time the children of Israel became entirely free from the temptations to idol worship and fully aware of the nature of God as Spirit. We do not dismiss the Old Testament because the story of Israel is tainted with idol worship. On the other hand, we find much value in the slow and toilsome growth of Israel towards clearer light about the nature of God and about the method of worshipping Him. The *bhakti* religion of India may be considered to belong to the spiritual level that is represented by the Old Testament. The faith and devotion and love which have been lavished on idols must be directed towards the one true God, especially as we know Him through His Incarnation in Jesus Christ.[10]

UNDERSTANDING BUDDHISM

Buddhism, in contrast to Hinduism, is more creedal. But it is also a religion that has been developing since the time of the Buddha in the sixth century before Christ.

The Buddha (the enlightened one) was born as Siddhartha Gautama in Lumbini (in present-day Nepal) in a princely family of the Sakya clan. The date of his birth is variously placed between 624 BC and 448 BC; the commonly accepted date is 560 BC. Gautama renounced his life as a householder at the age of twenty-nine and received enlightenment when he was thirty-six during a full moon night in the month of May. This happened in Gaya (in present-day India). Two months later, he delivered his first discourse near Varanasi, introducing the world to the Four Noble Truths. He died at the age of eighty; his death is referred to as *Parinibbana* (in Pali, the language in which all ancient writings of Buddhism are found), or final release.

The Four Noble Truths
The essential teaching of the Buddha comprises the following Four Noble Truths:[11]

1. *The Noble Truth of Dukkha* (suffering, dissatisfaction, stress): Life is fundamentally fraught with suffering and disappointment of every description.

2. *The Noble Truth of the Cause of Dukkha*: The cause of this dissatisfaction is *tanha* (craving) in all its forms.

3. *The Noble Truth of the Cessation of Dukkha*: An end to dissatisfaction can be found through the relinquishment and abandonment of craving.

4. *The Noble Truth of the Path Leading to Cessation of Dukkha*: There is a method of achieving the end of all suffering—namely, by following the Noble Eightfold Path that involves the practice of:
     right view;
     right resolve;
     right speech;
     right action;
     right livelihood;
     right effort;
     right mindfulness;
     right concentration.

To each of these Noble Truths, the Buddha assigned a specific task that the practitioner is to carry out:

1. The first Noble Truth is to be comprehended;
2. The second Noble Truth is to be abandoned;

3. The third Noble Truth is to be realized;

4. The fourth Noble Truth is to be developed.

The full realization of the third Noble Truth paves the way for the direct attainment of *Nibbana* (Sanskrit: *Nirvana*), the transcendent freedom that stands as the final goal of all the teachings of the Buddha. *Nirvana*, however, means nothingness or extinction.

The Eightfold Path

The last of the Noble Truths—the Noble Eightfold Path—contains prescriptions for the relief of our unhappiness and for our eventual release, once and for all, from the painful and wearisome cycles of birth and death (*samsara*). Humankind has been bound to these cycles for countless aeons through its own ignorance (*avijja*) of the Four Noble Truths. The Noble Eightfold Path offers a comprehensive practical guide to the development of those wholesome qualities and skills in the human heart that must be cultivated in order to bring the practitioner to enlightenment.

In practice, the Buddha expected his followers to adopt the Noble Eightfold Path according to a gradual system of training:

- Development of *sila*, or virtues (right speech, right action, and right livelihood), which are summarized in practical form by suitable precepts;

- Development of *samadhi*, or concentration and mental cultivation (right effort, right mindfulness, and right concentration);

- Development of *panna* or wisdom (right view and right resolve).

The practice of generosity (*dana*) serves as a support at every step along the path, as it helps foster the development of compassion and counters the heart's habitual tendencies toward craving. Progress along the path does not follow a simple linear trajectory. Rather, development of each aspect of the Noble Eightfold Path encourages the refinement and strengthening of the others, leading the practitioner in a forward spiral of spiritual maturity that culminates in awakening or enlightenment.

Seen from another point of view, the long journey on the path to awakening begins in earnest with the first tentative stirrings of right view, the first flickering of wisdom by which one recognizes both the validity of the first Noble Truth and the inevitability of the law of *karma,* the universal law of cause and effect. Once one begins to see that harmful actions inevitably bring about harmful results and wholesome actions ultimately bring about wholesome results, the person naturally grows to live a skilful, morally upright life and to take seriously the practice of *sila.* The confidence built from this preliminary understanding inclines the follower to put one's trust more deeply in the Buddha's teachings.

Common Buddhist Beliefs about Reality

There are three aspects common to Buddhist beliefs about reality: suffering (*dukkha*), nonpermanence (*anicca*), and nonsoulishness (*anatta*).[12]

Because the Buddhist does not believe in the identity of the soul (in contrast to the Hindu), reincarnation for the Buddhist is not transmigration of soul but rather the reassembling of constituent elements; thus, there is no continuous personal identity.[13] In fact, one of the issues that puzzled the followers of the Buddha was his reluctance to provide a definite answer to the question of afterlife.[14]

The follower becomes a Buddhist upon expressing an inner resolve to take refuge in the Triple Gem:

1. The *Buddha*: Both the historical Buddha and one's own innate potential for awakening;

2. The *Dhamma* (Sanskrit: *Dharma*): Both the teachings of the historical Buddha and the ultimate truth toward which they point;

3. The *Sangha*: Both the monastic community that has protected the teachings and put them into practice since the Buddha's day, and all those who have achieved at least some degree of awakening.

With one's feet thus firmly planted on the ground by taking refuge, and with the help of an admirable friend (*kalyanamitta*) to help show the way, one can set out along the path, confident that one is indeed following in the footsteps left by the Buddha himself.

A hundred years after the Buddha's death, the second council of Buddhist monks met at Vaishali, where the first schism occurred in ancient Buddhism. Those who did not accept the writings of the early Buddhists as authoritative branched off to form the Mahayana School of Buddhism, which became the dominant religion in China, Tibet, Japan, and Korea. Those who subscribed to Buddhist scriptures constituted the Hinayana School (*Theravada*). This branch of the religion has flourished in Sri Lanka, Myanmar, and Thailand.

There are various influences upon both forms of Buddhism that make classification difficult. As in the case of Hindus, we need to listen to the practitioner of Buddhism to decide on the correct approach of leading the person to the truth of Christ.

The difference between these two schools of Buddhism is given in the table on the following page.

POSITIVE CRITIQUE OF BUDDHISM

We should be willing to recognize the positive dimensions of Buddhism on which we are able to build bridges. This approach could provide a starting point in our dialogue with Buddhist friends and eventually lead them to Christ.

First, the reality of suffering as recognized by Buddhism is to be lauded. It is a good corrective against certain philosophies that deny the reality of evil, seeking to explain it away as illusion.

Second, the diagnosis of the problem as *tanha* (craving or desire) parallels the biblical view of 1 John 2:16.

Third, the discipline, both inward and outward, emphasized in the eightfold path is common to all religions and comprises admirable qualities for practical living.

In addition to the above, the need for a savior espoused by the Mahayana school is to be appreciated because it underlines the need for an external personal reality with whom the devotee can seek relationship.

NEGATIVE CRITIQUE OF BUDDHISM

We should also be willing to recognize the negative dimensions of Buddhism that could provide a starting point in our dialogue with Buddhist friends and eventually lead them to Christ.

For example, the essential diagnosis of life as one full of evil and suffering fails both philosophical and pragmatic tests. *Philosophically*, one cannot define a negative entity such as suffering or evil except as the absence of corresponding, positive entities, namely pleasure and good. If everything were suffering, we would not know it to be suffering! *Pragmatically*, Buddhism fails to appreciate the actual existence of positive aspects of life and thus turns out to be a pessimistic and nihilistic proposition.

In addition, while the cause of suffering is rightly identified as craving, its abandonment as the solution appears to be thoroughly impractical, again for philosophical and pragmatic reasons. *Philosophically*, the intention to get rid of all desires is itself a desire and suffers from a basic violation of the law of non-contradiction. *Pragmatically*, the resources to carry out this abandonment of all craving appear to be inadequate to the majority of seekers and within the reach of only a privileged few.

Next, while the steps of discipline in the Noble Eightfold Path appear to be praiseworthy, the human predicament seems to be one of incapacity to follow such endeavors. The problem is that we as humans know what is right but repeatedly find ourselves in the unenviable position of not being able to do what we know is right.

Theravada Buddhism, which is basically atheistic, suffers from all the weaknesses of classical atheism. A finite universe could not have come into existence except by a nonphysical, nontemporal cause outside of the universe. As the universe contains intelligence and moral tendencies, the First Cause (God) has to be infinite, powerful, intelligent, and just.

Mahayana Buddhism errs on the other side by deifying the Buddha and failing to acknowledge the frailty and finitude of Siddhartha Gautama as another mortal human being. As already stated, Gautama was unable or unwilling to address the issue of afterlife.

SHARING THE GOSPEL WITH BUDDHISTS

From the above survey of Buddhism and the accompanying critiques, it will be seen that the truths of the gospel can be presented simply and relevantly to the adherents of this faith. Several of the suggestions made in the context of Hinduism will be applicable here. Some of the additional features of our presentation are suggested below.

Because the Ultimate Reality with whom we have to do is the infinite, triune God who is holy and loving, suffering cannot be an ultimate quality of the universe as Buddhism maintains. The biblical view that suffering and death are the consequences of human disobedience is a far more plausible explanation.

Salvation is procured by Christ only because humans are incapable of saving themselves. This comes through clearly in the Christian message. The Buddhist view that one can get rid of craving by one's own effort is doomed to failure on account of the reality of human frailty.

While the Noble Eightfold Path is laudable in its reach, it has no moral frame of reference in the absence of an all-personal, all-relational God. The holiness of God's character is the only sufficient basis by which any moral standard of living can be adequately evaluated.

Mahayana Buddhism posits the Buddha as savior. It is not clearly stated what he saves us from in the absence of a valid standard for moral perfection. We fall woefully short of the blazing holiness of the God of the Bible (Rom. 3:23). In the absence of any notion of what God requires, the Buddha does not possess the resources to be the savior of humankind, nor does he proffer forgiveness for the one who is desperately conscious of his or her own moral evil.[15]

The gospel provides identity—both individual and communal—to the follower of Jesus Christ. This stands in marked contrast to a total lack of identity provided by the Buddhist version of reincarnation.

In positing Nirvana as the ultimate goal of life, Buddhism may not be able to provide a valid basis for life except in a purely escapist sense. The victory of Christ's death and his promised coming to bring history to a glorious climax stand in shimmering contrast to the nihilistic end that the Buddhist is offered in his belief system.

UNDERSTANDING THE NEW AGE MOVEMENT

There is an old adage that goes, "There is nothing new in theology except heresy!" Something similar can be said about the New Age movement as well, because there is nothing fundamentally new about this worldview; it has been around for a long time. Its essence can be summarized as follows: all the diverse realities that we see and perceive are, in actual fact, dim reflections and extensions of an infinite and impersonal reality. Some aspects of the New Age movement had their origins in some interpretations of Indian philosophy. One aspect of Indian philosophical thought, namely *Advaita Vedanta* (undifferentiated monism), is treated under this section.

The theology and philosophy behind the New Age movement is simple: an undifferentiated, undefined, and indefinable god (or universal principle) is all, and all is this god. It is therefore pantheistic in its outlook but multifaceted in its manifestations. This view can be traced back in the Western world to some forms of Platonic and Gnostic philosophies, for example those followed by the pantheistic European philosopher Baruch Spinoza and, more recently by Pierre Teilhard de Chardin, Aldous Huxley, Carl Jung, and Abraham Maslow.

In India, Sankara, a teacher who lived from AD 788–820, interpreted some of the early writings of Hinduism in a monistic way; that is, he used the term *Brahman* to denote an eternal, infinite, impersonal entity. (The word *Brahman*, which occurs in Hindu scriptures, is interpreted by early Indian scholars in different ways.) More recently, practices such as Zen Buddhism, Reiki healing, and some forms of alternative medicine, martial arts, and the like have explicitly taught that we are extensions of the infinite energy of the universe. Modern-day New Age gurus such as Deepak Chopra quote extensively from the New Testament but come up with nothing other than a purely subjective enterprise of finding God in our souls.[16]

In spite of the huge varieties of philosophies and practices, both East and West, there are certain underlying commonalities that influence New Age teaching. New Age "postulates that far from being a speck of dust, a machine, a monkey or even an image-bearer-of-God, the human self is in fact the Divine Self."[17] There are celebrities in the West who have made this philosophy popular. For example, Shirley MacLaine said, "The body is nothing more than a materialized thought . . . a dream. The universe is made up of our own mental images. I and the universe are one."[18] Although the two quotes appear to be very different, the underlying philosophy is the same: *the universe, including me, is an extension of the divine.*

Several factors, including some input from science, have contributed to this approach. Albert Einstein and Max Planck hinted that because of the very nature of sense perception, our knowledge of physical realities is derived indirectly. They did not deny the existence of the external world independent of the observer. But noted British physicist Sir Arthur Eddington took this idea further to speculate that the world of science was a symbolic world, a world of shadow. He went on to suggest that a Universal Mind was the only final reality.

Thus some of these scientists were actually playing into the ascendant New Age philosophers who were also insisting that the physical universe was nothing more than a construct of the human mind. Sir Arthur's senior contemporary, the mathematician-philosopher-theologian Alfred North Whitehead, further confirmed this. He drew the conclusion that if matter was really energy according to Einstein's theory, then mind and matter cannot be two distinct categories. Pierre de Chardin's interpretation of evolution as an emergent movement in a higher direction coincided perfectly with Whitehead's process philosophy and theology. Indian gurus and Zen masters who started influencing the West from the end of the nineteenth century have accentuated this move away from scientific materialism toward the esoteric, which would eventually embrace concerns as diverse as utopia, ecology, vegetarianism, and feminism.

Some Important Expressions of New Age

The mix of the New Age brew includes one or more of the following:

- The paranormal potential of the psychological theories of Jung and Maslow;
- People's experience of the psychic powers of healers;
- Widely reported encounters with extraterrestrial beings and science fiction, and Carl Sagan's search for extraterrestrial intelligence;
- A growing interest in the mystical experience of sex;
- The idea of the astrological Age of Aquarius;
- A reaction to the exploitative nature of modern society with its capitalist economic outlook and scant regard for the environment;
- A disillusioned youth culture susceptible to cults.

All that is needed to popularize the movement is to package the above to include in its agenda themes that resonate with the public mind. Brief summaries of some ways in which New Age expresses itself are given in the following paragraphs.

Intuitive Knowledge

In the New Age movement, there is a total rejection of cognitive knowledge, which is entirely replaced by intuitive knowledge. Thus, there is a clear-cut movement from logical thought (left brain) to feelings and intuition (right brain).

As one who worked with young people returning from hippie experiments in the East, Francis Schaeffer recognized the problem of removing all objectivity.[19] There was a further movement away to the dethronement of normal (waking) consciousness in favor of the transcendental and mystical. This latter was considered to be a superior altered state of consciousness (note that this terminology resonates with drug use). A third step would be to contact spirits and other media.

Astrology
The Age of Aquarius was popularized by the movie *Hair*. It was based on a rotation of the earth's axis, precession, once in about 25,800 years. The earth is supposed to be moving from its proximity to the constellation of Pisces to that of Aquarius; Aquarius is supposed to be the age of harmony, peace, universal brotherhood, joy, freedom (especially in ethics without any moral boundaries), science, accomplishment, and inspiration (especially in religion).

Three views result from the belief in the Age of Aquarius:

1. *Causal connections*: this belief results in a totally fatalistic worldview.
2. *Noncausal connections*: popularized by Jung, this view holds that our behavior is connected with the movement of stars at a preatomic vibrational level and can be used for therapeutic purposes.
3. *Spiritual connections*: astrology can make genuine, true predictions inspired by the demonic.

Spiritism
The emphasis of spiritism in the New Age movement includes the following:

1. *Magic*: performed by tricks such as sleight of hand.
2. *Psychic powers*: not yet fully understood capacities of certain individuals engaged in paranormal activities such as extrasensory perception.
3. *The demonic*: actual engagement with the powers of the spiritual world.

UFOs
In 1983, Arthur Koestler popularized the idea of UFOs as a religious experience. This idea was linked with the belief that extraterrestrial help would be needed to realize the optimism of an Aquarian future. UFOs are also sought after as an aid

to self-transcendence. Extraterrestrials are interested not so much in humans with all their sense of importance but rather in saving this planet from destruction at their hands. Thus, the environment enters the New Age agenda.

Sex

In New Age thought, sex is looked upon as holding the key to unlocking the mystery of the universe. Fritjof Capra implies as much in his book *The Tao of Physics*.[20] Perfection in sexuality is the discovery of the perfect balance in our androgynous nature, by uniting the male and the female by certain techniques. As the spiritual teacher formerly known as Bhagwan Shree Rajneesh said, "While making love to a woman, you are actually making love to Existence itself. The woman is just a door; the man is just a door."[21]

Ecology

New Age philosopher Fritjof Capra explains how closely related ecology is to the New Age movement: "The spiritual essence of the ecological vision seems to be to find its ideal expression in the feminist spirituality advocated by the woman's movement, as would be expected from the natural kinship between feminism and ecology, rooted in the age-old identification of woman and nature. . . . The earth, then, is a living system; it functions not just like an organism but actually seems to be an organism—Gaia, living planetary being."[22]

New Age spiritist David Icke personifies the planet, imbuing the earth with feelings that affect the planet's natural order. He claims, "The main problem for the earth [is] She is feeling unloved. . . . She is becoming confused. This is making her lose control and the natural order of the planet is falling."[23]

And Indian conservationist Sunderlal Bahuguna takes it one step further. He not only personifies the planet but identifies himself and the earth as one entity: "I hug the tree because I am one with the tree so that I can keep the illegal loggers from felling the tree."[24]

Vegetarianism

Vegetarianism as a religious phenomenon made its debut in India when Jainism and Buddhism revolted against the sacrificial system in Hinduism sometime before 600 BC. Mahatma Gandhi thought that nonvegetarianism made human beings cruel, aggressive, and passionate. But a fanatic vegetarian like Hitler proved to be an embarrassment to these proponents of vegetarianism, and Gandhi eventually abandoned that position. Monistic beliefs that say that all life is one and equally divine reduce humans to the level of grass or bacteria.

Reincarnation

The desire to live on and the possibility of meeting loved ones who have died have kept the lamp of reincarnation burning brightly in the hearts of many New Agers. It is therefore considered a liberating belief. Recent trends in science and philosophy do not encourage a purely reductionist, materialist view of life. The existence of the soul is now considered a distinct possibility. Instances of near-death experiences and past-life recalls have generated new interest in investigating claims to reincarnation. Hinduism and Buddhism have always taught reincarnation of the eternal soul, and recent interest in Eastern religions has further strengthened this belief.

BIBLICAL CRITIQUE OF NEW AGE

The God of the Bible is triune: one divine being of three infinite, relational persons. Thus in the being of God, both transcendence and immanence are implicit. The otherness between the persons is expressed as God's transcendence over his creation (Gen. 1:1); the perichoretic oneness between the persons is expressed as his immanence in creation (Ps. 104). (The Greek word *perichoresis* means "dancing around" and is used by early church theologians to describe the mutual indwelling of the Trinity.) New Age errs in sacrificing the transcendence of God at the altar of immanence!

The distinction between the persons of the Creator ensures the importance of identities in his creatures (Gen. 1:5, 8, 10) and the unique personalities of human beings who are made in his image. Thus there is no need for an identity crisis! In removing the distinction between human beings and nature as well among humans, New Age strikes a deadly blow to human dignity and individuality.

The Bible makes a clear distinction between God and his creation (Gen. 1:1). God made a real world and distinct identities within that world (Gen. 1:4, 6, 10–12, 18, 21, 24, 26–27). This is the objective basis for any scientific enterprise. In erasing this distinction, New Age destroys the basis of science.

The Bible gives the right place for reason: God created a reasonable world and made humans in the image of the Logos (John 1:1–3) so that they will be able to understand and harness nature. Outside of this worldview, there is no reasonable basis of how and why human beings are able to understand, conceptualize, and predict the course of nature. By confusing the distinctions within nature, New Age does not in any way promote the progress of science. Although Chopra makes profuse references to science and scientists,[25] he never seriously addresses the philosophical issues that undergird true science.

God created us for a relationship with himself (Gen.2:15–17), thus our understanding also has an intuitive, experiential dimension that is firmly rooted in the Being of God. The Bible nowhere advocates a pure rationalistic approach to reality, and it provides the only basis for the function of reason. Epistemology, therefore, has an objective-subjective axis on which it operates.

The spirit world is created by God. Angels are ministering spirits (Ps. 91:11; Heb. 1:14). Demons are fallen angels, and we are commanded not to dabble in any form of spiritism (Lev. 20:27). The Bible strongly affirms belief in spirit beings but prohibits any involvement with them.

We are commanded to trust in God and not to resort to divination or sorcery (Lev. 19:26). Predicted foreknowledge of the future paralyzes our freewill and prevents us from living as free beings under the providence of God.

God is the Creator of all things, including extraterrestrials if there are such beings! Our mandate is to look after the creation that God has entrusted to our care and not to show an unhealthy interest in celestial beings about whom little is revealed in Scripture (2 Peter 2:10–12; Jude vv. 8–10). This does not preclude legitimate scientific examination of evidence and research projects like the Search for Extraterrestrial Intelligence (SETI).

God created sex to be a fulfilling act of intimacy between one man and one woman in a marriage covenant. A monogamous, heterosexual relationship looks retrospectively at the unity of the Trinity and anticipates the marriage between Christ and the church (Gen. 1:26–27; 2:24; 1 Cor. 11:3; Eph. 5:31–32). We are neither to deify sex nor to despise it as evil. It is meaningful only because of the real distinction between men and women.

The Bible is a book that starts with creation of the environment and its beautifully balanced interdependence. The command of God to us was to responsibly look after what he had made (Gen. 1:28). If human beings are just part of the rest of creation and not at the head of a hierarchy of created beings, how can we justify our authority over the rest of nature?

God created animals and human beings as vegetarians (Gen. 1:29–30). Official sanction for a nonvegetarian diet appears in the Bible only in Genesis 9:2. The tone of this verse seems to suggest that meat consumption is a result of human rebellion. It is, however, for us to note that all ancient religions did have a sacrificial system in which the priest ate a portion of the sacrificed animal as a token that the offering had been accepted by deity. Of all ancient writings, the Old Testament is the only document that clearly enunciates the idea of a substitutionary sacrifice. In a real sense, all these sacrifices stand fulfilled on Calvary. In the new heavens and the new earth, the relationship between all creation will be vegetarian (Isa. 11:6–9; 65:25). The Christian faith is not a nonvegetarian faith; it may encourage vegetarianism on health, aesthetic, or sentimental grounds, but it would not necessarily object to it on theological grounds.

The view of time and history in the Scriptures is helical-linear. That is, there is a certain repetitiveness, but history is moving toward a grand climax. In this continuum, we have the chance of one life at the end of which we shall render account to our Creator (Heb. 9:27). Reincarnation robs the human individual of his dignity and identity apart from reducing morality to merely a cause-and-effect phenomenon.

PHILOSOPHICAL CRITIQUE OF NEW AGE TEACHING (PANTHEISM)

It should be clearly understood that New Age expressions of Buddhism and Hinduism are not the main tenets of these religions. However, certain schools of thought in these two religions have come out with philosophical speculation from some scriptures of these religions that have lent support to the New Age movement. This development, in recent times, has coincided with Western pantheistic thought as well as some aspects of postmodernism. I have used the generic term *pantheism* (already explained above) for the sake of brevity.

Positive Critique of Pantheism
Pantheism attempts to be comprehensive in its perspective. Swami Vivekananda was the Indian guru who transfixed the Parliament of Religions in Chicago in 1893. His English disciple, Sister Nivedita, refers to the swami's all-inclusive

vision as *advaitic* (nondualistic) and says, "If the many and the One be indeed the same Reality, then it is not all modes of worship alone, but equally all modes of struggle, all modes of creation which are paths of realization. No distinctions henceforth between sacred and secular; to labor is to pray; to conquer is to renounce; life itself is a religion. To have and to hold is as stern a trust as to quit and avoid."[26] Thus, this approach is not a fragmented philosophy but attempts to be an all-embracing view of the sum total of reality. In this sense, it is both metaphysical and comprehensive, two commendable dimensions essential to any worldview.

Pantheism also lays special emphasis on an ultimate dimension of reality that cannot be overlooked or denied, namely, unity.[27]

No adequate view of a God who is worthy of serious human interest can neglect his immanent presence and activity in the world. A God who is totally and completely other lacks relatability. Pantheism appropriately stresses that God is really in the world, at least within the depths of the human soul.

Pantheism acknowledges that only God is absolute and necessary. Everything else is less than absolute in the supreme sense, which God is. No part of creation is independent or ontologically detached; all is completely dependent on God, who is all in all. This insight is a valuable corrective for many forms of materialism and deism.

Pantheism invariably involves an intuitive epistemological emphasis,[28] which is often unappreciated by more empirically oriented minds. The stress on the direct and unmediated intimacy with the object of knowledge (especially God) is not only valuable but is unavoidable. Indirect or inferential knowing must rest finally on direct and immediate seeing. All justification must come to an end; first principles must be known intuitively. Hence, some form of intuitive knowledge is essential to knowing God, who is the ultimate principle in religion.

Pantheists place strong and appropriate emphasis on the *via negativa* (the negative way). God cannot be expressed in positive terms with limited meaning. God is infinite and transcendent, and all limitation must be negated from terms applied to him. Without the way of negation, verbal idolatry results in, namely, the finitizing of God.[29] Pantheists have preserved this important dimension of religious language.

Pantheism emphasizes the limitations of sense and concept perception (such as advocated by evidentialism and rationalism).

Negative Critique of Pantheism

Pantheism lacks logical consistency. It denies the fundamental canons of thought, but in so doing finds itself using the same laws of logic.

By insisting on the supremacy of intuitive thought and neglecting the use of conceptual thought, the pantheist finds himself in an incoherent epistemological quandary. "We become one with the truth, one with the object of knowledge. The object known is seen not as an object of outside the self, but as part of the self. What intuition reveals is not so much a doctrine as a consciousness; it is a state of mind and not a definition of the object. Logic and language are a lower form, a diminution of this kind of knowledge."[30] What is ignored is that to make this point known, logic and language have to be employed!

As the pantheist does not make any distinction between good and evil except in a temporary sense, there is no framework for absolute standards of ethics. Thus all values have to be considered to be relative. This does not mean that pantheists are immoral; it only indicates that this philosophy cannot provide a basis of true ethics.

Because of its insistence on the unity of all events, history is conceived of as a cyclical entity without any place for unique or significant events. The philosophy of history is cyclical, in line with belief in reincarnation.

There is no place for meaningful diversity of things in pantheism; thus science, which studies the interplay of differing types of entities, is provided no adequate philosophical basis. It presumably explains why Eastern civilizations, which were well advanced in empirical sciences, could not provide the conceptual basis for modern science.

Finally, pantheism has no explanation for the all-pervasive reality of evil. It only engages in the repeated denials of evil as a reality.[31]

Lessons for Christians from New Age

We should learn to combine transcendence and immanence of God in our attitude toward and worship of him. When Jesus taught his disciples to pray "Our Father in heaven," he was telling us that this was not a theological nicety but an amazing combination of reverence and familiarity in our approach to him. This is not available in any other faith! Our life must exhibit the insight that shows the world we are accountable to our Creator in our work and worship.

We need to celebrate our diversities without papering over them. This should be demonstrated in the Christian community and in our relationship with those outside. The Bible is clear that disharmony among individuals and communities is not sorted out by removing the real differences in their identities; it is rather by relating to one another in love that we begin to enjoy our distinctives.

New Age agenda is often a reaction against the wrong use of science and reason. We need to learn that the use of knowledge in these areas does not result in exploitation and control of people and resources but rather in serving them.

New Age (along with postmodernism) reacts against rationalism inspired by the Enlightenment. Christians, particularly apologists, are in danger of failing to distinguish between rationality (taught by Scripture) and rationalism, a by-product of the Enlightenment that seeks to enthrone reason at the expense of everything else, including God.

New Age is right in emphasizing the need of the subjective and experiential. A purely rationalistic approach on the part of Christendom in the past century tended to disregard the reality of the spiritual world and therefore engendered an unhealthy interest in it. We need to return to a biblical view of the spiritual world and the equipment God has provided for us to relate to it. Similarly, without undermining legitimate scientific enterprise, we should also be aware of principalities and powers and their agenda to subvert the rule of God over creation through us.

The Christian corrective to sexual perversions of all kinds is a robust return to the biblical understanding of sexuality. The Scriptures affirm all of life, and in this particular instinct with which God has created us, we are meant to demonstrate something sublime and beautiful. The Christian family and community are to be models in this all-important area of life. Our teaching should commence with the positive aspect of God's creation of us as sexual beings and not simply focus on the punishment for deviations.

The developed world—often perceived as Christian by others—has shown an appalling disregard for the environment. New Age has stepped into the gap left by a lack of concern on the part of Christians. It is time that we became good stewards of this planet: its animals, forests, oceans, and atmosphere.

CONCLUSION

In this chapter I have made a sincere attempt to identify the real longings of Hindus, Buddhists, and New Agers and to then show how these aspirations can be met in Christ and Christ alone. Followers of Hinduism and the New Age long for *relationship* with and between gods on the one hand and for ultimate reality to be infinite on the other hand. These two requirements are more than adequately met in the God of the Bible, who is infinite and personal—relational because he is Trinity. The gospel provides identity—both individual and communal—to the follower of Jesus Christ. It also stands in marked contrast to a total lack of identity provided by the Buddhist version of reincarnation.

As God's church, our final apologetic is the loving community of Christians that proclaims to the world that we are Christ's disciples (John 13:34–35). We need to identify with others as the apostle Paul did (1 Cor. 9:19–23). If Paul were writing to a Hindu context, he would probably have rewritten verses 20 and 21 thus: "To the Brahmin, I became like a Brahmin, to win the Brahmins; to the Shudras, I became like a Shudra, to win the Shudras."[32] Indeed, many Hindus and Buddhists have given their lives to Christ, not through philosophical arguments, but through the genuine love and friendship offered by their Christian friends. Over against the emphasis of yoga as merger with some indefinable reality, we can offer true relationship with the Infinite God through Jesus Christ and exemplify it through our own enjoyment of that sacred bond. Sadly, we sometimes portray Christianity as mere asceticism with a Christian slant and thus reduce to personal devotion alone what it means to follow Christ. The strongest argument against the attraction of Eastern religions lies not merely in an individual pursuit of Christian holiness but rather in the practice of a visible and demonstrable *Christian community.*

6

CHALLENGES FROM SCIENCE

John Lennox

Apologetics is the defense of the Christian message against competing worldviews.[1] Everyone (including scientists) has a worldview, attitudes about the big questions of life: origins, identity, meaning, and purpose. Broadly speaking, worldviews fall into three main categories: atheism, theism, and pantheism.

Atheism (principally materialism/naturalism[2]) holds that the universe is self-existent, self-contained, self-sufficient, and itself represents ultimate reality. *Theism* holds that ultimate reality is a personal Creator God who is independent of the universe. *Pantheism* holds, typically, that ultimate reality is impersonal and is essentially one with the inner self.[3]

BIBLICAL DOCTRINES CHALLENGED BY SCIENCE

The main contemporary challenge this chapter will address is the idea that science makes it impossible to believe in God. In particular, three fundamental biblical doctrines come under fire:

God Is the Creator of the Universe
There is an eternal, self-existent, and personal God who created and upholds the universe but is distinct from it (Gen. 1:1; John 1:1; Col. 1:16). Thus the

universe had a beginning; God did not. God is a person and not a force. Human beings were created in the image of God and therefore have unique value and dignity. Naturalism denies creation, holding that the universe is ultimately self-explanatory and that human beings are nothing special in the scheme of things—since, in fact, there is no scheme of things. Science is enlisted in support of this contention: "Darwin made it possible to be an intellectually respectable atheist," Richard Dawkins famously said.[4]

God Is Actively Participating in History

The grand miracle at the heart of Christianity is the fact that God became human in Jesus Christ, to which his miracles in general and his resurrection from the dead in particular bear witness (John 1:14). Naturalism, often citing David Hume, denies the miraculous in the name of science.

God Is Evident in Creation

At the start of the apostle Paul's most detailed statement of the Christian message, the letter to the Romans, he writes, "I am not ashamed of the gospel, because it is the power of God for the salvation of everyone who believes" (Rom. 1:16), a salvation that is necessary because of human guilt. This logically leads to the question, what evidence of God is there the rejection of which establishes that guilt? Paul gives various sources of evidence, the first of which is, "For since the creation of the world God's invisible qualities—his eternal power and divine nature—have been clearly seen, being understood from what has been made, so that men are without excuse" (Rom. 1:20).

Thus two things may be "seen" or perceived from the universe: first, that there is a God, and second, that he is powerful. Paul does not say that God's existence and power are *proved*, but rather *perceived*. For, strictly speaking, proof is only to be found in mathematics. Elsewhere it is proper to speak, not of proof, but of evidence, pointers, or indicators. However, Paul regards this evidence as substantial. He is not just saying that the created order supplies confirmation of the existence of God, in whom we believe on other grounds (although this is, of course, true). Paul is claiming that the evidence of creation is sufficient on its own to leave us "without excuse." The universe is not neutral; it contains evidence of its divine origin. Eminent plant scientist Sir Ghillean Prance FRS, former director of Kew Gardens in London, concurs when he describes God as nature's great architect. Science, he says, only confirms his faith. Naturalism admits that nature looks designed, but holds that such design is not real.

INTELLIGENT DESIGN

The current debate about intelligent design is vigorous but can be confusing since the expression is often taken to denote an unscientific form of creationist fundamentalism constructed for the one purpose of crippling evolutionary biology. And here, be it noted, creationism no longer simply means belief in a Creator but also in a whole package of additional ideas, the most dominant of which, based on a particular interpretation of Genesis, is that the earth is only a few thousand years old.

All of this has several unfortunate consequences. It obscures the fact that believing there is an intelligent cause behind the universe is very ancient and respectable. Also, it fails to do justice to the fact that there is divergence of opinion on the interpretation of the Genesis account even among those who ascribe final authority to the biblical record. The fact of creation can easily get lost in considerations of the timing of creation. And concentration on evolution alone can obscure the evidence from other scientific disciplines such as physics and cosmology.

In fact, the term *intelligent design* was originally used to separate the *recognition of design* from the *identification of the designer*. These are distinct issues. The second is essentially theological and agreed by most to be outside the provenance of science. The point of making the distinction is (or was) to ask whether science can help us with the first issue.

IS INTELLIGENT DESIGN SCIENCE?

Intelligent design is the hypothesis that the universe bears evidence of intelligent origin.[5] Now, we could say that theism is the hypothesis that there is a God and atheism that there is no God. Suppose we were now to ask the parallel questions: Is theism science? Is atheism science? Most people, including Christians, would give a negative answer to both. But if we now said that what we meant is whether there is any scientific evidence for theism (or for atheism), then we are likely to be faced with the reply, "Why, then, did you not say so?"

In light of this, the only sense I can make of the question about whether intelligent design is science is to rephrase the question: "Is there any scientific evidence for the involvement of intelligence in the origin of nature and its laws of operation?" That is, of course, a perfectly legitimate scientific question. Certainly, those scientists who argue on the basis of their science that atheism is the only intellectually respectable position scarcely have grounds to object to others using scientific evidence to support the opposing metaphysical position of theism. We shall look later at another possible interpretation of the question whether intelligent design is science in the sense of making testable scientific predictions.

THE MYTH OF CONFLICT
BETWEEN SCIENCE AND RELIGION

It is a widespread view that science and religion essentially conflict.[6] "Science and religion cannot be reconciled," said Oxford chemist Peter Atkins.[7] But if this were so, one would expect all serious scientists to be atheists—and that is not true. A 1996 survey by two scientists showed that the percentage of university scientists who believe, not simply in God, but in a personal God who answers prayer had remained more or less constant at around 40 percent since 1916.[8] Not only that but, at the very highest levels, there are scientists like Nobel Prize–winning physicist Bill Phillips and the director of the Human Genome Project, Francis Collins, who are convinced Christians.

The gulf between the two groups of scientists has little to do with conflict between science and religion but everything do to with their worldviews. One group espouses naturalism, the other Christian theism. Their conflict is a worldview conflict.

The key question is, therefore, with which worldview does science fit most comfortably? Influential entomologist Edward O. Wilson thinks that "scientific humanism" is "the only worldview compatible with science's growing knowledge of the real world and the laws of nature."[9] I disagree on the basis of three sources of evidence: the history of science, the philosophy and methodology of science, and the discoveries of science.

In this chapter, I deliberately leave the discoveries of science until last since the first two sources of evidence yield the most accessible and powerful arguments and since concentration on the discoveries of science alone can give the (false and dangerous) impression that faith in God is *solely* dependent on one's attitude to specific scientific discoveries.

EVIDENCE FROM THE HISTORY OF SCIENCE

The conviction that the universe is orderly is germinal to science. Melvin Calvin, Nobel Prize winner in biochemistry, has no doubt as to the origin of the universe: "As I try to discern the origin of that conviction, I seem to find it in a basic notion discovered 2000 or 3000 years ago, and enunciated first in the Western world by the ancient Hebrews: namely that the universe is governed by a single God, and is not the product of the whims of many gods, each governing his own province according to his own laws. This monotheistic view seems to be the historical foundation for modern science."[10]

This contrasts strikingly with the common tendency to trace the roots of contemporary science back only to the Greeks of the sixth century BC, and then to point out that, for science to proceed, the Greek worldview had to be emptied of its polytheistic content. Although the Greeks were the first to do science in anything like the way we understand it today, one implication of Melvin Calvin's statement is that the worldview of greatest help to science is very much older than the polytheistic worldview of the Greeks.

Sir Alfred North Whitehead observed that medieval Europe in 1500 knew less than Archimedes in the third century BC, and yet by 1700 Newton had written his masterpiece, the *Principia Mathematica*. Whitehead asked how such an explosion of knowledge could have happened so quickly. His answer: "Modern science must come from the mediaeval insistence on the rationality of God."[11] C. S. Lewis put it crisply, "Men became scientific because they expected law in nature and they expected law in nature because they believed in a lawgiver."[12]

Galileo (1564–1642), Kepler (1571–1630), Pascal (1623–1662), Boyle (1627–1691), Newton (1642–1727), Faraday (1791–1867), Babbage (1792–1871), Mendel (1822–1884), Pasteur (1822–1895), Kelvin (1824–1907), and Clerk-Maxwell (1831–1879) were all theists, most of them Christians. Their belief in God, far from being a hindrance to their science, was often the main inspiration for it. Johannes Kepler wrote, "The chief aim of all investigations of the external world should be to discover the rational order which has been imposed on it by God, and which he revealed to us in the language of mathematics."[13]

By contrast, Joseph Needham writing in the late 1960s ascribes the lack of scientific development among the Chinese to the absence of the concept of a lawgiver: "For them the idea that the universe could be governed by simple laws which human beings could and had discovered was foolish in the extreme. Their culture simply was not receptive to such notions."[14]

WHAT ABOUT GALILEO AND THE INQUISITION?

The story of Galileo's treatment at the hands of the Roman Catholic Church is often used to fuel the conflict view of science and religion. Historical research shows that this view is flawed. Galileo was no atheist. He believed in Scripture before he faced the Inquisition, and he believed in Scripture afterward. Galileo's "crime" was that he challenged the then reigning Aristotelian scientific paradigm, that a fixed and unmoving earth was at the center of the universe. This view, be it noted, was held both by the pagan philosophers of Galileo's day and by the churchmen who felt that it fit with their interpretation of Scripture.[15] They were all in error.

Ironically, it was Galileo, a believer in Scripture, who correctly challenged the then reigning scientific paradigm in the name of science. One important lesson is that those of us who take the biblical account seriously should be humble enough to distinguish between what the Bible says and our interpretations of it. The biblical text just might be more sophisticated than we first imagined, and we might therefore be in danger of using it to support ideas that it never intended to teach.[16]

In recent years, careful research has undermined the conflict thesis. Historian Colin Russell concludes, "The common belief that . . . the actual relations between religion and science over the last few centuries have been marked by deep and enduring hostility . . . is not only historically inaccurate, but actually a caricature so grotesque that what needs to be explained is how it could possibly have achieved any degree of respectability."[17]

EVIDENCE FROM THE PHILOSOPHY AND METHODOLOGY OF SCIENCE

We associate science with ideas like hypothesis, experiment, data, evidence, modified hypothesis, theory, prediction, explanation, and so on. But a precise definition of *science* is elusive. For instance, Michael Ruse says that science "by definition deals only with the natural, the repeatable, that which is governed by law."[18] On the plus side, this definition would certainly allow us to distinguish between astronomy and astrology. However, it would rule out most of contemporary cosmology as science. After all, the history of the universe is not repeatable!

Ruse's inadequate definition reminds us that not all science carries with it the same kind of authority. There is a danger of endowing inferences to the best explanation about unrepeatable past events with the authority of results derived from repeated experimentation.

To complicate matters even further, the Enlightenment ideal of the observer—one completely independent; free of all preconceived theories and prior philosophical, ethical, and religious commitments; doing investigations and coming to dispassionate, unbiased, rational conclusions that constitute absolute truth—is nowadays regarded as an idealized myth. In common with the rest of humanity, scientists have preconceived ideas and worldviews that they bring to bear on every situation. Even observations tend to be "theory laden"; we cannot take a temperature without having an underlying theory of heat. Also, theories tend to be underdetermined by the data; for instance, infinitely many curves can be drawn through any finite set of points. Furthermore, at the quantum level the very process of observation gives rise to disturbances that cannot be ignored. By its very nature, therefore, science possesses a certain degree of provisionality.

We hasten to add that this is far from implying that science is a totally subjective and arbitrary social construct, as has been suggested by some postmodern thinkers.[19] It is probably fair to say that many scientists are critical realists who hold that their theories, though not amounting to "truth" in any final or absolute sense, nevertheless give them an increasingly firm handle on reality. For example, consider the development of the understanding of the universe, from Galileo via Newton to Einstein.

The Limits of Science

Are there any limits to scientific explanation? At the materialist end of the spectrum, some hold that science is the only way to truth and can (ultimately) explain everything. According to Peter Atkins, "There is no reason to suppose that science cannot deal with every aspect of existence."[20] This view is called scientism.

If Atkins's claim were true, it would at once spell the end of many academic disciplines, such as philosophy, ethics, literature, poetry, art, and music. How could science tell us whether a poem is a bad poem or a work of genius? Science can tell you that if you add strychnine to someone's drink, it will kill her, but it cannot tell you whether it is morally right or wrong to put strychnine into your grandmother's tea in order to get your hands on her property.

Worse still, scientism is incoherent. Bertrand Russell wrote, "Whatever knowledge is attainable, must be attained by scientific methods; and what science cannot discover, mankind cannot know."[21] But Russell's statement is not a statement of science, so if his statement is true we cannot know it, which contradicts the very assertion that is being made! It is therefore incoherent.

Those who are committed to scientism regard all talk of God and religious experience as outside of science and therefore not objectively true, whatever the benefits claimed for it. But for them, thinking about God is like thinking about Father Christmas, dragons, or fairies. The fact that you can think about them does not mean that they exist. These scientists are (sometimes) happy to let people go on thinking about God and religion so long as they do not claim that God has any objective existence or that religious belief constitutes knowledge. The bottom line is this: science deals with reality, religion does not. Such a view is, of course, untenable for a Christian.

Aunt Matilda's Cake

An illustration may help. Let us imagine that my Aunt Matilda has baked a beautiful cake and we submit it for analysis to a group of the world's top scientists. The nutrition scientists will calculate the calories in the cake and tell us of its effect on the body; the biochemists will inform us about the structure of the proteins and fats in the cake; the chemists will describe the elements involved and their bonding; the physicists will be able to analyze the cake in terms of fundamental particles; and the mathematicians will no doubt offer us a set of elegant equations to describe the behavior of those particles.

Now that these experts have given us an exhaustive description of the cake, can we say that the cake is completely explained? We have certainly been given a description of how the cake was made and how its various constituent elements relate to one another, but suppose we now ask them *why* the cake was made. The grin on Aunt Matilda's face shows that *she* knows the answer, for she made the cake, and she made it for a purpose. But surely it is clear that all the scientists in the world will not be able to tell us why she made it. Unless Aunt Matilda reveals the answer, they are powerless. Their disciplines can cope with questions about the nature and structure of the cake but they cannot answer the "why" question.[22] Now, the artists among us will add that science is limited in another sense—it cannot comment on the sheer elegance and aesthetic appeal of the cake, nor could it comment on the quality and truth of a poem written about the cake. Many important aspects of reality are simply outside the provenance of science.

Nobel laureate Sir Peter Medawar writes, "The existence of a limit to science is, however, made clear by its inability to answer childlike elementary questions having to do with first and last things—questions such as: 'How did everything begin?'; 'What are we all here for?'; 'What is the point of living?'" He adds that it is to imaginative literature and religion that we must turn for answers to such questions.[23]

In light of this, we should take issue with Peter Atkins's statement: "Science has no need of purpose . . . all the extraordinary, wonderful richness of the world can be expressed as growth from the dunghill of purposeless interconnected corruption."[24] What would Aunt Matilda think of this as an explanation for the fact that she made the cake for her nephew Jimmy's birthday—to say nothing of it as an explanation of why she, Jimmy, and the birthday cake existed in the first place? She might just prefer a "primeval soup" to a "dunghill of corruption," if she were offered the choice.

It is one thing to say (correctly) that science cannot answer questions of ultimate purpose. It is quite another to dismiss purpose (and beauty and truth) as an illusion because science cannot deal with it. Atkins is simply taking his materialism to its logical conclusion—or perhaps not quite. After all, the existence of a dunghill presupposes the existence of creatures capable of making dung! Rather odd then to think of the dung as creating the creatures. And if it is a "dunghill of corruption" (as prescribed, one might suppose, by the Second Law of Thermodynamics), one might wonder how the corruption gets reversed. The mind boggles.

REASON VERSUS REVELATION?

Clearly it is absurd to hold that if science cannot tell us, then we cannot know why Aunt Matilda baked the cake. We can know why she baked it, if she chooses to reveal the answer to us. But if she doesn't, no amount of scientific analysis will help.

However, if she does reveal the answer to us, this does not now mean that reason is either irrelevant or inactive. We need our reason to understand and assess the credibility of her explanation. If she says she made the cake for her nephew Jimmy and we know that she has no nephew of that name, we will reject her explanation; if we know she has a nephew of that name, then her explanation will make sense.

In other words, reason is not opposed to revelation; it is simply that her revelation of the purpose for which she made the cake supplies to reason information that *unaided* reason cannot access. Reason is absolutely essential to process that information, even though it cannot create that information. The lesson is that in cases where *science* is not our source of information, we must not automatically assume either that *reason* has ceased to function or that *evidence* has ceased to be relevant.

Thus, when Christians claim there is Someone who stands in a similar relationship to the universe that Aunt Matilda stands to her cake, and that this Someone has revealed why the universe was created, they are not abandoning reason, rationality, and evidence at all. They are claiming that there are certain questions that unaided reason cannot answer. To answer them we need another source of information—in this instance, revelation from God. But to understand and evaluate that revelation, reason is essential. It was in this spirit that Francis Bacon talked of God's two books: the Book of Nature and the Bible. Reason, rationality, and evidence are essential to understanding both.

The Nature of Scientific Explanation

The success of science sometimes leads people to think that because we can understand the mechanisms of the universe, then we can safely conclude that there was no God who designed and created the universe in the first place. This reasoning commits a logical error in that it confuses mechanism and agency.

Consider a Ford motor car. It is conceivable that someone who was seeing one for the first time and who knew no science might imagine that there is a god (Mr. Ford) inside the engine, making it go. Of course, if he were subsequently to study engineering and take apart the engine, he would discover that there is no Mr. Ford inside it. He would also see that he did not need to introduce Mr. Ford as an explanation for its working; his grasp of the impersonal principles of internal combustion would be enough to do that. However, if he then decided that his understanding of the principles of how the engine worked made it impossible to believe in the existence of a Mr. Ford who designed the engine in the first place, this would be patently false. Had there never been a Mr. Ford to design the mechanisms, none would exist for him to understand.

It is equally mistaken to suppose that our scientific understanding of the impersonal principles according to which the universe works makes it either unnecessary or impossible to believe in the existence of a personal Creator who designed, made, and upholds it.

God of the Gaps?

In any discussion about science and religion, sooner or later the question of the "God of the gaps" will be raised: "We cannot explain it scientifically; therefore, God did it." We note that Mr. Ford is not to be found in the gaps in our knowledge about the workings of internal combustion engines. For Henry Ford is not a mechanism; he is the agent who is responsible for existence of the mechanism so that it *all* bears the marks of his handiwork—and that means the bits we do understand and the bits we don't. Nor is Henry Ford an alternative explanation to that of alternative combustion!

Nevertheless, influential authors like Richard Dawkins insist on conceiving of God only as an explanatory *alternative* to science—an idea that is nowhere to be found in serious theological reflection. Just as both Henry Ford and science are involved in a comprehensive explanation of the existence and workings of the car, so both God and science are involved in any comprehensive explanation of the universe.

Reductionism

The object of explaining something is to give an accessible and intelligible description of its nature and function. One obvious thing to try to do is to reduce the problem by splitting it up into separate parts, studying the parts and hoping that this will give insight into the whole. Such *methodological reductionism* is part of the normal process of science.

There is, however, another kind of reductionism, *ontological reductionism*. A classic example of it is given by Richard Dawkins: "The universe is nothing but a collection of atoms in motion, human beings are simply machines for propagating DNA, and the propagation of DNA is a self-sustaining process. It is every living object's sole reason for living."[25] Thus, everything can be reduced to physics and chemistry; there is an exhaustive bottom-up explanation for everything.

The words "nothing but" are the telltale signature of such thinking. Remove these words and we are usually left with something unobjectionable. The universe certainly is a collection of atoms, and human beings do propagate DNA. Both of these statements are statements of science. But if we add the words "nothing but," the statements go *beyond science* and become expressions of materialistic or naturalistic belief whose truth is highly questionable. Is there really nothing more to the universe and life than that? Are we going to say with Francis Crick, "'You,' your joys and your sorrows, your memories and ambitions, your sense of personal identity and free will, are in fact no more than the behavior of a vast assembly of nerve cells and their associated molecules"?[26]

What shall we think, then, of human love and fear, of concepts like beauty and truth? Are they meaningless? Is a Rembrandt painting nothing but molecules of paint scattered on canvas? On Crick's hypothesis, they are—and in that case, one further wonders by what means we would recognize it. After all, if the concept of truth itself is the product of "nothing more than the behavior of a vast assembly of nerve cells," how in the name of logic would we know the truth that our brain was composed of nerve cells?

John Polkinghorne describes such thinking as "ultimately suicidal. If Crick's thesis is true we could never know it. For not only does it relegate our experiences of beauty, moral obligation, and religious encounter to the epiphenomenal scrapheap, it also destroys rationality. Thought is replaced by electro-chemical neural events. Two such events cannot confront each other in rational discourse. They are neither right nor wrong. They simply happen. . . . The very assertions of the reductionist himself are nothing but blips in the neural network of his brain. The world of rational discourse dissolves into the absurd chatter of firing synapses. Quite frankly, that cannot be right and none of us believes it to be so."[27]

The Existence of the Universe

Science studies the universe. But science did not put the universe there. Why, then, is there something rather than nothing? Some scientists and philosophers think we should not even ask this question. There is no point in looking for a reason for the existence of the universe, since, they say, there simply isn't one.

Any chain of reasoning must start somewhere, so we might as well start with the existence of the universe. E. Tryton wrote, "Our universe is simply one of those things which happen from time to time."[28] That is an odd view for a scientist, as

Keith Ward points out, "to think that there is a reason for everything, except for that most important item of all—that is, the existence of everything, the universe itself."[29]

Peter Atkins's reductionism is breathtaking: "Spacetime generates its own dust in the process of its own self-assembly."[30] He calls this the "cosmic bootstrap," referring to the ludicrous idea of a person lifting himself by pulling on his own bootlaces. Keith Ward does not hesitate to say that Atkins's view of the universe is as blatantly self-contradictory as the name he gives to it, pointing out that it is "logically impossible for a cause to bring about some effect without already being in existence." Ward concludes, "Between the hypothesis of God and the hypothesis of a cosmic bootstrap, there is no competition. We were always right to think that persons, or universes, who seek to pull themselves up by their own bootstraps are forever doomed to failure."[31] Neither universes nor Aunt Matilda's cake are self-generating or self-explanatory. Atkins's "self-generation" explanation is demanded from him by his materialism, not his science.

Paul Davies's solution is similar. "There's no need to invoke anything supernatural in the origins of the universe or of life. I have never liked the idea of divine tinkering: for me it is much more inspiring to believe that a set of mathematical laws can be so clever as to bring all these things into being."[32]

It is strange that a scientist of Davies's standing confesses to deciding how things started on the basis of like or dislike. That is no better in principle than someone who says he likes to think there are fairies at the bottom of his garden. Furthermore, what could possibly be meant by *laws* bringing themselves or the universe into existence? Theories and laws cannot themselves cause anything. Newton's laws can describe the motion of a billiard ball, but it is the cue wielded by the billiards player that sets the ball moving, not the laws. The laws help us map the trajectory of the ball's movement in the future (provided nothing external interferes), but they are powerless to move the ball, let alone bring it into existence.

In the world in which most of us live, the simple law of arithmetic, $1 + 1 = 2$, never brought anything into being by itself. It certainly has never put any money into my bank. If I put one thousand pounds into the bank and then later another one thousand pounds, the laws of arithmetic will tell me that I have two thousand pounds in the bank. But if I simply leave it to the laws of arithmetic to bring money into being in my bank account, I shall remain bankrupt. The world of strict naturalism, in which clever mathematical laws all by themselves bring the universe and life into existence, is pure fiction.

The Nature and Role of Faith in Science

Lying at the heart of science is the conviction that the universe is rationally intelligible. But why is it so? It was Albert Einstein's astonishment at this that prompted him to make the famous comment, "The most incomprehensible thing about the universe is that it is comprehensible."

Eugene Wigner, a Nobel laureate in physics, was also struck by the mathematical intelligibility of the universe. He wrote, "The enormous usefulness of mathematics in the natural sciences is something bordering on the mysterious, and there is no rational explanation for it . . . it is an article of faith."[33] Science itself cannot account for this phenomenon. Why? Because in order to do any science at all, you must start by believing that the universe is rationally intelligible. In the words of John Polkinghorne, "Science does not explain the mathematical intelligibility of the physical world, for it is part of science's founding faith that this is so."[34]

Here are two eminent scientists, Wigner and Polkinghorne, explicitly drawing our attention to the foundational role that faith plays in science. Yes, *faith*. It is simply wrong to say with Dawkins that "faith" means "blind faith" and belongs exclusively to the domain of religion, whereas science does not involve faith at all. Faith is inseparable from the scientific endeavor.

If science cannot account for the rational intelligibility of the universe, then what can? Our answer will depend, not on whether we are scientists, but on whether we are theists or naturalists. And the fact is that the intelligibility of the universe is one of the main considerations that has led thinkers of all generations to conclude that the universe must itself be a product of intelligence.

Keith Ward commented, "To the majority of those who have reflected deeply and written about the origin and nature of the universe, it has seemed that it points beyond itself to a source which is non-physical and of great intelligence and power. Almost all of the great classical philosophers—certainly Plato, Aristotle, Descartes, Leibniz, Spinoza, Kant, Hegel, Locke, Berkeley—saw the origin of the universe as lying in a transcendent reality. They had different specific ideas of this reality, and different ways of approaching it; but that the universe is not self-explanatory, and that it requires some explanation beyond itself, was something they accepted as fairly obvious."[35]

The inference to the best explanation from the origin and nature of the universe to an underlying nonphysical intelligence has a long and impressive pedigree. Wigner is therefore wrong when he says there is no rational explanation for that intelligibility. The intelligibility of the universe is grounded in the rationality of God, who created both the universe and the human mind. Hence, it is not surprising when the mathematical theories spun by minds created in the image of God's mind find ready application in a universe whose Architect was that same creative Mind. Far from science abolishing the Creator, it is the existence of God that gives science its fundamental intellectual justification.

Evidence from Scientific Discoveries

Two warnings are necessary here. First, Christians sometimes hitch their wagons too closely to a particular scientist; think, for example, of the commitment to Aristotle in the time of Galileo. Then when science advances, they are left high and dry (in that case, until they saw that Scripture did not demand a static earth—so that science informed their understanding of Scripture). Thus it might be wiser to talk about convergences between our (current) understanding of Scripture and of science.

Second, we encounter two very different arguments about mainstream science. First are arguments that *proceed from an acceptance of mainstream science*. These have mainly to do with the physical sciences: cosmology, physics, and astrophysics. Then there are arguments that *call into question certain aspects of mainstream science*. These arguments have mainly to do with evolutionary biology. The latter arguments are much more controversial than the former and therefore attract much more public interest. The result, however, is that the first set of arguments (and, indeed, the arguments from the history and philosophy of science) may be completely ignored even though they may be much stronger. There is a great danger here of losing a sense of proportion.

ARGUMENTS FROM COSMOLOGY AND PHYSICS

Most scientists today believe that the universe had a beginning.[36] Yet for centuries, thinking was dominated by Aristotle's view of an eternal universe. Indeed, when evidence arose of a beginning to space-time, some scientists resisted it fiercely. Sir John Maddox, a former editor of *Nature*, pronounced the idea of a beginning "thoroughly unacceptable" because it implied an "ultimate origin of our world" and gave creationists "ample justification" for their beliefs.[37] It is rather ironic that in the sixteenth century some people resisted advances in science because they seemed to threaten belief in God, whereas in the twentieth century scientific ideas of a beginning were resisted because they threatened to increase the plausibility of belief in God.

Furthermore, one often hears the criticism leveled at scientists who believe in a Creator that they do not have a model of the universe that leads to testable predictions. But Maddox's comment shows that this is simply not true. His antipathy to the idea of a beginning was precisely because the creation model clearly predicts a beginning. The hypothesis of creation is testable. Arno Penzias, who was awarded a Nobel Prize for discovering the microwave background, makes precisely this point: "The best data we have are exactly what I would have predicted, had I nothing to go on but the five books of Moses, the Psalms and the Bible as a whole."[38]

The Fine-Tuning of the Universe

Science has shown that many of the fundamental constants of nature, from the energy levels in the carbon atom to the rate at which the universe is expanding, have just the right values for life to exist. Change any of them just a little, and the universe would become hostile to life and incapable of supporting it.

For instance, Paul Davies tells us that if the ratio of the nuclear strong force to the electromagnetic force had been different by one part in 10^{16}, no stars could have formed. Again, the ratio of the electromagnetic force–constant to the gravitational force–constant must be equally delicately balanced. Increase it by only one part in 10^{40} and only small stars can exist; decrease it by the same amount and there will only be large stars. Both large and small stars are needed; the large ones produce elements in their thermonuclear furnaces, and only the small ones burn long enough to sustain a planet with life.

According to Davies, that is the kind of accuracy a marksman would need to hit a coin at the far side of the observable universe, twenty billion light years away.[39] Yet even this example of precision-tuning is completely eclipsed by what is perhaps the most mind-boggling example of all. Our universe is a universe in which entropy (a measure of disorder) is increasing, a fact that is enshrined in the Second Law of Thermodynamics. Sir Roger Penrose writes:

> Try to imagine the phase space . . . of the entire universe. Each point in this phase space represents a different possible way that the universe might have started off. We are to picture the Creator, armed with a "pin"—which is to be placed at some

point in the phase space. . . . Each different positioning of the pin provides a different universe. Now the accuracy that is needed for the Creator's aim depends on the entropy of the universe that is thereby created. It would be relatively "easy" to produce a high entropy universe, since then there would be a large volume of the phase space available for the pin to hit. But in order to start off the universe in a state of low entropy—so that there will indeed be a second law of thermodynamics—the Creator must aim for a much tinier volume of the phase space. How tiny would this region be, in order that a universe closely resembling the one in which we actually live would be the result?[40]

He calculates that "the Creator's aim" must have been accurate to one part in 10 to the power 10^{123}, that is, 1 followed by 10^{123} zeros, a "number which it would be impossible to write out in the usual decimal way, because even if you were able to put a zero on every particle in the universe there would not even be enough particles to do the job."[41]

Faced with not one, but many such spectacular examples of fine-tuning, Arno Penzias concludes, "Astronomy leads us to a unique event, a universe which was created out of nothing, one with the very delicate balance needed to provide exactly the right conditions required to permit life, and one which has an underlying (one might say 'supernatural') plan."[42]

Many Universes?

However, some hold that the fine-tuning is to be explained not by the existence of a Creator but by the so-called many worlds hypothesis: that there exist infinitely many, parallel universes in which anything that is theoretically possible will ultimately be actualized. This hypothesis suggests, consequently, that there is nothing surprising in the existence of a universe like ours. This is the view opted for by astronomer Sir Martin Rees.[43]

Cosmologist Edward Harrison reacts very differently: "Here is the cosmological proof of the existence of God—the design argument of Paley—updated and refurbished. The fine-tuning of the universe provides *prima facie* evidence of deistic design. Take your choice: blind chance that requires multitudes of universes, or design that requires only one. . . . Many scientists, when they admit their views, incline towards the teleological or design argument."[44]

Arno Penzias puts the argument the other way around: "Some people are uncomfortable with the purposefully created world. To come up with things that contradict purpose, they tend to speculate about things they haven't seen."[45]

ARGUMENTS FROM BIOLOGY

There is no doubt that the living world gives an overwhelming *impression* of design. Richard Dawkins even defines biology to be "the study of complicated things which give the impression of having been designed for a purpose."[46] But that, say he and many other scientists, is all it is: an impression of design, admittedly a strong impression of design, but nevertheless not real design.

Such statements provoke the question, if it looks like a duck, waddles like a duck, and quacks like a duck, why not call it a duck? Why are such scientists not prepared to draw the obvious inference, and say that living things look as if they are designed, precisely because they are designed?

Dawkins claims that there is no need for a divine watchmaker. In his words, "The only watchmaker in nature is the blind forces of physics, albeit deployed in a very special way. A true watchmaker has foresight: he designs his cogs and springs, and plans their interconnections, with a future purpose in his mind's eye. Natural selection, the blind, unconscious, automatic process which Darwin discovered, and which we now know is the explanation for the existence and apparently purposeful form of all life, has no purpose in mind. It has no mind and no mind's eye; it does not plan for the future. It has no vision, no foresight, no sight at all. If it can be said to play the role of watchmaker in nature, it is that of the blind watchmaker."[47]

The argument, then, is that if evolutionary mechanisms can account for the apparent design in the universe, then the inference to an intelligent origin is false. Thus we are offered a straight choice between God and evolution. Since everything can be accounted for by evolution, there is no Creator. Darwinism implies atheism. Let's have a look at the logic.

The deduction clearly depends on the *simultaneous* validity of the following assertions:

Assertion #1: Biological evolution is incompatible with the existence of
a Creator.
Assertion #2: Biological evolution accounts for the existence of all of
life's complexity.

For many, there is nothing to discuss. For them, both statements are true; the first almost self-evidently and the second as a result of scientific research. Yet two awkward facts insist that things really cannot be quite that simple. First, there are many scientists who deny the first assertion and accept the second—that is, they believe in God as well as in evolution (for instance, Francis Collins, the director of the Human Genome Project). Second, as publishing activity shows, *scientific* questions are being asked (and not only by believers in God) regarding the precise status of the second assertion.[48]

Analysis of Assertion #1

The idea that God and biological evolution are mutually exclusive conceptual alternatives implies first of all that God and evolution belong to the same category of explanation. But this is plainly false. Evolution purports to be a biological *mechanism*, and God is a personal *agent* who designs and creates mechanisms. Further, as we saw before, just because we understand the mechanism by which a Ford car works is not in itself an argument for regarding Mr. Ford himself as nonexistent. As Sir John Houghton puts it, "The fact that we understand some of the mechanisms of the working of the universe or of living systems does not preclude the existence of a designer, any more than the possession of insight into the processes by which a watch has been put together, however automatic these processes may appear, implies there can be no watchmaker."[49]

In other words, the evolutionary viewpoint, far from invalidating the inference to intelligent origin, arguably does nothing more than move it back up one level, from the organisms to the processes by which those organisms have come to exist, or, if you like, from primary to secondary causation. Think of a man who, on seeing a car for the first time, supposes that it is made directly by humans, only later to discover it is made in a robotic factory by robots, which in turn were made by machines made by humans. His initial inference to intelligent origin was not wrong; rather, it was his concept of the nature of the implementation of that intelligence that was inaccurate. To put it another way, direct human activity was not detectable in the robotic factory because it is the existence of the factory itself and its machines that is, ultimately, the result of intelligent human activity.

On the basis of this kind of reasoning, many scientists accept evolution as the Creator's way of producing life's diversity. God designed the universe and its laws; their outworking has led to life. Thus when we look at the living cell, it looks designed because it has been designed in that sense. Darwin himself had such scientists among his supporters, including the distinguished Harvard botanist Asa Gray, a Christian, who was the first person outside England to whom Darwin revealed his theory and with whom he kept in constant touch.[50]

Analysis of Assertion #2

This argument carries little weight with biologists like Richard Dawkins and Daniel Dennett. For them, natural selection somehow *designs without itself being designed* or having any purpose in view. Says Dennett, "Love it or hate it, phenomena like this [DNA] exhibit the heart of the power of the Darwinian idea. An impersonal, unreflective, robotic, mindless little scrap of molecular machinery is the ultimate basis of all agency, and hence meaning, and hence consciousness in the universe."[51]

But is this really true? That is, we can rephrase the content of assertion #2 as: *does the evolutionary mechanism bear all the weight that is put on it?* Experience shows this is a risky question to ask for two main reasons. First, some sort of evolution is a logical necessity for the materialist or naturalist. In other words, if all we have is matter/energy, the forces of physics and time, there is only one logical option: these forces over time have produced life unaided via evolution of some sort. This argument was understood in ancient times; the Greek philosopher Epicurus deduced an evolutionary theory from the atomic theory of Democritus.

Second, the word *evolution* is used in several different ways. It can be used to describe mere change without any implication of the kind of mechanism or intelligent input (or lack of it) involved in bringing about the change. In this sense we speak of the evolution of the motor car, where intelligent input is necessary, or the evolution of a coastline, where it isn't.

Next, there is artificial selection. Many different kinds of roses and sheep have been developed from basic stocks, by very careful selective breeding methods. This process involves a high degree of intelligent input; and so, although often cited, in particular by Darwin himself, it is a poor model for evolution by *unguided* processes.

Next comes microevolution: variation within prescribed limits of complexity, quantitative variation of already existing organs or structures. This aspect of the theory is scarcely controversial as such effects of natural selection, mutation, genetic drift, and so on are constantly being recorded.[52] One classic example with which we are, sadly, all too familiar around the world is the way in which bacteria develop resistance to antibiotics.

However, the word *evolution* is used in two further senses that are controversial. The first of these is macroevolution: the coming into existence of qualitatively new organs, structures, and genetic material so that a marked increase in complexity is involved. The second is molecular evolution. Indeed, strictly speaking, evolution presupposes the existence of self-replicating genetic material so that "prebiological natural selection is a contradiction in terms."[53] However, the term *molecular evolution* is now commonly used to describe the emergence of a living cell from nonliving materials.[54] This language usage can easily obscure the fact that the word *evolution* here cannot mean what it means elsewhere.

Macroevolution has been challenged in detail by Michael Behe in his book *Darwin's Black Box*.[55] Darwin once wrote, "If it could be demonstrated that any complex organ existed which could not possibly have been formed by numerous, successive, slight modifications, my theory would absolutely break down."[56] The point is repeated by Richard Dawkins, who says that if such an organism is found he will "cease to believe in Darwinism."[57] Behe responds by arguing that there exist many such irreducibly complex molecular machines, like the bacterial flagellum. The debate he has stimulated is likely to rage for a long time.

A MATTER OF INFORMATION

Molecular machines are made from proteins, which are in turn made out of very long chains of amino acids, twenty of which occur in living organisms. Think of the amino acids as the twenty "letters" of an alphabet. Then a protein is an incredibly long "word" in that alphabet in which every amino acid letter must be in the right place. Similarly, the letters in an ordinary word or the keystrokes in a computer program must be in the correct order for the word to mean what it should mean or for the program to work.

A living cell is, therefore, not merely matter. It is matter replete with information. Like a computer hard disk, DNA contains the database of information and the programs to produce the proteins. Bill Gates wrote, "DNA is like a computer program, but far, far more advanced than any software we've ever created."[58] This statement carries with it the implication (already exploited scientifically in myriad ways in recent years) that biological machines are open to mathematical analysis in general and information—theoretic analysis—in particular.

It is to this analysis we now turn to consider the question of whether molecular machines (of whatever kind) can generate novel information. Léon Brillouin, in his classic work on information theory, has no doubt where the answer lies. He asserted, "A machine does not create any new information, but it performs a very valuable transformation of known information."[59]

Twenty years after Brillouin's writing, Nobel laureate Peter Medawar wrote, "No process of logical reasoning—no mere act of mind or computer-programmable operation—can enlarge the information content of the axioms and premises or observation statements from which it proceeds."[60] He deduced from this observation that some kind of law of conservation of information must hold.

Kurt Gödel, one of the greatest mathematicians of all time, indicated that he also thought that some kind of conservation of information was characteristic of living things. He said, "The complexity of living bodies has to be present in the material [from which they are derived] or in the laws [governing their formation]. In particular, the materials forming the organs, if they are governed by mechanical laws, have to be of the same order of complexity as the living body."[61] Gödel's own formulation runs as follows: "More generally, Gödel believes that mechanism in biology is a prejudice of our time which will be disproved. In this case, one disproval, in Gödel's opinion, will consist in a mathematical theorem to the effect that the formation within geological times of a human body by the laws of physics (or any other laws of a similar nature), starting from a random distribution of the elementary particles and the field, is as unlikely as the separation by chance of the atmosphere into its components."[62]

Nobel laureate Ilya Prigogine and Isabelle Stengers argue that order can arise spontaneously by *self-organization* out of chaos and disorder.[63] However, Stephen Meyer is surely right when he says, "Self-organizational theorists explain well what does not need to be explained. What needs explaining is not the origin of order . . . but the origin of information."[64] Now if there is any truth in the ideas of Medawar and Gödel, we would expect that any origin of life simulations that claim to get information "for free" by purely natural processes must somehow, in spite of their claim, be smuggling that information in from outside. That this appears to be the case has been convincingly argued by many authors, including William Dembski.[65]

The existence of complex specified information, therefore, provides a very substantial challenge to the notion that unguided natural processes can account for life and makes scientifically plausible the suggestion that an intelligent source was responsible. Such an inference to an intelligent source, based on the nature of DNA, is not simply an argument from analogy. Many classical design arguments were of that kind. In them, an attempt was made to reason back from similar effects to similar causes, so that the validity of the arguments often turned on the degree of similarity between the two situations being compared. This circumstance was famously discussed by David Hume.

But the design inference from DNA is much stronger than its classical predecessors for the following reason: "DNA does not imply the need for an intelligent designer because it has some similarities to a software program or to a human language. It implies the need for an intelligent designer because . . . it possesses an identical feature (namely, information content) that intelligently designed human texts and computer languages possess."[66] We are not, therefore, arguing from analogy; we are making an inference to the best explanation.

The astronomer Carl Sagan thought that a single message from space would be enough to convince us that there were intelligences in the universe other than our own. Now, if we are prepared to look for scientific evidence of intelligent activity beyond our planet, why are we so hesitant about applying exactly the same thinking to what is *on* our planet? Is the scientific method not applicable everywhere? Once we put it this way, is it not obvious that the next question to ask is, *what, then, should we deduce from the overwhelming amount of information that is contained in even the simplest living system?* Does it not, for example, give evidence of intelligent origin of a far stronger kind than did the argument from the fine-tuning of the universe, an argument which, as we have seen, convinces many physicists that we humans are meant to be here?

At the public announcement of the completion of the Human Genome Project, its director, Francis Collins, said, "It is humbling for me and awe-inspiring to realize that we have caught the first glimpse of our own instruction book, previously known only to God."[67]

DIVINE ACTION AND THE GOD OF THE GAPS

It is frequently objected that the design inference is an argument from ignorance and, possibly, intellectual laziness, postulating design (and therefore, by implication, a Designer) to cover a gap in the present state of our scientific knowledge rather than getting on with the hard scientific work of finding out. Let me therefore strongly emphasize that the main thrust of the design argument is from what *we know*, not from what we don't know: the rational and mathematical intelligibility of the universe, its fine-tuning, and so forth.

When it comes to the special areas like the origin of life, we need to investigate the "God of the gaps" charge more closely. In particular, we need to distinguish between gaps that are *closed* by science and gaps that are *revealed* by science; perhaps we could call them "bad gaps" and "good gaps," respectively. As an example of a bad gap, we might think of Newton's suggestion that God occasionally had to tweak some of the orbits of the planets to bring them into line. That kind of gap we would expect to be closed by science because it falls within the explanatory power of science to settle. Good gaps will be revealed by science as not being within its explanatory power. They will be those (few) places where science as such points beyond itself to explanations that are not within its purview.

Supporters of the SETI program would not find convincing the idea that postulating an alien intelligence as the source of an information-rich message that had been received was tantamount to postulating an "alien of the gaps." And we find no difficulty in inferring an intelligent author as the source of writing, since we know the futility of attempting to give a reductionist explanation in terms of the physics and chemistry of paper and ink. Putting it another way, when it comes to fully explaining writing on paper, there is a gap in the explanatory power of physics and chemistry. This is not a gap of ignorance but a gap in principle—a "good gap" that is revealed by our knowledge, and not by our ignorance, of science. It is because we know that, even in principle, physics and chemistry cannot give an adequate explanation of writing, we reject a naturalistic explanation, and we postulate an author.

Alvin Plantinga has pointed out that it is a matter of logic that if there is a God who does anything in the world indirectly, he must ultimately act directly. And once we admit that God has acted directly at least once in the past for the original creation of the world, what is there to prevent him acting more than once, whether in the past or in the future? After all, the laws of the universe are not independent of God; they are (our) codifications of the regularities that he has built in to the universe. Therefore, it would be absurd to think that the laws of the universe constrain God so that he could never do anything special. Plantinga summarizes,

"Could we not sensibly conclude, for example, that God created life, or human life, or something else specially" if, of course, the evidence demands it?[68]

That is the crux of the matter. Are we prepared to follow where the evidence leads—even if it goes against naturalistic explanations? If there is an active Creator God, then it should not surprise us if our attempts to understand the universe on naturalistic presuppositions are for the most part very successful.[69] Rather, we find that there are some areas (particularly associated with origins) that not only do not yield but become increasingly opaque to any naturalistic methodology.[70]

John Polkinghorne, who like Plantinga emphatically rejects a God of the (bad) gaps theology, nevertheless insists that we must not "rest content with a discussion in such soft-focus that it never begins to engage our intuitions about God's action with our knowledge of physical process. If the physical world is really open, and top-down intentional causality operates within it, there must be intrinsic 'gaps' (an envelope of possibility) in the bottom-up account of nature to make room for intentional causality. . . . We are unashamedly 'people of the gaps' in this intrinsic sense and there is nothing unfitting in a 'God of the gaps' in this sense either." As to the nature of God's interaction, in his view it is "not energetic but informational."[71]

However, if God has done some things directly, he is responsible for some energetic action or interaction. After all, the law of conservation of energy tells us that energy is conserved. It does not tell us where that energy came from in the first place—a fact that is usually overlooked. Furthermore, the central pillar of orthodox Christianity, to which Polkinghorne publicly subscribes, is the resurrection of Christ, an event within history that involved a direct and extraordinary input of divine energy (see Eph. 1:19–20).

The Complexity of God

Richard Dawkins objects, "To explain the origin of the DNA/protein machine by invoking a supernatural Designer is to explain precisely nothing, for it leaves unexplained the origin of the Designer. You have to say something like 'God was always there' and if you allow yourself that kind of lazy way out, you might as well just say 'DNA was always there', or 'Life was always there', and be done with it."[72] If you do that, he suggests, you have an end of science. For science, in his view, must always explain the more complex in terms of the less complex.

However, simplicity is not the only criterion of truth. Quantum electrodynamics is not simple. Yet scientists believe it because of another important criterion of truth: explanatory power. Imagine I am exploring a cave in China with an archaeologist. On the cave wall there are a couple of scratches and she suddenly says, "Human intelligence!" I say, "Don't be absurd; those are just a couple of scratches. Why do you need something as complex as the human mind to explain something as simple as that?" She replies, "It is clear you know nothing of semiotics. These two scratches are the Chinese character 'ren,' which means a human being. Therefore, I am sure they were produced by human intelligence." Suppose I reply, "But that is no explanation at all, since the human brain is infinitely more complex than the two scratches." That would be silly. And it would be even sillier to go on to suggest that we had reached an end of science. The scratch marks may well be important clues as to the identity, culture, and intelligence of the people who made them.

Similarly, the notion that belief in a Creator God who created and who upholds the universe would bring science to an end is false.[73] Believing that the engine of the car had been designed by Mr. Ford would not stop anybody from investigating scientifically how the design worked. In fact, it might well spur them on to do so.[74] James Clerk-Maxwell was certainly thinking like that when he had inscribed over the door of the famous Cavendish physics laboratory in Cambridge the words: "Great are the works of the LORD; they are pondered by all who delight in them" (Ps. 111:2).

Incidentally, is it not to be wondered at that our archaeologist immediately infers intelligent origin when faced with a few simple scratches whereas some scientists, when faced with the 3.5 billion-letter sequence of the human genome, inform us that it is to be explained solely in terms of chance and necessity?

CONCLUSION

The scientific intelligibility of the universe points to the existence of a Mind responsible both for the universe and for our minds so that we are able to do science and to uncover beautiful mathematical descriptions. Not only that, but our increasing insight into the fine-tuning of the universe in general, and of planet earth in particular, is surely consistent with the widespread awareness that we are meant to be here. This earth is our home.

The really big outstanding question is, *why are we here?* True science recognizes that it is not equipped to answer such questions. How shall we find out? In light of the above, it is surely not illogical that one of the major reasons we have been given minds is not only that we should be able to explore our fascinating universe, but that we should be able to understand the Mind that has given us this universe. Furthermore, we humans are capable of giving expression to the thoughts of our minds and communicating them to others. It would therefore be very surprising if the Mind from which we are derived should be any less capable of self-expression and communication than we are.

This leads us at once to the question, is there any evidence that that Mind has ever spoken into our world? Many ancient cosmologies populated the universe with gods of every kind. These deities were usually thought to emerge from the primeval material chaos of the universe, so that they were ultimately part of the basic stuff of the universe itself. They cannot be the answer to our question since we are, by definition, looking for a Mind that exists independently of the universe.

The Greek philosopher Aristotle formulated the concept of an "Unmoved Mover," which, though changeless itself, imparted change to other things. Regarding as absurd the idea that the principle of change should be inside it, he believed that this Unmoved Mover was in some sense outside the universe. However, Aristotle's Unmoved Mover was much too remote and abstract to have been interested in speaking into the world.

Long before Aristotle, the book of Genesis was penned. It starts with the words, "In the beginning God created the heavens and the earth" (Gen. 1:1). This statement stands in complete contrast with the other mythical cosmogonies of the time, where the gods were part of the stuff of the universe, and the world was made out of a god. Genesis claims that there is a Creator God who exists independently of the universe. The Christian apostle John puts it this way: "In the beginning was the Word, and the Word was with God, and the Word was God. He was with God in the beginning. Through him all things were made; without him nothing was made that has been made. In him was life, and that life was the light of men" (John 1:1–4).

In Greek, the word translated "Word" is *logos*, which was often used by Greek philosophers for the rational principle that governs the universe. But what lies behind the universe is much more than a rational principle. It is God, the Creator himself. It is no abstraction, or even impersonal force, that lies behind the universe. God, the Creator, is a person. And just as Aunt Matilda is not part of her cake, neither is God part of the stuff of his universe.

Now, if the ultimate reality behind the universe is a personal God, this has very far-reaching implications for the human search for truth, since it opens up possibilities for knowing ultimate reality and not merely the scientific study of things. Persons communicate in a way that things do not. Being persons, we can get to know other persons. Therefore, we next ask, *if the Creator is personal, has he spoken directly?*

At this point, we encounter the biblical claim that God has spoken in the most direct way possible. He, God the Word who is a person, has become human, to demonstrate fully that the ultimate truth behind the universe is personal. "The Word became flesh and made his dwelling among us. We have seen his glory, the glory of the One and Only, who came from the Father, full of grace and truth" (John 1:14).

These are things that the natural sciences cannot tell us and should not claim to. However, as with so many other things beyond the competence of science, this does not mean that there is no evidence for them. Indeed, presenting that evidence would take us far beyond the scope of this present chapter into history, literature, and experience. I must therefore content myself with allowing Nobel Prize-winning physicist Arthur Schawlow to give the direction: "We are fortunate to have the Bible and especially the New Testament, which tells us so much about God in widely accessible human terms."[75]

Inevitably, of course, not only those of us who do science, but all of us have to choose the presupposition with which we start. There are not many options—just two, really. Either human intelligence ultimately owes its origin to mindless matter, or there is a Creator. Strange, is it not, that some people claim that it is their intelligence that leads them to prefer the first to the second?

PART ONE
Giving an Answer

SECTION TWO
Addressing the Questions Behind the Questions

7

CONVERSATIONAL APOLOGETICS

Michael Ramsden

Credo quia absurdum or "I believe because it is absurd" is a dangerous creed to follow. Yet for many who place themselves decidedly outside of the Christian fold, this creed sums up everything they feel in relation to "faith." It expresses the thought that the Christian faith has not so much failed to reflect reality, as that it never attempted to do so in the first place. Such a conviction leads to the conclusion, or the fear, that faith not only fails to make sense of life philosophically, existentially, or morally, but that it has never even tried to do so.

So has the Christian faith failed, or has it been misunderstood? This chapter briefly examines three areas where some people believe the Christian faith has—or fear will—fail them. We will look at these areas from the viewpoint of one who doubts, and much of what is to follow should be read with this perspective in mind.

PHILOSOPHICALLY FRIGHTENED?

Many Christians and curious skeptics nurse philosophical fears about faith. These tend to revolve around the concern that faith has nothing to do with truth or reality. Some would argue that this is precisely why Christianity is called "faith" in the first place—because it lacks both truth and reality. It is something, people argue, that others are made to believe (often at a young age) or something that they are able to believe (because of some need) in the absence of any evidence as to its veracity. Richard Dawkins comments, for example, that faith is "blind trust in the absence of evidence, even in the teeth of evidence."[1]

In the absence of truth and reality, faith soon collapses into the merely psychological: God is not there to believe in, yet somehow we are still able to believe in him. The question of faith becomes asking not whether it is true or false, but whether it is psychologically possible for people to believe in such absurdity. The debate about God is not to ask for evidence for God's existence, but rather to find explanations as to how people came to hold to this belief at all.[2] Such beliefs characterize the one who has philosophical fears about faith.

This conviction that faith has nothing to do with either truth or reality is very common. Faith is seen as a persuasion of the mind that falls short of the truth. In which case, faith is construed as the ability to believe in things even when you have *no idea* whether they are true or not, but would like them to be. A strong faith then would consist of being able to believe in things that you actually *suspected* weren't true or real, yet were still firm in your convictions. And the strongest possible kind of faith that you could have, therefore, would be *knowing* that something isn't true or real, and still being able to believe it. How strong a faith would be required for that!

On this analysis, faith disappears in the presence of knowledge. Once you realize that your faith has had a psychological benefit in absence of reality, it is akin to awakening to the fact that you have been taking a spiritual placebo. Now that you know that faith is not real, the psychological benefit is lost.

Faith Is Not Wishful Thinking

This conviction is often expressed most politely in the following form: "Michael, I'm so happy that you're a Christian, and I wish I could believe what you believe, but I can't." In my experience, what most people mean by this is: "Michael, I am so happy that you are so happy. There seems to be a joy and completeness in your life that I find attractive. But the reason you are happy is because you are a Christian. In other words, you believe in things that are not true or real." (Now, what do you call people who believe in things that are not there? The answer is: *lunatics.*) So what they are saying is, "Michael, you are actually insane. But the main thing is that you are happy and insane. And I am happy that you are happy.

As a matter of fact, I'm so desperate to be happy, that I too would embrace insanity just to join you, but I can't do it. I've thought about it, but I just can't."

Faith Is Not Speculation

Thankfully, this is not the Christian understanding of faith. Yes, the Bible does say that faith is a gift, but it is not the gift of stupidity. It is not being able to believe in things that are not there. Nor is it a blind leap into the dark.

For example, if I were to say to you, "I have faith in the British prime minister," you would not hear me saying, "I wish to postulate at a philosophical level the existence of an ontological metaphysical entity, which I am labeling 'British prime minister.' I further wish to postulate that, given his existence, I am justified in believing in him." No one would ever understand me to be saying such a thing. Instead, when I say, "I have faith in the British prime minister," what they would hear me saying is two things: one, that there is a real person who is the British prime minister—he actually exists—and two, that I have grounds to trust him—that I know him to be true to his word and so on.

It is only in this sense that the Bible uses the word *faith*. It never carries with it the idea of speculation at a philosophical level. The statement "I have faith in God," carries the same meaning as the statement "I have faith in the British prime minister." That is, I trust in someone who really exists and who is true to his word and character—a being who is worthy of being trusted.[3]

The question then is this: *is God real and worthy to be trusted?*

Faith Is Not in Something but Someone

When Christians talk about having faith, they mean they have put their trust in someone who is both true and real. "Faith in" or "trusting in" is the only honest response to the God who is both true and real. Faith is nothing less than that; it is more than that, but it is nothing less than that. In the letter to the Hebrews we read, "Without faith it is impossible to please God" (11:6).[4] And since the book is being written by someone who wants to please God, and since it is impossible, he says, to please God without faith, then it is rather important to define faith. Rather handily, that is exactly what he goes on to do. "Without faith it is impossible to please God, because anyone who comes to him must believe that he exists [God is real. He exists], and that he rewards those who earnestly seek him [he is true to his promises and character, worthy of faith, and trustworthy]."

Do you know that kind of reality with God in your own life? Do you know him? Faith is not speculation that God is; it is *knowing* that God is. There is a big difference between the two. Without these elements of reality and truth, there is no faith.

In summary, faith is not wishful thinking. It is not hoping that God is there. It is not a leap into the dark. As a matter of fact, if you read the Bible you will see that there is no such statement that faith is a leap into the dark. Rather, faith is described as stepping into the light, a light allows you to see and be seen.[5] But sadly, many Christians (or many people who think they are Christians) find themselves in a position where they neither know the truth nor the reality of Christ. They may even have a secret hope that it is true. But all that means is that they do not actually have faith in Christ; they do not know him.

Do You Truly Know Him?

Over the last few years, I have had many conversations with people who fall exactly into this category. Several of these conversations have lasted many hours, and in some cases have even been spread over days and months. These are people who have been brought up in church, read their Bibles almost every day, try to pray every day, have been to church every Sunday, have married in church, and now their children go to church, but who are not Christians. They have never known Christ in their lives—because you cannot put your faith in someone if you believe that he does not exist, or if you think that he cannot be trusted.

People sometimes try to persuade themselves that they are something that they are not. They are scared to even ask questions, because if questions are asked in the light of such a faith, their faith will collapse. However, if people lose this kind of faith, they have not proved that God is not real; rather, they have simply proved that he was never known to them in the first place. You cannot lose what you never had. All they have proved is that their faith was not real, not that God is not real.

Knowing and Knowing

There is really only one basic response to this challenge, which can be divided into two parts. The first is at the level of reality: do you *know* that Christ is God, and can it be known that Christ is God? Anybody can claim anything, and anyone can *claim* to be God. Perhaps you are familiar with the story of the psychiatrist who is transferred to a new wing in a psychiatric hospital. As he is doing his first rounds, he comes to a patient who really perturbs him. Eventually he asks,

"Excuse me, just who do you think you are?" The patient replies "Napoleon." The psychiatrist probes deeper. "That's very interesting," he says. "Who told you that you are Napoleon?" He replies, "God told me." At this point, the man sitting in the bed next him says, "I most certainly did not!"

Anybody may claim to be God, yet the question is, how can such a claim be meaningfully sustained? This is why, for example, prophecy is so important in the Christian faith. The prophetic is not just a statement of what will happen before it happens, but it is also an explanation as to why it will happen before it happens. It is just one of the ways we can begin to find out whether there is something more to the Christian faith than a state of mind. Jesus claimed to come in fulfillment of hundreds of prophecies about who the Christ would be, where he would be born, how he would die. Have you ever looked into it? This kind of apologetic enquiry is as important to the Christian trying to understand his or her faith as it is to the non-Christian, who is honestly moved to examine these kinds of issues. The Christian faith claims to be rooted in reality, and hence in history. That being the case, what evidence do we have for this claim? Is it reliable? What does it say? Can it be trusted?

The second part of the response is that God is not an idea. We can meet him. We can talk to him. The greatest gift that God has given to humankind is himself. We can know him because he has given himself to us. This is different from the kind of knowing talked about in the paragraph above. We can have faith in him, not just because of what he has done, which is very important, but because he is, and because he makes himself known. This is the kind of faith that does not disappoint because it is not speculation about someone; it is faith in someone.

For the Christian, this is helpful in that it reminds us that the basis of faith is Christ. For the non-Christian, especially if one has some kind of Christian background, it is important to realize that unless faith is in response to and results in trust in the person of Christ—and not just one's ideas or hopes about the person of Christ—then there is no biblical faith. Again, you cannot lose what you never had. So for the person who says that he has lost his faith, we must first properly ask about the nature of his faith in the first place. What was it? Reliance on an idea? Or a personal relationship with the risen Christ?

In his book *God Is the Gospel,* John Piper quotes Jonathan Edwards, who observes: "There is a difference between having an *opinion* that God is holy and gracious, and having a *sense* of the loveliness and beauty of that holiness and grace. There is a difference between having a rational judgment that honey is sweet, and having a sense of its sweetness."[6] Piper adds, "If a person comes to the gospel and sees the events of Good Friday and Easter and believes that they happened and that they can bring some peace of mind, but does not see and savor any of this divine glory, that person does not have saving faith."[7]

EXISTENTIALLY DISAPPOINTED?

The second reason people think that maybe the Christian faith has failed them flows from the first and is existential. I have sometimes remarked that at the human level, there are normally two main categories of people who lose their faith for existential reasons. One group consists of people who have gone to church and discovered they didn't like their pastor; the second group includes pastors who have gone to church and found out that they didn't like their people. However, there is much more to it than this. The famous playwright Dennis Potter has said that he would like to write dramas in which religion is not a bandage applied to a wound, but rather is the wound itself.[8] D. Z. Philips, commentating on Potter's plays, says that for Potter, "It is not enough to say that what religion offers is idle language. It does too much damage for that."[9]

Professor Alister McGrath, in his excellent book *Dawkins' God: Genes, Memes and the Meaning of Life*, tracks professor Richard Dawkins's definition of *faith* over the years. In 1976 Dawkins's definition of *faith* was "blind trust that goes against the evidence." McGrath then shows how his position hardens: it becomes a "mental illness" in 1989, and then seven years later "one of the world's great evils, comparable to the smallpox virus but harder to eradicate."[10] In Dawkins's recent book *The God Delusion*, his emotional tirade hits a climax. The accusation mirrors the sentiment of Dennis Potter's: the Christian faith is not simply misguided; it is morally reprehensible.

Trying to speak to these issues in a comprehensive way is almost impossible because of the sheer range of different experiences people have had. But let me just say this before we move into a different aspect of the same problem. Writing to the church in Galatia, the apostle Paul was very concerned that they be able to distinguish true Christians from false Christians, and true Christianity from false Christianity. He pointed out that one of the ways this is done is by examining the fruit of people's lives. The word he uses for "fruit" is singular; there is one fruit to look for, but it has a complex taste. He then describes that fruit as love, joy, peace, patience, kindness, goodness, faithfulness, gentleness, and self-control (Gal. 5:22–23). What he is saying is that if you come into contact with people who taste like this, then this is a good indication that they are who they say they are. But if what you taste is different from that, if it leaves a bitter taste in the mouth, then what you have experienced is not really Christian. In other words, those who have put their faith in Christ look and "taste" like Christ.

I have no doubt there are many people reading this who know people who claim to be Christian, yet the fruit seems to be absent. The frightening thing is that when Paul writes to the church in Galatia, he is writing in a context where there are people who are claiming to be and, indeed, are, leaders of so-called churches—and he is saying that they are no leaders at all. The type of fruit is determined by the type of plant. If the fruit is not there and the desire to bear such fruit is not evident, then we have the right and duty to question whether they are at all what they claim to be.[11]

The Real Deal

I have the privilege of working with Dr. Ravi Zacharias. I know him as *Ravi-ji*. In India, the word *ji* is a title both of respect and affection. The reason I call him "Ravi-ji" is because I love and respect him. I do not love and respect him because he is perfect; he is not perfect. The reason I love and respect him is because he is real, because he is honest. It is because I have known him for many years. We are close. I know that who he is in private is also who he is in public. Do you know people like that? If you are reading this and you are not a Christian but you are interested, my guess is that you do. But if you are reading this and you are not really interested, my guess is that, sadly, you may not know such people. What is the fruit that you have tasted? If it has been poisonous and it has disillusioned you, it may well have not been Christian fruit at all.

Disappointment with God

There is another side to this problem that needs to be highlighted. We do not experience disillusionment and disappointment at a human level only, but at a spiritual level with God himself. And the way that this normally is expressed is along these lines: "Look, God, I have been a good person. I have gone to church, I have prayed. I have listened to hours of boring sermons. I have tried to be nice to people, and I've asked for a couple of things, but where are you? I have upheld my side of the bargain, God. But you haven't upheld yours."

If the criticism is phrased this way, it will always produce a wrong answer. The Latin motto *do ut des* ("I give so that you may give") expresses what many people feel about sacrifice and the Christian faith. This conviction often proves to be an ongoing source of disappointment with God for many Christians, who feel they have upheld their end of a spiritual bargain but God has failed to uphold his. There are interconnected elements in play here—namely, that obeying a system of divine law makes God indebted to us and that there are good people who do not deserve to experience certain events.

What Makes You Think You Are Good?

This is a very difficult and almost painful thing to say, but the simple truth is that there are no good people. I know that we often may think of ourselves as being good people, especially when we compare ourselves to other people whom we do not like. Someone came to Jesus once and said, "Good teacher, what must I do to inherit eternal life?" (Luke 18:18).[12] What he was saying was, "You're a good person. You're obviously going to go to heaven. What must I do? Tell me, good teacher, what are the good things that I must do so I can go too? How do I attain eternal life?" Jesus looked at him and said, "Why do you call me good?" And then he added, "No one is good but God alone." Think about this: if you have to be good to go to heaven and only God is good, who is going? God and . . . no one else. In other words, Jesus is saying, "Your application to join the Trinity has been refused."

Now, sometimes we find this type of statement offensive, but if you are reading this and you really believe that you're perfect, there's only one solution to that predicament: you need to get married. If you are married, then you need to start listening! We need to be honest with ourselves. We may try to be good, but we know that we are who Jesus said we are: sinners.

He Knows Who Has Been Naughty and Nice!

Do you know the story of the boy who wanted a bike for Christmas? On Christmas Eve he hunted around the house and realized that none of the parcels was big enough to contain a bike. He started to worry that maybe his bike was not going to materialize. So that night he got down on his knees and said, "God, I really want a bike for Christmas. I really do. More than anything else I want a bicycle. And God, if you give me a bicycle for Christmas, I promise I will be good for a month. For one month, God, I won't do anything wrong. I will please only you." He then got into bed, and he started to think his bargain with God was not very realistic. After all, a month is a very long time. So he got out of bed and got back on his knees and said, "Okay, God. I'll tell you what. I will give you a week. I will be good for a whole week if you give me a bicycle for Christmas." He got back into bed and started thinking about his sister—about how annoying she was, about that little turn of phrase she has that really winds him up and makes him mad. So he realized that's not going to work either. He got back on his knees and said, "Okay, God, I'll tell you what. How about a day, okay? You give me a bike tomorrow for Christmas. I'll be good for a day." Then he started thinking about his mother and how he had to keep his room tidy and all the other kinds of things he didn't do, and how he might fail. So he concluded that this was not going to work either. And then all of a sudden, a thought occurred to him. Suddenly he remembered that just off the street where he lives was a small, formal chapel. He sneaked out of bed and hurried across the street. He opened the door to the chapel. Just on the left was the little stone basin for holding water, and above that there was a small statue of Mary. So he took the statue off the pedestal, went back through the church door, dashed across the street, sneaked upstairs, and barricaded himself in his bedroom. He put the statue in his wardrobe, closed the door, and got down on his knees and prayed, "Okay, Jesus. If you ever want to see your mother again . . ."

The reason we laugh at that story is we know that any such bargain is ridiculous. If we are simply prepared to be honest enough with ourselves, to even try to approach God in this way is foolish. The letter that the apostle Paul wrote to some of the very first Christians in Galatia may well be the earliest Christian piece of literature ever written.[13] As Paul begins his letter, he makes reference to two different gospels, except one of them, he says, is actually no gospel at all—it is not good news in any sense of the word.[14] He writes, "I am astonished that you are so quickly deserting the one who called you by the grace of Christ and are turning to a different gospel—which is really no gospel at all. Evidently some people are throwing you into confusion and are trying to pervert the gospel of Christ" (1:6–7). The false gospel, he goes on to say, teaches that by obeying the law through human effort, you can earn favor with God (see 2:15–16). He will smile on you and everything will go well.

Curses and Blessings

Paul says that not only is this view actually no gospel at all, but that all those who try to live that way will bring a curse on themselves; those who rely on works of the law are under a curse (Gal. 3:10). Paul uses very strong language. He is in effect saying, "If that is what you are trying to do, your life will not be happy; it will be cursed." Later in his letter, he actually does challenge them on this very ground: "Even though my illness was a trial to you, you did not treat me with contempt or scorn. Instead, you welcomed me as if I were an angel of God, as if I were Christ Jesus himself. What has happened to all your joy? I can testify that, if you could have done so, you would have torn out your eyes and given them to me" (4:14–15). Paul describes an extreme joy that the Galatians had known but was now gone as they mistakenly tried to complete what had been started by God.

Return to Joy?

The other gospel, Paul says, which is the only real gospel, the only good news, is that God has become a curse for us. Having told them that those who rely on the law are under a curse, Paul counters, "Christ redeemed us from the curse of the law by becoming a curse for us" (3:13). The reason I believe many people think that they are Christians and feel that God has failed them is that they think they have upheld their end of the bargain. They have tried to obey the law, so surely they should now be rewarded by God for all their effort. However, everything in the Christian faith is *a gift*. You cannot earn any of it. And once you realize it is all a gift. Once you realize that you do not deserve anything, but in Christ you have now been given everything, then you are able to experience joy.

When Paul says that Christ became a curse for us, he is saying that Christ took on himself the full weight and consequence, in every possible way, of our sin. Sin is not a "regrettable lapse," but "hostility to God."[15] When we sin, we are saying that we neither recognize God nor need God nor heed God. As a matter of fact, when we sin, it is because we want to be God. When we believe that we can earn our own salvation by adherence to a certain standard, we are also rejecting the provision that God himself has made that we might know him, and this puts us under a curse. Christ however, came to earth and became that curse that we ourselves might be free from it, and so know him.

I will return to this subject again at the end of the chapter. But I should say that this is why the apostle Paul reminds the Galatians that they received the *gospel of grace* with such great joy—because it liberated them from this curse. He then confesses his astonishment that having been so liberated and having received this liberation with such great joy, that they should allow themselves to be removed from it, and return to the bondage they had escaped from!

MORAL QUALMS?

The third reason that some people feel the Christian faith has failed them is due to what I am going to call "moral qualms." Now there are so many legitimate aspects to this moral category that I'm going to have to leave almost all of them alone and pick out just one—namely, the conviction that if someone becomes a Christian or that by being a Christian and embracing Christian morality, he or she actually becomes a morally *bad* person. Many people fear that to be truly Christian, to truly trust in Christ and stand firm in that faith, is to become a morally reprehensible person.

I was asked to speak at an event a couple of years ago in which the audience wrote down all the difficult questions that they could think of and then the questions were drawn out of a basket at random. At the end of the event, a woman who embraced Buddhism came up to me. She said, "Michael, I've enjoyed this evening, but I'm a Buddhist and something bothers me. I want to ask you about it." I invited her to continue. She said, "You didn't say it expressly, but you seemed to assume in your answers, that there is only one way to God, through Jesus Christ. Would that be correct?" I said, "Well, yes. It would be correct." She said, "Well, I could never agree with you—I could never become an intolerant person like you by saying that other people are wrong."

I said, "You're a Buddhist, right?" She said, "Yes." I continued, "Tell me, didn't the Buddha say that Hinduism was wrong? Did he not reject the caste system, which is central to Hinduism, and state that the Vedas, their scriptures, were not divine?" And her face fell. She said, "He did say that. I read it this morning in my devotions." I said, "My question to you is really quite simple. If you're prepared to entertain the words of the Buddha, even though he said that millions of people were wrong, why are you not prepared to entertain what Jesus has to say when he says that some people are wrong?" She quickly replied, "I don't like where this conversation is going." I said, "I can appreciate that, but will you answer my question?"

The next morning she attended a church in which I was preaching on the subject of forgiveness. At the end, she sat in silence for a few minutes and then burst into tears. For the first time she realized that the Christian faith she had left behind for Buddhism was not true Christianity at all. She had simply exchanged one way of life for another; she had actually never known Christ, despite having gone to church almost every day of her school life.

The Evils of Monism

Professor Isaiah Berlin was a leading professor at the University of Oxford and, during the sixties and seventies, was a dominant intellectual figure in Europe. When he died, the obituaries about him in the major newspapers ran to full-page articles. He was considered a genius. Isaiah Berlin wrote about many subjects, but there were two areas to which he kept returning. One was freedom—what does it means to live in a free society? And the other one was monism—the belief that there is just one single truth into which all other truths must be made to fit. He argued that freedom needs pluralism in order to exist. Interestingly, in his last essay before his death, he wrote,

> The enemy of pluralism is monism—the ancient belief that there is a single harmony of truths into which everything, if it is genuine, in the end must fit. The consequence of this belief (which is something different from, but akin to, what Karl Popper called essentialism—to him the root of all evil) is that those who know should command those who do not. . . . To cause pain, to kill, to torture are in general rightly condemned; but if these things are done not for my personal benefit but for an ism—socialism, nationalism, fascism, communism, fanatically held religious belief, or progress, or the fulfillment of the laws of history—then they are in order.[16]

Monism, he argued, was one step away from despotism. If you meet someone who believes he knows he has the truth, then he is only one step away from being a despot. I can remember reading that essay for the first time, coming to the end of it, and writing just one sentence at the bottom of the page, *What about a truth filled with grace?* When you say that someone is graceful, you are saying that there is something beautiful to their physical movement. When you describe someone as being gracious, you are saying that there is something beautiful about their inner movement. Jesus was described as someone "full of grace and truth" (John 1:14).

We may wrongly assume that because there is such a thing as morality, and hence moral judgments, then there cannot be grace. Indeed, one of the most common complaints about God and of the Christian faith in particular is that it is judgmental. "How can a loving God judge us?" is the continual refrain.

Have you read the novel *Pride and Prejudice* by Jane Austen? It tells a love story between a young woman, Elizabeth, and a certain Mr. Darcy. At one point Mr. Darcy comes to inform this beauty who has captured his heart of his feelings for her. He starts out well when he says, "My feelings will not be repressed. You must allow me to tell you how ardently I admire and love you."[17] However, he finishes spectacularly badly when he informs her that he loves her—even though it goes against his will, against his reason, against his character, and against his upbringing!

Feeling surprised when his declaration of love is rejected, Mr. Darcy asks Elizabeth how she can so freely and easily reject him. She responds by saying, "You are mistaken, Mr. Darcy, if you suppose that the mode of your declaration affected me in any other way, than as it spared me the concern which I might have felt in refusing you, had you behaved in a more gentleman-like manner."[18] She also gives the reason that she finds his declaration offensive: "I might as well enquire . . . why, with so evident a design of offending and insulting me, you chose to tell me that you liked me against your will, against your reason, and even against your character."[19] In other words, Elizabeth is complaining that Mr. Darcy told her that he loved her against all better judgment. It is ironic, isn't it? Most of us are looking for intimacy, and we spend our lives of trying to project an image of someone we are not in order to get people to like us and to love us. But it is impossible to find love and intimacy that way. When someone loves you, truly loves you, it is not because they don't know who you are, it is because the person does know exactly who you are and what you are like, and still loves you. That is one vital aspect that makes love meaningful.

In the song "Where Is the Love" by the Black Eyed Peas, which was a number-one hit around the world, they raise many pertinent issues about love in a broken world. People are killing and people are dying, they say. Children are hurt, and you can hear them crying. As the refrain comes in, it is always punctuated with two questions: will we practice what we preach? Will we turn the other cheek? The questions are followed by a cry to "Father." A cry for him to guide us from above, because people are making him ask one final question, "Where is the love?" They give a long list of complaints: issues with politicians, the media, and our selfishness. However, one line in particular makes you sit up and pay attention. After saying that many people sweep truth under a rug, they make the observation that if you have "never known truth" in your relationships, then you have also "never known love."

They couldn't be more right. The words "I love you" mean something when the person who utters them knows exactly what you're like and still cares for you. Love does not exist in the absence of judgment; true love exists when someone has passed the correct moral judgment on who you are and is under no illusions as to what you're like, but still loves you.

That is the way God loves us. God does not love us in the absence of judgment. He knows exactly what we're like. He sees who we are. He loves us in truth. This is why the Bible says that while we were still God's enemies, he manifested his love for us by giving us his only Son (1 John 4:9–10). God did not love us because we were lovely; rather, in love he gave himself and so has now made us lovely because of what we have received. We were, by nature, objects of God's wrath (Eph. 2:3). Yet now, through Christ, we have become partakers of the divine nature (2 Peter 1:4).

Moral Complaints and Compassion

The song by the Black Eyed Peas is a long, moral complaint against the society in which we live. Sadly, the song never progresses beyond its complaint, and so it never finds the answer to the question it asks: where is the love?

Interestingly, the word *compassion* comes from ecclesiastical Latin—that is, Latin that was inspired by the Christian faith and used to help govern and guide the church behavior. The word means to make a moral judgment about a situation, and to do so with empathy and a passion to respond. So when you see poverty and you say, "That's wrong. People should not live this way," you have passed a moral judgment about the situation. However, in order for this response to be compassionate, it needs to be followed both with an appropriate emotional response and a conviction to do something about it. When you see injustice and call it such, you pass a moral judgment. You say, "That is wrong. It should not be this way." But if you are compassionate, you will decide to do something about it. Compassion and love cannot exist apart from moral judgment. We do not make the world a more loving place by getting rid of morality, but we certainly would make it a lot less caring and a lot less compassionate.

Hope of Transformation

I was speaking in a Muslim country a short while ago. At the end of my talk, a psychiatrist asked a question I have never been asked before. He said, "Michael, in your talk you told us that we need to put our trust in God. But I have a question for you. Can God trust us?" It was a good question. I said to him, "You know, in the Gospel of John it says that Jesus didn't entrust himself to the crowd because he knew what was in their hearts. But if you ask me, God does want to trust us and indeed, entrust us with something very valuable. But before he can trust us, he must first transform us."

The reason God shines his light of moral judgment into our hearts is not to expose and shame us, but to *transform* us, because he is a gracious and compassionate God. God's love for us does not exist without judgment because without it, true intimacy and love with him would be impossible. God's love for us also cannot exist without transformation because we are in no state to enjoy him and have fellowship with him. Again, on the cross, Christ became a curse for us, taking the punishment of God on our behalf so that we may be redeemed from the curse that we were under and so through Christ be reconciled to God by being transformed by him.

In other words, the reasons that many people become disillusioned with their faith should actually be *the very reasons that they should rejoice*, once those reasons are properly understood. The gospel is about the God who is true and real. It is about the God who sees the situation we are in and passes judgment on it. He sees the pain. He passes judgment on our sin and shame, and yet, he so loves us and has compassion on us that he came into this world to be broken for us, so that we can know wholeness in him. And my prayer is that if you do not know it already, that wholeness may be yours also, and that you may be reconciled to God, the only true source of hope and joy in this world and the next.

8

Broader Cultural and Philosophical Challenges

Joe Boot

Now faith is being sure of what we hope for and certain of what we do not see. This is what the ancients were commended for. . . . And without faith it is impossible to please God, because anyone who comes to him must believe that he exists and that he rewards those who earnestly seek him.

—Heb. 11:1–2, 6

Faith gives the understanding access to these things, unbelief closes the door upon them. . . . A right faith is the beginning of a good life, and to this also eternal life is due. Now it is faith to believe that which you do not yet see; and the reward of this faith is to see that which you believe.

—Augustine of Hippo

In our contemporary climate of skepticism and doubt, the role of belief and authority in human knowing often goes unrecognized. Our world demands proof for knowledge, as far as it goes, but I want to suggest that believing in Christ leads us to true understanding and wise living. The apologetic task is first and foremost a spiritual conflict that sometimes shows itself through competing worldviews that seek to undermine faith in Jesus Christ. That is why our apologetic must rest upon the orthodox Nicene faith, the faith embraced by our fathers and mothers who lived very early in the life of the church, and the faith that has continued to be embraced by Christians in all the years since. This great cloud of witnesses can help us grapple with the doubt so prevalent in our time, one good example being the fifth-century North African seeker, pastor, and theologian Aurelius Augustinus, or Saint Augustine.

Augustine's apologetic method can assist us practically as we engage our culture with its many competing worldviews. In it we find a way in which the value of *faith in the authority of Christ for life and knowledge* brings light to the blind alleys of unbelief. Scripture summons us to search for God, even as it promises us that, if we do, we are guaranteed to find him. Rather than trying to discover knowledge through pure reason, strict empiricism, or absolute doubt, we have the *assurance* of finding knowledge in the person of Jesus Christ. Here, I believe, we discover the superiority of the Christian story, where belief leads to understanding and faith gives way to sight.

ENTERING THE FRAY

The reality is that all Christians are engaged in a cosmic conflict, a struggle for the ultimate victory of Christ's church and the kingdom of God in the world. The children of faith have been caught up in the conflict between light and darkness ever since Cain killed his brother Abel. Jesus taught this. Evangelism is energized by beholding the contrast between what Augustine called the City of God and the Earthly City. These cities have two ultimate principles, two kings, and two destinies; one revolves around the love of self, while the other elevates the love of God. And while it is sometimes easy to underestimate these distinctions because we don't want to divide people, biblical doctrines about creation, sin, ruin, and redemption are at the core of our faith. They often cause an upset, even when we are gracious. That is why, in a critical passage dealing with the cost of discipleship, Jesus employs the metaphor of a sword to highlight the divisive nature of his identity, allegiance to which may separate even close relatives (Matt. 10:32–39). Yet these central components of the Christian paradigm speak truth into the confusion of our world. We must not, therefore, lose sight of them even when they are unpopular.

DELIVERED FROM WHAT?

Now, one immediate problem that Christians face as they desire to dialogue with their neighbors is the absence of any contemporary understanding of sin. The good news of Christ is a message of deliverance, but in the West's gleaming tomorrowland is there anything left to be delivered from? Theologian and philosopher Peter Kreeft talks about this:

> In the past, the difficulty in accepting Christianity was its second point, salvation. Everyone in pre-modern societies knew sin was real, but many doubted salvation. Today it is the exact opposite: everybody is saved, but there is no sin to be saved from. Thus what originally came into the world as "good news" strikes the modern mind as bad news, as guilt-ridden, moralistic and "judgmental." For the modern mind is no longer "convinced of sin, of righteousness and of judgment" (John 16:8). Yet the bad news is the only part of Christianity that is empirically verifiable, just by reading the newspapers.[1]

Without an awareness of our fallen human condition, there is no good news and consequently no conflict. Nevertheless, the pain, violence, and confusion that fill human experience demonstrate that the Bible tells us the truth about ourselves. Jesus' historical redemption offers a hope more real than any promise of human salvation through scientific progress or political policy. Yet we must always be mindful that this is not a battle waged against human beings but against "the rulers, against the authorities, against the powers of this dark world and against the spiritual forces of evil in the heavenly realms" (Eph. 6:12). These spiritual forces establish key strongholds, and Paul tells us what they are. "The weapons we fight with are not the weapons of the world. On the contrary, they have divine power to demolish strongholds. *We demolish arguments and every pretension that sets itself up against the knowledge of God,* and we take captive every thought to make it obedient to Christ" (2 Cor. 10:4–5; emphasis added).

There are several prominent arguments and pretensions we face today in the struggle against our spiritual foes. One is uncritical religious pluralism. This perspective wants to accept all religious beliefs as equally valid and deny any method of judging between them. We also face varying degrees of relativism, which consider truths about reality or ethics to be dependent on the individuals or cultures that endorse them. Our culture also contains a great deal of skepticism about our ability to have knowledge at all.

Underlying each of these views is an attitude toward knowledge that fundamentally challenges the value and surety of faith in Christ as revealed in Scripture. Each is built on the illusion of *neutrality* (that it is possible to decide one's beliefs from a neutral, noncommittal position) and *autonomy* (that there is no higher authority than human beings and their reasoning). However, this belief in the secular, the notion that there is a space that is neutral and void of religious commitment, is itself a religious confession. Our culture's religious allegiance is to the authority of the human mind. Broadly, it is this cultural and philosophical challenge of autonomy—independence from authority—and skepticism toward the Christian story that I will address here. I hope to tease out a direction of thought and practice that may stir the skeptic from his or her indifference and inform the Christian persuader seeking to fulfill the command of 1 Peter 3:15 to "be prepared to give an answer."

A WAR OF INDEPENDENCE

As a whole, Western culture eschews moral responsibility even as it rejects the notion of a transcendent creator—continuing the revolt against God begun by our first parents. Under the historical influence of thinkers like Frederick Nietzsche and Jean-Paul Sartre, and swayed by pop atheists like Richard Dawkins and Sam Harris, it has chosen to live in a universe where matter and energy are all that exist. But there are other models.

Christian theology has always understood that being (everything that is) depends absolutely for its existence upon God's creative, sustaining presence and goodwill. It has simultaneously drawn an absolute distinction between Creator and creation—our being and God's are *not* equal.

For a long time, much of Western thought followed a similar path, accepting the notion of *participation*, in which all that exists participates in God and depends on him for its existence while God remains independent, distinct, and transcendent. However, beginning in the Middle Ages, philosophers began teaching that everything that is exists in the same way and in the same sense. They denied any validity to transcendence, or they ignored it. And this attitude has continued in different forms through the present day. It is the basis for our pervasive secularism.

See, whether one is a modernist or postmodernist,[2] both of these philosophical attitudes hold explicitly to the idea that whatever exists, from smallest to greatest (and including people), can be described independently of a transcendent God and his revelation. Human beings are a law unto themselves, independent and autonomous. They, therefore, mentally inhabit a similarly neutral realm, a position that affects how knowledge is obtained and justified.

It was René Descartes in the seventeenth century who most clearly divorced knowledge from revelation and laid the foundations upon which many after him would build. Descartes sought to establish certainty by doubting everything that could be doubted in order to reconstruct knowledge on unquestionable foundations. His method fueled an entire movement in Western culture and philosophy called the Enlightenment. Catholic theologian Hans Küng describes the result: "With Descartes, European consciousness in a critical development reached an epochal turning point. Basic certainty is no longer centered on God, but on man. In other words, the medieval way of reasoning from certainty of God to certainty of the self is replaced by the modern approach: from certainty of the self to certainty of God."[3]

Descartes proved a perhaps inadvertent midwife in producing our cultural moment of skepticism. Following Descartes, what counts for knowledge today no longer seeks its ultimate criterion in God and revelation, but it remains centered on the subject, deconstructing everything else by means of corrosive doubt.

As children of this method, people today have no real certainty of the self, never mind God. When we cut off the possibility of the transcendent, we lose our ability to hear from God by revelation. The only authority we are left with is ourselves, and the result of this blind faith in our own reason has been disillusionment, confusion, and violence.

Such results raise many questions: Has intellectual independence proven worthy of the trust we placed in it? Has it brought us any closer to real knowledge about God, the world, or ourselves? Does secularism make good on its own claims to knowledge? And, though philosophical skepticism denies that we have knowledge, how can it be so confident that it *knows* nothing can be known? These questions must not be overlooked.

Peter Kreeft, in his book *Christianity for Modern Pagans*, compares the episte-mological projects of Descartes and Blaise Pascal. Kreeft observes that Descartes sought certainty, utility, and ease, while Pascal was content to set aside rational certainty for the kind of knowledge and understanding that comes through faith in Jesus Christ:

> His [Descartes's] chief critique of the ancients was that they lacked certainty, or "a sufficient criterion". Certainty, in turn, was his means to the end of utility, or efficiency, or "the conquest of nature". This technological conquest, in turn, was a means to the "relief of man's estate", that is, ease, comfort, the abolition of suf-fering. Yet these are precisely the three things his philosophy, and the civilization that has been seduced by it, not only fails to deliver but destroys. Life has never been so full of confusion and uncertainty. The average person has never felt so weak and helpless; and all social indicators show we feel exactly the opposite of ease and comfort. . . . Pascal is a prophet. Descartes is a false prophet.[4]

Küng agrees: "There is nothing specifically Christian about [Descartes's] phi-losophy: Jesus Christ does not appear to have played any part in it."[5]

Amazingly, many Christian apologists have accepted Descartes's method of doubt. They have tried to arrive at intellectual certainty or establish the idea of God by building arguments based on human reason. Because of this, some Christian thinkers today have dismissed apologetics as finished, but they have simply misunderstood the heart of apologetics.[6]

Apologetics goes wrong when it follows Descartes and grasps for certainty by beginning with the self and doubt. It should, instead, remember the example of Augustine: apologetics does not begin with doubt, but with prayer to Christ. What is desired is wisdom, a broader and less mechanical object than Descartes's certainty. The Christian apologist should never forget that any perspective that puts the human mind in the place of authority is making a huge faith commit-ment, and a dangerous one.

We all nurture a worldview that must rest upon a given authority, purport-ing to answer the big questions about the nature of human life. And though these are often called philosophical problems, they are, in essence, religious. Not everyone's worldview is the same, but everyone must choose between them. Thankfully, we are not left to choose arbitrarily. At the heart of knowing how to choose between competing stories lie fundamental questions: Which faith leads to understanding? Which faith gives us a view of the world that makes sense of and justifies our experience? *Which faith teaches us the truth that will set us free?*

In answering those questions, Christians must remember that the story of the Bible is a *good* story. The Word, the *logos,* was made flesh and dwelt among us (John 1:14). Our story centers not on the self as ultimate, but with the *mystery* of Christ, our "all in all" (see Col. 3:11). This story is a sweeping epic, beginning at creation, being caught up in the conflict between darkness and light, and culminating in truth incarnate and the triumph of the heavenly city, the kingdom of God. It is a history of revelation and cosmic conflagration that must be told and retold for our time.

The story, or the epic, that has captured the minds of our generation says that human beings have been thrown into existence by chance and bear the huge responsibility of finding knowledge, creating meaning, and improving the world by their own efforts. This is a story that can only end in despair. The Bible has the better story to tell, and we must learn to tell it well. Whatever is coming to pass in our time under God's providence, if we would win the epoch, we must win the epic.[7]

Calling Upon the Cloud of Witnesses

So then, as we tackle this faith-stifling atmosphere of skepticism, cynicism, and despair, where can we look to find help and inspiration? I see the creative process in apologetics as a form of recycling the best insights we can find among past masters from times that are suggestive of our own. We stand at the head of a long line of witnesses, many of them martyrs. Their message is our trust; the message we preach did not begin with us. Those who believe themselves to be so original that they wrap a new gift are not innovators but idolaters according to Scripture. C. S. Lewis wrote, "No man who bothers about originality will ever be original; whereas, if you simply try to *tell the truth* (without caring two-pence about how often it has been told before) you will, nine times out of ten, become original without ever having noticed it."[8]

As Lewis notes, "to tell the truth" makes Christian originality truly possible. Orthodoxy is not a straitjacket to prevent creativity. It is, instead, a vast playing field where one finds new ways to communicate the faith.

In the same way, apologetics is not a *science* in which we apply a particular method again and again. Rather, it is a *craft* in which we learn to adjust our methods to fit different situations, all the while remaining faithful to the truth. In science, anyone given the same conditions will achieve the same result. But a craft is not like that. To practice a craft is to be guided by a set of skills and practices handed down from one person to another, slowly mastering and being mastered by a knowledge that enables one to uniquely contribute to the craft as a whole. Jesus was a master craftsman. He presented the faith not in syllogisms but in powerful stories and with all manner of creative argument and persuasion. His divine eloquence and rhetoric was captivating! In the same way, we are to take the faith of those who have gone before us and present it to today's culture with all the passion, creativity, and ingenuity we can muster.

We are, perhaps, on the brink of an epochal turning point. The cyberneticists have now become the guides and influencers in our society. Liberty without responsibility and enjoyment without community are universally available courtesy of cyberspace—a private universe accessible through the keyboard. But, tragically, it is not freedom but new forms of slavery that are the end result. We have "come of age," succumbing all over again to the temptation of our first parents "to be like God," each one doing as he [sees] fit" (Gen. 3:5; Judg. 17:6).

Saint Augustine of Hippo lived, ministered, and defended the faith at another epochal turning point in history, during the fall of Rome (AD 410) and the transition from the ancient to the medieval era. In his day, as in ours, Christians were being blamed for the world's problems and both paganism and humanism were popular. I believe Augustine's voice is both prophetic and instructive for our cultural moment. Smith incisively summarizes his remarkable contemporary relevance: "There is a sense in which Augustine's cultural situation mirrors our own postmodern predicament. . . . Like Augustine we are constructing theology and engaging in Christian witness in the shadow of both a dominant empire and a religious pluralism. In short, for Augustine there is no secular, non-religious sphere as construed by modernity; there is only paganism or true worship."[9]

This is illustrated powerfully for today's reader in the *Confessions*, in which Augustine moves seamlessly between philosophy, theology, prayer, and praise. As Küng notes, "Descartes' *Discours* and Augustine's *Confessions* are brilliant autobiographical justifications of each other's way of life. But we need to read only a few pages of either to sense a completely different mental atmosphere. Between them lies not only a millennium but a whole world."[10]

Thus when we respond to the irrational rationalism of contemporary thought, we must do so from a distinctively Christian platform and starting point.[11] If we do not, we will find ourselves using the same autonomous method that is wholly inadequate to arrive at the desired destination: God, truth, and meaning. Alvin Plantinga notes, "I say Christian philosophers should address these questions and topics starting from the Christian faith, using all that they know, including Christian teachings . . . according to the Augustinian tradition. . . . What we need and want, in studying a given area, is the best total understanding we can get, using all the resources at our command."[12]

Is Doubt the Best Foundation?

That said, how do we begin to address a society awash in doubt? Doubt is a fundamental reality, and we should not be afraid of it. We do not need a course in philosophy to recognize this, because doubt is not a purely rational phenomenon; all of us experience doubt in our hearts and minds. We live in a world full of tragedy. Furthermore, our own lives fail to meet our hopes or even our expectations and so we experience frustration and disappointment. We all know what it is like to believe something and then find out we were mistaken. It is an experience that shakes our confidence in knowledge and causes us to wonder what else we might be wrong about.

Doubt is woven into the fabric of our fallen lives. Hence, the offer of salvation in Christ must address our lives, not just our reason. And, indeed, it does. The truth of Christ is not a matrix of facts, but an address delivered to the whole person, requiring the openness of one's entire being to God. Küng observes:

> For both Augustine and Pascal, final existential certainty is rooted not in the "cogito" of pure reason but in the "credo" of the biblical message. The radical remedy for skepticism is in the biblical faith guaranteed by the church . . . for him [Augustine] what is decisive is crede, ut intellegas, "believe in order to know" . . . For both Augustine and Pascal, it is never a question of an irrational but always rationally justifiable faith; not rationalism, but rationality; not blind, but reasonable, submission. . . . Faith is necessary not only in regard to questions of Christian revelation but also in regard to questions of everyday life . . . as faith has to do with reason, so reason also has to do with faith.[13]

Modern philosophy, including that which is often called postmodern, does not recognize or acknowledge that it is the *heart's* commitments that control the rational life. This being so, the skepticism of our time requires a comprehensive approach to its dilemma. We need to unify the spheres of faith and reason and intertwine philosophy and theology so that, when we are thinking, we are believing, and when we are believing, we are thinking. There are too many artificially constructed, absolute distinctions between what is believed and what is known. As Küng concludes, reflecting on the biblical harmony in Augustine's thought: "Such a 'Christian philosophy' is therefore not grounded in thinking as such but is reflective self-interpretation of the Christian faith, especially in regard to God and the human soul. Consequently, *submission to divine authority is prior to all searching and researching*. It is understandable that in this view—as opposed to the Cartesian—the principle *credo, ut intelligam,* 'I believe in order to understand,' should be mainly stressed."[14]

Our contention must be that only the Christian faith can adequately describe and account for laws of thought, reasoning, and the very idea of proof; otherwise the world collapses into a meaningless void. God is the *origin* of the laws of thought and inference—the rules of rationality that govern our minds. Reason by itself cannot be trusted. The world, by its wisdom "did not know God" (1 Cor. 1:21). That is why, as Merrill Callaway says, "No matter how much we strive, we cannot know or reach [God] on our own, within the world system. Conversely, every worldly philosophy and false religion seeks completeness and by so doing becomes inconsistent. . . . As long as humanity reasons in a vacuum, no matter how skilled its thinkers or how sophisticated the reasoning, human effort will fail."[15]

Reason is only trustworthy when it finds its place under God's authority. Without trust in God, we have to assume that the laws of logic are valid without any guarantee or justification for this assumption. The *presence* of the divine logos, the very Word of God, is necessary, and Jesus is revealed as the logos—the word from which we derive the term "logic"—in John 1. Jesus is the self-existent one, the ground of all being. He is the truth and the life (John 14:6). He alone can bring completeness to our reasoning. Only in him is there a truly transcendent source of knowledge that illuminates the minds of creatures. Without him there is no completeness. When we accept his truth by faith, we can have a logically consistent worldview. God's truth in the world and his Word, both in the created order and special revelation, are one. They are interrelated and connected, and so taken separately cannot adequately be known. We must begin any pursuit of knowledge with confident submission to God and his Word.

No better summary of the choice before us could be given than this as we engage with the contemporary challenges to our faith. We must reach back a millennium past Descartes and there locate our true evangelical and catholic heritage in the apostolic witness to Christ. Here we can find answers in a time when Enlightenment rationalism has notoriously failed. Albert Wells effectively summarizes our current state of affairs:

> Nothing could be clearer than that a better way needs to be found for understanding reality than that which the modern philosophical tradition has offered. Representatives of that tradition have persistently hesitated to attribute any philosophical importance to the biblical revelation. They have perpetuated the prevailing conception of philosophy as a rational discipline that cannot admit any other source of authentic knowledge than what can be immediately known by the autonomous mind. . . . The record is clear that the modern philosophical tradition has not been able to provide an intellectual approach to reality that is adequate to the vastness, the diversity, and the complexity of reality, to say nothing of the ultimate meaning. Nor does the current existentialist posture in itself offer a permanent solution.[16]

In our day, we may begin by exposing some of the assumptions about knowledge and reality that skeptics hold but they have not justified. We also need to expose the religious commitments that secular humanism and postmodernism hold, trusting in the human self and denying the authority of God for life and thought. Whether I am speaking with a student, dialoging with a professional, or formally debating a professor of philosophy at a university, I find people quite unaware of these religious commitments until they are exposed. And when they are exposed, people are quite bewildered in dealing with the challenge of finding real meaning in the context of their own worldview. Time and again, I have found that skeptics are unable to respond effectively to these foundational questions and make intelligible sense of their worldview without the transcendent God to give depth and meaning to reality.

I believe that, by recovering the value of faith in Christ for knowledge, we can face our skeptical, doubt-filled time with confidence and find our way out of the humanistic quagmire. Otherwise, even with the best intentions, we will become impotent allies of secularism. I believe that Augustine, Pascal, and others who have a similar direction of thought—placing faith commitment prior to true understanding as the sun by which all other facts are illumined—help to give us the tools needed in our day.[17] As an apologist who has defended the faith in many contexts, I am utterly convinced that we need to *return to the transcendent, triune God made manifest in Jesus Christ as our criterion in both apologetic message and method.*

Augustine and Apologetics by Stealth

So then, how can we call people in today's situation to *believe* in order that they may *understand*? First, few things are more obvious to those engaged in sharing and defending the faith than that the messenger and the method are as important as the message. As we have seen, our task is to "take captive every thought" (2 Cor. 10:5). Whichever way you slice it, this is often seen today as a hostile act, an act of violence. But the reality of the Fall makes people captives of sin and, according to the apostle James, an enemy of God in their hearts (James 4:4). This necessitated Christ's coming to defeat the powers of darkness. Hence, we need strategic minds and sensitive hearts as we, in cooperation with the Spirit, attack all speculations that set themselves up against the knowledge of God. We need to be "shrewd as snakes and as innocent as doves" as we obey Christ's commission (Matt. 10:16). To me, it is precisely at this point that the *sight of faith* comes to the forefront—but we will return to that later.

There are obvious things we can learn from everyday human psychology about successful persuasion. I have learned as a husband and as a father, not to mention as an apologist, that there are approaches to discussion and persuasion that are virtually doomed to failure before I start; they erupt in nonproductive and emotion-filled argument. In adult conversation, there are ways of trying to persuade our discussion partner that do not involve attacks, arrogance, or unwillingness to listen to his or her perspective.

If the common root of skepticism is primarily a heart condition and not force of argument, if it is not so much a question of rational warrant but emotive concerns that gets in the way, then feelings must be taken into account as we persuade others. According to Christ, those who truly seek will find (Matt. 7:7). That means, ultimately, that the reason nonbelievers do not believe is that, for various reasons, they are not seeking Christ or they have had insufficient time to seek him. How then can we encourage them to truly become seekers, which involves an initial faith step, or to keep seeking by the help of the Holy Spirit?

Because the claims of Christ are total, they leave out nothing. They are profoundly personal, life transforming, and lifestyle challenging. The gospel is fundamentally a call to reorient every aspect of life toward Christ. Thus, we are not coming to the skeptic with a distant or abstract hypothesis that may be coolly weighed on unbiased scales. There can be no neutrality with respect to Christ, no fence sitting. If we are conscious of this, it will help us see that presenting the faith to the skeptic is much more like a marriage proposal than a garage sale negotiation or a political debate. My attitude, posture, manner, and plea will be very different in these cases. Christ is inviting people to be his bride, the church, not to buy from him a time share in a lake country cottage. So we recognize that a direct and assertive "attack" that regards the nonbelieving person primarily as an "opponent" to be defeated instead of someone blinded by illusions who needs Christ is usually counterproductive. As Ravi Zacharias often says, there is little point in cutting off someone's nose and then giving him or her a rose to smell.

On this subject, Søren Kierkegaard writes with insight:

> A direct attack only strengthens a person in his illusion and, at the same time, embitters him. There is nothing that requires such gentle handling as an illusion if one wishes to dispel it. If anything prompts the prospective captive to set his will in opposition, all is lost. And this is what a direct attack achieves, and it implies moreover the presumption of requiring a man to make to another person, or in his presence, an admission which he can make most profitably to himself privately. This is what is achieved by the indirect method which, loving and serving the truth, arranges everything dialectically for the prospective captive, and then shyly withdraws [for love is always shy], so as not to witness the admission which he makes to himself alone before God—that he has lived hitherto in an illusion. . . . However, if I am disposed to plume myself on my greater understanding, it is because I am vain or proud, so that at bottom, instead of benefiting him, I want to be admired. But all true effort to help begins with self-humiliation.[18]

We should also be aware of the worldview from which a person speaks. The underlying presuppositions of nonbelievers are hidden, cherished, and often undefended. Since they feel that these need no defense, they are usually taken for granted. These beliefs and assumptions govern nonbelievers' thoughts and determine what is acceptable or unacceptable evidence or forms of argument for them. Because people are emotionally and psychologically attached to these beliefs in a deeply personal sense, it often proves futile to attack them directly. Even when people can see intellectually that they are wrong, they often still cling to their opinions simply as a matter of personal pride. We should not presumptuously present ourselves to them as their teachers, but rather as fellow learners pointing to the Teacher.

We also need to be cautious about our motives whenever we enter apologetic discussion. As C. S. Lewis, an apologist of singular gifting, poignantly reminds us with his own evening prayer:

> From all my lame defeats and oh' much more
> From all the victories that I seemed to score;
> From cleverness shot forth on Thy behalf,
> At which, while angels weep, the audience laugh;
> From all my proofs of Thy divinity,
> Thou, who wouldst give no sign, deliver me
>
> Thoughts are but coins. Let me not trust, instead
> Of Thee, their thin-worn image of Thy head
> From all my thoughts, even from my thoughts of Thee,
> O thou fair Silence, fall, and set me free.
> Lord of the narrow gate and the needle's eye,
> Take from me all my trumpery lest I die.[19]

Our priority in apologetics is not to make the nonbeliever listen to *us*, but to help the person be ready to listen to God and be taught by *him*. If listening to us were the end game, then battering people with argumentative direct attacks might suffice. However, we do not use words simply for the sake of speaking. Rather, they are signs that call for a hushing of the restless heart, giving shape to the silence and mystery of Christ who speaks in a still small voice. Our faith teaches us that God reveals himself to people in his good time, when they have been prepared in one way or another to meet him. Jesus was clear that "no one can come to me unless the Father who sent me draws him" (John 6:44).

Indeed, God's revelation of himself to people presupposes that in a certain sense, God is at first concealed from people with a particular attitude of heart; there is no revealing without first a concealing. This concealing is a result of people's fallen condition and God's character. We all have a sickness of the inner eye that prevents us from taking in the brightness of his light until the healing hand of faith restores our sight. Our Lord thus emphasizes that only those who seek God find him, and further, that all those who truly seek him will certainly find him. These conditions destroy the pretensions of rationalism, which despises the search, and this promise nullifies skepticism, which despises the destination!

The great problem facing a skeptic, then, is him- or herself, not a lack of evidence or adequacy of reasons to believe. We tend to find only what we want to find and to see only what we want to see. The fallen human desire to escape the reality of God is very strong. Reflecting this bizarre human malady, Gregory Benford, professor of plasma physics and astrophysics at the University of California, writes: "Why is there scientific law at all? I have a possible answer but as yet no proof of it. We physicists explain the origin and structure of matter and energy but not the origin of the laws behind them. Does the idea of causation apply to where the laws themselves came from? . . . One can imagine a universe in which laws are not truly law-full. Talk of miracles does just this, invoking God to make things work. Physics aims to find the laws instead."[20]

In this desperate search to find the origin of laws, Benford goes on to speak of the possibility of an infinite number of universes that obey any kind of law you can imagine—ours just happens to have these regularities—but then writes this off as too counterintuitive and a cop-out. Instead, he recognizes that our universe is fine-tuned and that order surely assumes an ordering principle. But the notion of God proves intolerable, so he suggests that prior intelligences "made" other "smart" universes with the right fixed laws to produce ever grander structures! Notions of intelligences that evolved in some other reality and then created our universe seem to be a more attractive faith than trust in God even though they can never be proven.

The problem is seen again and again: men and women do not want to meet

God. Yet with amazing audacity they try to claim that their disinterest is because our faith is irrational or we invoke miracles while their faith is a realistic, scientific one. C. S. Lewis writes:

> Men are reluctant to pass over from the notion of an abstract and negative deity to the living God. I do not wonder . . . it is always shocking to meet life where we thought we were alone. . . . An "impersonal God"—well and good. A subjective God of beauty, truth and goodness, inside our own heads, better still. A formless life force surging through us, a vast power which we can tap, best of all. But God Himself, alive, pulling at the other end of the cord, perhaps approaching at an infinite speed, the hunter, king, husband—that is quite another matter. There comes a moment when the children who have been playing at burglars hush suddenly: was that a real footstep in the hall? There comes a moment when people who have been dabbling in religion ["Man's search for God"!] suddenly draw back. Supposing we really found him? We never meant it to come to that! Worse still supposing he had found us? So it is a sort of Rubicon. One goes across; or not. But if one does, there is no manner of security against miracles. One may be in for anything.[21]

The Clear Sight of Faith

Given this inbuilt reluctance of the skeptic to "pass over" to the living God and "go across" at the call of the king, we have much to learn from people like Augustine and Pascal. The next step is to show that faith is inescapable, rational, and reasonable. Then we go on to show how attractive the Christian faith is, not only in how it meets the deepest existential longings of the human heart, but also in how faith brings real understanding and allows us to find confidence and intellectual satisfaction. Only by faith is the problem of knowledge resolved and beauty, truth, and virtue discovered in the triune God.

Let us explore first then *the rationality of faith.* When people are looking for the truth in matters of ultimate concern, they immediately face a problem since we all live in the midst of an array of clamoring voices. If we know who it is that has truth, we must already know, to an extent, what that truth is! But the one who is searching is, by definition, uncertain about who has the truth, or at least has not yet come to an understanding of it.

Consequently, when asking about what is true, we are invariably in search of reliable guides. No one is an island. We have to trust in some authority or another. What subject did you ever learn in university or school that did not involve trusting a guide, whether living or dead? History itself could not be known without authority and faith in those who recorded it and those who interpret their writings. People often dismiss the Christian faith without ever having understood it or having sought a guide to help them comprehend it. They are quick to treat Christ in a way they would not even have treated the trivial knowledge needed to pass a college exam. We all need to trust others in our search for truth. But how do we judge who is reliable?

Modern treasure hunters pursue their task with enormous passion, seeking riches on the ocean floor. The paths to the treasure lie hidden beneath the waves, and the only way to uncover them is an unflinching diligence coupled with an overwhelming desire to find the buried riches. Many of us do not find the treasure of truth because we have no love for the treasure promised and we are too apathetic to seek out the hidden path. As Peter Kreeft notes, "If we do not love the truth, we will not seek it. If we do not seek it, we will not find it. If we do not find it, we will not know it. If we do not know it, we have failed our fundamental task in time, and quite likely also in eternity."[22]

The precondition of a treasure hunt is the firm belief that there is treasure to be found. A certain kind of belief always comes before discovery. Scripture tells us that "anyone who comes to [God] must believe that he exists, and that he rewards those who earnestly seek him." (Heb. 11:6). Is this credulity? People often think that to believe or to accept authority in questions of religion is totally unacceptable. But clearly all belief is not simply ignorant credulity. On the contrary, if "belief" is wrong, then it is unforgivable to believe a friend's word, a witness's testimony, a spouse's vow, a businessperson's handshake, or any other kind of unproven claim or unsubstantiated promise. I do not need to see the truth of my wife's marriage pledge to me in her mind to verify it empirically; I believe it on faith, but not without reason. This is not foolish credulity because there is a different type of reason that has earned my trust.

We may think we "know" what we have understood with our reason, and that may be so in some cases, but we believe countless things purely on the basis of authority because we have grown to trust the source of knowledge. Further, doesn't belief or faith often prepare our minds for seeing something clearly for ourselves? Years ago I believed my philosophy teacher could help me understand the classical arguments for God's existence; this conviction brought me to his classes and soon I "saw" it for myself. Belief prepares us for knowledge. Belief in God prepares us for the knowledge of God; the love of God assures us of it.

There are three different ways we can approach our lack of certainty. There are those who think they know what they do not know. Second, there are those who are conscious that they do not know, but they may or may not use the right method to find out. Last, and most tragically, there are those who do not think that they know at all and are not bothered about finding out!

I believe on the basis of historical testimony that the great Christian leader, William Wilberforce, triggered the abolition of slavery in the British Empire, but I do not "know" it in the same way that I know five plus five equals ten. Indeed, I know there is no way I can know it or prove it for certain. These things I take on authority with good reason. So we see that anyone who says we should not believe anything we do not *know* is not thinking clearly. For in such a case, that person would be very short on working knowledge in any field to say the least. In fact, everyone has numerous *beliefs* about every aspect of life.

Or consider our use of reason and logic itself. Some thinkers, both ancient and contemporary, claim they only believe things that a full empirical proof can verify or that sound reasoning has justified. However, philosopher David Hume showed that even the inductive principle we use in reasoning is a belief that cannot be proved. The inductive principle is a way of reasoning that moves from many occurrences of a particular thing to general conclusions.

Science is based on this principle. For example, since we observe consistent patterns in nature, we label those patterns and call them laws. We then make predictions for how things will behave in the future based on those laws. However, there is no logical proof that nature will continue to follow the same patterns we have observed. Just because a scientist has repeated an experiment a hundred times with the same result, there is no logical guarantee that the same result *must* occur. Just because we have observed that on earth apples fall whenever they are dropped, we cannot prove that nature will behave the same way and follow the law of gravity tomorrow. We simply believe this. And this kind of empirical evidence is extremely valuable in discovering many things about our world. But *this principle itself* must first be believed before it becomes useful.

Furthermore, in a universe without God, how can we be sure of any of our rational capabilities like logic, mathematics, or value judgments in ethics? Pascal writes of them, "We cannot be sure that these principles are true [faith and revelation apart] except through some natural intuition. Now this natural intuition affords no convincing proof that they are true. There is no certainty, apart from faith [revelation], as to whether man was created by a good God, an evil demon, or just by chance, and so it is a matter of doubt, depending on our origin, whether these innate principles are true, false or uncertain."[23]

Is our human software to be trusted? Without God, can we trust our minds? Unless they are creations of a good God, can they be relied upon? If our brains are the result of blind processes, why should we trust their conclusions? Surely we can only depend upon our reasoning if it is created by a transcendent God, who relates our thoughts (mental processes) to a real world of experience. Reasoning and thinking about this chapter, for example, presupposes faith, because to rely on your reason is ultimately an act of faith and not an act of reason or empirical observation.

So how can reason be validated and made intelligible? Kreeft notes that there are only three possibilities.[24] First, it could be by something subrational—less than rational—like animal instinct? But how can something *inferior* validate something *superior?* Second, reason could be validated directly by a piece of reasoning. But this is circular. Given that all reason is on trial, a piece of reasoning cannot justify all reasoning. Consequently, the only remaining possibility is an indirect validation by something super-rational—more than rational—like faith in God and his revelation. Only through belief in God and his assurance that we are made rational, in his image, capable of understanding our world and knowing truth, can we have any basis to trust reason.

Some have sought to escape this by just saying they will presuppose the validity of reason because it seems to *work*. But what warrants that assumption? How do we define what works? "By what *brings you to truth*," comes the typical response. But, then, one has simply begged the critical question without offering any warrant for confidence at all. In fact, if naturalism is true, we have every reason to doubt reasoning and therefore all the deliverances of our minds!

It is important to note that reason and logic are *components* of a worldview, not a total synoptic view of reality. Consequently, intelligibility rests on the origin of logic and reasoning within that worldview, which skeptics either reduce to chance or admit they simply cannot tell us. The chance explanation obviously seeks to use the subrational *inferior* to validate the rational *superior*, which I have already noted lacks explanatory power. In any case, to form a logical argument to presuppose logic as an ultimate foundation is to use a piece of reasoning to validate the whole, which simply begs the question. Once again, faith is found to be indispensable to reason. We cannot prove, without God, that our minds convey any truth at all. The Christian proof itself is *indirect* by showing that the exclusion of the transcendent God is unintelligible and absurd as it destroys all reasoning, collapsing all reality into pure physics. Michael Robinson writes:

> If there is no God, we are just molecules in motion, and we have no sense and no mind; we are just the random firing of chemicals in the brain. If our minds are composed only of physical matter, then our thoughts are, as Doug Wilson wittily quipped in his debate with atheist Dan Barker, just "brain gas." . . . If our minds are just the result of chemical reactions, then in the debate over pop cans, God's existence can rightly be settled by shaking the two soda pop cans simultaneously. Labeling one can "atheism" and the other "theism"; after shaking the cans, the one that fizzes the most wins the debate. If our minds are simply the fluctuations of proteins, neurotransmitters, and other brain biochemicals, then an intellectual debate is equivalent to the chemical reactions that occur when one shakes up a couple of cans of soda.[25]

Given that we believe so many things we cannot know for certain, should we, then, be guided by those who say we cannot know God and offer arguments to tell us why we cannot know him? The nonbeliever does not accept many of the evidences for the God of Scripture because he cannot recognize the signs that point us to him. How could he? For if you have no knowledge or you suppress the knowledge of the *thing itself,* which the signs are indicating, how can you recognize them as pointing to him? How could I recognize the meaning of a word sign in Cantonese if I have no knowledge of the language? We can detect external things, material things, with our eyes and our other senses, even if we have seen nothing similar before, but this is not true with what the inner eye (intellect) perceives regarding the immaterial. What it perceives is in the mind, like 5 + 5 = 10, *so seeing it* is the same as *knowing it.* Remember math class? You either "see it" and know the solution, or you do not. Merely looking at material indicators on the chalkboard does not enable you to see the solution; the inner eye must grasp it. It has to make sense to you.

Therefore, when it comes to Christian truth about the immaterial, transcendent God, the skeptic needs *grace* to get out of his or her predicament. Nonbelievers in some sense know God, and in another important sense, they do not know God. They do not see God with the eyes of the heart as the believer does because they do not "have" him. Given that they do not *have* God and consequently do not *know* him, they cannot recognize the signs of him without grace. If I am tested color-blind to red and blue, I will not see those colors anywhere in the world. The cure for our disease can only come from God. Again, Hebrews 11:6 reminds us that when we come to God, we *must believe that he exists* and rewards those who sincerely seek him. Augustine writes, "Unless we believe both that he exists and that he can be invoked by the human mind, we should not even look for the true religion. What are we trying to investigate with such great effort? What are we hoping to achieve? Where do we want to arrive? At some place that we do not believe exists or do not believe has any relevance to ourselves? Nothing could be more perverse than a mentality like that. . . . Do you come then asking to find out about religion, even though you think that God does not exist, or, if God does exist, that he does not care about us?"[26]

The Value of the Search

In Luke 11:9, Jesus teaches that only those who seek will find and only to those who knock will the door be opened. Even when it comes to material possessions, anyone who has ever lost anything valuable knows how tiring, frustrating, and painstaking an effective search can be. Yet when we find what we have lost, a great relief comes over us, and the great value of what we find is reinforced to us. However, skeptics usually do not know or will not accept that they have lost anything, and so they do not know what they ought to search for. They do not search because they do not recognize the value of what is lost. *And one cannot find without searching.*

This is where authority and faith are so important. Jesus Christ in the mystery of incarnation reveals God to humankind. As the God-man, he is humanity's God. The person of Christ confronts us at every turn. On the historic testimony of Scripture and the authority of his church down through the centuries, he commands us to believe—to begin by believing and then to seek. He reveals a glimpse of the treasure in himself, through the testimony of his Word, and invites all people everywhere to seek him, further promising that they will find him. In the search, we can see that the evidences for the faith of God's church are very strong and valuable. We can speak of historical, textual, archaeological, prophetic, and miraculous corroboration of the message in great detail. Yet we do not claim it amounts to ironclad proof, for what can be proved in those terms?

As we have seen, the very concept of reasoned proof depends upon faith in God. Furthermore, only this faith has the explanatory power to account for the rudimentary realities we take for granted like energy, consciousness, and rationality. However, the Christian evidences are sufficient to encourage many seekers to begin in belief, like the man who said to Jesus, "I do believe; help me overcome my unbelief!" (Mark 9:24), and embark on the search on the foundation of Christ's own promise: "Ask and it will be given to you; seek and you will find; knock and the door will be opened to you" (Matt. 7:7).

Of course, faith is distinctive in a way that reason is not. Revelation comes to us as a gift, and faith itself comes as the gift of God. Many contemporary skeptics are irritated, even enraged, at these gifts because they are of supernatural and special quality. People demand that the playing field be entirely level; the Christian must be just like everybody else and dependent upon reason alone. Why should people have to commit their whole mind and heart in sincerity to a search based on special revelation? The answer is not difficult: the myth of neutral, secular reasoning has proved itself weak and helpless, leading only toward a meaningless void. The search itself has an effect that only the one who has truly found can explain. The secret is that, to truly know God, *the way and the goal are one in Christ Jesus.* Our Lord Jesus Christ, who says "I am the way" (John 14:6), is also our end; he is both the road and the destination. The only way to know God is to discover that Jesus is the way; that he and the Father are indeed one.

To this task the honest seeker should dedicate all his or her resources, for this is what Christ requires. The search itself trains the mind of the seeker to grasp the one it discovers. Clearly, belief that the object of your search exists is psychologically important for a real search. People would not search or drill for oil in the North Sea unless they believed there was oil there. Thus, those who approach God in Christ must do so with belief, with faith in his authority. That faith "comes from hearing," without which "it is impossible to please God" (Rom. 10:17; Heb. 11:6).

Faith and reason are like two blades on a pair of scissors that cut together toward truth when "wrought in God." To accept the word of those who urge you not to believe on faith is merely to take their word on faith instead! If we will not believe on Christ without direct proof offered on secular criterion, we must of necessity believe some other authority without any kind of proof. And we must be influenced and directed by that person's reasoning. Such blind guides build a foundation for rationality upon the grounds of irrationality and yet demand our allegiance. This way offers no hope of knowing God! The Christian apologist must instead urge you to believe, even though at this time you do not know, so that the seeds of truth can be sown and bloom into a harvest of the knowledge of God.

A Superior Story

Most skeptics today would not deny that Christ was a real person and quite possibly a "good man" and a "moral teacher." Some of the world's most ardent skeptics have acknowledged that to deny Christ's existence is ridiculous; he was no legend. But they would offer a different account of his identity because they do not believe that Scripture is the Word of God. What they know of Christ as a moral teacher or a good man, they know from the Bible. They accept its testimony in part but not the whole, for their own philosophical confession will not permit it. Yet, if a witness in court is found to be lying in part, he or she is entirely discredited.

People are often happy with a certain kind of Christ. Their knowledge of him, such as it is, is directly or indirectly stolen from Scripture and reshaped according to their moral desires. But they will not have the Christ-story of Scripture, which has been proclaimed by his church down the centuries. Instead, antagonists urge others to not believe the testimony of Christ about himself, or the testimony of the church. People are to believe their own narrative on faith and, in reward for this faith, they obtain a lukewarm ignorance—or despair!

In responding to such objections we can have great confidence, for our faith offers a much better account of reality. James Smith's comments are instructive: "Christianity offers a much better story. The mode of cultural engagement in the marketplace of ideas, then, is not syllogistic demonstration but narrative persuasion. . . . This narrative persuasion as a "new apologetic" begins by pointing to the mythical status of competing ontologies [theories of reality] and narratives and offers a counter-narrative from the Christian story that is embodied in practice. . . . *This does not negate the possibility of critique.*"[27]

So the apologist creatively retells the Christian epic while exposing the inconsistencies of alternative stories and their failures to justify their own assumptions about reality. Having done that, the Christian persuader must *proclaim* so that the Word of Christ will be believed until faith gives way to sight and the search makes us capable of knowing something of the divine mystery by the Spirit's regeneration of the human heart.

We know that sometimes we are looked down upon as naive fools for being led by this faith and not by secular "sight." But what does this so-called sight amount to but tragic blindness? By their own authority, nonbelievers call people back from faith, while Christ calls us to believe on God's authority. In fact, Jesus gave highest praise to people with great faith. The world mocks us and yet the faith spreads to more and more people. Augustine writes,

> So he who brought the remedy that would heal . . . established authority with miracles, won belief with authority, held the masses with belief, endured through the masses and made religion strong by enduring. . . . Then, by responding to authority, people would first have their lives and conduct purified and in that way grow capable of being given understanding. . . . By his miraculous birth and deeds he won our love, but by his death and resurrection he drove out fear. In all the other things . . . he showed himself for us to see how the divine mercy can reach out and human weakness be lifted up.[28]

These things we believe. We claim that we know God, while the contemporary skeptic says we do not, and that we are deluded into believing it. So then we are liars, or we are deluded, or we have the truth. The antagonist claims not to know about God, usually denying it is possible to have any knowledge of God. But if that is the case, why does the atheist tell us that God does not exist, or the agnostic assert that God cannot be known? These are surely claims to know something about God! Both of these claims are grand, metaphysical *confessions of faith* about the capacity of other human beings, reality as a whole, and God. To such a skeptic, Augustine urges that transcendent authority, not human authority, is the only hope for lifting us to wisdom:

If God's providence does not preside over human affairs, there is no need to be concerned at all about religion. If, however, the outward appearance of everything [which we surely must believe emanates from some source of true beauty] and a certain inner consciousness combine, publicly and privately as it were, to urge all minds to look for God and serve God, then we should not abandon hope that there is some authority established by that God himself to be like a fixed step on which we may stand to be lifted up to God.[29]

Furthermore, how has this authority been seen and established so that we have such confidence to set out upon the search in faith that prepares the heart for understanding? Augustine continues,

This has been brought about by divine providence through the utterances of the prophets, through the humanity and teaching of Christ, through the journeys of the apostles, through the derision, crosses, blood and death of the martyrs, through the exemplary lives of the saints, and in all cases, as appropriate for the time, through miracles befitting such great deeds and virtues. When therefore we see such great help from God, so productive and so beneficial; shall we hesitate to hide in the bosom of his church?[30]

We must, then, urge skeptics in today's world to commit themselves to the search and to commit themselves to the teaching and authority of Christ. As the lens of truth in Christ purifies and heals the eyes of the heart by faith, understanding and knowledge will emerge. Then faith will see wisdom's reasons, and the reason of faith will be seen in Christ in the same way that all of the beauty of this world is revealed by the sun. Christ must be presented both as the *way* and as the *destination*. If Christ is only presented as the destination and reason is put forward as the way, we will end up arriving at an entirely different destination. Christ is not merely a conclusion at the end of an argument. He is the argument and the conclusion. In faith, hope, and love, we should urge those who seek to pray, as well as to read and think, so that by grace they may come to see the truth in Christ. Without belief, there is no understanding. Nothing can be seen in its true light outside of the enlightening of Christ, "the true light that gives light to every man" who came into the world (John 1:9)!

CONCLUSION

Belief of some kind is inescapable; faith is necessary. As such, authority is a governing reality in all of our lives. Christ established his authority as God speaking to his creatures with power. The Scriptures reveal how he established authority through miracles, won followers with authority, and is continuing to establish and make his church strong. We trust him and call others to trust him, not in blind credulity, but in proper confidence. He is the only foundation of intelligible experience and of reason itself. And has provided manifold evidence for those who will seek with an open heart. Our faith promises certain fruit that is fulfilled in the believer.

As we invite skeptics on this search, we do so in humility and for their benefit, not so that we may pride ourselves on our superior understanding. The search itself purifies the heart, by the grace of God, as men and women are drawn to see and are made capable of understanding the reasonableness of our faith. True faith always seeks understanding. That faith and understanding unite us in love to God in Christ, who is both our way and destination, and give us a sure and certain hope. That certitude surpasses a confidence in evidences. It is grasped in a way analogous to the way a mathematical truth is grasped: it is an axiom that appears beautiful and inescapable. Then, finally, faith gives way to sight, for "when he appears, we shall be like him, for we shall see him as he is" (1 John 3:2). Our hearts long for his glorious appearing when we will finally be united with him—our Lord, our Life, our Way, our End.

In all our apologetic efforts and the constant struggle to share our faith effectively with the nonbeliever, amid all the contemporary challenges hurled at Christians, and as we war against our spiritual foe in heavenly places, let us remember that the battle is the Lord's. Ultimately, it all depends upon him. Without his power, our efforts are feeble. If we do not depend upon Christ, if we build upon any other foundation, if we rest on our arguments and abilities, we will utterly fail, for Christ is the wisdom and power of God. He is the image of the invisible God and the repository of wisdom and knowledge; all else is wood, stubble, and straw to be burned in the fire. Without love for Christ first and foremost—no matter how strong our efforts—we will be only a resounding gong or a clanging cymbal (1 Cor. 13:1). May God deliver us from our pride and use us graciously in his mercy.

9

EXISTENTIAL CHALLENGES OF EVIL AND SUFFERING

Ravi Zacharias

It has been said, "Never morning wore to evening but that some heart did break." A famed preacher once noted, if you preach to a hurting heart, you will never lack for an audience. Pain, suffering, and evil are indisputable realities and present the sharpest edge of criticism against God's existence. In fact, all one needs to do is wake up and read the newspapers and one would wonder where God is in the grand scheme of things. History unfolds before our eyes and suffering is writ large in the human experience. There is an old joke: What do you get when you play a country music song backward? Answer: you get your house back, you get your pickup back, you get your wife back . . . and so on. Country musicians write songs about their losses. Rock musicians write songs asking God the reason for their losses.

Justin Hayward, years ago, said it well:

> Why do we never get an answer
> when we're knocking at the door?
> With a thousand million questions
> about hate and death and war?[1]

If we were to direct those songs to God, we may be tempted to ask what we would get back if God were in control. In that question lies the heart and mind of the problem. What kind of world are we asking for? What shape would things take if we were in control? Certainly, we would wrestle with the idea of a world free from pain and suffering. Until we get there, we keep asking, *Why this kind of world?*

We readily notice one feature that emerges every time the question is raised. A long list of tragedies or atrocities is presented—from famines and floods to rapes and murders. Why and what purpose do these serve? I remember well as a young man visiting Vietnam during the tense days of war in the early 1970s. To stare at the darkness so close at hand is an overwhelming feeling. To read the history of the First World War or even the Second World War, when life was snuffed out by the thousands within hours, was to have an onlooker changed forever. Many a skeptic has said that the First and Second World Wars changed humanity's attitude toward God and the world. Those who have seen the pictures of Hiroshima or the D-Day landing with the immense loss of life within a matter of hours cannot but be sobered by it all.

As I respond to this daunting question, I will try to do a few things. Over the years I have attempted, in different articles and other publications, to respond with different approaches. In this instance I shall try to pull some of it together. The strange thing about this question is that although the heart of it never changes, the face of it does. If one has suffered a personal tragedy or grief or witnessed some horrific sight, the face is a new one for the age-old heart-piercing query. First and foremost I will try to establish that when a skeptic raises the question, he also smuggles in the Judeo-Christian worldview. He may try to bypass that assumption, but I'm not sure it can be done.

The Mystery of Evil

I recall after the tsunami hit in December 2004, principally in India and Indonesia, the terror that struck millions was hard to verbalize. Its timing was somewhat ironic as far as the West was concerned. In America, most of the month of December had one story or another about whether Christmas carols could be played in public places. Government offices and public schools faced lawsuits from individuals who found the public display of such belief in violation of their rights to not have to use taxpayers' money for such purposes. One woman in New Jersey even objected to Christmas tunes being played at the school her children attended because they reminded her of the words. At Capitol

Hill, for the first time the Christmas tree was called "The People's Tree" to appease the irreligionists. These stories were in the news, and one network in particular had one commentary after another on whether the Christian faith was being singularly targeted by the atheistic segment of society.

Then on December 26, 2004, the tsunami hit with a vicious force, sweeping thousands of people to their deaths. What was the first question raised by the antitheistic thinker? "Where was God during the tsunami?" The ironic thing about the question is that the Muslim wasn't asking it in Indonesia. In India the devout Hindu or in Thailand the Buddhist resigned him- or herself to karma. Moreover, the naturalist ought not to be raising the question as a moral problem because in a naturalistic framework, morality is very subjective. So in a real sense the only one who can justifiably raise the question is the one within the Judeo-Christian framework. Granted, the naturalist has in recent times repositioned the question to make it more sophisticated in order to justify it. We will get to that as well.

That will be the second task of my response. I will demonstrate that within the Christian worldview are both an explanation of the reality and an answer to the mystery.

I use the word *mystery* carefully because the problem of evil is more than just a problem; it is a mystery. There is a very important reason to brand evil a mystery. Gabriel Marcel defined a mystery as "a problem that encroaches on its own data."[2] By that he meant that the questioner unwittingly becomes the object of the question. One cannot address the problem of evil without ending up as a focus of that problem. Skeptics calmly bypass this reality and proceed as if they were spectators observing a phenomenon, when in reality they are part of the phenomenon. We are not merely observers of the reality of evil. We are involved in it beyond any mere academic discussion. Peter Kreeft, professor of philosophy at Boston College, comments, "Getting to Mars is a problem. Falling in love is a mystery."[3] Evil, like love, is not a problem. It is a mystery. It subsumes the questioner within the question.

Let us look at the breadth of the struggle before us.

The Reality of Evil

The eighteenth-century philosopher David Hume, who spared no ink in his attack upon the supernatural, summed it up in these words:

Were a stranger to drop suddenly into this world I would show him as a specimen of its ills, a hospital full of diseases, a prison crowded with malefactors and debtors, a field strewn with carcasses, a fleet floundering in the ocean, a nation languishing under tyranny, famine and pestilence. To turn the gay side of life to him, and give him a notion of its pleasures; whither should I conduct him? To a ball, to an opera, to court? He might justly think that I was only showing him a diversity of distress and sorrow.[4]

Hume complains elsewhere that it is impossible to square such a world with an ultimate purpose of love. This is possibly better posed than Hume even realized, for he hinted at an explanation even in the question. The thrust of his question is forthright.

One does not have to be a profound philosopher to feel this deeply as the most soul-felt of all questions to God. But as we think of the question, one must also question the question. G. K. Chesterton summed up this counterpoint well when he suggested that when belief in God becomes difficult, the tendency is to turn away from him—but in heaven's name to what? This is a candid and needed reminder. Of course I would personally like to see a different set of circumstances at work. But the more I ponder the weight of the question and see the story line behind our human experience, the more I am convinced that the answers God has already given strike me as the real answer and not the wide-eyed, imaginary, simplistic answers we would like to give. That is why I say that the questioner often forgets the smuggled-in assumptions within the question. In short, the problem is real and our questions hint at the answer.

THE UNIVERSALITY OF EVIL

The Bible does not shy away from the universal problem of evil and suffering. The book of Job is one of the oldest in the Bible and addresses this problem from the point of view of a theist. The prophets of the Old Testament raised this very issue as well. Habakkuk asked, "Why do you make me look at injustice? Why do you tolerate wrong?" (Hab. 1:3) David cried out, "Hear me, O God, as I voice my complaint; protect my life from the threat of the enemy. Hide me from the conspiracy of the wicked" (Ps. 64:1, 2b). Jonah was fearful of the violent Ninevites and wanted them wiped out. Jeremiah challenged the Lord, saying, "I would speak to you about your justice; why does the way of the wicked prosper?" (Jer. 12:1). Furthermore, Buddhism was founded because of the nature of suffering.

So let us remember that *every* worldview—not just Christianity—must give an explanation or an answer for evil and suffering. Either evil categorically proves that God does not exist, as the atheist avows, or evil is not ultimately real evil, as the pantheist claims, or evil is most coherently explained by the Christian view of God and his purpose in creation. In short, this is not a problem distinctive to Christianity. This problem of evil is one to which we all must offer an answer, regardless of the belief system to which we subscribe. The atheist argues laboriously on the extent of the problem, and no worldview is more impoverished in its answers than the atheistic one. To quote a professor of mine: "They are better at smelling rotten eggs than laying good ones." The questions raised cut across time and cultures and worldviews.

THE COMPLEXITY OF EVIL

When one raises the specter of evil, the question encompasses a wide array of happenings. There is the physical side of the problem. Natural disasters, tragedies, and cataclysmic events are ironically called "acts of God." Oddly enough, a bumper crop, a beautiful day, a close brush with what should have been death but wasn't, the wonderful joys and pleasures of life are given no such benevolent source. Malevolence is God's doing; benevolence is "evolutionary wisdom." Strange, isn't it? To attribute rational thought to a predicate without a subject provides not just philosophical problems but grammatical ones as well. But that we shall leave for a later discussion. Then there is the metaphysical side of the question. What is the source of it? Finally, there is the moral side of it. How can there be an all-loving sovereign power that permits such events?

Apart from these facets of complexity, there is a "relevance" dilemma in answering the question. There are two main approaches that confront the one who seeks to provide an answer—the logical or intellectual side and the emotional or existential side. Both are vitally important. To address one to the exclusion of the other may meet a particular need but will do so at the cost of ignoring the rational foundation on which an answer must stand. On the other hand, to make it so cerebral that the emotional side is denied is equally troubling. Since so much has been written on the philosophical side of the subject, notably by scholars such as Alvin

Plantinga, Paul Feinberg, and others, I will attempt to principally address the existential side of this problem, but will do so without ignoring the logical side. As daunting a task as it may be, I do not for a moment believe it is anywhere near as insurmountable a problem as it is for the skeptic.

It is here that I must point out again that every worldview has the responsibility of explaining this, not just the Christian. What is more, enveloped in each person's answer is the affirmed purpose of life itself. Evil and suffering cannot be explained without assuming life's purpose.

As soon as the atheist begins his or her answer, there are *three clear challenges placed before the theist.* None of them succeeds. Each one ends up in conflict of a major sort.

The First Exit: The Presence of Evil and the Extinction of God

The first challenge is *the presence of evil equates to the extinction of God.* The most demanding form of the question posed to theists is what is called the evidential argument from evil. This implies that evil is not only a problem for the theist to explain, but, in fact, the absence of any moral order seen in the universe actually disproves the existence of God. Several atheistic philosophers have argued this. Some do it in more sophisticated ways than others, but the bottom line is the same. Placing it in a syllogistic form, this is the way their argument runs:

1. There is evil in the world.

2. If there were a God, he would have done something about it.

3. Nothing has been done about it.

4. Therefore, there is no God.

This is traditionally the way the argument has been made. But clearly, the third premise is not self-evident. It is susceptible to strong counterarguments because it is a deduction in itself and in need of inductive support. All kinds of evidence can be shown that God has done something about it. It may not be to the critic's way of thinking and liking, but that just pushes the question into a different realm. So the criticism can be shown to fail the test of truthfulness and validity because it reveals the presuppositions of an individual. That is, it says nothing about whether God exists or not, but only that if he did, he would do things "our way."

Proponents have therefore refashioned this argument when they realized it was self-contradictory. I shall address this newer form later, but for now the traditional one is presented as it has always been. For starters, the logical ground on which a theist would walk presents at least two options.

Approach #1

1. Yes, there is evil in this world.
2. If there is evil, there must be good (a problem the atheist has to explain).
3. If there is good and evil, there must be a moral law on which to judge between good and evil.
4. If there is a moral law, there must be a moral lawgiver.
5. For the theist, this points to God.

With this approach, theists can mitigate the force of the argument from evil and then address the underlying assumptions. They can show that some assumptions are not consistent with an atheistic worldview. Lastly, theists may then present the arguments for God's existence and explain what God has said—and done—about the problem of evil.

However, there is one step that we must address here—and one that I am often asked about in an open forum. Many people ask, "Why is it that because there is a moral law, one must conclude that there be a 'moral lawgiver'? That is, why does the argument move from an idea to a person?"

The fascinating thing about the one who questions this step is that the questioner himself or herself does not ignore that the question is posed not ideationally but *personally*. Can a moral precept be posited in abstraction without the value being intrinsic to the one doing the positing? Can a value-laden world be so without the person being intrinsic to that value-laden reality? Can humanity be worthless but the question of evil be worthy?

In short, can personhood of worth be attributed without attributing worth to the first cause? Must not that first cause also have personhood essential to that worth? Positing a moral law without a moral lawgiver would be tantamount to raising the question of evil without a questioner. One may as well talk of the supreme ethic being love, but no entity exists with the capacity or need for it. Such values are meaningless without being rooted in personhood.

As such, let's look at another approach the theist can consider.

Approach #2

1. There is evil in the world.
2. There is also the reality of freedom to choose; and where there is freedom to choose, evil will always be a possibility.
3. In fact, concepts of love and goodness are unexplainable unless there is freedom to choose.
4. Since love is the supreme ethic, its possibility necessitates freedom.
5. Where there is freedom, there will be the possibility of evil.
6. This is precisely the paradigm of creation by God in the Bible.
7. Therefore the biblical model of a loving God, who creates for the possibility of the supreme good, may be defended on reasonable and existentially persuasive grounds.

From here theists begin their arguments for the existence of God. Atheists may counter each argument, but they soon run into the very assumption of objective moral values, which is illogically inferred from a naturalistic universe and only argued from intuitive certainty. They end up in self-stultification. More on this as we progress.

Invisible Order, Implausible Reasoning

There are two doors through which the individual raising the question of God's existence tries to escape from the entailments of disbelief with some sense of reason. I am afraid, nevertheless, that these doors are marked No Exit.

The first is this refashioned argument—namely, that no moral order is seen in this world, therefore there simply is no basis to posit God. One questioner wrote our office some time ago quite vehemently stating that God does not follow his own moral law so he should not be worshiped or consequently doesn't exist. Indeed, regarding the 2004 tsunami, Sam Harris, author of *Letter to a Christian Nation*, writes, "If God exists and takes an interest in the affairs of human beings, his will is not inscrutable. The only thing inscrutable here is that so many otherwise rational men and women can deny the unmitigated horror of these events and think this is the height of moral wisdom."[5]

Here is Harris again:

Somewhere in the world a man has abducted a little girl. Soon he will rape, torture and kill her. If an atrocity of this kind is not occurring at precisely this moment, it will happen in a few hours, or days at most. Such is the confidence we can draw from the statistical laws that govern the lives of six billion human beings. The same statistics also suggest that this girl's parents believe—as you believe—that an all-powerful and all-loving God is watching over them and their family. Are they right to believe this? Is it good that they believe this?

No.

The entirety of atheism is contained in this response. Atheism is not a philosophy; it is not even a view of the world; it is simply a refusal to deny the obvious. In fact, "atheism" is a term that should not even exist. No one needs to identify himself as a "non-astrologer" or a "non-alchemist."

Examples of God's failure to protect humanity are everywhere to be seen. The city of New Orleans, for instance, was recently destroyed by a hurricane. . . . But what was God doing while Katrina lay waste to their city? Surely he heard the prayers of those elderly men and women who fled the rising waters for the safety of their attics, only to be slowly drowned there. . . . Do you have the courage to admit the obvious? These poor people died talking to an imaginary friend. . . .

It is time we acknowledged how disgraceful it is for the survivors of a catastrophe to believe themselves spared by a loving God, while this same God drowned infants in their cribs. Once you stop swaddling the reality of the world's suffering in religious fantasies, you will feel in your bones just how precious life is—and, indeed, how unfortunate it is that millions of human beings suffer the most harrowing abridgements of their happiness for no good reason at all.[6]

There is so much philosophical hollowness in this outburst that one actually wonders where to begin. Notice several points in this statement.

First, the writer does not wish for atheism to be seen as a philosophy. If there is any doubt whether Sam Harris is an atheist, just read his books. "One does not describe himself as a 'non-alchemist' or a 'non-astrologer'"—that is actually quite a humorous statement. If you are in a discussion about your future life and someone looks at your hand, asks for your date of birth, and says he will study the planetary alignment on that day, it might be to your advantage to know whether he is an astrologer or a pizza maker who reads palms as an avocation. If you are having some serious health issues and you are given a potion by a stranger to drink, it would be of interest to know whether this is an alchemist or a pharmacist you are dealing with. So when you delve into every definition of life ranging from origin to destiny, it does make sense to know whether you hold to an atheistic worldview or not. Sam Harris just does not like to be categorized the same way he comfortably categorizes others, including God. But this is not atypical of atheists. They shun categorization of anything they hold. The reason is that *it does not hold.* They look for a universal solvent to dissolve the notion of God and end up dissolving their own worldview.

Take a look at the next assertion: "What was God doing when Katrina lay waste?" Or else the rape instance. What is he saying? Is he saying that such an act is evil, ought to be evil, or ought not to be allowed by a loving God? In any of the three assertions he at best says, "I do not see a moral order at work here." Says who? Sam Harris or Adolf Hitler? Hitler's very point was that the destruction of the weak is a good thing for the survival of the strong and that nature intended it that way. For Sam Harris to convince us that Hitler is wrong, he would have to borrow from an objective moral framework to make his point stand. There is no way for him to break the stranglehold of determinism or subjectivism. That is the very reason his own genre of writers, in naturalism's frame of reference, say that moral reasoning is not rational without God. Their philosophical escapism is fraught with stifling unreason.

Finally, if Sam Harris says that God breaks his own laws, he is selectively borrowing from the biblical revelation while ignoring the entire story of human purpose and value. There is one fundamental difference between God allowing death when he has the power to restore life and my taking a life when I don't have the power to restore it. The story of evil is one part of a greater narrative. To ignore the greater narrative is to continue to raise particulars without accepting the general.

Whose Moral Right?

Allow me to give an illustration here. Some years ago, I was on a radio talk show at Ohio State University, answering questions along with the well-known astronomer Hugh Ross. We were talking about some theme related to the origin of the universe when a woman called in quite angry and attacked us with a volley of words. Her basic charge was that all this discussion was nothing more than a smokescreen for reversing *Roe v. Wade* and taking away the right to abortion from women. The outburst was odd since that was not even the topic of discussion. She continued to repeat the line, "It's my moral right to do what I choose to with my body." Finally, I said, "All right, ma'am, since you brought it up, I'd like to ask you a question. Can you explain to me why if a plane were to crash and some die while others live, that a skeptic calls in and questions God's moral nature if he at his whim chooses some to live and others to die; yet when it is your choice to allow a child within you to live or die, it is your moral right to make that determination? Does that not sound odd to you? When God decides, he is immoral. When you or I decide, it is our moral right."

There was pin-drop silence. The questioner may cavalierly say that she does not see a moral order. But I strongly suspect it is not the absence of the moral order. Rather, it is an intuitive sense of morality that at the same time wishes to arrogate to itself the right of moral self-determination. Let's face it. The absence of a moral order ought to also assume what a moral order would look like. But why should the moral order look like the skeptic's and not anyone else's? Besides, if there is no visible moral order, then the very enforcement of one is sheer pragmatism and open to any challenge for other pragmatic reasons. If, on the other hand, the charge is made that the God of the Bible violates his own moral order, then ought not one heed the fact that the same God who gave the moral law also gives his reasons for why he allows the reality of pain and suffering? Why do they accept the revelation of his moral law as factual but the reasoning as not?

Some time ago I read an article about a little girl who suffered from a rare malady of insensitivity to pain called congenital insensitivity to pain with anhidrosis (CIPA). The victim does not feel any pain, nor does she sweat or shed tears. There are only one hundred known cases in the world. A recent story was told about a five-year-old in Big Lake, Minnesota. Little Gabby Gingras is watched constantly in her class. At four months old, her parents noticed that she would bite her own fingers till they bled, and she would do so without any expression of discomfort. At age two, her parents had to have her teeth removed to keep her from biting herself into a fatal heavy bleed. She could put her hand on a hot plate and burn that hand off without feeling a twinge. She always has to wear safety glasses because in one instance she had scratched her cornea badly and would have blinded herself had she not been seen in the nick of time. She plays sports with an abandon, fearless of crashing into anything. She says sometimes she feels like crying but can't. The life of this little one is in perpetual danger. An average lifespan for a CIPA child is twenty-five years. Parents of children with CIPA have one prayer: that they would feel pain.

If it is possible in our finite world with limited knowledge to see just one benefit of pain, is it not possible for God to design this characteristic within us to remind us of what is good and what is destructive? As horrendous as the illustrations may sometimes be, can we not see the moral framework that detects atrocities and resists tragedies? Could there not be a greater answer than just saying, "There is no God"?

Why Call Anything Good?

The denial of God leads us to preposterous conclusions that in the end, the amoral world of the skeptic, who simply cannot explain good, is worse than that of the theist who has an explanation for evil. This network of argumentation is actually quite fascinating when you evaluate the skeptic's challenges to theism. Over the years, naturalists first denied *causality* as an argument to prove God's existence: *Why do we have to have a cause? Why can't the universe just be? Why can't the Big Bang have just happened?*

Then they denied *design* as an argument for God's existence: *Why do we need a designer? Why could it not have all just come together with the appearance of design? Besides, so the eye is complex, but look how poorly designed the backbone is.* (I can't resist: as one with serious back problems and who has undergone radical surgery, I have yet to see a neurosurgeon who can replace this one with a better design.)

Now they deny *morality* as an argument for God's existence: *Why do we need to posit a moral law or a moral law source? Why can't it just be a pragmatic reality?* This I find fascinating! They want a cause for suffering or a design for suffering, but they have already denied that either of these is necessary to account for every effect.

Not one proponent of evolutionary ethics has explained how an impersonal, amoral first cause through a nonmoral process has produced a moral basis of life—especially as they simultaneously deny any objective moral basis for good and evil. Does it not seem odd that of all the permutations and combinations that a random universe might afford we should end up with the notions of the true, the good, and the beautiful? In reality, why call anything good and evil? Why not call them orange and purple? That way, we settle it as different preferences. By the way, Bertrand Russell tried that latter approach and looked quite pathetic at it.[7]

The truth is that we cannot escape the existential rub by running from a moral law. Objective moral values exist only if God exists. Is it all right, for example, to mutilate babies for entertainment? Every reasonable person will say no. We know that objective moral values do exist. Therefore, God must exist. Examining those premises and their validity presents a very strong argument. In fact, J. L. Mackie, one of the most vociferous atheists who challenged the existence of God on the basis of the reality of evil, granted at least this logical connection when he said, "We might well argue . . . that objective intrinsically prescriptive features, supervenient upon natural ones, constitute so odd a cluster of qualities and relations that they are most unlikely to have arisen in the ordinary course of events, without an all powerful God to create them."[8]

Therefore, the conclusion must be agreed upon that nothing can be intrinsically, prescriptively good unless there also exists a God who has fashioned the universe thus. But that is the very Being skeptics want to deny because of the existence of evil. Listen also to the words of Canadian philosopher Kai Nielson, prolific in his writings on atheism: "We have been unable to show that reason requires the moral point of view or that really rational persons unhoodwinked by myth or ideology need not be individual egoists or classical amoralists. Reason doesn't decide here. The picture I have painted for you is not a pleasant one. Reflection on it depresses me. . . . Pure practical reason, even with a good knowledge of the facts, will not take you to morality."[9]

So Sam Harris, evaluated by his own terms, is either engaging in moral reasoning, which is only valid if God exists, or he is being irrational in his assertions. Little wonder that Bertrand Russell admitted that he could not live as though ethical values were simply a matter of personal taste and therefore found his own views "incredible." "I do not know the solution," he said.[10] What such antagonists end up proving is that there is an intuition within them that finds such acts reprehensible. But how does that intuition come about? Let us even grant him a little ground there. What, then, is he asking? That anytime a tragedy or catastrophe is about to hit, God puts a staying hand on it? What kind of world is he asking for? No freedom, only compulsion or robotic acts? Can such a person do anything loving in such a world?

"In counterpoint," the skeptic asks, "why couldn't God have made us to always choose good?" Philosopher Alvin Plantinga of Notre Dame, in his powerful book *Warrant and Proper Function*, responds to the question of evil and argues that God simply cannot do that which is mutually exclusive.[11] Omnipotence does not mean "everything." It only means that which is *possible* to do without making omnipotent to mean omnivolitional, meaning God can will anything. No, God cannot make square circles because the definitions lose their parameters in the process. God cannot will himself into extinction. God cannot make a stone so large that he cannot lift it because the question poses a mutual exclusivity. The problem is not with God; the problem is with the question. If it were the case that God could do anything and everything, even that which is mutually exclusive, then he could also contradict his character, rendering the problem of evil moot. The very reason we raise the question is because we seek coherence.

The reality is that in a world where love is the supreme ethic, freedom must be a reality, and where freedom is true freedom then the possibility to reject that love and live with the entailments must also be there.

Once again, even thinkers hostile to Christianity inadvertently assert truths that agree with Christian thought. For example, Jean-Paul Sartre writes in *Being and Nothingness*, "The man who wants to be loved does not desire the enslavement of the beloved. He is not bent on becoming the object of passion, which flows forth mechanically. He does not want to possess an automaton, and if we want to humiliate him, we need try to only persuade him that the beloved's passion is the result of a psychological determinism. The lover will then feel that both his love and his being are cheapened. . . . If the beloved is transformed into an automaton, the lover finds himself alone."[12]

How insightful! Love compelled is a precursor to loneliness. Having the freedom to love when you may choose not to love is to give love legitimate meaning. This is why I said earlier that David Hume had more of an answer in his question on the problem of pain than he may have known. His closing statement on that question was, "Honestly, I cannot see how you can possibly square these with an ultimate Purpose of Love."[13] Not only that, Hume also conceded that even the pleasures we clasp end up leaving us more desolate. So there is something systemically wrong with the human condition where our definitions of love, freedom, and evil do not meet the quest for coherence. To ask that we be denied freedom and only choose good is to ask not for love, but for compulsion and for something other than humanity.

Sartre is absolutely right here. When love is a compelled state of mind enforced by design, it is not love and in fact with reasoning actually is a precursor to loneliness. Love by choice within the parameter of the trust that is sacred is a guarantee of legitimate meaning. To desire love without the freedom not to love is to ask for something other than human. It has been said that all of our human miseries are really a reflection of our grandeur. May I dare suggest that the very reason we ask the question of our miseries is because of our grandeur, and that is not the intrinsic bequest of naturalism.

THE SECOND EXIT: THE ABSENCE OF GOD AND THE EXTINCTION OF EVIL

The first exit door to flee from God was opened, and the escape route was blocked by intuition or reason. They push at a second door that is patterned on the first. The skeptic approaches the question a little more carefully now, knowing that the question carelessly worded actually necessitates the existence of God. The challenge is now positioned by saying that no moral order is seen in the universe; therefore, there is no moral first cause. Certainly the God of the Bible cannot exist, who seems to kill at whim and is ruthless in judgment.

This position is so nihilistic that it still borrows from a rejected worldview in order to press home the point. The deduction is staggering. Here are the words of Richard Dawkins: "In a universe of blind physical forces and genetic replication some people are going to get hurt, other people are going to get lucky, and you won't find any rhyme or reason in it, nor any justice. The universe we observe has precisely the properties we should expect if there is, at the bottom, no design, no purpose, no evil and no other good. Nothing but blind pitiless indifference. DNA neither knows nor cares. DNA just is. And we dance to its music."[14]

Do you see what sleight of hand there is in this argument? Since no order is seen, there is no such thing as evil. Starting with a long list of emotion-straining tragedies and atrocities to make God look like a killer, they then proceed to tell us all these things are really not evil after all. If they were evil, God would not have committed them. But if they were evil and he did commit them, he is not worthy of our respect. Suppose you take the latter. All that proves is that respect is due to something worthy of honor. But since this is not worthy of honor . . .

But wait a minute: why do we say this is not worthy of honor unless we presuppose what is honorable, which is the very thing we deny actually exists? We cannot flee from intuitive certainty because it is simply wrong to do some things. Hence, the ultimate denial of the existence of evil. Evil isn't. God isn't. We are, and we just dance to our DNA. So Hitler should be called to task not because he did something evil but because he danced to a DNA we do not like. So we dance to the moralizing skeptic's tune or no tune at all.

This is supposed to be an answer? If DNA neither knows nor cares, what is it that prompts our knowing and our caring? Why even freely ask the question? Are we just embodied computers, overvaluing our senses? If our feelings have no bearing at all on the reality of this question, then maybe ours is the artificial intelligence and the computer's is the genuine one—for it has no feeling; it has only information. Computers do not care. They do not grieve over evil and are, therefore, closer to reality.

Is this what we have come to? We must be warned that there are no brakes on this slippery slope once we step onto it. The denial of an objective moral law, based on the compulsion to deny the existence of God, results ultimately in the denial of evil itself. Can you imagine telling a raped woman that the rapist merely danced to his DNA?

The question is irrepressible: why not allow God to dance to his DNA as well? No, that would be unacceptable, so Dawkins comes to the rescue again. Why do we even think of God? In his lectures delivered to the British Humanist Association, Dawkins declared that the idea of God is a virus, and we need to find software to eradicate it. A virus scrambles the data within the human gene and spits out this misinformation. Somehow if we can expunge that virus that led us to think this way, we will be purified and rid of this bedeviling notion of God, good, and evil.[15] One would like to ask Dawkins, are we morally bound to remove that virus? Let us not forget that Dawkins himself is, of course, somehow free from the virus and can therefore input our moral data.

The problem has encroached upon itself. In an attempt to escape what they call the contradiction between a good God and a world of evil, skeptics exorcise the mind of theistic notions, only to be entered and overcome by contradictions sevenfold. They try to dance around this huge contradictory system by introducing terms like *evolutionary ethics*. The one who raises the question against God in effect plays God while denying he exists. In that sense Sam Harris is right. They are not really atheists—they just arrogate to themselves the authority of God. They are surrogate theists transferring the power to themselves.

Though I have often quoted G. K. Chesterton in his criticism of this kind of thinking, no one says it better, so I would like to quote him again:

All denunciation implies a moral doctrine of some kind; and the modern [skeptic] doubts not only the institution he denounces, but the doctrine by which he denounces it. Thus he writes one book complaining that imperial oppression insults the purity of women, and then writes another book . . . in which he insults it himself. . . . As a politician, he will cry out that war is a waste of life, and then as a philosopher, that all life is waste of time [sic]. A Russian pessimist will denounce a policeman for killing a peasant, and then prove by the highest philosophical principles that the peasant ought to have killed himself. A man denounces marriage as a lie and then denounces aristocratic profligates for treating it as a lie. . . . The man of this school goes first to a political meeting, where he complains that savages are treated as if they were beasts; then he takes his hat and umbrella and goes on to a scientific meeting, where he proves that they practically are beasts. In short, the modern revolutionist, being an infinite skeptic, is forever engaged in undermining his own mines. In his book on politics he attacks men for trampling on morality; in his book on ethics he attacks morality for trampling on men. Therefore the modern man in revolt has become practically useless for all purposes of revolt. By rebelling against everything he has lost his right to rebel against anything.[16]

In striking contrast, the Christian message recognizes the horror of evil and seeks to offer a morally justifiable reason for God to allow suffering. Let us turn to the Christian response, so that we may see the difference.

LIFE AND ITS STORY

When all that the Scriptures have said is pulled together, there are six elements that combine to give an explanation that is coherent and unique. No escape is sought, either in the denial of the question or in the implications of the answer.

The Author of the Story

First, *God is the author of life.* The God of the Bible reveals himself as the author of life and as the Being in whom all goodness dwells. There is nothing self-destructive in God. To use philosophical language, *it is impossible for him to not be.* But this is more than a fact about existence; this is descriptive of his very nature. All life coheres in God. He is perfect and uncaused. The heart of what describes him is in the Hebrew term for holy, *kadosh* (see, for example, Isaiah 6:3, where the word is used three times). That is at the core of the narrative. Holiness is more than morality; it is more than just doing right. It is the essential quality that defines what it means to be in perfection of goodness. It is the distance between humanity and God. To us in the West, this concept has become so foreign that we actually mock it. The idea of the sacred is inimical to our freewheeling, hail-fellow-well-met culture.

Sometime ago I bought my wife a beautiful piece of jewelry. It was handmade with a combination of gold and some semiprecious stones. I had bought it when I was overseas from a specialist in that kind of jewelry; it was one of a kind, and I guarded it carefully. At the planned moment, I gave it to her one night when I was home. We admired it and talked about it, described each stone and set it aside. Next morning, I woke up early to do some writing. I went into the kitchen to make myself a cup of coffee. All of a sudden, I heard a crunching sound. I looked over toward where my daughter's puppy was lying and suddenly realized she had the necklace in her mouth and was delightedly chewing on it like a juicy bone. I dropped everything. When I saw what she had done with it, I could only stand and feel the tears well up within me. What was there to be said? To go and bring a gemologist's manual and show the puppy the value of each stone? Or else, go and pick up the bill of sale from my briefcase and tell her the money I had spent on it? Hardly!

You see, there is a difference between the puppy's view of value and mine. As a dog, she could only look at the jewelry. She couldn't look through it. She could only look at my tears; she couldn't look through them. She only knew it was not what I had wanted done with it. She couldn't understand why. She had no clue of the beauty and the worth of what had been mangled. That is the way we human beings look at holiness. We have no idea what it is we have violated. Morality suggests to us it's ours or God's. The disenchantment we sense is that it was a "no-no." We can look *at* the idea of holiness but we cannot look *through* it. Looking through it points to the essence of what life was designed for and strains to catch a glimpse of the one who himself is the essence of all that is true and good and beautiful.

There is an old humorous story about a man who died in a flood in a small town when the rivers overflowed. Upon his arrival in heaven, he walked around looking rather angry. Finally, one of the apostles asked him how it was that he should walk about with such a disgruntled appearance in heaven. He replied, "Why should I not be upset? Does anybody here know what I went through? Do they have any idea of that tragedy? When the riverbanks overflowed, there I was helplessly trying to stay afloat. Do you know how perilous a flood can be?" The apostle tried to calm him down. "All right," said he. "We'll call a meeting tonight and gather the masses. You can share your story from your town and your experience. Will that help?" That seemed to calm him down. Then the man said to the apostle, "One more thing. I'd like to have a question and answer time too, to answer any tough questions on how my faith withstood it and all that." "Fine," said the apostle and that evening a huge meeting was convened. The apostle introduced the speaker and said that they were going to hear a story of extraordinary proportions and he could field any question they wanted to ask after he finished. As the man stood up to speak, the apostle whispered, "They are very eager to hear from you, especially the man in the front row—his name is Noah."

As questioners, we think we understand evil and its nature. We only do to a limited extent—and it is like seeing a candle when God sees the devastating power of evil as a lightning bolt to the soul. We only grasp in small measure how heinous evil is. We look at the symptom; God looks at the disease. We look at the rape as a violation of one person; God looks at the violation of the one as the violation of the very image of God. We look at moral issues that hurt society; God looks at the profane heart that desecrates everything in the process. We look at laws that will make life mutually livable; God looks at the regenerate heart that will make life in itself pleasurable.

The Script of the Story

Second, God is not only the author in description, but *he is also the author in prescription*. He has given us the story of who we are and why we are here. The Bible is a descriptive and a prescriptive book. God is a God who speaks and who tells. The Hebrew prophets spoke the word even when it was a self-indictment. The written word was not just a self-attestation. It was a revelation sustained by reason and tested by time and character. Unlike Muhammad, whose personal life was anything but pure, and who in effect became exalted into some kind of demiurge, the writers of the Hebrew Scriptures pointed not to themselves but to the God who made us and revealed himself to us. The writers never claimed perfection; they pointed outside of themselves to the Holy One.

The story line of the Bible is very clear. God has fashioned us in his image: we reflect a moral and self-determining propensity. Yet in the condition of our uprightness, we chose to rewrite the laws of God and become the god of God. The response of God was to show that his Word is and was true. We do not violate God's laws without the entailments of brokenness. Life is broken on every front because it is broken within. Desiring that everything we touch become gold, we found out that the body could not live on gold. There is a light side and a dark side to life. The words of Pascal are true: we are the glory and the shame of the universe.

There is a very simple way to illustrate this. Andrew Lloyd Webber's *The Phantom of the Opera* was one of the most successful musicals on Broadway. The music is superb, and the story line is riveting. I recall that when I first heard some of the music over the radio, I was surprised that portions of it seemed discordant, sometimes even shrill. How could the same composer orchestrate both the delightful and the jarring? I could not blend the two until I finally saw the play. Then it all fit together—the magnificent and the pathetic, the harmony and the discord, the hideous and the beautiful. Why? Because there was a script to explain it.

When one comes to grips with the story of God's plan and purpose born out of his holy and pure character, both good and evil speak within its context. God has a script. He has spoken of it in his Scriptures. Without God, there is no story, and nothing makes sense.

To the follower of Jesus Christ, that story unfolds in two significant events. First, *God spoke through the prophets and the apostles*. The Bible is often seen as some kind of new kid on the block of revealed truth. That is not true at all. The revelation through Moses began centuries before Jesus. In the first three chapters of Genesis we see several things:

God speaks.

God commands.

God creates.

God separates.

God provides.

God complements.

God evaluates.

God blesses.

The creation and the Fall sum up the beginning. God created us for a purpose. That purpose was given boundaries. Everything true and good and beautiful is potentially violable. When that violation takes place the entailments bring the false, the evil, and the hideous. In choosing to redefine God's law we entered the existence of evil and suffering. All of creation is fallen, and all people are affected. To have it any other way is to fragment existence in absurd ways. Imagine a world where half are "fallen" and the other half "perfect." How would the perfect ones explain to the fallen ones that they are fallen? What portion of the world will have evil and what good? Will only the fallen ones encounter pain and the perfect ones be insulated from it? What if there is a dinner in the home of a perfect one, and some fallen ones are at the dinner and a tsunami hits? Will only the fallen ones be drowned and the perfect ones remain afloat? The absurdities of a half-fallen world are unimaginable. The Scriptures tell us, "The whole creation has been groaning" (Rom. 8: 22). Thankfully Genesis 1–3 is not the only portion of the script; it is more than just a script with bad news. The redemption and transformation of the human heart is the way back.

In *A Preface to "Paradise Lost,"* C. S. Lewis offers this brilliant insight into heaven and the nature of good: "It is in their 'good' characters that novelists make, unawares, the most shocking self-revelations. Heaven understands Hell and Hell does not understand Heaven, and all of us, in our measure, share the Satanic, or at least the Napoleonic, blindness. To project ourselves into a wicked character, we have only to stop doing something, and something that we are already tired of doing; to project ourselves into a good one we have to do what we cannot and become what we are not."[17]

That transformation of being is what our redemption is all about. That redemptive answer is in turn enfleshed.

Second, the Scriptures tell us that *God spoke through his Son, Jesus Christ.* "In the past God spoke to our forefathers through the prophets at many times and in various ways, but in these last days he has spoken to us by his Son, whom he appointed heir of all things, and through whom he made the universe" (Heb. 1:1–2). Everything God creates is at best similar to him. Only that which God begets is identical to him. That is why the writer goes on to say, "The Son is the radiance of God's glory and the exact representation of his being, sustaining all things by his powerful word" (Heb. 1:3). That incarnate figure of Jesus reflects everything God intended for us to be like. We are fashioned to resemble him. This aspect of the revelation of God is unique in the Christian faith.[18]

The key point I am making here is that God in his essence is a "Being in relationship." That part of the story is key to understanding evil. When the relationship is broken, evil is expressed in brokenness in every other relationship. Love, language, trust, respect, hope, fidelity—all end up in the heart of deceit and selfishness. Evil at its core is that which breaks purpose from the metanarrative and that which in its self-will separates and divides illicitly. God put boundaries and markers to keep the sacred. When those boundaries are removed, a different division takes place. It is the division of the profane—a violation of your essential worth and right. God is all for human rights because some things are right and others wrong. Finding the script moves us closer to solving the mystery.

The Point of the Story

Third, *if there is a story, what is at the heart of it?* Not only is God holy, but he reveals to us the sacred nature of love, to which he beckons us. And from this sacredness of his love must flow all other loves.

The important aspect of this logical flow is that *intrinsic sanctity* provides both the reason and the parameters of love. The inability to understand the mystery of evil leads to an inability to understand the sacredness of love. A deadly mistake I believe our cultures make in the pursuit of meaning is this illusion that love devoid of the sacred, a naked love, is all we need to carry us through life's tests and passions. Religions that promote polygamy confuse love with compassion and benevolence. Islam is one of those. Muhammad himself had multiple wives and concubines. The reasoning runs something like this: he was caring for their needs and provided for them. Without that care, they would have been destitute. All that sounds very gallant, doesn't it? But love is greater than that. Muhammad could well have cared for these women without the consummation for himself. Love binds itself, and it is the nature of love to bind itself with exclusion and demarcation of relationships. The very statement that we are to love God with all our heart and soul tells us that we shall have no other gods beside him. Love that is pure transcends itself by making God supreme.

What does all this have to do with suffering? Everything. You see, when the skeptic asks why God did not fashion us so that we would only choose good, he or she completely misses—drastically misses—what goodness is in God's eyes. *Goodness is not an effect.* If an effect is all that is important, of course God could make us that way. There is nothing logically contradictory about making us as automatons. But if life is born out of sacredness, neither goodness nor love alone is the goal. It is love conjoined with reverence, and it must be chosen even when it is hard and costly. In the old Anglican wedding service, the pledge was worded, "With my body, I thee worship." There was a reverential exclusivity to the physical, consummate act. Worshiping God is the ultimate of reverence with life itself as a gift at his altar. This kind of love is a choice to let the sanctity of life and its affections dictate the commitment of the will. This kind of reverential love can look upon suffering and see it beyond the clutches of time and through the victory of eternity.

I have a colleague in Malaysia. He and his wife have three children. Their youngest is seven years old. Jonathan was born with a perilous condition of being microcephalic—having a small head. The doctors had advised them to abort the baby. They chose to carry the child. Jonathan was not supposed to live this long. But he has and everywhere the family goes, he is wheeled in a special chair and sits beside either his father or mother. Sometimes he looks as though he is staring into nothing. But he knows who his parents are. He becomes part of the conversation of the waiters and waitresses when they ask what happened. It is fascinating to see the care the family gets when they hear the story. Friends and strangers reach out without voices, and their hearts are deeply moved that such a love exists that sacrifices every moment to care for one who will not live long and who lives in such a deprived condition.

Yes, the Peter Singers of this world (professor of ethics at Princeton) would consider this boy less than an animal, as they have avowed in their own writings.[19] Yet his parents named him Jonathan: "gift of God." The Peter Singers of this world in the name of altruism will destroy and kill the less fortunate. Jonathan's parents, unknown in the academy, make this world a better place even for the maimed and weak. The Peter Singers of this world with one fist clenched at God call him evil for not stopping the births of such people. With the other fist they mock and kill these very ones in the name of moral reasoning. We all recognize a sacred love when we see it, and we long for it. We all recognize arrogance and selfishness when we see it too. Sacred love is not without boundaries. There are lines that commitment will not cross because when they are crossed it ceases to be love.

Douglas Coupland, in his book *Life After God,* gives a sobering reflection of a generation, himself included, that wandered in the wilderness of life without God. He cuts through the hype and the velvety veneer of absolute freedom. At the end of his book he writes a surprising postscript: "Now, here is my secret: I tell you with an openness of heart that I doubt I shall ever achieve again, so I pray that you are in a quiet room as you hear these words. My secret is that I need God, that I am sick and can no longer make it alone. I need God to help me give, because I no longer seem to be capable of giving; to help me be kind, as I no longer seem capable of kindness; to help me love, as I seem beyond being able to love."[20]

This is so instructive. A bare love on its own does not really stand on anything except the will. Worship is the rationale of existence. It is the ground from which love emerges unique and strong, with convictions and reverence. Worship provides the posture of the heart and harnesses the inclination of the will. We stand together as a community before God, but we also stand in communion first with the triune God who himself is a Being in relationship.

Only when holiness and worship meet can evil be conquered. For that, only the Christian message has the answer.

The Centerpiece of the Story

This brings us to the fourth step. *How is it possible for the sacred to acknowledge the reality of evil and still be able to offer a morally justifiable explanation?*

The core of the Christian message posits a way that by all estimates has been a unique and matchless expression in the face of evil. Jesus described his journey to the cross as the very purpose for which he came. His death in that manner brings a message with double force. It demonstrates the destructiveness of evil, which is the cause of suffering and, in Jesus' example, the ability to withstand suffering even though it is undeserved.

Suffering and pain did not spare the very Son of God. Looking at him on the cross were the very ones who sang songs of joy at his birth. Surely, for Mary, this had to be an utterly traumatic moment. The One who was conceived of God was now at the mercy of man. But I suspect she knew in her heart that something had yet to be completed in the script.

Looking at the cross, evil becomes a mirror of fearsome reality. But by carefully looking into the cross, we discover that it is not opaque but translucent, and we are able to glimpse true evil through it. The suffering of Jesus is a study in the anatomy of pain. At its core, evil is a challenge of moral proportions against a holy God. It is not merely a struggle with our discomfort. Here, two staggering truths emerge.

The first is how God himself expressed his love in such absolute terms. In his expression, all of the emotions and struggles of the human heart converge. Some time ago, I was asked to address the United Nations ambassadors on their Day of Prayer. The subject I was assigned was "Navigating with Absolutes in a Relativistic World." The setting was, of course, quite restrictive because there would be people of all faiths in attendance, and the standard "preaching" approach just would not do. With the strictures presented, I spoke on the search for absolutes in several areas of which I selected four.

1. Every now and then, some nation brands another *evil.* Who is to define that?
2. As a world administrative body, *justice* is so often sought. How does one arrive at it?
3. Every member there comes with some cost of separation. They miss their loved ones. They all hunger for *love.*
4. Every now and then, one of them is caught in an ethics violation and seeks *forgiveness.*

Evil, justice, love, and forgiveness. I illustrated the search for these answers in all of our lives. I ended by suggesting to the ambassadors that there was only one event in history in which these four converged: in the crucifixion of Jesus Christ. Only on the cross of Jesus Christ do love, justice, evil, and forgiveness converge. Evil, in the heart of man, shown in the crucifixion; love, in the heart of God who gave his Son; forgiveness, because of the grace of Christ; and justice, because of the law of God revealed. That is at the heart of the Christian story. God has done something about evil. It is too profound for our simplistic answers to understand.

Eleonore Stump, professor of philosophy at Saint Louis University, has written an outstanding essay titled "The Mirror of Evil." Unfolding her own personal journey toward God, she has brought a fascinating argument to the forefront. In the beginning, she recounts Philip Hallie's struggle on the same issue, as he described it in his book *Lest Innocent Blood Be Shed.* Hallie was struggling to work through human depravity. The appalling wickedness that changed his whole life was in coming to terms with the unmitigated brutality in the Nazi death camps. His despair reached its limit when he wrote: "My study of evil incarnate had become a prison whose bars were my bitterness toward the violent, and whose walls were my horrified indifference to mass murder. Between the bars and the walls I revolved like a madman. . . . Over the years I had dug myself into hell."[21]

As he became immersed in this man-made hell, Hallie noticed a hardening in his own heart. He ceased to feel the horror of evil. But as a prisoner to his own indifference, something happened. He came across the heart-gripping work of the people in a small French village, Le Chambon, and found himself responding to their supererogatory acts—acts of extraordinary kindness in the face of evil. Undaunted by the cruelty around them, the Chambonnais repeatedly risked their own lives to rescue those most directly under the Nazi scourge and to alleviate their suffering.

As Hallie read of their deeds of mercy, he found himself almost unconsciously wiping away a tear, then two, then three, till his face was covered with tears. Surprised by such an uncorking of emotion from a heart he thought had died to the schemes of men, he stopped himself and asked, "Why am I crying?" Had something released him from behind the bars of bitterness and indifference? Had the translucent mirror of evil let through just enough light from the other side that he could see not only the face of wickedness, but also a faint possibility beyond the mirror, the countenance of God? Had some light shone forth from the darkest corner of the world and directed the path of this one, trapped by fear?

On the verge of seeing himself stripped of all feeling in the pit of wickedness, the merciful had opened up a spring of tears. The Chambonnais had become a symbol of all that was contrary to the hell unleashed by the Third Reich. There was no more perplexity for him. There was only one antidote. He saw through the wickedness and for himself, Hallie wrote:

We are living in a time, perhaps like every other time, when there are many who, in the words of the prophet Amos, "turn judgment to wormwood." Many are not content to live with the simplicities of the prophet of the ethical plumbline, Amos, when he says in the fifth chapter of his Book, "Seek good, and not evil, that ye may live: and so the Lord, the God of Hosts, shall be with you." . . . We are afraid to be "taken in," afraid to be credulous, and we are not afraid of the darkness of unbelief about important matters. . . .

But perplexity is a luxury in which I cannot indulge. . . . For me, as for my family, there is the same kind of urgency as far as making ethical judgments is concerned as there were for the Chambonnais when they were making their ethical judgments upon the laws of the Vichy and the Nazis. . . . For me the awareness of the standard of goodness is my awareness of God. I live with the same sentence in my mind that many of the victims of the concentration camps uttered as they walked to their deaths: "Shema Israel, Adonai Elohenu, Adonai Echod." "Hear O Israel, The Lord your God is one."[22]

Borrowing that lesson from Hallie, and thinking of tears in response to goodness, Eleonore Stump then applies it in her own way. She proves Hallie's point by giving another illustration:

A woman imprisoned for life without parole for killing her husband had her sentence unexpectedly commuted by the governor, and she wept when she heard the news. Why did she cry? Because the news was good, and she had been so used to hearing only bad. But why cry at good news? Perhaps because if most of your news is bad, you need to harden your heart to it. So you become accustomed to bad news, and to one extent or another, you learn to protect yourself against it, maybe by not minding so much. And then good news cracks your heart. It makes it feel keenly again all the evils to which it had become dull. It also opens it up to longing and hope, and hope is painful, because what is hoped for is not yet there. So, in an odd sort of way, the mirror of evil can also lead us to God. A loathing focus on the evils of our world and ourselves prepares us to be the more startled by the taste of true goodness when we find it and the more determined to follow where it leads. And where it leads is to the truest goodness of all—the goodness of God.[23]

This existential reality is powerful. In a world full of harsh expressions of hate and pain, it is very easy to get hardened. In fact, the constancy of such exposure only leaves us dead to the true extent of pain. Something in the heart needs to soften in order to react with wisdom and resolve. The cross presents just such a spectacle. It is no wonder that one of the thieves crucified beside Christ cried out for mercy and the centurion used to inflicting pain succumbed under the power of such majesty and muttered of Christ: "Surely this man was the Son of God" (Mark 15:39).

Perhaps this is what Malcolm Muggeridge meant when he said, "Contrary to what might be expected, I look back on experiences that at the time seemed especially desolating and painful, with particular satisfaction. Indeed, I can say with complete truthfulness that everything I have learned in my seventy-five years in this world, everything that has truly enhanced and enlightened my existence, has been through affliction and not through happiness, whether pursued or attained. . . .This, of course is what the cross signifies. And it is the cross more than anything else, that has called me inexorably to Christ."[24]

In fact, one of the most forgotten realities emerges from the Scriptures. Jesus struggled with the burden of having to be separated from his Father in that momentary event of his crucifixion, as he bore the brunt of evil. He cried out, "My God, my God, why have you forsaken me?" (Matt. 27:46). The incredible truth was that at the very moment his Father seemed farthest from him, Jesus was in the center of his Father's will. That is precisely what an understanding of the cross means. Only when one comes to the cross and sees both in it and beyond it can evil be put in perspective.

What emerges from all of these thoughts is that God conquers not in spite of the dark mystery of evil, but through it.

Mahatma Gandhi made the comment that of all the truths of the Christian faith, the one that stood supreme to him was the cross of Jesus. He granted that it was without parallel. It was the innocent dying for the guilty, the pure exchanged for the impure. This evil cannot be understood through the eyes of the ones who crucified him, but only from eyes of the Crucified One. It is the woman who has been raped and not the rapist who understands what rape is. It is the one who has been slandered who understands what slander is, not the slanderer. It is only the One who died for our sin who can explain to us what evil is, not the skeptics. The cross points the way to a full explanation.

This leads to the "so what?" of it all.

The Shock of the Story

Fifth, if all that has preceded this is true, then the focus of evil should shift dramatically. *Evil is more than an exterior reality that engenders universal suffering. It is an internal reality from which we run.*

As I mentioned in the introduction to this book, I recall talking to a very successful, wealthy businessman who throughout the conversation repeatedly raised this question, "But what about all the evil in this world?" Finally, the friend sitting next to me said to him, "I hear you constantly expressing a desire to see a solution to the problem of evil around you. Are you as troubled by the problem of evil within you?" In the silence that followed, the man's face showed his duplicity.

The longer I have encountered this question about evil, the more convinced I am of the disingenuousness of many a questioner. During a forum that I took part in on this very subject of evil and suffering, an atheist asked me, "If you found out that God did not exist after all, what would you immediately do that you are not doing now out of fear of him?" How tragic that we see God as the inhibitor when his Word reminds us of the utter fulfillment we find in doing things his way. One may as well ask, what would you do if you found out you'd never be found out? Imagine a world of such deceit.

Evil is to life what contradiction is to reason. If an argument is contradictory, reasoning breaks down and you can no longer expect the argument to hold. If life is swallowed by evil, life breaks down. This is actually at the core of our very question. The evil that we get so upset about doesn't seem to upset us very much when we perpetrate it. That which is internal is nowhere near as heartbreaking to us as when we want to lay it all at the feet of God. One of the shortest letters written to an editor was by G. K. Chesterton. It read, "Dear Sir: In response to your article, 'What's wrong with the world,'—I am. Yours truly, G. K. Chesterton." The skeptics of our time forget that human depravity is at once the most empirically verifiable fact that is and, at the same time, the most intellectually resisted.

The Sting in the Tale

This brings us to our sixth and final point in the process of sustaining the Christian worldview regarding evil. The surest evidence that evil is not the enemy of meaning is this inescapable existential reality: *meaninglessness does not come from being weary of pain but from being weary of pleasure.* This obvious truth is conspicuously absent in the arguments of skeptics. But they hint at it. Was this not David Hume's point that away from the hospitals and the broken bodies, what would he show the stranger visiting this planet? Take him or her to some dance or some pleasure haunt? Was not that also in some way so empty? Hume spoke volumes in that question. It is not pain that has driven the West into emptiness; it has been the drowning of meaning in the oceans of our pleasures.

Pleasure gone wrong is a greater curse than physical blindness. And blindness to the sacred is the cause of all evil.

CONCLUSION

In the ninth chapter of John's gospel, some questioners come to Jesus and ask him whether a blind man was born blind because of his own sin or his parents' sin. Jesus said, "Neither . . . but that the work of God might be displayed" (v. 3). There is no way to understand blindness of the soul until you are humble enough to know that only God can bring healing. Jesus went on to say that the real tragedy was not the blindness but the tragedy of those who thought they saw but were actually blind.

The problem of evil has ultimately one source. It is the resistance to God's holiness that blankets all of creation. It is a mystery because we are engulfed in it—spiritual blindness. And there is ultimately only one antidote, the glorious display of God at work within a human soul, bringing about his work of restoration. That transformation transforms and tenderizes the heart to become part of the solution, not part of the problem. Such a transformation begins at the cross.

But like the skeptics of Jesus' day, some want to find a reason to deny who Christ is and the healing he can bring. Like the neighbors, the curious masses wish to know how it happened. Like the parents, those who come into close contact will witness the transformation that Christ brings. And like the blind man, those who have personally experienced Christ's power to transform their lives will understand the greater blindness from which they have been rescued.

God is the author of life. God is not merely presented as good, but holy. That is essential to understanding why life is, therefore, intrinsically sacred. The essential component of goodness is not just an effect as much as it is the will expressed with the real possibility of choosing otherwise.

If God is the author, then there is a script. There is a story. We either let God's purpose be freely expressed, or we reject that purpose and the floodgates of evil swing open. Skepticism by its own admission does not know the script or the story. You repeatedly hear, "We must come up with this ourselves." The wide range from egocentric humanism to nihilism provides the options for them. Violence and evil with these options can become not just legitimized but intrinsic to the process.

What is the story for the Christian? There are two clear indicators. First is the response of worship. Second is the response of love. Worship brings coherence within; love impels a unity without.

But this brings us to the crux of the matter. How is such love possible? Suffering is at the heart of the answer. The centerpiece of the Christian message is the cross. In the cross of Christ is presented the Christian counter-perspective to every other worldview. Even those who are not Christians have stated the extraordinary nature of Christ's answer. Here we may see the ultimate paradigm shift. Here we see the concrete expression of what the rejection of God's order does. Wickedness was at its most visible when pure love was resisted and crucified.

With the cross at the center, the focus shifts dramatically. The problem of evil is first an internal issue before it is a cosmic one.

The most difficult aspect of suffering and evil is what we call physical evil, when no human agency is to blame. But here is where we see the solidarity of life's sacredness. The created order can only be in keeping with human rebellion. To disconnect the two is to construct a scenario that separates what God has intrinsically joined together. In fact, natural disasters may at some time be the only means of reminding us of our finitude.

Finally, I reject the notion that suffering is the cause of meaninglessness in this world. There are many who have experienced no suffering, for whom life is still empty. That by itself ought to be a clue.

As we saw at the beginning of this chapter, Justin Hayward's song asks why we never get an answer when "we're knockin at the door." The song ends with these words:

> I'm looking for a miracle in my life.
> I'm looking for someone to change my life.[25]

The answer Hayward sought was in an inner miracle. That is what Jesus offers to answer the problem of evil, because it began within.

10

CROSS-CULTURAL CHALLENGES

I'Ching Thomas

It was the middle of a late summer night in 1999. Most everyone in the Kocaeli region of Turkey were well into dreams that suddenly turned into nightmares. In a matter of seconds, an earthquake measuring 8.5 on the Richter scale devoured tens of thousands of lives and left even more in a desolate and hopeless state. Shock, loss, devastation, pain, and tears had, without warning, seized the lives of many. And what had previously seemed like sturdy blocks of apartments had crumbled like sandcastles at the sea.

Two days later, I rode on a minibus driving through the rubble of the collapsed city with wailing mothers who were hoping against hope for the survival of loved ones. I sat next to Leyla, a Turkish lady garbed in a headscarf, and her eight-year-old daughter. Trying to speak above the roaring siren of ambulances outside, I asked if the earthquake had affected her.

"Yes, my brother's entire family, except him, died in the earthquake. It is too bad," Leyla replied matter-of-factly.

Surprised by her indifference and feeling at a loss for words to say to one who had just experienced such tragedy, I listened sympathetically as she continued. "I believe in God. I believe that he is in sovereign control of all things and that he is merciful."

I nodded as I found myself in agreement with Leyla. We were well into our discussion on the sinfulness of man and the greatness of God when she added,

"However, we have sinned against Allah as we have not been living according to the teachings of the Prophet. Therefore, God willed this disaster upon us as he is venting his wrath on us. I am grateful that my immediate family was spared, but we have to be careful not to provoke God again. We have to stop sinning and start living right by fulfilling all our religious duties," she concluded.

At this point, I realized that we were talking about two distinct Gods who are worlds apart in attributes and teachings. I could see how our view of the world parted ways here. Though we were both using the term *God* in our discussion, we were referring to very different beings.

ONE GOSPEL FOR EVERY NATION, TRIBE, PEOPLE, AND LANGUAGE

In the first century AD, when the apostle John was exiled to the rocky and treacherous island of Patmos, the Lord gave him the privilege of beholding one of the most beautiful visions of humanity ever revealed. He writes of his vision in the book of Revelation:

> After this I looked and there before me was a great multitude that no one could count, from every nation, tribe, people and language, standing before the throne and in front of the Lamb. They were wearing white robes and were holding palm branches in their hands. And they cried out in a loud voice: "Salvation belongs to our God, who sits on the throne, and to the Lamb." All the angels were standing around the throne and around the elders and the four living creatures. They fell down on their faces before the throne and worshiped God, saying: "Amen! Praise and glory and wisdom and thanks and honor and power and strength be to our God for ever and ever. Amen!" (Rev. 7:9–12)

What an awe-inspiring vision it must have been for the apostle! And what a sight it will be when the day finally arrives and all of us, representing our native cultures, our mother tongues and tribes, will assemble before the throne to worship the Lord with one voice bearing testimony to the faithfulness of the Lamb. Yet as we await that glorious day, the task is still at hand for us to go in the authority and power of Christ to proclaim the good news and make disciples of all nations with their distinct cultures and worldviews.

Today, most of us need not go far to fulfill that calling. Our world, and each of our communities, is becoming increasingly pluralistic in its culture and ethnicity. Many of us have friends and colleagues of different ethnic origins and of varying religious commitments who share our public space and life. Indeed, for some of us, carrying out the Great Commission among people of all nations no longer requires us even to go beyond the next office cubicle or house on our street!

However, along with these accessible opportunities for cross-cultural evangelism comes the challenge of communicating the truth of the gospel in ways that are meaningful and relevant to someone who is foreign to what is familiar to us. Thus we may find ourselves being either misunderstood as intolerant of other belief systems or drawn into a web of other issues when we attempt to give an objective justification of the Christian faith.

Harold A. Netland, a professor of philosophy who lived many years in an Asian country, maintains that the Christian faith should be communicated and defended according to the related cultural context. Namely, we must both respect the nature of the questions addressed and the manner in which they are engaged if we want to persuade someone to consider the truth of Christianity against his or her existing belief system in a cross-cultural and multicultural setting.[1] The issues and the questions concerned will, of course, vary from culture to culture. For example, among Muslims in most contexts, the existence of God is not a critical issue. On the other hand, this is a significant question for adherents of other nontheistic or naturalistic worldviews.

However, we should be careful to note that the category of *worldview*, used to describe the various ideological systems or religious commitments, is still a very broad classification. That is, within each worldview there are subschemes and different ways of perceiving life and reality. Additionally, one's culture, ethnicity, history, and temperament all factor into the complexity of a person's *Weltanschauung* (conception of life).[2]

It is very difficult for one person to persuade another to consider changing his worldview even when both have the same cultural background. This is not surprising, given the fact that such discussions focus on the deepest and most meaningful questions of life. Thus, when the participants also come from a different culture, the barriers to effective, meaningful communication and dialogue are raised even higher.

Challenges to Cross-Cultural Conversations

Let us now turn to examine some of the issues that often hinder the communication and defense of the gospel across cultural boundaries. Hopefully, a better awareness of these challenges can help us to lower these barriers.

Mind Your Language!

When I was in grade school, there was a British situation comedy that I loved watching on television. *Mind Your Language* was set in a night language school in London where the teacher, Mr. Brown, attempted to teach the English language to a class of foreigners from China, India, Germany, Pakistan, and so forth. Much of the humor of the show revolved around the problems the students had with the English language, including their oftentimes offensive speech patterns and their comical mispronunciations of English words. The show was produced at a time when political correctness was not as widely advocated, and it lightheartedly made fun of national stereotypes and their views of the world. For example, the character from China was always quoting Chairman Mao, whereas the Indian and Pakistani men were often provoking each other to fight.

While we laugh at their hilarity, the difficulties that Mr. Brown faced in teaching his motley crew of students portray rather vividly the communication challenges we encounter when we share the gospel and defend our faith cross-culturally. The account of my brief exchange with the Turkish lady is an example of how we could agree a great deal about God with a non-Christian—only to learn much later that all the time we were speaking about very different understandings of God himself!

Often we use terms like *salvation, sin, eternal life,* and even *God* in our conversations and are confident that they hold the same meaning for the person to whom we are talking. In fact, we do this all the time without much deliberation. However, when we are speaking to someone from another culture, familiar terms that we think convey what we mean may not be communicating precisely what we want to say. This suggests that we must carefully define what we mean by our terms and concepts in our evangelistic conversations.

Whenever we introduce a new term to explain the Christian faith, we must first establish if our intentions behind the term are the same. For instance, take time to elaborate the Christian view of original sin and explain what you mean by our "sinful nature" when talking to a Muslim or to someone whose worldview is influenced by Confucian thinking. Otherwise, you will find that though the other person may be using the same words, you are not speaking on mutual terms. You see, there is no doctrine of original sin within the Islamic worldview, and Confucian teaching on sin refers only to acts of man's conscious volition that can be desisted from by an act of the will.[3]

Additionally, when you speak about hell to a Buddhist-Taoist, you need to define it clearly as "a place of God's final retributive punishment" because many nominal Buddhist-Taoists believe that hell is a parallel universe to this world where the deceased wait to be reincarnated.[4] Therefore, it is not necessarily a place to shun. Traditional Buddhist-Taoist death rites evidently reflect this belief. In these rites, paper models of houses, maids, household appliances, cars, and other luxuries are burnt so that the deceased will receive them for their life in hell. A lot of spirit money (also called "hell money") is burned so that the deceased will have enough to spend in the afterlife as they await reincarnation.

The late Christian statesman and missionary Lesslie Newbigin aptly points out that the task of evangelism today is no longer merely recalling people back to their spiritual roots.[5] Up until two decades ago, we shared a commonality with our nonbelieving neighbors in the West. Their fundamental assumptions about life and reality were rooted in the Judeo-Christian worldview. Evangelism in such contexts was more of a call to revival, a call to return to the committed Christian way of life. However, this is no longer the case, as we find the worldviews of communities around us are increasingly distinct from the Judeo-Christian heritage.

THE DYNASTY FACTOR

From observing the portrayal of Westerners in television and movies, people of other cultures frequently mistake those who merely participate in Western traditions with Judeo-Christian roots, like Christmas and Easter, for bona fide Christians. Furthermore, it is easy to find friends of Muslim, Hindu, or Buddhist backgrounds who are much more pious than our average Christian neighbors. Many of these non-Christians are also very devout in fulfilling their religious duties. In such circumstances, evangelism takes on a different meaning than conventionally understood in the West. With such communities, we are seeking to introduce a whole new paradigm of perceiving life and reality into their existing worldview and spirituality. Unlike engaging in a conversation with someone familiar with the Judeo-Christian worldview, we have to recognize that many from other cultural traditions have scant, if any, idea of what the Christian faith is about. I remember a Turkish college student once asking me why Christians are so immoral if Jesus had taught them otherwise. Baffled at her question, I asked to know what had prompted it. Apparently, she got her impression of Christians from watching *Dynasty*, a popular television soap opera in the 1980s!

Another problem is that some people from other cultures have only been exposed to some form of Christianity, but not one that is representative of biblical orthodoxy. Often, what is being carried in the news is taken to epitomize orthodox Christian beliefs. Once when I was speaking at an interfaith forum at a university in Malaysia, a male student of Middle Eastern descent came forward with a strong critique of Christian morality. He said, "Christians have always taken pride in their rigid and self-righteous moral code. However, recently, it seems the church has shifted its stand by allowing practicing homosexuals into the clergy. Tell me, how can I believe that the Christian religion is true when its principles are so easily compromised according to social pressure?"

Clearly, the young man's complaint against Christianity was based on what he had been reading in the news about a certain denomination's acceptance of gay priests. However, he had taken this liberal departure from orthodoxy (and orthopraxy) to be true of all Christian churches.

Such a misunderstanding of the Christian faith among believers of other religions is more prevalent than we think. What is typically known about Christianity is usually an assumption rather than the correct interpretation of the essentials of the faith. A recent encounter with a young Muslim evangelist and apologist further confirmed this.

Steven is a highly respected Muslim intellectual and speaker in his community. Born a Malaysian, he converted to Islam when he was a college student in the United States eight years ago. After Steven found out what I do, he asked to know what the differences between Christianity and Catholicism are. Despite the fact that he had lived most of his life in a culturally and religiously pluralistic environment, he had little knowledge about what Christians believe. It was even more ironic when I discovered that Steven was actually born into a Catholic family!

Straw Men and Stereotypes

Before we continue to assume that this is only a problem with non-Christians, we must confess that we are equally culpable, in that few of us have really examined what our neighbors of other religions believe. For example, how many of us can truly say we know the distinction between a Shiite and a Sunni Muslim? Granted, the expression of religious belief varies according to community, society, or even individual, but this should not be an excuse for us to be uninformed of the basic differences among the various religions and sects within them.

Engaging in cross-cultural apologetics is indeed a difficult and sensitive task that must be undertaken with insight, discretion, and genuine respect for the other's convictions.[6] In so doing, it would be wise for us to avoid attacking "straw men" of other religions and belief systems. Just as we are frustrated when those from other religions unfairly criticize the Christian faith by using a misrepresented or isolated case, we must be careful not to do the same by making generalizing stereotypes. We must be mindful to regard other religions and traditions with care by being willing to acknowledge what is good and true in these worldviews just as we would speak against what is false within them.

Nonetheless, Netland rightly describes the task of apologetics in cross-cultural contexts as not merely showing that Christian belief is reasonable, but also that it is *preferable* to other alternatives. He advises, "We might do this by arguing for the truth or plausibility of certain Christian core beliefs or by arguing that there are compelling reasons for concluding that certain central beliefs of other religions are false."[7] Hence, just as we would expect nonbelievers to see the credibility of the Christian faith, we also have the responsibility to examine the alternative worldviews and learn of their strengths and weaknesses (as well as our own biblical worldview).

Understanding the Religious Dynamics Attached to a Culture

I had just finished conducting a workshop on a Christian response to ancestral veneration when Don came up to tell me his story. He expressed his appreciation for my lecture as it had helped him unravel an incident with his dad that had left him perplexed for a long time. Here is his story:

I work as a chemical engineer for a multinational corporation in Malaysia. Being a Malaysian of ethnic Chinese background, my family professes to be Buddhist-Taoist, but we rarely practice any of the traditional religious rites and rituals except maybe on occasions like Chinese New Year or the Hungry Ghost Festival.[8]

When I left to study engineering in Australia, I was the pride of my father, who had invested most of his savings in my education as I am his eldest son. After my first year in college, I came to believe in Jesus through some friends.

A few years ago, after I had completed my studies, I returned to Malaysia to work. I moved in with my parents as I wanted to be closer to them since they were advancing in age. One of the first things I hoped to do upon my return was to share the gospel with my family members, especially my parents. I wanted to share the good news of my new life in Christ with them. Just as Christ has changed my life, I would like to see my father come to experience the salvation I found in Jesus.

I still recall vividly how thrilled I was when the opportunity came one evening for me to break the news to my father. I remember going to great length and detail in explaining the plan of God to redeem his own through the Messiah and how that salvation is available to us today.

However, the response I received was not what I had expected at all. After I finished speaking, my father remained silent as he did throughout the whole time. I was not sure of what to make of his reaction until I noticed that tears were welling up in his eyes.

He then spoke with a sorrowful, trembling voice, "As my firstborn, you know how much you mean to me. I gave you my best to see that you have a good life. However, it seems that I no longer hold any place in your life. You have today disowned me as your father!" He left the room immediately. We have never spoken about the episode ever since.

When it happened, I was naturally shocked, as I have never seen my father cry and could not figure out what I had said that hurt him so much, until today.

Ethnic Chinese, wherever they are found in the world, typically honor loyalty to family and community greatly. Much seriousness and effort are placed upon respecting the older generation, particularly parents and grandparents. The family value of filial devotion has its roots in Confucius' teaching.[9] He taught that filial piety is among the greatest of virtues, and this obedience and respect is an unconditional obligation to be shown toward both the living and the dead.

This obedience and respect is an unconditional obligation and is expected to evolve into veneration or even worship once the elderly pass on from this world.

Though filial devotion is based on the central doctrine of Confucianism, the practices of veneration of ancestors performed today are based on a syncretism of Taoism, Confucianism, and Buddhism, and are steeped in superstition.[10] For example, it is believed that our ancestors will have many chances to be reborn until they achieve enlightenment. Some of the things one can do to be assured of a reincarnation are the performance of certain death rites that one's descendants can do in proxy. Therefore, if a child truly venerates his parents, he would perform as many of such rituals as possible upon their death to ensure that they would be reincarnated.

It is little wonder that many who have converted to Christianity would completely reject the tradition of veneration of the dead. It is typical to find that one of the main objections to the conversion of a family member, especially the son, is that the teachings of Christianity conflict with the individual's absolute loyalty to his family and heritage. For this reason, when a Christian child informs a parent that he has become a Christian, what the parent actually hears is, *My child will not be able to take part in any death rituals upon my death and hence will not be able to help me escape from hell through reincarnation.* One may thus understand the despair such knowledge of conversion brings to the parent.

A friend told me recently of an encounter he had with a woman who was convinced of the truth of the gospel but was struggling to accept it for herself. The main obstacle that was hindering her from accepting Jesus Christ was the fate of her late mother: "If what Christianity claims about God and reality is true, and Jesus is the only way to eternal life," she explained, "then I will have to live with the dreadful thought that my mother, who died a Buddhist, is now lost forever and I will never see her again. This is a truth too painful for me to accept."[11]

Similarly, many ethnic Chinese I know have parents or relatives whom they long to come to salvation, but this conception of death and afterlife stands as a main obstacle to their accepting the Christian faith. Therefore, we must address the question, *Is it possible to reconcile the Chinese value of filial piety and its various expressions with our Christian beliefs regarding death and afterlife?*

Lit-Sen Chang, the late Chinese apologist, claimed that the tradition of filial piety has been misinterpreted and distorted to imply ancestor veneration.[12] Classical Confucian sources seem to indicate that there is no logical relation between filial piety and ancestor worship. For example, a noted scholar and statesman in the Sung dynasty (AD 960–1279) wrote, "It is more important to provide respectfully and affectionately for the needs of the parents when they are alive; rather than worship them by burning paper money and spreading a feast before the ancestral tablet—a mere superstitious practice."[13]

Chang concluded that filial piety only refers to the respect of parents while they are alive, and faith in Jesus is not in contradiction with true filial piety. In fact, filial piety should culminate in the reverence of our Father in heaven.[14] Of course, much more can be said about the complex issue of ancestral worship, but it is an example that underscores the need for us to recognize some of the underlying cultural implications in our cross-cultural dialogues. This awareness will help us understand the questions and dilemmas that confront someone from a Chinese background when it comes to committing one's life to Christ.

ENGAGING CHERISHED TRADITIONS AND CORE BELIEFS

Therefore, the challenge for us is to figure out if there is a way to locate some of the traditional values of other cultures within the Christian worldview. This means the onus is on us to learn and study about competing worldviews and religions, and their cultural expressions. Consider how to ask probing questions tactfully and learn to listen attentively as you seek the help of the Holy Spirit to discern the core issues at hand.

We should be familiar with at least the fundamental affirmations of the worldview and religion that we are engaging. This knowledge will equip us to differentiate the various religious elements that are so closely entangled in the culture. This is crucial, since no matter where an interreligious encounter takes place, it always occurs in contexts influenced by culture, history, and the associations of the past coupled with present realities. These dynamics sometimes help and at other times stymie mutual understanding. We have to realize that when we present the truth of the gospel to someone from another culture, we are essentially asserting that much of what he or she has been informed and known about life and reality is flawed. What's more, we are suggesting that he alter his worldview by abandoning erroneous values and beliefs to conform to the truth. We have to empathize with the person in that this is a major decision that will affect his social and cultural identity.

Thus, it is imperative that we are sensitive to this reality when we evangelize and engage in cross-cultural apologetics.[15] Ultimately, a better appreciation for various cultural and religious expressions will enable us to communicate meaningfully and tactfully as we persuade our friends from other cultures to seriously consider the truth and the relevance of the Christian worldview. This should also spur us to commit ourselves to walk alongside a new convert from another religion as she struggles to emerge as a new person in Christ from her old belief system, which is so closely bound to her cultural and ethnic identity.

CHRISTIAN TRUTH AMONG OTHER TRUTHS

It is not often that I get the opportunity to have a deep discussion about God with one of my cousins, Kaye. Like me, she was born into a third-generation Buddhist family where popular Buddhist-Taoist rituals are staunchly kept and performed, though there is little understanding of the significance of those practices.

Having grown up in an ethnically and religiously diverse society like Malaysia, Kaye is used to living beside neighbors who have very different ideas about performing their religious duties. Besides, for as long as she could remember, she has always been told that she should be tolerant of other people's beliefs, as everyone has the right to practice religion in his or her own way. Furthermore, she believes that all religions have similar teachings on how to be an ethical person and everyone has the right to choose what works for him or her, and this is usually predetermined according to a person's ethnicity.

This particular evening, Kaye had taken a special interest in the Christian's claim that God is love. While the various Buddhist-Taoist gods her family worships are perceived to be powerful and effectual, love has never been one of their traits.

"Why do Christians claim that their God is love?" she inquired.

My explanation of God's love led our discussion to Christ's offer of salvation.

"Tell me about this salvation that Christians always talk about. What do we need to be saved from?" she asked.

After my lengthy account of the Fall and God's plan of redemption through the death of his Son on the cross, Kaye finally asked if Jesus is the only way to God. I felt a surging sense of excitement over the possibility of her coming to believe in Jesus. I jumped at the opportunity and asked if she would like to become a Christian.

She quickly responded, "Oh no, I am a Buddhist."

"How so?" I asked her, "You neither understand nor believe in the Buddha's teachings. Even when you take part in those customary practices, they mean little to you!"

"That is not the point. Don't you understand? I am born into a Buddhist family—I am a Buddhist. The past two generations in my family have been Buddhists. Why would I consider changing my religion now when it has worked for us all this time? Besides, it's obvious that both Buddhism and Christianity similarly teach about holiness and morality. So, I see no reason for me to be a Christian as long as I am sincere in my commitment to be a good and moral person."

Though Kaye was clearly persuaded by the credibility and the truth of the gospel, she saw no compelling reason to embrace Christianity since the most important thing is not which religion one espouses but that one lives a morally upright life. She feels that as long as she is sincere about her beliefs, there is no need to convert to another religion, as every culture and ethnicity has its prescribed religion.

Increasingly in the West, and certainly in most parts of Southeast Asia, *tolerance* is the most upheld virtue in any discussion about religion and God. We strongly believe that within a pluralistic society where there exists a diversity of ethnicities, cultures, and religions, we are to respect the right of others to believe and practice their faiths so that we can live harmoniously as neighbors. Though we may not subscribe to another's religious commitments, as civil members of a multicultural society, we must be tolerant of our cultural and religious differences.

It is undeniable that tolerance is an essential attribute within a culturally and religiously pluralistic society. While we do not agree with our Hindu neighbors regarding their beliefs, we respect their right to embrace that religion. Unfortunately, however, in most contemporary contexts the virtue of tolerance has been naively understood as the "simplistic notion that the most civil manner in which to respond to other religious traditions is the complete suspension of judgment of any kind; don't make value judgments of any kind, positive or negative; simply allow the other religions to carry on in their own way."[16]

Closely related to this mistaken conception of tolerance is the definition of *religious pluralism*. The term can often be understood in two senses. On the one hand, when used descriptively, religious pluralism simply means religious diversity—the reality that people do espouse different religions.[17] This fact is undeniably true, especially in most contemporary societies. Furthermore, this form of plurality is usually present in contexts of cultural diversity as well. Religious and cultural pluralism in this sense is not problematic in itself. In fact, having been born and lived most of my life in multicultural and multifaith Malaysia, I have found the experience of being in a pluralistic society most enriching and unique.

On the other hand, the phrase *religious pluralism* is also used to refer to the view that truth about God and salvation can be attained through any of the varied world religions. It is alleged that all religions are equal with regard to truth and soteriological effectiveness ("all roads to God lead to salvation"). Netland describes this type of pluralism as "a distinctive way of thinking about religious diversity that affirms such diversity as something inherently good, to be embraced enthusiastically."[18] It is obvious that this second view poses a challenge for us Christians who believe that it is only through Jesus, the Son of God, that we can be redeemed and attain salvation. It is not uncommon that we are accused of being arrogant and wrong because we hold to such a particularistic view of truth and, further, are regarded as intolerant within this understanding of pluralism. When Christians make an exclusive claim to truth against other religious traditions, pluralists assume that this evaluation of other belief systems is really no more than the conclusion of the Christians' subjective and limited perspective. Hence, the Christians' conclusion cannot be considered authoritative in any objective sense, as pluralists assume they are merely making a value judgment from within the perspective of their Christian worldview.[19] Consequently, we are exhorted to cease from making any claims to objective truth and to be tolerant and accepting of all traditions and their belief systems.

BATTLING RESIGNATION AND PRAGMATISM

Among Christians brought up in culturally diverse societies like I was, this simplistic brand of religious tolerance has bred passivity, apathy, and even fear when it comes to our task of evangelizing our nonbelieving friends. Since dialogue about God and religion may seldom lead to a rigorous inquiry or critique of other religious worldviews, what, then, is the point of such discourse? In fact, discussions that are seen as attempts to proselytize are considered inappropriate, and are even illegal in some contexts.[20] As such, we may refrain from dialoguing with friends of other religious backgrounds and become quite comfortable with the status quo; our neighbors continue with their annual *kurban* (sacrifice) of the goat, and we with our cell group fellowship every Friday evening.

However, we must ask, are all truth claims about religious beliefs merely subject to the narrow perspective of our own culture, ethnicity, and traditions? Are we really incapable of assessing the truthfulness of ideas in the marketplace without succumbing to cultural bias? Is it at all possible to completely suspend value judgments concerning other religions? Netland argues that it is misleading to think that one can—or even should—withhold judgment about a given religion; for in reality, people do make evaluations about other religions. It is simply impossible for any educated person not to make at least some implicit value judgments about religion in general as well as religious traditions in particular. Besides, a person who claims indifference and who subscribes to an ambivalent view of religion cannot avoid making at least some implicit value judgments about religious beliefs. For in making such a claim to indifference, he implicitly accepts at least one value judgment—namely, that participation in religious traditions is not worthy of one's commitment.[21]

Therefore, regardless of one's attitude toward religion or toward other religions, one cannot escape making some kind of value judgments in this regard. Thus, Christians are not alone in making value judgments about other religious traditions, as such assessments are inevitable within a religiously pluralistic environment. The issue then is no longer *whether* we should make judgments about other religions, but rather, *on what grounds* we should do so.

A common basis for evaluating religious beliefs is whether a religion "works." *Pragmatism* or pragmatic views of religion perceive the goal of religious beliefs as merely the means to an end. For example, religious practices and values that require discipline will inculcate positive moral values, as in, "religion makes bad people good." I remember I was eight years old when my mother, who was a staunch Buddhist-Taoist then, would ask my uncle, a Baptist, to bring me to Sunday school. "Take her to church with you," she said. "Maybe there she will learn some values and grow up to be a good person!"

Alternatively, people participate in religious practices as a means of finding peace, order, and meaning in the midst of crises or traumatic events in life. This view of religion is quite common among Diaspora Chinese, as they are characteristically pragmatic in their outlook on life. For many, the chief purpose of life is to do well financially, have good health, and maintain harmony within the family. Therefore, if a certain religion has been proven to work for their parents and grandparents, then there is no good reason to convert to another religion.

When I was teaching at a church in Singapore recently, a lady strongly disagreed with my approach in challenging the coherence and truthfulness of the nonbeliever's belief system. "We always claim that Christianity is true and that Jesus is the Son of God," she told me. "But what does that mean to my non-Christian friends? They will tell me that their gods are more genuine as they respond to the prayers of their worshipers—when they pray to them for deliverance from an illness, for example. It does not matter that their beliefs are incoherent as long as they work. Hence, there is no way I can contend that the Christian God is true, as he does not seem to always answer our prayers accordingly. The Christian's belief in God does not appear to work!"

When the validity of a belief system is based on whether or not it "works,"[22] the doctrinal consistencies—or inconsistencies, for that matter—of one's religion are not pertinent as long as the believer sees favorable results. It follows that a *positive response to an appeal or request* (such as healing of a sickness, changing of one's fate, or financial blessings) is *preferred* over the coherence of the belief system. In other words, the efficacy of the "god" is more important than the truthfulness of the belief.

Unfortunately, many Christians today also believe for various reasons apart from a concern for truth. They believe faith is true "because it works," because they "feel it is true in their experience," because they sincerely believe it is "true for them," and so on. Such a pragmatic, subjective, and relative view of the Christian faith, according to sociologist Os Guinness, produces a "sickly faith deprived of the rude vigour of truth."[23]

However, when we assert that the Christian message is true, it is not true because it works. Rather, *the reason it works is because it is true.*[24] Truth is true even if no one believes it, and falsehood is false even if everyone believes it. The truth of a belief or claim is not dependent on its popularity or on the believer's culture, sincerity, or preference. Something is true only if it corresponds with reality. Thus, if we claim that the central beliefs of Christianity are indeed true, then we have a moral obligation to share this good news with others, regardless of their culture or tradition. We are to boldly but sensitively challenge our friends from other religious traditions and worldviews to seriously examine their beliefs against the truth claims of Christianity.[25]

In a religiously pluralistic environment where many live by the assumption that there can be no certainty about religious beliefs, it is all the more imperative for Christians not only to proclaim Christ as the way, the truth, and the life, but also to contend that the Christian message is justifiably true in its claims. Thus, whenever other contenders in the marketplace of beliefs clash with Christianity, those other views are, in the final analysis, and with all due respect to their adherents, mistaken.

CROSSING OVER THE CULTURAL CHASM

When I was a missionary in the Middle East, one of the first evangelism techniques I learned was to present my personal testimony of how God had transformed me and given me a purpose for my life. I was told that when I share from a personal experience, it is difficult for the nonbeliever to negate the reality of what God had done in my life. While this worked a few times, it did not take long for me to encounter a Muslim who had a similar testimony of the good that Allah had brought into her life. I realized that merely sharing my personal story as the reason for my belief in Jesus was inadequate. For example, while the positive spiritual transformation I experienced after becoming a Christian is real, my Buddhist neighbor could easily relate her parallel experience of how spiritual discipline according to the Buddha's Noble Eightfold Path had brought her inner peace and strength.

It soon became obvious to me that any approach to Christian witness that is limited to sharing personal testimonies *without* the validation of the truthfulness of the gospel is deficient. Netland comments that any use of personal stories in our evangelism should be substantiated by other corroborating factors since "Christian witness based merely upon personal experience or the pragmatic benefits of conversion would have little to say concerning why the woman ought to abandon Buddhism and embrace the Christian faith."[26] In a cross-cultural setting, the testimony of our subjective experience with God, apart from reference to the objective truthfulness of the Christian faith, is insufficient. The truth value of the gospel is both personal and universal. It is universal in that it is objectively true for all people, regardless of where they are located.

Fundamentally, the Christian faith is grounded in the fact that the Creator of the heavens and earth has revealed truth about himself and humankind.

Moreover, this truth, which is centered in the person and work of Jesus Christ, needs to be both believed and acted upon if human beings are to be restored to a proper relationship with God. The universality of the Christian gospel lies in the fact that all humankind, irrespective of ethnicity, culture, or religion, are sinners. All are in need of redemption by God's grace. And God desires the salvation of all through a particular person, Jesus Christ, the absolutely unique incarnation of God, who took upon himself the sins of the world.[27] Therefore, the justification for such an exclusive view of God requires more than our personal experience with Jesus.

Throughout the apostle Paul's ministry, he is often recorded as reasoning, presenting evidence, and trying to rationally persuade others to become Christians. He never failed to emphasize the truth and universal relevance of the gospel; he did not merely appeal to felt needs. Often when we share the gospel, we condense it into a simple story that affirms the basics of our faith: "God loves us and has a wonderful plan for our lives. But we have sinned and are therefore separated from him. Jesus Christ on the cross is the answer to our sinful state, and if we will accept him as our personal savior, we will have eternal life." Though exact in what it highlights, such a simplified presentation can wrongly convey the idea that the gospel is primarily about our own fulfillment and satisfaction: "God loves *you* and has a wonderful plan for *you*." A truncated message like this seems to place *us* in the center of the gospel, and not Jesus.

On the contrary, the heart of both the Old and New Testaments is the fulfillment of God's plan. The story of our redemption is God's complete and multifaceted movement through history among all peoples and nations. This cannot be reduced to the mere background of "God's wonderful plan for *you*" without compromising the reach and heart of God's redemptive mission.

The apostle Paul, for one, clearly understood he had to be precise in the way he shared the message of Christ's atonement. We can take a cue from his encounter with the Athenians in Acts 17. The text suggests that Paul found himself among a community that was highly pluralistic, with worldviews that were very diverse and distant from the Judeo-Christian tradition. The cultural and religious environment in Athens at that time is strikingly similar to ours today, where idolatry is ubiquitous and many different types of religion and philosophy abound.[28]

Note the breadth of Paul's message: After he courteously esteemed the

Athenians' reverence for God, he prefaced his message by going back to the beginning—to the drama of *creation*—and identified the Creator of all as one who is transcendent and personal, holding command over the history of his creation. Then he went on to describe God's *mercy* in relation to the human condition, setting the stage for the climax of his message: *redemption* through the death and resurrection of Jesus, and the need for all people to repent.[29]

Another interesting point is that in his speech, Paul did not explicitly quote the Hebrew Scriptures. Instead, he quoted from the writings of pagan Greek poets with which his audience was familiar (Acts 17:28). Likewise, sometimes we need not quote verses from the Bible outright to bring across the redemption message. There will be instances when the audience will be more receptive to the truth of the gospel when contextual expressions like cultural folk stories or anecdotes are used as illustrations.[30]

In addition, James Sire observes that though Paul understood God's judgment of man's sinfulness is crucial, he did not start his speech at Athens on that that point. Rather, Paul presented the grand history of humanity to demonstrate the relevance of the Christian worldview and how the message of redemption is true to its own claim. Ultimately, the Christian way has to be preached and defended on the basis that it is the only true and right way to live and to interpret all of life. As Lesslie Newbigin correctly maintains, "The Christian faith is— as often said—a historical faith not just in the sense that it depends on a historical record, but also in the sense that it is essentially an interpretation of universal history."[31]

ENGAGING IN *AGAPE* APOLOGETICS

The mandate to evangelize and make disciples of all nations should always be approached with the attitude of compassion and authenticity. This requires evangelism that is undergirded by apologetics and dressed in love and humility. It is worthwhile to always examine our motivation for undertaking the task of apologetics—is it in fact grounded in truth and compassion for the other person, or is the motive something else? If our motive is rightly inspired by *agape* love (the term the New Testament uses for God's self-giving love), and if we take our mission to preach the gospel with full seriousness, then it is imperative that we walk according to the example set by the apostle Paul, who wrote, "Though

I am free and belong to no man, I make myself a slave to everyone, to win as many as possible. To the Jews I became like a Jew, to win the Jews. . . . To the weak I became weak, to win the weak. I have become all things to all men so that by all possible means I might save some. I do all this for the sake of the gospel, that I may share in its blessings" (1 Cor. 9:19–20, 22–23).

Paul's approach to reaching the lost requires us to adapt our style and paradigm of doing evangelism and apologetics according to the cultural context specific to the audience or person we are engaging. Therefore, it is critical to learn how we can respectfully ask probing questions with genuine interest. Earlier I proposed that we take the study of other religions and worldviews seriously; however, this knowledge should not merely be facts about beliefs and practices. It is equally crucial that we *establish vibrant relationships* with people of other cultures and religions. As Netland rightly stresses, our knowledge of other cultural traditions should involve actually knowing followers of other religions in a personal manner where the humanity and intrinsic dignity of the other person is experienced.[32] This requires us to identify with the questions and struggles that confront our friends in their native cultures; then, hopefully, we will be able to walk alongside them and lead them to consider the truth of the gospel. Ultimately, a relationship of mutual trust and acceptance is the only proper and valuable ground for any cross-cultural evangelism and apologetics discourse.

Theologian Michael Green affirms, based on his experience in Asia, that "the principle of practical kindness without strings attached lies very near the heart of the gospel. We must find culturally appropriate ways of embodying that principle. We need to overflow with grace!"[33] The good news of Christ should always be communicated in word and in deed, for acts of kindness, grace, and generosity will never betray the message of the cross.

Our defense of the propositional truth of the gospel must correspond with the truth embodied in us. The reality that we proclaim to be true must be evident in the way we live and love. As D. A. Carson puts it so succinctly, "While trying to think through what to say, we must think through how to live."[34] After all, the Greatest Commandment is summed up in a two-pronged call to love: "'Love the Lord your God with all your heart and with all your soul and with all your mind.' This is the first and greatest commandment. And the second is like it: 'Love your neighbor as yourself'" (Matt. 22:37–39). Our professed love for God should always compel us toward authentic agape love for others, and it is in this love for others that we are to carry out the mandate of the Great Commission.

Finally, although many young people maintain a superficial commitment to traditional religious customs and beliefs, their significance has faded in the context of modern materialism, hedonism, and other cultural ideologies that compete for young people's allegiance. Regardless of one's cultural background, ethnicity, or religious commitment, the yearning for purpose and the restless ache of the heart is very real at one's existential core. This is the desire for the Creator that cannot be denied and longs to be fulfilled. It is encouraging to recognize that the grace of God reaches people where they are, with their particular dispositions and characteristics, rooted in their social and cultural contexts with all of the associated influences.[35] Our role then, as ones who have come to experience the transformational love and truth of Christ, is to lead our fellows, regardless of where they are located, to the spring of living water so that they, too, will drink of the new life that is only found in Christ.

PART TWO

*Internalizing the Questions
and Answers*

II

THE TRINITY AS A PARADIGM
FOR SPIRITUAL TRANSFORMATION

L. T. Jeyachandran

Classical apologetics has generally assumed a common starting point outside of God for developing arguments for God and Christ. This assumption is a gigantic one in today's world where postmodernism and New Age have virtually wiped out the possibility that there can be an agreed view of perceiving reality. The classic Indian story that punctuates many conversations about the exclusivity of Christ is about six blind men who go to "see" an elephant. They touch different parts of the elephant and reach six different conclusions about the animal, depending upon the parts they have felt: the elephant is like the trunk of a tree, a broom, a sieve . . . and so on. The point of this illustration is that there is only one God, who is perceived differently by different faiths and traditions.

However, what is often overlooked in this story is the fact that even if the six blind men had had a committee meeting after touching the elephant, they would still not have been able to fit the pieces together correctly. Indeed, the only one who knows that there is a whole elephant out there is the one with sight, and no one—including, ironically, the one who tells the story—is supposed to have seen it!

This parable, then, actually points to the prior necessity of revelation of something that we are not able to perceive correctly or adequately. That is definitely true of God, if not of anyone or anything else.

In this chapter, I propose that God is the basis of all reality. If this is so, what he is like in his being and through his activity should provide an adequate explanation for all that we see and experience.[1] It should be helpful to see that the Christian Scripture is not only didactic and prescriptive; rather, the major part of the Bible is a narrative that outlines God's encounter with his people in creation and redemption history. Paul's statement in Romans 1:20 ("For since the creation of the world God's invisible qualities—his eternal power and divine nature—have been clearly seen, being understood from what has been made, so that men are without excuse") could, therefore, be read and applied in two ways.

First, we can work backward from creation to conclude, by induction, what God the Creator is like. This is the route that has been taken by classical apologetics and is not without its difficulties. One of the main problems is that of the starting point of the apologetic (as stated above). From a moral and theological point of view, it has often been contested that fallen reason can never reach a correct conclusion about God, as the context of this verse seems to suggest.

Second, if we could start from the point of who God is in accordance with biblical revelation and work forward, we should be able to provide an adequate explanation of all reality. In fact, we could provide a study of other religions from their understanding of God and verify which of the many alternative theologies has the best explanatory power.

The first part of this chapter takes the latter approach. Although this can be labeled *presuppositional apologetics*, I intend to take this argument farther than is normally done in an apologetic study. The word "God" falls rather flat in its normal connotation and provides only a one-dimensional and abstract justification for being, design, and morality. Also, the conventional way of describing God in abstract and negative terms—absolute, infinite, immortal, invisible, impassible, and so on—has tremendous merits but does not actually say what God *is* like. I suggest a more detailed exploration of God as a trinitarian being and have chosen to describe this God as an all-personal, all-relational being. From this starting point, I seek to show that we can arrive at a more robust, full-orbed explanation of reality without falling into the errors of various dualisms.

The second part of this chapter deals with our response to this awesome God in terms of the transformation of our character exhibited by our social behavior.

My main argument in this context is that our emphasis on devotion to God tends to be an individualistic one and, in more than one unfortunate sense, is no different from the pursuits of many Eastern religions. Religious showmanship today is often taken to be a sign of true spirituality. Against this backdrop, I submit that in the exercise of spiritual disciplines of every sort, we need to give to and receive from one another and thus, truly reflect the trinitarian God whom we worship. Further, the Bible presents the understanding of true virtue as *relational*—summed up by the simple word *love* (1 Cor. 13; 2 Peter 1:5–7; 1 John 4:7–12, 16), which cannot be actualized except in relationships.

It is a sad fact that the doctrine of the Trinity has been believed in but rarely preached on in our churches. Living these last few years in Singapore, sandwiched between the two Islamic countries of Malaysia and Indonesia, I have half-humorously, half-seriously commented to Christian leaders, "We all believe in the Trinity, but we pray to the Trinity that nobody would question us about the Trinity!" The doctrine is felt to be irrelevant if not an outright and unnecessary complication imposed on the simple belief in the One God. Karl Rahner rightly said, "Should the doctrine of the Trinity have to be dropped as false, the major part of religious literature could well remain virtually unchallenged".[2] At the other end of the equation, we need to gratefully acknowledge before God the fact that in the recent past, a spate of good trinitarian books has been published.[3] As Bruce Ware suggests, "The doctrine of the Trinity is both *central and necessary for the Christian faith*. Remove the Trinity, and the whole Christian faith disintegrates."[4]

GOD'S REVELATION OF THE TRIUNE GODHEAD

As a common prologue to both sections of this chapter, it would be pertinent to consider the fact that the doctrine of the Trinity was not arrived at by theological or philosophical speculation *ab initio* ("from the beginning"). Rather, the triune God met his people at discrete points in time revealing the plurality of the persons in the Godhead. It is also significant that the first Christians were Jews and therefore strict monotheists. As Robert Letham notes, "[The words of Deut. 6:4–5] and the whole law of which it is a part, trenchantly repudiate the polytheism of the pagan world."[5] It is therefore futile to allege that trinitarianism had Greek and Roman polytheistic origins. The one sin the Israelites were rid of during the Exile five centuries earlier in Babylon was pagan, polytheistic idolatry.

An extremely significant fact that often escapes our notice is that the first Christians were strict monotheists. We can justifiably speculate that the early church struggled to reconcile their belief in one God with the following distinct encounters with persons, each of whom they could not but conclude to be God.

God in the Old Testament

At one time, about two million men, women, and children heard the audible voice of God. They requested Moses, their leader, to go up the mountain and hear God because they were scared that they would die if God should continue speaking to them.

This is a story (Ex. 20:18–21) that Jewish children would have heard from their parents and grandparents as they sat around their meal tables. This invisible being, whose back alone Moses is privileged to see (Ex. 33:17–23) does show himself visibly in a number of ways, their parents assured them, but we are hard put to explain who he really is or what he looks like! God manifests himself in Genesis 18:22, 23; 32:22–30; Deuteronomy 34:10; and Joshua 5:13–15. There are also mysterious uses of the plural when God refers to himself (see Gen. 1:26; Isa. 6:8). We encounter a plurality of divine persons in some of the references, one of whom is considered by the Jews to be the promised Messiah (Ps. 2:7–9; 45:6–7; 110:1 [quoted by Jesus in Matt. 22:41–46]; Prov. 8:24–31; Isa. 48:16).

God on the Dusty Streets of Palestine and Jerusalem

The disciples of Jesus, the men and women who followed him, had no doubt that he was a man. Jesus was hungry, thirsty, and tired like the rest and probably shared with them some of the temptations he had faced and won. But they soon realized that there was something unusual about this Man. He excluded himself from praying the prayer (Matt. 6:9; Luke 11:2) that he taught them to pray, obviously because he had not committed any sins that needed to be forgiven. On the other hand, he claimed to have the authority to forgive the sins of others (Mark 2:10). He spoke to the stormy waves as if he was their Creator (Matt. 8:26–27). He did not seem to have to pray to the Father but exercised his authority over nature directly. He addressed Yahweh as Father (John 5:17–18) and claimed that a number of predictions in the Jewish Bible had been fulfilled in him (Luke 24:27). The disciples hear Jesus pray to the Father (Matt. 11:25–26; John 17) and also hear the Father speak to and about him (Matt.

3:17; 17:5; John 12:27–29). Jesus spoke and taught as if he possessed original, and not delegated, authority in matters of theology and moral law (Matt. 7:28–29). He raised dead people back to this life, but when he himself rises from the dead, there is no need for the gravestone to be removed.

The contrast with the resurrection of Lazarus is striking and should not be missed. We read in Matthew 28:2–6 that the stone to Jesus' tomb was rolled away; this was not to let Jesus out, but to let us in. The grave clothes around Jesus' body had been unwound (John 20:5–8), whereas when Jesus called Lazarus from the tomb "his hands and feet [were] wrapped with strips of linen, and a cloth around his face" (John 11:44). Jesus rises to a different order of life, and forty days later when he ascends to heaven, he is taken out of our dimensions by a cloud (Acts 1:9). The question that confronted his disciples then was, is this man Jesus a demigod or, in some mysterious sense, also God?

God in an Upper Room in Jerusalem

Ten days after Jesus ascends to heaven, the disciples have an amazing experience as they wait in the Upper Room in Jerusalem according to the advice of Jesus. They are filled with the Holy Spirit; Jesus had spoken to them about the Holy Spirit as a Person (John 14:16–17, 26; 15:26; 16:13) and Peter and Paul would later imply the same (see 2 Peter 1:21; Eph. 4:30). It was important for Jesus himself to go away to the Father so that he could send the Spirit (John 7:39; 16:7); the Spirit would represent the Father and Jesus to them in an intimate and personal way (implied in John 14:23). The Holy Spirit would now be *in* them, whereas up to that point he had only been with them (John 14:17); he would lead them into all the truth Jesus wanted them to know (John 14:25–26; 15:26; 16:13). The disciples had heard and read about the Holy Spirit, but his work had hitherto been outside the person of the believer—*extrapersonal*. Now for the first time in human history, the Spirit is present in them *intrapersonally* and, in a very special sense, represents Jesus to and in them. Ravi Zacharias refers to the Holy Spirit as "God at his most empirical"![6]

What is the early church to make out of these encounters with God? Are they three independent, autonomous gods, as the surrounding pagans believe? Or are they three different modes in which a unipersonal God has manifested himself? If the first alternative were true, each of the three independent gods could not be infinite.[7] The second alternative would be experientially absurd because the disciples hear Jesus praying to the Father and the Father speaking to Jesus. (What words they hear may be intimated, but on occasion—such as at Jesus' baptism and Transfiguration—the disciples are clearly privy to the Father's words.) Further, Jesus refers to the Spirit as the One who will come to the world only after he, Jesus, goes back to the Father. And truly enough, the disciples experience the indwelling presence and power of the Holy Spirit in their ministry.

It is precisely at this point that the crucial role of Jesus can truly be appreciated. When Philip, one of his disciples, requests Jesus to show the Father to them, Jesus chides Philip for not recognizing who he was in spite of being with him for so long (John 14:8–11). Jesus then goes on to explicitly tell him that those who have seen him have seen God! This claim is amazing, to say the least. Jesus describes his relationship to God in a way that no human being in his right mind has ever come close to saying. He and the Father are in a relationship that is so intimate—one is in the other and vice versa—that to see Jesus is to see God. Indeed, earlier in John's Gospel, Jesus declares, "I and the Father are one" (10:30).

The analogy that comes to my engineering mind is that of a cube, wanting to identify with a two-dimensioned world, becoming a square. It should be noted that it is still 100 percent cube in three dimensions and 100 percent square in two dimensions, but this is possible only because the square is the image of a cube in two dimensions. Being God and human at the same time is not like a mixture between salt and sugar where one would be n % of the whole and the other $(100 - n)$ %; rather, it is a unique relationship between two entities that have a special relationship with each other—one is the image of the other. So in Jesus Christ, divinity and humanity combine without any confusion, and it is manifested in the seamlessly integrated life of this simple Galilean carpenter as recorded in the first four books of the New Testament.

Jesus said that he and the Father were one. He prayed to the Father that the "oneness" of the disciples should reflect the "oneness" that he himself enjoyed with the Father (John 17:11, 21–23). The word *one* in these verses is in the neuter gender in the Greek language (*hen*). It implies oneness in *essence* and not sameness of persons. If Jesus had meant the latter, then John would have used the Greek masculine gender for the word *one* (*heis*). What is implicit in these verses of Scripture is that the agent of this oneness in God and his community—the church—is God the Holy Spirit.

An overwhelming number of Scriptures attribute full divinity to all three persons.[8] Thus the early church is driven to the only option: that these three distinct persons in some way constitute the one divine being. Over the next centuries, the church came to articulate the doctrine of God as *Trinity*—a word not found in canonical Scriptures—by semantically combining both the unity of the essence of the Godhead and the three distinct personalities of Father, Son, and Holy Spirit.[9]

A TRINITARIAN PARADIGM FOR APOLOGETICS

The aspects of God that have the most fundamental applications for apologetics are his *being (identity), character,* and *knowledge.*[10] As already discussed briefly, the attributes of God have often been stated in negative terms—absolute, infinite, immortal, invisible, impassable, and so on. This approach has the important advantage of not equating God to anything that belongs to finite creation, thus avoiding the possibility of verbal idolatry. However, it creates two huge problems. One, we know what God is not, but who *is* he, and what is he like? Two, if the infinite is defined as the absence of the finite, we also have a philosophical problem. That is, should the infinite depend upon the finite for its understanding?

In the amazing providence of God, he stands revealed not in platitudes and abstract universals, but in a breathtaking narrative recorded for us in the Bible. We shall now proceed to reflect upon the trinitarian revelation of God in the three aspects listed above.

Freedom and Identity of God

What is the application of the fact of the Trinity to our understanding of God as well as his creation in terms of *freedom* and *identity*? The identity of a person or thing to be himself/herself/itself also involves the freedom to exist. We make the important distinction that in God, freedom translates as sovereignty, but in God's creation, the freedom is contingent (dependent) and is our distinct identity as people and things. The Bible makes the additional, all-important point that in all of creation, humans are made in God's image. Thus, we do have real freedom to make moral choices and engage in loving relationships.

Trinitarian theology provides the very starting point of what it means to be a personal being.[11] *Personality* has been defined frequently as comprising three basic faculties: intellect (thought), emotion (feeling), and will (volition). These qualities have very often been referred to as if they are stand-alone qualities, but are they? Are they not meaningless in a world where there are no relationships? What use is my intellect if there is nothing to think about? How would I experience emotion if there were nothing to feel? What is the meaning of will if there were no possibility of decision making? Thus, we are forced to conclude that these are *relational* qualities and have no meaning in isolation. In other words, in God, qualities of personality can be actualized only if there is an actual, eternal relationship in him prior to, outside of, and without reference to creation. Only in that way would God be a personal being without being dependent on his creation.

When Moses asked God for his name, the answer he got was least expected: I AM (Ex. 3:14). This amazing mystery of the name (identity) of God solves a problem that we may not always be aware of: *God is his own frame of reference.* We have already considered the fact that the infinite cannot be defined with reference to the finite. God, therefore, has to be self-referencing. This would be an absurd proposition but for the fact that, in the being of God, there is a plurality of infinite persons and each can define himself with reference to the other. God can truly be said to be self-existent only because he is the all-personal, all-relational being. Jesus introduces the first and second persons of the Godhead in familial terms of Father and Son. It is not an accident that the Father derives his fatherhood only because of the Son and vice versa.

We can look at the subject of identity and freedom from another angle as well. The sovereignty of God—his *freedom* to act according to his will—should be seen as a relational quality. Simple human experiences can illustrate this aspect of freedom. A space traveler stranded at 22,500 miles away in zero gravity is not free; he is paralyzed because he is unrelated to anything. On the other hand, we who are subject to gravity and friction are free to move because we are related to planet earth!

Similarly, a soccer team is not *free* to shift the goal posts—there will be no meaningful game if such a freedom is exercised! The rules of the game enable them to relate to each other and free them to play the game. Thus, if God is to be free, he has to be a relational being, and that is possible only in a trinitarian understanding of God. The Father is free to be Father, and the Son be the Son through the Holy Spirit, for where the Spirit of the Lord is, there is freedom (2 Cor. 3:17). The Holy Spirit, who binds the Father and Son, also provides the space for each to be himself.[12]

The application to comparative religion of this one point is enormous. At one end of the spectrum of religions, pantheism and its modern-day New Age relatives insist that everything is divine and God is all. Thus, God is portrayed as extending himself in his creation, and he is of necessity bound to do so. This idea of God makes him a slave of his creation, and religions arising from this belief are, not surprisingly, fatalistic. In this worldview, creation has to lose its identity in the divine and has no freedom to exist as creature! The other alternative of a unipersonal god (as in Islam) could result in an equally fatalistic view of life where humans are no more than mere pawns in the hands of an arbitrary deity.

Defining God as infinite once landed me in a peculiar problem. After one of my lectures, a Hindu colleague of mine from the Indian government asked an important mathematical question: "Infinity is not an actual number; it is larger than the largest actual number you can think of. How can you talk about an *actual* God who is *infinite* at the same time?" The question may sound purely academic, but the way we approach it has immense applications for apologetics. For the infinite to be an *actual being*, he has to be pulsating with life. One of the titles of God in the Bible is that he is the *living God*, the great I AM! From a trinitarian theological perspective, the Trinity—the eternal generation of the Son by the Father and the eternal procession of the Spirit from the Father and the Son—accounts for this dynamism. The simple word *God* does not quite carry the same actuality that the trinitarian relationship accounts for.[13]

A further application in apologetics could be the way the created order exhibits the unity in diversity of the Creator. There is an undeniable identity to each entity in creation; note the fact that God names various entities in Genesis 1. In spite of their independent identities, each is dependent on another for its existence and utility. This phenomenon can also be observed in the fact that the components of the universe that are so different from one another are, at the same time, made up of the same protons, electrons, neutrons, and the same chemical elements!

Philosophers, ancient and modern, have struggled with the issue of finding integration between plurality and unity. Heraclitus was the philosopher of the former, Parmenides of the latter. Colin Gunton wisely argues that the "opposing alternatives for thought and order presented by [these two philosophers] have left to Western thought a legacy of a dialectic in which the rights of neither the one nor the many are adequately sustained."[14] In today's cacophony of voices, the fragmentation of postmodernism (that denies the existence of a grand integrative metanarrative) and the undifferentiated synthesis of New Age provide the counterpoints. The revelation of the being of God, who combines real unity at one level with real diversity at another, comes as a breath of fresh, cool air in this philosophical desert!

It is only in a trinitarian understanding of God that his transcendence over creation can coexist with his immanence in creation. The real otherness that exists between the distinct persons of the Godhead explains how God can really be other than and therefore transcendent over his creation. Simultaneously, the perichoretic oneness of the triune God makes his immanence in creation a reality. (The Greek word *perichoresis* means "dancing around" and is used by early church theologians to describe the mutual indwelling of the Trinity.) The weaknesses of alternative views of God are obvious: either God is hopelessly part of his creation (because creation is an extension of his being), or he is unapproachably remote. Ironically, in both these cases, the idea of God is functionally impersonal—one who cannot be related to. We can confidently assert that trinitarian theology provides the springboard to a comprehensive ontology (the study of being) by bringing together the possibility of transcendence and immanence.

The Holiness and Character of God

Let us now consider the *holiness* and *character* of God.

In the course of a Bible study for college students in Delhi, a Hindu girl asked me what I consider to be a brilliant question: "How can you Christians say God is good? Good is the opposite of evil; evil is not eternal; therefore, good cannot be eternal as well." Without going into her definition of evil as the opposite of good, it should be conceded that the question is a legitimate one. The Christian insists that God exists without reference to evil and rejects the dualism of positing good and evil as equal and opposite. But how can the Christian sustain this position philosophically and existentially?

If I were awakened suddenly in the middle of the night and asked this question, "What is holiness?" my instinctive answer would be "Absence of sin!" Although that may be enough of an answer for our understanding of holiness because of our fallenness and familiarity with sin, it would be inadequate as a definition of the holiness of God. He is holy without any reference to sin. How do we define *that* kind of holiness? We cannot define *good* with reference to evil because good is the original of which evil is the counterfeit—a problem parallel to defining the infinite in terms of the finite. Evil is an aberration. We need to look for a positive definition of good without reference to evil.

Very significantly, the answer lies in the trinitarian being of God. Love is the epitome of all virtue and the highest expression of holiness. And God should not have to depend upon his creation to actualize his capacity to love, for that would make creation as important as the Creator because the Creator would be incomplete without his creation. But the Bible introduces love as an interpersonal quality requiring a subject-object relationship that is available in the Trinity because of the Father-Son relationship through the Holy Spirit. The trinitarian God is complete in his love relationship without reference to his creation. The Father loves the Son before the creation of the world (John 17:24). The infinite personal medium through whom this love is communicated is the Holy Spirit, and he is the one who pours the love of God in our hearts as well (Rom. 5:5). The final answer that I could give to this college girl was to appeal to the Trinity, where good always existed without any reference to, outside of, and before evil.

What is the application to apologetics of this amazing truth? At the philosophical level, this is the fundamental basis of all studies of values, what is called *axiology*. This branch of philosophy deals with the study, among others, of *aesthetics* and *ethics*. The holiness of this trinitarian God is the basis on which all ethics are grounded. Trinitarian theology becomes the proper starting point of all theorizing about ethics. At another level, the study of beauty involves unity in diversity such as a painting or a symphony. If both the diversity of the elements and the unity of the final product do not have real significance, these could reduce to meaningless pursuits. That significance is provided only because in our Creator God, diversity (the distinction between the Persons of the Godhead) and unity (the Oneness of the Godhead) are both meaningful and significant. The pursuit of pleasure in variety that is the hallmark of today's society is the most observable symptom that we are a bored generation! Christians are not exempt, either, because we have learned to look at the creative arts at the purely pragmatic and utilitarian levels. I do not mean that one must hold an eternal perspective in order to meaningfully engage in the arts. All I intend to communicate at this point is that beauty and harmony are best explained only when ultimate reality, God, is the ground of both unity and diversity.[15]

A trinitarian understanding of holiness avoids two errors. At one end of this spectrum of errors, the classical moral argument in favor of God talks about him in rather flat, one-dimensional terms as a much-needed frame of reference for any system of moral values. However, the plea that God is the infinite, moral standard (as he is often referred to in these arguments) does not tell us who this God is. At the other end of the spectrum, we have no alternative except to posit a dualism where good and evil are seen as equal and opposite. But it is quite obvious, even from a philosophical point of view, that good cannot simply be stated as the absence of evil. In fact, the opposite is the case. But then, we need to establish how good can be defined without any reference to evil. Indeed, this is the substance of the question posed by the college student quoted at the beginning of this section.

The Ten Commandments that God gave to his people (Ex. 20:1–17) sum up God's requirement in terms of *relationships*—with him and with one another. The Old Testament also sums up the commandments as love relationships with God (Deut. 6:4–5) and among his people (Lev. 19:18). In other words, holiness by God's own definition (Lev. 19:2) is summed up in the relational commandments that comprise the rest of that chapter. Holiness is therefore not the stand-alone ascetic quality that is the hallmark of some Eastern religions but a community of people in right relationship to one another. Thus, a trinitarian interpretation of holiness gives us a positive and robust understanding without the anemic contentlessness of the first error and the destructive dualism of the second.

In conclusion, then, it should come as no surprise that the psalmist tells us that God is to be worshiped in "the beauty of holiness" (Ps. 29:2 KJV). As we have seen, both these qualities require harmony and relatedness.

Knowledge of God

We will now consider God in terms of his *knowledge*—that is, his omniscience.

We normally take God as an *Object* who is really there,[16] who can be talked about and who leaves telltale evidences of his existence that can be investigated. We can thus be sure that he is unchanging as the object of our knowledge. The adjective *objective* is one that springs to mind whenever we engage in an apologetic discussion of God. But the moment we begin to consider the fact that God could be all-knowing, we are introducing a problem perhaps without realizing it.

If I say that I know this laptop computer on which I am typing this chapter, I am the subject and the computer is the object of my knowledge. My computer does not change—it is an inanimate object only capable of responding to my keystrokes—but I, the subject, do change (particularly when I am adjusting to a new computer!). When we say that God is all-knowing, we are actually positing him as the supreme *Subject*. The question is, how can God be all-knowing and still be unchanging?

If God's capacity to know depended upon creation to be actualized, we would have a problem similar to what we considered in the previous section on love. But the Bible leaves us in no doubt on this score. In Matthew 11:27, Jesus says that no one knows the Son except the Father and no one knows the Father except the Son. Both the Subject and the Object of this knowledge are infinite, eternal, and personal. Further, the use of the Greek present tense in this verse suggests continuous action. Thus, this verse can also be translated in this way: "No one keeps knowing the Son except the Father, and no one keeps knowing the Father except the Son." We can safely conclude that there is a dynamic reciprocity in this amazing relationship within the Trinity. Here again, the divine personal medium through whom this knowledge is communicated is the Holy Spirit (1 Cor. 2:10–16).

We can discern applications of this astounding truth at several levels. At the philosophical level, this mutual knowledge in the eternity of God is the starting point of all epistemology. This branch of philosophy deals with the subject of knowing and finds an adequate starting point only in trinitarian theology, where the subject and object of knowledge exist eternally!

In the area of divine knowledge, this complementary knowing parallels the simultaneous existence of transcendence and immanence in the study of the being of God. Passages in the Old Testament that we consider to be anthropomorphic—for instance, when God is described in human terms in Genesis 18:20–21 and Exodus 3:7–8—can probably be better explained as the mysterious combination of the reality of God's omniscience and his immanent interaction with his creatures in space-time. We shall thus avoid the twin errors of fatalism and open theism.

As an application to apologetics, the trinitarian being of God combines the objective reality of the external world with a healthy subjective way in which we can be involved in what we study and examine. The inescapable aspect of subjectivity that is a part even of the scientific enterprise has been well argued by Michael Polanyi.[17]

We can also legitimately surmise that in the coming together of the apparent determinism of classical macrophysics and the uncertainty at the quantum level, even inanimate nature reflects the complementarity in the being of God. The enjoyable paradox that exists at the interface between a sovereign God and the real freedom of humans made in his image is the highest level where we see this mystery displayed for human experience.

A TRINITARIAN PARADIGM
FOR SPIRITUAL TRANSFORMATION

We shall now turn to a consideration of our response as human beings that this trinitarian God expects from those whom he freely chose to make in his image, who are capable of free, loving relationships. What we often call "spiritual disciplines" are nothing more than what God requires of us in response to who he is and what he does—that is, again, his *being, character,* and *knowledge.* It may be noted that my treatment of our response to God is intended to correspond to the discussion in the previous section.

Worship

In one word, our reflection on the enthralling being of the triune God should result in true *worship.* This is simply the response of who we are to who God is. Unfortunately, in our present Christian climate, what we *do* in our worship services seems to take precedence over everything else! Yet our thinking, feeling, and willing capabilities actually flow out of the fact that we *are*—our being. My particular emphasis in the context of worship will be limited to the consideration that our being is shaped and maintained by relationships.

We are born to our parents, and we grow in our understanding of ourselves as we learn to relate to parents, siblings, and friends. Simply put, I can't be *me* without someone else; you can't be *you* without reference to someone else. What makes a person a person is her (or his) capability of interpersonal relationship. In fact, we derive our most fundamental sense of identity by relating to God and other human beings. Moreover, the identity that we seek from impersonal entities such as achievement, fame, pleasure, and possessions—the hallmarks of today's consumerist, shopping-mall existence—can be extremely inadequate and frustrating. To add to the confusion, we are deep into the use of gadgets and cybertechnology that is accelerating this tendency to depersonalization. Information technology seems to be providing the basis for our philosophy of life; everything, including people, can be digitalized and miniaturized and reduced to megabytes on a microchip. The spate of science fiction movies suggests and aggravates these very tendencies.

It is not surprising that in this rather lonely environment, the Christian pursuit of worship has been made a purely individualistic endeavor. Christian disciplines do not appear to be any different from the aspiration of Eastern religions except that Christian words have been inserted. Are we guilty of baptizing alien methods of spirituality into the Christian church by reducing the totality of Christian worship to nothing more than Christian forms of the lonely soul's *Nirvana*?

Most of today's Christian worship songs are in the first person singular—*I, me,* and *my*—with scant thought of the fact that our Christian walk has so much to do with others. We no longer include in our hymnody songs like the following by Bernhardt S. Ingemann:

> Through the night of doubt and sorrow
> Onward goes the pilgrim band,
> Singing songs of expectation,
> Marching to the promised land.
> Clear before us through the darkness
> Gleams and burns the guiding light:
> Brother clasps the hand of brother,
> Stepping fearless through the night.
>
> One the light of God's own presence,
> O'er His ransomed people shed,
> Chasing far the gloom and terror,
> Brightening all the path we tread:
> One the object of our journey,
> One the faith which never tires,
> One the earnest looking forward,
> One the hope our God inspires.
>
> One the strain that lips of thousands
> Lift as from the heart of one;
> One the conflict, one the peril
> One the march in God begun:
> One the gladness of rejoicing
> On the far eternal shore,
> Where the one almighty Father
> Reigns in love for evermore.

Onward, therefore, pilgrim brothers,
Onward, with the cross our aid!
Bear its shame, and fight its battle,
Till we rest beneath its shade.
Soon shall come the great awaking,
Soon the rending of the tomb;
Then the scattering of all shadows,
And the end of toil and gloom.[18]

The lack of trinitarian thinking and preaching has exacerbated the prevailing individualism of our culture and has brought it right into our Christian life and practice. If we do not think of God as a relational being in himself, we cannot appreciate the point that we are made to reflect his image in our relationships with one another. More often, we only consider God as relational insofar as what we can get out of him in a utilitarian sense. We need to depend on one another to help us comprehend the majesty and love of God and respond in true worship as a community (Eph. 3:14–21).

Many of the psalms are in the plural and not necessarily sung to God but to one another (see, for instance, Pss. 95–100; 122–126; 132–144). The idea of worship today is that every individual Christian is supposed to ride on an emotional high all the time. Each is supposed to lift him- or herself by some mysterious emotional bootstraps to maintain a steady state of high excitement. What is not emphasized is that it is simply not possible—happily so, in my opinion, because that kind of a sustained emotional state is recipe for a mental breakdown! On the other hand, the Scriptures teach us that when we are discouraged, we encourage one another to lift up our feeble hands in adoration to God. In so doing, we begin to reflect our dependence on one another and thereby reflect the being of God in our corporate worship.

There is another aspect to our consideration of God as part of our worshipful response. No true worship of God is possible without the qualities of transcendence and immanence existing together in him. He is worthy of worship only because he is transcendent; we can truly relate to him in worship only because he is close to us (immanent)! Jesus admirably combined these complementary qualities in the opening line of the prayer that he taught his disciples to pray: "Our Father [immanence] in heaven [transcendence] . . ."

The Pursuit of Holiness

Our response to the holiness of God is to reflect his character in our lives—in one phrase, *the pursuit of holiness*. In our endeavor in this direction, however, we need to be careful to note that what we have come to call *personal holiness*—what is inward—is only a potential that has to be constantly actualized in interpersonal relationships. The time I spend with God must enable me to relate to a world of people and things in the right way. In fact, I can be holy when I am by myself; it is when I come out of my room and meet the world of people and things that I run into serious problems! I am afraid that the emphasis on holiness that we often talk about is my preoccupation with my hands being clean and my conscience clear for my own sake, and that happens to be a pretty selfish motive. A selfish motive to be selfless, indeed! It would be almost as if Moses, on coming down from Mount Sinai, began to enjoy his shining face in a mirror!

Holiness, in the final analysis, is otherward and unselfish. I have been fascinated by the trinitarian example from John 5:19–27; 16:13–14. The Father entrusts all things to the Son: his authority, his power over life, and judgment. But the Son will not do anything by himself; he will only do what he sees the Father doing. The Spirit will not speak of himself nor seek his own glory. He will bring glory to Jesus by taking what belongs to Jesus and showing them to us. Three self-giving, self-effacing persons constitute the amazing God whom we worship! It is this aspect of God's character that we seek to reflect in our life and walk as the church of Jesus Christ.

We should carefully consider the answer that Jesus gives to the question that a smart lawyer poses to him (Matt. 22:34–30; Mark 12:28–33). Jesus summarizes the Ten Commandments in two relational aspects: love for God and love for others. Morality is always defined in the Bible in the context of relationships (see Lev. 19, for example). The connection between the commandments is also intriguing, to say the least. If we had been there to ask Jesus why he gave us more than one commandment when we were looking for only one, the greatest, his reply may have taken this direction: "Without obeying the first, you do not have the ability to obey the second; but obedience to the first is secret between you and God. Thus obedience to the second, which is open for public verification, is the evidence that you have obeyed the first. So both commandments are equally important" (see 1 John 4:20).

I often wonder whether our individualized view of holiness reduces the

Christian faith to nothing more than the ascetic, lonely pursuits of Eastern religions like Hinduism and Buddhism. We make statements like "We should be holy *and* work on our relationships," implying that the first is somehow more important than the second and the second is nothing more than an optional extra to the Christian life! I will have more to say on this in the concluding section of this chapter.

The Pursuit of Truth and Transparency

What is our response to the knowledge (omniscience) of the triune God? In one phrase again, it should be the *pursuit of truth and transparency* in all of our relationships. We seem to have driven an unsightly wedge between these two aspects; *truth* is often categorized as an academic pursuit and *transparency* as a moral one. But is this really correct? I shall attempt to indicate otherwise.

At the behavioral level as Christians, we have already seen the centrality of relationships. But this aspect has an added element in knowledge. In the Hebrew language, knowing a person is to relate to that person in an intimate manner; the verb *to know* is often used in the context of the intimacy of a husband-wife relationship. But this kind of knowledge is not possible to the knower unless the known is willing to reveal himself. And that kind of self-revelation is not possible unless a degree of trust is present. The fact that Adam and Eve were naked and they were not embarrassed about it (Gen. 2:25) is a commentary on their state of innocence. Conversely, the first symptoms of their autonomy were shame before each other and guilt before God (Gen. 3:7, 10). (Their making coverings of fig leaves for themselves could very well have marked the beginning of the fashion industry!) It is obvious that while relationship of a person to things is so easy, relationships between persons require trust and openness. Supremely, God has made himself known in his amazing self-revelation in nature, Scripture, and Jesus Christ. He invites us now to take the risk of vulnerable relationships through which we introduce others to God and to one another. Our lives of faith are lives of knowledge that begins with trust in a relational, trinitarian God and should lead us to similar trusting relationships with others.

In commanding and empowering Adam and Eve to have dominion over the earth (Gen. 1:28), God is indicating to us through his Word that an enjoyable pursuit of knowledge and truth in all of life is part of his mandate for us. Knowledge for its own sake is commendable and should not be reduced to purely utilitarian considerations. We should be careful that our knowledge of the material world does not lead to a mindless plundering of the planet's resources for human consumption and unbridled economic growth. I have already referred to Michael Polanyi to make the point that our knowledge of the physical world contains an inescapable subjective dimension. In our moral response to this knowledge, we need to exhibit care for the environment—the amazing fauna and flora of our "privileged planet"[19]—on behalf of its Creator. We seem to have let this item slip away from an evangelical agenda and be taken over by the New Age movement.

During the Q&A session after one of my open forums in India, one of my questioners argued that animals and humans have the same kind of sentience and so it would be wrong to consider human beings to be superior to animals. I alluded to Project Tiger—a government of India program to keep the tigers from extinction—and made the following comment: "When I look at a tiger, I know that he can harm me but I should not shoot him dead unless he attacks me; on the other hand, when the tiger looks at me, his sentiments are quite different—he considers me as potential lunch! How can you explain this difference in attitudes except to see an obvious hierarchy where we are situated in a position to take care of the rest of created order?"

CONCLUSION

I draw my thoughts on the Trinity to a conclusion by highlighting the fact that Jesus preferred to put forward a relationship criterion as what would distinguish his disciples rather than religious criteria (see John 13:1–17, 34–35). I think this is surely the need of the hour because we have probably shed more blood in the name of religion in the last one hundred years than in all previous centuries of human history combined.

We need to recognize the fact that there is one aspect of apologetics that involves presentation of truth, taking into account philosophy, history, science, arts, and so on. But there is another aspect of apologetics—the expression of love within the Christian community—that is the final proof that we are the disciples of the Lord Jesus (John 13:34–35; 15:9).

It is the love within the Trinity (John 17:24) that overflows into the world (John 3:16). In the same way, the love of the community of Christian believers should overflow to a lost and hurting world. Love for the saved precedes love for the lost. Indeed, some people find it easier to love their enemies than to love their wives!

The community of loving Christians is seen by the watching world, not as a collection of perfect individuals. While it would be great to have such a community, few individuals are able to relate to perfect people! The acted parable of John 13 portrays imperfect people in relationships that reflect the mutual sharing of the Trinity. Jesus washes his disciples' feet and says, "I have set you an example that you should do as I have done for you" (v. 15). Jesus' disciples are to wash one another's feet (admitting that we each have dirty feet), and the world is attracted by the fact we are willing to relate to one another in this amazingly practical way. As I wash your feet and you wash mine, the world comes to see us as two imperfect people in a perfect relationship!

But we have two problems. First, I do not want to wash anyone else's feet. And second, I do not want anyone else to wash my feet! The problem is mutual and reciprocal. A God who exhibits mutuality and reciprocity—namely, the triune God—is the One who can deal with this problem.

Our Christian communities are like the Indian bureaucracy (with which I am most familiar), where some people are indispensable but most people are unnecessary. In God's kingdom, however, everyone is important but no one is indispensable; no one is so senior that he has nothing to receive, no one so young that she has nothing to give! The mutuality of the foot-washing illustrates this reality perfectly.

In washing his disciples' feet, Jesus was making it clear that he was not just exhibiting his humility and servanthood. He tells Peter that unless he washed Peter's feet, he could not truly relate to Peter. At the same time, Jesus did not bathe Peter because Peter was already clean; he only needed to have his feet washed. This shows that we, the disciples of Jesus, need to minister moral and spiritual cleansing to one another as well.

But with what attitude shall we offer this cleansing to one another? The clean one has to take the position of the servant (weakness) and accord to the dirty one the place of the master (strength). In other words, our ministry to one another has to be nonthreatening. The wrongness of our attitudes can destroy the rightness of our words and deeds. As we apply this lesson to the some thirty-six "one another" passages of the New Testament—accept one another, forgive one another, be kind to one another, and so on—we begin to show something of the self-giving Trinity. One other related lesson that the world needs to see in our post-9/11 world is that violence is a sign of weakness and vulnerability is a sign of true strength. After all, our Victor gave himself over to be Victim, didn't he?

But in order to be able to emulate the self-giving relationships of the Trinity, we need to cultivate the following four qualities by the grace of God and the help and support of one another (John 13:1–3).

First, we should be aware of God's timing (*kairos*) in our lives (v. 1). We tend to be too coldblooded on the one hand or too impulsive on the other. Jesus moved in line with God's timing and his hand upon his life. The Christian life is very demanding, and without this awareness we are not likely to succeed and may end up as burnouts.

Second, we need to have a prior commitment to one another before we can embark upon this costly adventure (v. 1). This is similar to the commitment Jesus had made to the Twelve at the beginning of his ministry when he chose them out of the many who were following him.

Third, we need to be willing to wash the feet of a possible Judas who may be present in our company (v. 2). If Jesus had not washed Judas's feet and if he had discriminated against Judas during the three and a half years of his ministry, it is quite possible that five disciples could have followed Judas and five could have followed Peter, and the first church could have split down the middle! In the event, of course, it is Judas who goes out into the night (John 13:30). When love becomes unbearable, it poses a choice to the offender—to return to the fold or to leave forever.

Fourth, Jesus had an identity before he embarked upon the foot-washing enterprise (v. 3). That is, he did not seek to derive an identity from service, as we so often are wont to do. He could rise from supper, take off his robe of divine privileges and authority, and clothe himself in the apron of a servant only because he was sure of his identity as God's Son.

I am often reminded of two famous women who died within eight days of each other in August and September 1997. As I looked at their photographs printed on facing pages of an issue of *India Today* (a popular newsmagazine in India), I realized this: both women did a lot for the poor. One woman who did not find love in her parents' home or her husband's home frantically tried to compensate her inner emptiness by serving the poor; the other was full of the compassion of Christ and served the poor in an amazingly unself-conscious way. One, a wealthy woman of fame and fashion; the other, at her death, had nothing to her credit but two blue-bordered white cotton saris and a plastic bucket!

How then shall we live and speak in a society that is increasingly secularized and is keen on deconstructing all that the Christian faith has to say? We need to rightly represent our God in our talk and in our walk as a community of his worshipers.

Loving God with our minds should involve thinking more on his trinitarian being—our "reason reflecting on his revelation"[20]—and applying those insights in our understanding and critique of our culture. As I have attempted to show in this chapter, a trinitarian understanding of reality has amazing explanatory power over the many alternatives that surround us.

Our life has to shift away from its individualistic focus toward more of our relationship with one another in the body of Christ. Christian spirituality is the very opposite of religious showmanship or one-upmanship. Our relationships with one another are the *only* ways that our relationship to God is shown to the world. Over against the postmodern tendency to level cultures or exaggerate their differences,[21] the Christian community affirms our different identities and cultures while celebrating our oneness in our understanding and devotion to our triune God. Relationships within the Christian community are therefore seen as central to spirituality rather than a peripheral and desirable option.

Will we be perfect in this life in achieving the above? No! However, we shall persevere here in this world, waiting with a longing hope for the coming of Christ. Then, in union with him we, the church, will begin a never-ending journey of discovery of the mystery of the triune God.

12

THE ROLE OF DOUBT AND PERSECUTION
IN SPIRITUAL TRANSFORMATION

Stuart McAllister

It seemed like yet another routine border crossing in what was then Communist-ruled Czechoslovakia. The year was 1981; Leonid Brezhnev was the head of the Soviet Union, and half of Europe languished under the Communist vision and control. As a young, enthusiastic, and eager Christian, I had joined a mission whose primary task was to help the church in Eastern Europe. This involved transporting Bibles, hymn books, and Christian literature to believers behind what Winston Churchill called the "Iron Curtain."

It was indeed an iron curtain: a vast barrier made of barbed-wire fences, mine fields, exclusion zones, guard towers, heavily armed soldiers, and dogs. Although designed allegedly to keep the West out, it was in actuality a vast system of control to keep those under this tyranny *in*. On this occasion my task was to transit through Czechoslovakia into Poland to deliver my precious cargo of Bibles and books to a contact there.

The literature was concealed in specially designed compartments, and my colleague and I had gone through our routine preborder procedures. We checked everything to see that it all appeared normal. We checked that everything was closed, locked, and secure. We bowed our heads and prayed that God would protect us and make seeing eyes blind—not literally, but unable to detect our hidden cargo. We then proceeded to the border crossing between Austria and Czechoslovakia.

It was a cold, bleak, early winter day. It all seemed normal. We entered Czechoslovakia, and the huge barrier descended behind us. We were now locked in. As usual, the unfriendly border guards took our passports, and then the customs inspector arrived. I had been trained to act casual, to pray silently, and to respond to questions. I sensed this time it was different. The man ignored me, concentrated on the structure of our vehicle, and was soon convinced we had something concealed. I became quite tense.

My colleague and I were separated. The guards demanded we show them what we had, and they tried to force me to surrender the keys to the vehicle. I resisted verbally, conscious that they were armed. I was a Christian and did not want to give anything away, yet I had to try to act as a normal tourist would in such circumstances. They eventually took the keys from me and locked my colleague and me in separate rooms. The guards broke into the special compartments in our vehicle, where they discovered the Bibles and literature.

I prayed for wisdom. I asked God to guide me and to lead me in whatever came next. For several hours I was interrogated. *Who sent us? Where were we going? Did we work for a Western government or agency?* I had determined based on previous experience that if caught, I'd concentrate on witnessing, as all the other details they needed were in my passport. They were neither amused nor interested. Several hours later, we were collected by some plainclothes officials and driven to a prison outside the city of Brunn.

My colleague and I were handcuffed, not allowed to speak to each other, and put in separate cells with people who spoke no English. The small rooms smelled of disinfectant and had only two bunk beds and a hole in the floor that served as the toilet. The light was kept on all night and some basic food was brought three times a day. The rules were rigid and enforced: no sitting or lying on the beds during the day. This meant shuffling backward and forward for hours in a highly restricted space, then facing a difficult night as we sought to sleep under the glare of the constant light.

Time became blurred. Was it morning, day, evening? I found myself alone, in a hostile place, without anything to read, without anyone to talk to, without any idea when or if we might be released, and with seeming unlimited (and empty) time on my hands. There is nothing like empty time and constricted space to bring to the surface feelings, questions, and doubts.

I did not choose this path for adventure; I was well aware of what we were up against and what might happen if we were caught. I was surprised by my intense feelings brought on by boredom and uncertainty—how long would this imprisonment last? Contrary to some of the more starry-eyed testimonies I have read, I did not experience overwhelming grace or a profound sense of God's presence. I did have the assurance that he was there, that he knew what was going on, and that "my times were in his hands" (see Ps. 31:15). My feelings, however, became a source of torment.

Why? For some reason I had an initial impression that we would be released quickly and expelled from the country. As the first few days passed with no communication and I had no idea what was happening, I began to wrestle to some degree with doubt. It was intense, it was real, and it was filling my mind and clouding my thoughts and my heart. My doubts seemed to focus on uncertainty as to what God was doing and whether I could actually trust what I thought was his leading. I also was struggling with how much I might be asked to face. I only had prayer and memories of those in Scripture who had faced similar things and the training sessions we had passed through in our team sessions in Vienna to resort to, so I struggled to regain focus and to rest and trust in God.

I can well remember a point of surrender. After several days, I resigned myself to the possibility that my imprisonment could last for years. I might not get out for a long time, so I had to make the best of what was and to rest in God. It is a point where we accept the hardship, where we still believe in greater good, and where we surrender to what seems like inevitability. I think I came to relinquish my sense and need for control (I had none anyway) and simply accept that God would be there as promised, and therefore, to rest in him.

I had crossed an important point that I subsequently discovered in the writings of Dietrich Bonhoeffer, Richard Wurmbrand, Alexander Solzhenitsyn, and Vaclav Havel. Scholar Roger Lundin remarks,

To Bonhoeffer, this is the distinctive "difference between Christianity and all religions." Our suffering, wrote Bonhoeffer only months before his 1943 arrest, teaches us "to see the great events of world history from below, from the perspective of the outcast, the suspects, the maltreated, the powerless." The interpretive key to human experience is to be found not in our preference for Eden but in our power to share in the sufferings of God and the world: "We have to learn that personal suffering is a more effective key, a more rewarding principle for exploring the world in thought and action than personal good fortune" (*Letters*, 17). *This* is what it means to see with a "god's-eye" view of things. From such a vantage point, Bonhoeffer asks, "How can success make us arrogant, or failure lead us astray, when we share in God's sufferings through a life of this kind?"[1]

In Matthew 11:1–4, we read the account of John the Baptist in prison. From the early part of the Gospels we often assume a picture of this robust prophet sent in advance of the Messiah, announcing boldly the one who is to come. Here, however, John is in prison. He does not know what will happen or how long he will be there. He faces a life that is out of control and unpredictable. From within the dark prison, he hears of Jesus' miracles and he begins to wonder. He is now not so sure and sends a messenger to ask Jesus, "Are you the one who was to come, or should we expect someone else?" (v. 3).

We cannot ignore John's earlier experiences and his announcement of who Jesus was in John 1:19–34. This same John is now in prison, now in very different circumstances, and he has doubts. Yet notice that Jesus does not launch into a harangue or respond, "How dare you doubt." He tells the messengers, "Go back and report to John what you hear and see: The blind receive sight, the lame walk, those who have leprosy are cured, the deaf hear, the dead are raised, and the good news is preached to the poor. Blessed is the man who does not fall away on account of me" (Matt. 11:4–6). Jesus provides some information and invites John to reflect on what is happening and to draw his conclusions from the great narrative of redemptive history and prophecy that John was aware of and of which Jesus was clearly implying he was a part.

That is, John's circumstances did not just descend on him in a vacuum. He was imprisoned because of his commitments and convictions, and above all, because of his identity and calling. His life was marked by God; he had a clear sense of destiny, and yet he did not know—*nor did he expect*—that it would turn out this way. Moreover, some time later he faced the day when an executioner in response to an embarrassed ruler came to take his head. This reality is a far cry from the easy believism or "Christianity lite" that is often trumpeted as the normal Christian life. John faced, and paid, the ultimate price of his calling.

As those raised in comfort and convenience, the very nature of all this may frighten or repel us. If the message we have believed or the model we have been taught has raised false expectations, then we are going to be subject to doubt and fear, and worse, reject the whole thing. The gospel and Christianity are concerned with reality, and hence with truth. By this I mean what the true nature of life really is and means. Christianity is not an escape system for us to avoid reality, live above it, or be able to redefine it. Christianity is a *way* that leads us to grasp what reality is and, by God's grace and help, to navigate through it to our eternal home.

Nothing quite hits home during our soulful experiences of doubt, pain, frustration, and disappointment. A friend of mine used to say, "Trials will make us bitter or better," and I have seen this demonstrated in many lives. Trials, persecutions, and problems may surface unresolved fear.

Perhaps we fear that all we believe is just an illusion, a lie, or a mere projection of our deepest desires (as Sigmund Freud asserted). Or perhaps we fear abandonment; we keep on believing God is there, but he seems to ignore us. Or maybe we fear that we do not have what it takes to suffer or endure, and so we face the personal battle of failure and ultimately, shame.

To anyone familiar with apologetics, C. S. Lewis stands out as a prominent figure. His philosophical reflections in *The Problem of Pain* are well known and stand within the long tradition of Christian thought on this topic. His work *A Grief Observed*, written in the furnace of intense suffering upon the sickness and death of his wife, Joy Davidman, reveals another dimension to this whole equation. Lewis writes in *The Problem of Pain*:

> Everyone has noticed how hard it is to turn our thoughts to God when everything is going well with us. We "'have all we want'" is a terrible saying when "'all'" does not include God. We find God an interruption. . . . Now God, who has made us, knows what we are and that our happiness lies in Him. Yet we will not seek it in Him as long as He leaves us any other resort where it can even plausibly be looked for. While what we call "'our own life'" remains agreeable we will not surrender it to Him. What then can God do in our interests but make 'our own life' less agreeable to us, and take away the plausible source of false happiness? It is just here, where God's providence seems at first to be most cruel, that the Divine humility, the stooping down of the Highest, most deserves praise.[2]

Like the psalmist, Lewis is honest; he expresses anger, doubts, and questions. He asks God for comfort and assurance, yet at times he feels as if heaven is closed for business, the doors locked and double bolted.

In such circumstances we are forced to face what we mean when we speak of faith. Do we have to believe in spite of the evidence to the contrary? Do we believe no matter what? How do we handle the deep and pressing questions our own minds bring as our expectations and reality do not match? For me, in my time in prison, I expected God to do certain things, and to do them in a sensible way and time. I expected that God would act fairly quickly and that I would sense his intervention. My reading of Scripture, my grasp of God's promises, my trust in the reliability of God's Word, the teaching I had received, and the message I had embraced led me to expect certain things, and in a particular way. When this did not occur in the way I expected or in the timing that I thought it should, I was both confused and angry.

Was God ignoring me? Was there some higher, hidden purpose that I was to somehow fulfill yet was denied any access to what it was? Had I been sold a lie? God in his mercy allows us to express our fears, our doubts, our anger, yet he also leads us to face the true nature of reality, of his character and ways, and the true nature of spiritual warfare. What did I learn in the furnace of doubt?

First, I learned *the role of prayer.* I found that prayer is an active, ongoing, and vital conversation with God in the midst of struggle and doubt.

Second, I learned the *role of reflection.* I thought about the great stories of the Bible and God's promises. In this, my memory of Scripture, songs, testimonies, and promises was crucial. What did they mean, and how did they apply here and now?

Finally, I learned *the role of struggle.* As much as I disliked it, there was no denying that struggle was all through the Bible, in the life of Jesus, and across church history.

The great story of Shadrach, Meshach, and Abednego in Daniel 3 captures this lesson powerfully. Though prisoners of a militaristic empire, these three believers find themselves in the employment of the top government. Then the king passes a decree that puts their primary loyalty to God in question and demands their full obedience. Yet their convictions will not allow them to deny their God, compromise their faith, and commit idolatry. When faced with their uncompromising stance, King Nebuchadnezzar does what many power-addicted rulers do: he threatens them with an all-or-nothing choice. "Furious with rage, Nebuchadnezzar summoned Shadrach, Meshach and Abednego. . . . 'If you are ready to fall down and worship the image I made, very good. But if you do not worship it, you will be thrown immediately into a blazing furnace. Then what god will be able to rescue you from my hand?'" (Dan. 3:13–15).

In this cameo, we see a scenario that has been repeated across history time and time again. It is okay to believe so long as you know and accept the limits permitted. You can believe what you want privately, but when a public demand intersects with your "personal" convictions, you are expected—no, you are *required*—to conform to society's demands, and to do so quickly and without reservation. There are many examples of this.

Dietrich Bonhoeffer was quick to grasp the totalitarian nature of the Nazis and the way that theology, church leadership, and state power could all be used to demand total subservience to the Nazi state and its policies. As with many in the time of the Roman Empire, the issue was who was king: Caesar or Christ? Hitler or Jesus? Bonhoeffer not only resisted Hitler's policies, but he was also actively involved in an attempt to stop him. Bonhoeffer's theological reflections, honest questions, and prayers before God invite us to weigh the implications of truly trying to follow Christ, even unto death.

Alister McGrath astutely observes,

> God is revealed and human experience is illuminated through the cross of Jesus Christ. Yet, as the believer contemplates the appalling spectacle of the suffering and dying Christ, he is forced to the recognition that God does not appear to be there at all, and the only human experience to be seen is apparently pointless suffering. If God *is* to be found in the cross of Christ, then he is hidden in the mystery; if human experience *is* illuminated by that cross, then the experiences which are illuminated are those of suffering, abandonment, powerlessness and hopelessness, culminating in death. Either God is not present at all in this situation, or else he is present in a remarkable and paradoxical way.[3]

When the time came to face the hangman's rope, Bonhoeffer committed his soul into the hands of God and went quietly to his death. Likewise, Shadrach, Meshach, and Abednego gave an astonishing answer to King Nebuchadnezzar and his ultimatum, and thus revealed something even more potent: "If we are thrown into the blazing furnace, the God we serve is able to save us from it, and he will rescue us from your hand, O king. But even if he does not, we want you to know, O king, that we will not serve your gods or worship the image of gold you have set up" (Dan. 3:17–18).

Here is a classic case of speaking truth to power. These men were thrown into events they had no control over, yet their faith rooted them in God and gave them the courage and determination to choose the right thing in spite of the obvious consequences. I am confident that silent prayer, deeply ingrained memories, and their reflection of God's character contributed to their ability to stand. Specifically, these three men knew that God was real, holy, and in control. They recognized that their lives were in danger, yet they were not willing to compromise. They knew God *could* deliver them, but they did not know if he *would*. Either way, they would not compromise or dishonor God.

Maybe we want to psychoanalyze Shadrach, Meshach, and Abednego and ask why they were so extreme. Perhaps we assume they were just among the courageous few we see occasionally in history. I don't think so. I think this narrative in Daniel 3 is given to cause us to reflect deeply on the nature of reality and truth. If we don't have some sense of what is really real, then we cannot live truthfully or in correspondence with reality.

Once again, Alister McGrath captures this well: "In effect we are forced to turn our eyes from contemplation of where we would like to see God revealed, and to turn them instead upon a place which is not of our own choosing, but which is given to us. As the history of human thought demonstrates, we like to find God in the beauty of nature, in the brilliance of an inspired human work of art or in the depths of our own being—and instead, we must recognize that the sole authorised symbol of the Christian faith is a scene of dereliction and carnage."[4]

Shadrach, Meshach, and Abednego learned that this is a God-created and a God-governed world. Because it is created, they knew that living in conformity to God's will was the only way to truly function. Their view of reality was fuller than that of Nebuchadnezzar, and because of this they were confident that *doing* the right thing *was* the right thing. Because God governs the world, they knew that justice was ultimately in God's hands, not the king's. They were, therefore, willing to make a hard choice no matter where it would lead.

Many times as we traverse the world speaking to diverse audiences, we are questioned on issues related to God, truth, and other religions. These questions come from a worldview and life view perspective, as does our response. The question is whether our view deals adequately with reality and is, in fact, truthful.

In their useful book *Ten Theories of Human Nature*, Leslie Stevenson and David L. Haberman delineate four elements that they discovered as a common structure in a wide variety of philosophical systems and religions.[5] They are the core questions that lie at the heart of the diverse views of our human condition. What are these four elements, provided by life's experiences and our reflections on them?

1. A background theory of the universe.
2. A theory about the nature of man.
3. A diagnosis of what is wrong.
4. A prescription for putting it right.

Since I had never given any conscious thought to worldviews in general or mine in particular, I was unaware how many unexamined assumptions I was living by. I did not realize how little change had penetrated my heart, and under pressure the gaps were painfully revealed and felt. From the perspective of time, I can now answer these questions meaningfully, but I needed the experience of doubt and hardship to show me how much I did not know or was not rooted in the biblical answers to these core questions. A worldview that merely answers questions intellectually is insufficient; it must also meet us existentially where we have to live.

Persecution, struggle, and pain force us to face what is the nature of reality. How do things really work? What kind of a world is this? As I went into the Czechoslovakian prison, it was with several deep convictions. I believed that God really exists, that he is the Creator and sustainer of the world, that he oversees reality, and that he is present with us by the Holy Spirit. I believed (and still believe) he is a God of purpose, and his will is paramount in history. Even if we cannot discern what is at stake, God is present and working in strange places and in unseen ways.

Yet significantly, the beliefs that brought comfort also became part of my struggle. What should I expect from God? How might he intervene and in what way? I found that I had to let go of demands, expectations, and frustrations, and to embrace uncertainty, helplessness, and silence, even though it was hard. The limitations of my human perspective seemed to press in on me at times with a weight I wished I could overcome. I was to a large extent unable to grasp how deep and how sinister were the implications of living in a disordered, disrupted world until these unwanted experiences surfaced levels of doubt or questions, until then hidden from my own consciousness.

Martin Luther used the term "the God of glory" to describe the God who animates most believers' imaginations and hopes. That is, we want a God who intervenes on demand, smashes our enemies, relieves our sufferings, and solves all our problems quickly, painlessly, and finally. Luther was well acquainted with the god of the philosophers and with the many speculations of theologians regarding who God was, what God could or could not do, and how things really worked. Luther found that the everyday Christian was unimpressed and unhelped by what he described as "the naked God" of the philosophers. This is a god of our imaginations, of our desires, of our own creation. This god could come from deeply rational theology or from significant philosophical reflection, but the portrait is not one given from the Scriptures but rather from human effort, reflection, and imagination. What God had given, what his answer was, was the clothed God in Jesus Christ (John 1:14–18). Jesus was, and is, the center of reality, the lens through which we must view and interpret all things. The incarnation and the cross were not mere sideshows in the grand cosmic drama. They were and are the central event. All of reality, all of experience, all of life, must be weighed in the light of these crucial happenings.

Luther's remedy was not in a system, in an idea, or in concepts. His call was to look to Christ and to embrace his way. Clearly Luther experienced a significant transformation in his own life, and his preaching, writing, and actions have influenced many since. In 1518, as Luther addressed his fellow Augustinian monks on his theology of the cross, he alluded to Exodus 33 and what he called "the back parts of God." What we often think is the absence of God, because of our contradictory experiences, turns out to be something else.

In the foreword to Alister McGrath's *The Mystery of the Cross,* scholar James Atkinson writes, "But it is of decisive importance to see what Luther taught was not that God was somehow there, *in spite of* defeat, sorrow, pain, humiliation, anguish, failure, sin and death. Not at all! He taught that God himself confronts us in person and makes his presence near *in and through* defeat, sorrow, pain, humiliation, anguish, failure, sin and death."[6] This is the part I also struggled to grasp and to accept. That God was really present in my weakness, in the experience of powerlessness, in the inability to help myself in any significant way.

Atkinson continues, "The 'contrary things' of failure, sin and death constitute the raw material which God transforms into his own self in the human heart. God reveals himself through a contrary form. It is the back of God which is revealed—but it *is* God, and not another. To learn this is to learn Christ. To know this at first hand, to have the mystery of the cross so explained, is to have tapped the very source and spring of Christian faith."[7]

One aspect that came to the fore and that is central to all I have been writing is the nature and problem of evil and suffering. One of the expectations raised by the Christian view of life is what degree of transformation we can or should expect now. Like Luther, I have high views of God, Scripture, and of God's purpose in history. Yet there is much at stake in the gap between expectation and life as it unfolds.

It seems that because I expect more from God for life, I believe I should see more answers, intervention, and change than I actually do! This desire often leads to a vast internal or analytical quest. Are my beliefs inadequate or flawed? Am I lacking insight into how to put it all into practice? Is there something I have not grasped or that I am unwilling to grasp?

I find it personally helpful to reflect on history and on major events. I try to imagine what it was like to live then, what it would have been like to face some of the challenges that others have faced. In the early 1990s, a friend joined me at a conference in Germany, and when it was over, we left on what was to be a brief historical and philosophical tour. I wanted to show him where Adolf Hitler addressed the mass Nazi rallies in Nuremberg. I wanted my friend to see Nietzsche's archive in Weimar, and then we would go on to Berlin and look at the impact of the Nazi and the Communist years.

At one point, we stood in Zeppelin Field—one of the places designed by Hitler's architect Albert Speer—at the very podium where Hitler had stood in the 1930s and proclaimed his Thousand-Year Reich. Though this regime was long gone, having lasted a mere twelve years, it brought untold brutality and suffering on the world. A few days later we stood beside a dilapidated building in former East Germany where I had also been interrogated and arrested. We stood outside the window of the very room where I was questioned for several days. In that moment I was overcome with emotion, and I well remembered Malcolm Muggeridge's comments on these "powers" now all gone with the wind (see Isa. 40:21–25).

My dear friend Chip and I discussed the seeming invincibility of these human systems. When the Nazis and the Communists ruled, they were overwhelming, brutal, and domineering. Yet in God's time, they suddenly came to an end. As I reflect on this now, I realize how difficult it is for many of us to balance the immediate and the eternal. In other words, we are children of our time, and our expectations and desires are often governed by a sense of the immediate, the short term, the now. We lack or we do not develop a historical and long view approach to things.

Without devaluing any of the individual suffering that occurs, we need a big-picture view of suffering as well, in which we consider the whole drama. Indeed, one of the reasons Shadrach, Meshach, and Abednego could respond to Nebuchadnezzar with such boldness was their assurance that God is the Creator and sovereign over all, who holds all history, rulers, and events in his hands. This ability to see beyond, to believe in the face of darkness, to triumph through suffering is a vital aspect of the Holy Spirit's transforming role in our lives and in the reframing of our view of reality, and therefore, of truth.

As a Christian facing such difficulties, the battle with our emotions becomes crucial. Did Daniel's friends experience fear and doubt? Did John the Baptist? Did Bonhoeffer? The answer, I think, is *yes*. It is part of what it means to be human. Yet it is also one of the vast hurdles to be faced in our time. This is the age of therapy, the domination of market values, where looking good and feeling good replace being good and doing good—and most people don't know the difference. Feelings and emotional states have been elevated and promoted to such a degree that the domination of emotions and the demand for good feelings, all the time, is imbibed with the air that we breathe.

If we think *this* is reality, and if we are submerged in perpetual stimulation from media and advertising that says it is true, then we face an uphill battle with the demands and expectations we then encounter in our relationship with God. What we think and feel is reality, is in fact, a system of alternatives and deceit that serves to blind us to our real condition. Ephesians 2:1–3 is a powerful commentary on how the Bible unveils reality for us. We live in a context that keeps us as slaves of a hidden power (remember *The Matrix*?) and prevents us from asking the right questions or pursuing the path that leads to real (but difficult) life. Second Corinthians 4:4 reveals that we must face active, living, intelligent, and malevolent forces of evil that interfere to prevent us from seeing. It is hard to recognize and admit that the world is indeed corrupted, disordered, damaged, and dangerous.

In a very real sense, part of the journey of transformation in the believer's life is becoming aware of our false expectations and the true nature of the world we have to live in and face, which the Bible reminds us is still afflicted by dark powers and forces (Eph. 6:10–12). Throughout our lives and our journeys, we are compelled to ask questions of our beliefs, our values, and our experiences. Perhaps the question is, how does God work in forming us and transforming us? Do these experiences of pressure, suffering, and doubt actually contribute to our growth, and more, are they (in reality) part of the ways and means God employs to achieve his ends?

Something in us seems to recoil at this. Well, let me qualify that: something in the Western mind, excluding those reared in the Catholic tradition, recoils at this. However, I think we must admit that it is justified biblically; it is supported by experience, history, and testimony; and it makes sense if we situate our thinking in the biblical data and worldview.

The Christian view of life and history sees all of life as contested (see Eph. 6:10–12). This aspect of the story is not tangential; it is central. We indwell a great cosmic conflict that rages 24/7 and knows no neutral zones or cease-fires. One thing I learned in my experience in prison was the reality of truth, goodness, and beauty. I had taken these for granted; I assumed I knew what they were and that they were common to everyone, that they were shared. In the confines of my atheistic prison, I learned that other values, beliefs, and priorities superseded these and by their very absence were affirmed! The pressures came at the level of self-doubt, like an internal, tormenting voice, constantly whispering, *Why endure this? Is this really worth it?*

When circumstances restrict our choices and unpredictability reigns, we are forced to come to terms with the nature of reality. I found that my experience raised questions that forced me to clarify my own beliefs, sharpen my own thinking, and to decide what really mattered in life.

I had no idea that the interrogations I endured would provide a model for how I would later share the gospel publicly. The apostle Peter exhorts us to be prepared to give answers for the hope that we have (1 Peter 3:15). My colleague in England, Michael Ramsden, argues that this hope is specific. This hope is unique. This hope is inseparable from Christ and his cross. I learned in the press of life that whether or not this hope was real and true was, in fact, the core issue.

I needed to cultivate the skills and the thinking that would allow me to intelligently respond to questions, but also enable me to dwell comfortably in the gospel and to own its implications and its costs, even if that involved suffering, pain, and possibly death.

Shortly after my colleague and I were released from the Czechoslovakian prison, we spent a few days at a retreat center in Austria. We were quite weak from our imprisonment, but we were also soon energized by being together and with our other teammates, and by being able to share our testimonies and to pray freely. I cannot honestly say we were deeply affected at the time by the whole experience—perhaps due to our youth—for we quickly absorbed it and considered it a small price to pay for the privilege of serving our Lord.

At the Austrian retreat center I took the opportunity to write to my parents, who at that time did not follow the Lord as I did. I realized that there was a real possibility that I might end up a long time in prison or worse. I did not want that to happen, and I did not seek it, but it became more and more evident that it was an intrinsic aspect of following Christ in a fallen and often hostile world. I wanted my parents to understand that if they received news one day that I had been arrested, and if my life was taken in the course of this kind of ministry, they needed to know I had chosen this with full awareness of the potential cost.

I was not coerced; I had not been brainwashed. I was not being driven to prove something. If the worst were to happen, I told them I would embrace it willingly because of the reality of Christ in my life, the assurance of his will for me, and my hope in his ultimate destiny for me. I sent the letter, and it brought an immediate response from my parents. They understood what I was saying, and though concerned, they supported my resolve.

I wish I could say that it has been easy to maintain this assurance, but I cannot. The ongoing struggle with doubt is a painful one, and one that hits certain types of personalities with a force that others do not feel. I have seldom doubted God, or his Word, or the arguments for the Christian message. My doubts tend to come as a result of disappointment with people, from hypocrisy (my own and others'), and from the mess and muddle of life. My doubts have been fueled at times in regard to the residual and ongoing battles I have had in my own heart and mind. Why do I still do such selfish things? Why do I say such hurtful things at times? What does it take to enter into a more gentle, meek, gracious, and kind life and way?

These existential questions have a powerful weight to them, and in my reflective and rational moments I see clear answers:

- The biblical description of the Fall and its ongoing impact with the redemption of our bodies (Rom. 8:19–23).
- The current presence of active, intelligent, and malevolent powers arrayed against God's people, way, and kingdom.
- Living in the presence of those who both reject Christ and who follow other "lords."

- Living in a context where values, lifestyles, and views vastly contradictory to truth, goodness, and beauty are often the norm.
- The tension of living in hope and being willing to endure until the work of God is completed.

Paul speaks in Romans 8 of the "anxious longing" of the whole creation. He compares this suffering to the pains of childbirth. He says that even as we "groan within ourselves," we also "wait eagerly." He reminds us of the Spirit's role and work: he helps us in our weakness (Rom. 8:26). This presence of God with us is a vital key to how we face life and how we can endure.

The Trinitarian vision of God has served to sustain me in many different ways. What do I mean? As I journeyed into my life of faith I came to grasp (not very well) the historic teachings regarding the nature of God. To see that God is a community of love, that he existed in self-giving relationships before the creation, and that he took on himself flesh in order to redeem us, was an awesome discovery. The gift and life of the Holy Spirit was the final link in tying together what was for me, a vague notion. This universe is a relational order, and I was now tuned in by virtues of God's grace, mercy, and enabling love. This understanding of God allowed me to dwell on God the Father, the Sovereign, the ruler, the God who humbled Egypt and led his people in the wilderness. It also allowed me to consider Jesus as the incarnate one, the suffering servant, who although God in the flesh, restrained himself, sought out sinners, and gave his life in such an unselfish way. The Father ruling, governing, guiding; the Son in his example, service, and sacrifice, followed by the Spirit in his comfort, keeping, power, and presence (John 14:26). All these have been vital in my reflections.

How has this helped practically? It has meant that many times I could rest in the assurance of God's ultimate and good control over life and circumstances. Even though I had to face questions, I recognized my limitations and found comfort in the sense of God's sovereign rule. The example of Jesus continues to inspire and fuel a longing to be more like him: to follow his way, to respond as he responded, to treat people as he treated them, to love as he loved. The assurance of the Spirit's presence and help has met me in many ways, as I travel, preach, face questions, and seek to wrestle through issues.

The metaphor of the journey has also been very important to me, and is, I believe, an important feature of the biblical message. John Bunyan famously pictured this in *The Pilgrim's Progress,* and C. S. Lewis followed in his *The Pilgrim's Regress.* The metaphor of the journey reminds me of a beginning, a setting out, the need for provisions, rest, and sustenance on the way. It also raises issues of direction, delays, dangers, and of course, all that is involved in completing the journey safely and successfully.

My journey began in Glasgow, Scotland, when at the age of twenty-one I was challenged by the existence of God and specifically by the person of Christ. My initial revulsion turned to curiosity and then to surprise as I surrendered to Christ and was changed by him. Once the reality of God was clear to me, everything else was up for grabs. My life and lifestyle began to change. I began to learn of new values, new ways of being, and of things that had to go in my life. It did not all happen at once, but what began, remained steady.

I had no idea that the journey would take me so far or that it would involve so much. It was 1977 when I began to follow Christ, and in 1978 I was on my way to full-time Christian service to the then Communist bloc (all of Eastern Europe, and the Soviet Union). The journey would lead me to places, people, and situations where growth was demanded and where I would have to learn how to respond to specific questions and to face challenging situations or threats.

I learned several things through facing persecution, struggle, and doubt.

- I needed to face my inadequacies and work at what Scripture calls the renewing of my mind (Rom. 12:2; Eph. 4:23).
- I needed to explore other ideas, worldviews, and systems and see how I could respond effectively to their claims.
- I needed to address my own spiritual needs and work on prayer, trust, self-awareness, and whatever disciplines were necessary to shore up my heart.
- I learned that because I did not have an answer or could not give an answer, it did not mean that an answer did not exist that someone else could give!
- I learned that the Christian life is reasonable, it is sufficient, but it is not safe (if we mean a guarantee of problem-free living).

Reality as I had understood it was "other" than I thought. It was not just my journey from an unbelieving, atheistic worldview to a Christian one; it has been progressive exploration, correction, and transformation of what was often an idealized and romanticized Christian one. Reality, I have learned, is harder, more difficult, more demanding, and more complex than I was willing to admit or embrace. My illusions, false beliefs, and sincere but wrong thinking have been challenged and changed, often in the furnace of adversity.

One of my favorite word pictures from C. S. Lewis is the one in *The Lion, the Witch, and the Wardrobe*, where the Pevensie children hear from Mrs. Beaver about Aslan, the great king of Narnia, who they discover is a great lion. In a wonderful exchange, Lucy asks, "Is he safe?" Mrs. Beaver replies, "Oh no dearie, he's not safe, but he is good."[8] This aspect of God is something I have had to come to terms with, and one I suspect that many refuse to fully embrace. We want a God of predictability, a God of order, a God we can understand and figure out.

Thus, it is profoundly disturbing to our theologies, well-honed beliefs, and carefully considered positions that God seldom does what we expect and even more rarely what we demand. He is a God of surprises, of true holiness, of great wisdom, power, and love. He is also God alone, and by nature of his being, position, holiness, and power, he is not required to respond to our every whim or demand for more information or better explanations!

One of my colleagues often responds to a situation or some difficulty with the statement, "It is what it is." He exhorts us to accept the reality of things (often some kind of difficulty) and to move on. Perhaps this is one of the central lessons of persecution and doubt: the Holy Spirit comes to us in times of struggle and sorrow and tells us, "It is what it is"—not so that we surrender to some form of fatalism or determinism, but so that we can then invite God, by his grace, to intervene and to lead us on. God sometimes changes the situation, but more often, he changes us in the situation. It is not an either/or issue, as I am happy when both the circumstances and my attitudes are changed!

God's intervention does not always come in ways we expect (though sometimes it does); however, it does come. Here again Alister McGrath is insightful:

> For Paul, death and life, weakness and strength, suffering and glory, wisdom and folly, sorrow and joy, are all interwoven in the remarkable event of the cross. Paul's understanding of both the mission of Jesus Christ and Christian existence itself is dominated by such cross-centred themes of life in death and strength in weakness. The full force of Paul's insights is missed if we interpret him as teaching that we

can have life *despite* death and strength *despite* weakness: for Paul, the remarkable meaning of the enigma of the cross is that life comes *through* death and strength *through* weakness.[9]

It may be a direct experience of grace; it may be mediated through another person, book, or sermon. The point is, in a God-governed and purpose-driven cosmos, nothing is in vain and nothing should be ignored or neglected. Bill Smith, a friend of mine, often exhorts people to cultivate the "gift of noticing." By this he means actively looking for God's presence and grace in the everyday things we often ignore.

It may be in the beauty of creation, in the smile of a friend or a spouse, in the aroma and taste of a good meal, in the joy of robust laughter, in the pleasure of a good book or movie. When we work at noticing, we begin to "see" more, to enjoy more, and to celebrate more.

Daniel's three friends became aware of a presence in the midst of the furnace and in the midst of their trial. Bonhoeffer also wrote touchingly of his experience in the Nazi prison and in the face of death. It was not just the ability to endure, but the transforming work of God in their lives that was crucial and practical. We see God at work in the big picture, even at times as we may lose perspective or sight in the details. To me this is one of the greatest lessons and the biggest challenges we face.

As I sat thinking, praying, and hoping in the custody of the Czechoslovakian authorities, I was surprised one day when the door opened and I was summoned forth, signaled not to speak, and then led out to a waiting car with my colleague, whom I was just seeing after ten or eleven days. We were driven in silence to the border. We were handed our passports and our severely damaged vehicle, and we were then expelled from the country.

We crossed into Austria and were able to talk for the first time in nearly two weeks. We shared our stories, and we stopped and prayed. We heard missing details; we discovered ways that God worked in us. We shared how we could witness and testify. We spoke of our struggles, our doubts, and our overall confidence. We did not doubt God was there, or that he had a purpose in our arrest, interrogation, and imprisonment. We sensed that somehow, in some way, we were part of an ongoing cosmic drama in which these events played a small but meaningful role. It was not an experience we would choose, and it was not the way we expected, but it was God's will for us at that time and we could see and testify that it had changed us.

It was many years later that I read things that made sense of many of my experiences. I find that the theology of the cross is one of the most vital lessons in coming to terms with the true nature of reality. Alister McGrath sums it up well:

> The "word of the cross" is not to be identified with God—it points beyond itself to the greater personal reality underlying it. It identifies a pattern of divine presence and activity, supremely disclosed by the cross and resurrection, which both illuminates and transforms human existence. It invites its hearers to read this pattern of divine presence and activity into their own existence, to make the connection between the death and resurrection of Jesus Christ and their own situation. It is an invitation to read the story of our own lives in the light of the cross and resurrection, in order that we may realise the "word of the cross" addresses *us*.[10]

It would be presumptuous to turn our limited experience and insight into a major pattern for all, yet in the midst of it we were able to detect broader strokes, hidden meanings, and real possibilities. Like Joseph so many centuries before, we could look back on all that happened, reflect on it and say, "They meant it for evil, but God meant it for good" (Gen. 50:20).

13

IDOLATRY, DENIAL, AND SELF-DECEPTION:
HEARTS ON PILGRIMAGE THROUGH THE VALLEYS

Danielle DuRant

In this chapter we will consider idolatry, denial, self-deception, and the various valleys in which we may find ourselves on our journey with God. In *The Pilgrim's Progress,* John Bunyan envisions some of these settings in Christian's passage to the Celestial City: the Valley of the Shadow of Death, By-Path Meadow, Vanity Fair. Like Christian, we may feel fearful of or want to settle in certain places. Yet thankfully, as Bunyan details, Christian had Faithful and then Hopeful to accompany him on his journey. Likewise, we have the Counselor, the Spirit of truth, who reveals God's Word (John 14:16–17) and the fellowship of believers as companions. Such relationships are vital if we are to grow in Christlikeness and persevere in faith through the valleys. Indeed, the Scriptures insist that our knowledge of God, our world, and ourselves is relational and reciprocal. We are dependent creatures made in our triune God's image: Father, Son, and Holy Spirit in relationship with one another. We are persons in relation to other persons, and we know subjects in relation to other subjects.

In his seminal work *Personal Knowledge,* scientist Michael Polanyi contends that all knowing is personal: each of us brings tacit assumptions and our own art of knowing as we relate to information and formulate questions and views. Even a scientist comes to an investigation with particular skills, imagination, and interests that may inform or limit his or her discovery. Additionally, we do not know mere propositions out there—for example, "the universe exists"—for to know this truth necessarily implies some sort of relationship with the subject. Christian philosopher Esther Lightcap Meek explains, "Knowing involves statements, but it doesn't mistakenly divorce those statements from the knower who is affirming them. . . . Knowing is, at its heart, an act. To act is to live, embody, knowledge. The act of knowing is a profoundly human one. And it is a struggle toward coherence."[1]

John Calvin begins his first chapter "The Knowledge of God the Creator" in *Institutes of the Christian Religion* with this subheading: "The Knowledge of God and That of Ourselves Are Connected." He continues, "*Without knowledge of self there is no knowledge of God.* Nearly all the wisdom we possess, that is to say, true and sound wisdom, consists of two parts: the knowledge of God and of ourselves."[2] Calvin observes that we know ourselves only as we come to know God, and we know God as we in turn gain knowledge of ourselves through his Word, the work of his Holy Spirit in us, and the fellowship of his church. This knowledge is integrative and mirrored in relationship. It's not just that we know, but also that *we are known and begin to live in the light of this awareness.* Consider, for instance, when you first really took notice of your spouse-to-be or a dear friend. Once, the person was just a name, a face, and shared information, but seemingly overnight his smile brings you a delight you had not known in his company before, and his eyes disclose a part of you that you had not seen. You begin to see him in a different light, and you yourself are different in the light of this knowledge.

Yet in this earthly journey, we see and know only in part (1 Cor. 13:12). Perhaps the late Christian apologist Greg Bahnsen overstates his explanation, but even secular scholars concur with his assessment of our complex souls: "There is something of a cognitive mess at the core of our lives. We are inconsistent in our choices, incoherent in our convictions, persuaded where we ought not to be, and deluded that we know ourselves transparently."[3]

By way of introduction then—taking my cues from the authors cited above— I want to suggest that one accurate measure of our relationship with God and our understanding of ourselves may be assessed by our prayer life. Our words are witnesses, both revealing and concealing what we believe about God and ourselves in relation to him. And my thesis is this: *Our knowledge of God and the degree to which we are willing to entrust ourselves to who he has revealed himself to be can limit or foster our spiritual growth.* If we have a false or inadequate understanding of

God, we may guard ourselves from him or find counterfeit comfort in our imagined idea and thus not give ourselves to him fully. When I speak of "our knowledge of God," I mean essentially our *relationship with him* and our *understanding of ourselves in relation to him,* for we have seen thus far that all knowing is personal. So we may stagnate or grow depending upon *both* our "knowledge of God and of ourselves." Using the biblical metaphor of pilgrimage, we will examine the subtle valleys of idolatry, denial, and other places we may find ourselves in the sometimes painful journey of spiritual growth. Lastly, we will want to consider how we experience transformation.

Words Left Unspoken

"My name is Ruth. I grew up with my younger sister, Lucille, under the care of my grandmother, Mrs. Sylvia Foster, and when she died, of her sisters-in-law, Misses Lily and Nona Foster, and when they fled, of her daughter, Mrs. Sylvia Fisher."[4] So begins *Housekeeping,* the highly praised first novel by Marilynne Robinson, who was awarded the 2005 Pulitzer Prize for her second novel, *Gilead.* The story takes place in Fingerbone, a small town set on a glacial lake, and is told through the teenage Ruth, whose hesitant voice is often understated. For instance, notice in her one sweeping sentence not only what has been said, but also what has *not* been said. Where is her mother? Where is her father? And what do we make of "when they [her great aunts] *fled?*" Ruth's words both reveal and conceal, taking the form of confession and denial. The story's setting upon icy waters is an apt metaphor for the coldness this young girl has endured. "Memory is the sense of loss," says Ruth, "and loss pulls us after it."[5] Thus throughout the novel she carefully reconstructs her life story to keep the dark undercurrents of loss and confusion at bay.

I have been consistently humbled by this truth: the sentences we speak about our lives to others, and especially to ourselves, shape our understanding of who we are and who we hope to be. This is no less the case in prayer. The words we utter when we come before God are a reflection of what we believe and what we hope from him. Yet this reflection is like seeing ourselves refracted upon the surface of a lake: it is not quite accurate. "Everything that falls upon the eye is apparition, a sheet dropped over the world's true workings," suggests young Ruth.[6] Similarly, Esther Lightcap Meek writes, "We labor under the misimpression that we see what we see, that seeing is believing, that either I see it or I don't."[7]

For example, several years ago I picked up Catherine Marshall's book *Adventures in Prayer.* I vaguely recall reading the first chapter, "Prayer Is Asking," concluding, "Well, of course it is," and setting the book aside.[8] It was not until recently that I discovered that simple truth—prayer is *asking*—suggests we set our whole hearts before God, to name our questions, longings, and fears and to entrust them to our sovereign and all-knowing Creator. But I was not ready to do this with any specificity, let alone consider what I really thought about the One whom I was asking—though, having a master of divinity degree and long-term vocation in ministry, I could provide an accurate theological answer.

Identifying unspoken assumptions and presuppositions involves the law of identity, one of the first tasks of apologetics. I labor with this truth regularly, at least at a cognitive level. This law states that everything that exists has a *specific* nature—for example, B equals B or a sheep is a sheep (and not a cow). If someone remarks rather casually, "Sure, I believe in Jesus," we rely upon the law of identity when we ask w*ho* this Jesus is: "Do you mean the Jesus portrayed in the New Testament or in *The Da Vinci Code*?" Or we might follow up by asking the person to tell us what he or she means by "believe." In such conversations we discover that "belief in Jesus" may be radically different than what the Bible presents. Thus, it is critical to examine unspoken assumptions.

Recently I read Marshall's book again and came face-to-face with these sentences on prayer in her first chapter: "Soon we discern that asking involves more than verbalization. Our lips do not always communicate accurately the heart's true cry. In some instances, that's because we are so out of touch with our own emotions that our prayers deal in unrealities. Sometimes we are divided within ourselves about what we actually want, so that we cannot ask wholeheartedly. Or perhaps we do not even know enough about our hopes and dreams to make our asking specific."[9]

In other words, our prayers may resemble Ruth's glossing over her family's history. We may readily set our hearts before God yet circumvent or minimize certain doubts. Sometimes we avoid spelling out what we think and feel because we are not even cognizant of these thoughts and emotions. We may have a sense of uneasiness or anger, so words are left unspoken. This then begs the question Marshall alludes to: why don't we verbalize certain beliefs to God, and paradoxically, even to ourselves?

The apostle Paul tells us that "since the creation of the world God's invisible qualities—his eternal power and divine nature—have been clearly seen" (Rom.

1:20), but we "suppress the truth in unrighteousness" (v. 18 NASB). Paul is not only describing the confusion of unregenerate hearts, but he is also cautioning believers who know the truth of God to respond to it accordingly (see especially his argument in Rom. 2:1–24). He goes on to say, "They exchanged the truth of God for a lie, and worshiped and served created things rather than the Creator" (v. 25). So why do we sometimes suppress the truth or what we believe to be true? New Testament scholar F. F. Bruce poses a similar question in his commentary on Romans: "What is the cause, [Paul] asks, of this appalling condition that has developed in this world? . . . It all arises, he says, from *wrong ideas about God.*"[10]

INTO THE VALLEYS

The biblical writers suggest that wrong ideas about God may lead us to protect ourselves from him or mistakenly find comfort in a false view of him. It is critical to note at this juncture, however, that I am *not* saying—nor do I believe F. F. Bruce or, moreover, the Scriptures propose—that it is *always* the case that we don't verbalize certain beliefs because we "suppress the truth in unrighteousness" or have "wrong ideas about God." We may have several areas of unarticulated or underdeveloped knowledge of ourselves and God, akin to what Polanyi identifies as "tacit knowledge." As Michael Polanyi quips, "We know more than we can tell."[11] Over time our awareness can deepen as we begin to live in the light of knowing and being known through God's Word, church, and Spirit. We will examine this point further near the close of this chapter yet will also want to bear it in mind as we proceed through the complex terrain of idolatry, denial, and self-deception.

We may arrive at a distorted view of God through unorthodox doctrine or weak theology. Our misbeliefs amount to an inadequate understanding of him at best. We might ascertain that if God is all-knowing, wise, and loving, then surely he will fix this situation or respond in a certain manner. Perhaps we most often draw faulty conclusions about God through unmet expectations and painful experiences in our first relationships, especially with our parents. Often we carry these views into subsequent relationships. For instance, if we have been abandoned by betrayal or loss, we may not only filter our perception of others through such experience, but our perception of God as well. If we have matured in our faith, we might say that God knows best yet live with persistent, unspoken doubts whenever we come to him in prayer. Or maybe we have gone years without questioning his goodness and sovereignty only to find our faith unravel when enduring the death of a loved one or a particular crisis.

Left unexamined, such misbeliefs and heartaches can carry us into difficult valleys. Of course, let us not lose sight that peaks and valleys are part of the undulating landscape of our Christian journey, as Christian's passage in Bunyan's allegory so vividly reveals. This world is not our home. Scriptures tell us we are passing through as "strangers and exiles on the earth . . . seeking a homeland," "a better country, that is, a heavenly one" (Heb. 11:13–14, 16 ESV). Let us also hold fast to the promise that wherever we may be in our pilgrimage and whatever companions we know or lose along the way, we are *never alone*. We read of God in Psalm 139 that "if I make my bed in the depths, *you are there*. If I rise on the wings of the dawn, if I settle on the far side of the sea, even there your hand will guide me, your right hand will hold me fast. If I say, 'Surely the darkness will hide me and the light become night around me,' even the darkness will not be dark to you; the night will shine like the day, for darkness is as light to you" (vv. 8–12; emphasis added).

CREATOR OR CREATED GOD?

We have suggested that *our knowledge of God and the degree to which we are willing to entrust ourselves to who he has revealed himself to be can limit or foster our spiritual growth.* Our wrong ideas about God can take us into valleys where we may want to keep our distance from him or to settle in greener grasses where he appears controllable and always responds to our desires, whatever they may be. No matter our circumstances, our view of God will be consistently challenged, as even the prophets propose: "Who has understood the mind of the LORD, or instructed him as his counselor? Whom did the LORD consult to enlighten him, and who taught him the right way? Who was it that taught him knowledge or showed him the path of understanding? . . . To whom, then, will you compare God? What image will you compare him to?" (Isa. 40:13–14, 18).

In chapter 40, Isaiah portrays God as both a shepherd who "gathers the lambs in his arms and carries them close to his heart" (v. 11) and mighty Creator who "calls [the stars] each by name" (v. 26). Elsewhere we encounter other striking antonyms for God. He is the Lion and the Lamb, warrior and suffering servant. Ultimately, he is the Holy One (Isa. 40:25), the eternal I AM who is altogether unlike us (Ps. 50:21) and "who alone is wise" (Jude 25). So Isaiah rightly asks, "To whom, then, will you compare God?" Likewise, Job ultimately confesses to God, "You asked, 'Who is this that obscures my counsel without knowledge?' Surely I spoke of things I did not understand, things too wonderful for me to know" (Job 42:3).

Consequently, a relationship with God will necessarily involve awe, reverence, humility, and surrender. For us to ignore such a reality is to deny his very nature. Yet according to the Scriptures, as human beings, we are prone to do just that; we often believe we fully understand our desires and goals and may question God's wisdom and justice when they are thwarted. Whether deliberately or unconsciously, we sometimes operate under the misimpression that our desires are ultimate and that God is just another means by which we may accomplish our plans. We may suppress the truth of God and his sovereign claim upon our lives through misdirected affections, unexamined beliefs, and willful denial. Suppressing this truth, the skeptic attempts to resist the signs of God's existence, though "his eternal power and divine nature have been clearly perceived, ever since the foundation of the world" (Rom. 1:20 ESV), whereas the believer may attempt to avoid God and seek his or her own desires.

Notice that this is essentially what Paul argues in Romans 1: "They exchanged the truth of God for a lie, and worshiped and served created things rather than the Creator" (v. 25). F. F. Bruce comments, "These wrong ideas about God did not arise innocently; the knowledge of the true God was accessible, but men and women closed their minds to it. Instead of appreciating the glory of the Creator by contemplating the universe which he created, they gave to created things that glory which belongs to God alone. *Idolatry is the source of immorality . . . it is a deliberate ignorance. . . .* The truth was accessible to them, but they suppressed it unrighteously and embraced the 'lie' in preference to it."[12]

THE VALLEY OF IDOLATRY

Bruce contends that the Scriptures have a name for wrong ideas about God, whether misbeliefs or "deliberate ignorance": *it is idolatry*. This may seem a strong indictment, but the biblical writers consistently show that false beliefs and misdirected affections may sometimes lead us into the valley of idolatry. For example, why do the Israelites construct a golden calf in Moses' absence? Because they wrongly conclude that God has forgotten them. Why does Israel enter into alliances with other nations though God explicitly forbids them? Because in fear they entrust themselves to another sovereign whom they hope will protect them. Why does the craftsman fashion an idol of silver and gold? Because he foolishly ascribes to these inanimate elements the power that belongs to God alone. Regarding this person, Isaiah declares pointedly, "He feeds on ashes, a deluded heart misleads him; he cannot save himself, or say, 'Is not this thing in my right hand a lie?'" (44:20). This valley of idolatry is not mere metaphor: wayward Israel even sacrifices its own children to pagan gods in the Valley of Ben Hinnom, *gehenna* in the New Testament—the word Jesus uses for hell (see 2 Kings 23:10; Jer. 7:3–31, 19:1–6; Matt. 5:22).

What is idolatry? It is "treating what is not ultimate as though it were ultimate, making absolute what is only relative," says Emory professor Luke Timothy Johnson.[13] Whenever we deem a particular relationship or goal an absolute necessity—I *must* have *this*—we are in danger of idolatry. According to Martin Luther, whatever your heart clings to and relies upon, that is your God. "An idol is something within creation that is inflated to function as a substitute for God," suggests Dick Keyes.[14] "Since an idol is a counterfeit, it is a lie. Deception is its very identity. . . . Rather than look to the Creator and have to deal with His lordship, we orient our lives toward the creation, where we can be more free to control and shape our desired directions."[15] David's seizing Bathsheba for his own pleasure and Jacob and Rebekah's scheming for his brother Esau's birthright are two further biblical examples.

Idolatry distorts our knowledge of God, ourselves, and others. Since the Scriptures repeatedly address this concern, we will examine this valley's topography in greater detail than the others. God reveals himself in his Word most often through the language of marriage and kingship; as such, it is not surprising that idolatry is seen as a challenge to God's exclusivity. After the golden calf incident in Exodus 32, God reiterates his covenant and instructs Moses to again warn his people, "Do not worship any other god, for the LORD, whose name is Jealous, is a jealous God" (Ex. 34:14). He declares that he alone is—and is to be regarded as—Israel's faithful husband and trustworthy king. Nonetheless, time and again his people spurn his steadfast love and protection and surrender their affections and allegiance to false gods, whether golden idols or hardened hearts. "Idolatry is a meaningful concept only within the framework of radical monotheism," Johnson astutely reasons. "If we believe that there is only one ultimate Power from whom all things derive and toward which all things are ordered, not as independent entities but as creatures, then the service of any creature as ultimate must be regarded as deception and distortion. . . . Idolatry [is] the Big Lie about reality."[16]

We suggested first that false beliefs and misdirected affections may manifest themselves in idolatry. Second, *idolatry often exposes our deeply held fears and longings.*[17] Exodus 32:1 tells us what led to the construction of the golden calf: "When the people saw that Moses was so long in coming down from the mountain, they gathered around Aaron and said, 'Come make us gods who will go before us. As for this fellow Moses who brought us out of Egypt, we don't know what has happened to him.'" The Israelites are fearful without a visible representative of God. Moses is chosen by God to deliver his people and guide them to the Promised Land, but he is still a mere human, and his absence does not render God inattentive and powerless. The Israelites wrongly ascribe to Moses what God alone is able to do; it was God himself—and not Moses—who brought them out of Egypt. Moreover, even with Moses among them, they doubt God's presence with them in the wilderness. So God provides manna each morning, quail, and the promise of his dwelling in the tabernacle that he instructs Moses to build (ironically in the chapters just previous to this incident). Nevertheless, the Israelites struggle to trust God and demand his continual presence—or rather, *their understanding of what this should look like*—in order to assure them of their safety and security. They insist upon this as an absolute necessity—we *must* have God in *this way*—and become idolaters.

Johnson writes with bullet insight in his book *Faith's Freedom: A Classic Spirituality for Contemporary Christians,*

> We can speak of idolatry in functional terms as the centering of human life around some perceived power. We thereby are provided a diagnostic tool of the first importance for the life of the Spirit. Idolatry in this sense is not an abstract set of erroneous opinions, but the most concrete structuring of human life. . . . And since idolatry is essentially a form of compulsion protecting us against existential fear, we can also move analytically from the deployment of our defenses to the point of our greatest vulnerability. . . . We each structure our lives to possess what we regard as most powerful and important, or conversely, to avoid what we most fear.[18]

Third, in Israel's story we witness the *illusive promises and irrational persuasion of idolatry*. Impatient and fearful because Moses is "so long in coming down from the mountain," they reason, *If only we "make gods who will go before us" we will feel safe and secure to live as we wish* (Ex. 32:1). So Aaron fashions the golden calf, and the Israelites now ascribe their deliverance from Egypt to this idol (v.4). "Afterward they sat down to eat and drink and got up to indulge in revelry" (32:6; in the Hebrew, this indulgence is clearly sexual perversion). How glaringly distorted their picture of God has become. They willfully choose to ignore his first two commandments: "You shall have no other gods before me. You shall not make for yourself an idol in the form of anything in the heaven above or on the earth beneath or in the waters below. You shall not bow down to them or worship them; for I, the LORD your God, am a jealous God" (Ex. 20:3–5; see also v. 23). They distort God's words prohibiting "gods before me" and demand "gods who will go before us."

Fourth, *idolatry can render us deaf, dumb, blind, and senseless*. Scripture repeatedly tells us that we become like what we worship, whether comfort that we passively await, or pleasure that we aggressively pursue. Psalm 115 provides a striking description: "Their idols are silver and gold, made by the hands of men. They have mouths, but cannot speak, eyes, but they cannot see; they have ears, but cannot hear, noses, but they cannot smell; they have hands, but cannot feel, feet, but they cannot walk; nor can they utter a sound with their throats" (vv. 4–7). Furthermore, an ominous portent follows: "Those who make them will be like them, and so will all who trust in them" (v. 8). This psalm graphically contrasts the lives of those who worship idols with those who fear and "trust in the LORD" (stated three times in vv. 9–11). "The LORD remembers us and will bless us," declares the psalmist (v. 12). He also contrasts these impotent idols to the living God: "Our God is in heaven; he does whatever pleases him" (v. 3). For those who trust him, "He is their help and shield" (also found three times in vv. 9–11).

Fifth and finally, we see *the emptiness and confusion that idolatry ultimately brings*. Namely, it is critical to stop a moment and ask this question: *What would it take for God to do in order for the Israelites to trust and surrender to him fully?* Like Jesus' pointed question to the two blind men on the road to Jericho in Matthew 20, it is most reasonable to ask, *"What is it that you want?"* What is it that you think will bring you an absolute sense of God's presence and protection? We must wonder whether the Israelites could even verbalize what they really wanted from God. Like the golden calf before them, they are unable to reason. Their idols are security and a constant sense of God's presence. Their unspoken assumption is that they could construct a visible, controllable god so that they would never feel fearful, forgotten, and void of God's presence. But does such an image—or any earthly thing for that matter—really have the power to fully assuage our fears and longings? As frail human beings we may try to cover and surround ourselves with what promises security, yet we cannot avoid this truth: we are *naked before God.*

One of the most startling depictions of this reality can be seen in Renaissance artist Masaccio's fresco of Adam and Eve called *The Expulsion from Eden.* Their shame and horror are evident: Adam buries his face in his hands, while Eve, with her head lifted to the heavens in agony, tries desperately to cover her naked flesh. As the biblical story goes, their response is the dreadful realization that they have sinned against God and spurned his goodness. Less than a hundred years after Masaccio completed his fresco, Martin Luther ascended the tower steps trembling under this same reality: man's utter inability to withstand the weight of God's devastating holiness. In his presence we rightly tremble before this One who "does whatever pleases him" (Ps. 115:3) and which "no plan of [his] can be thwarted" (Job 42:2).

Johnson argues, "The roots of idolatry lie deep within the human heart, in the terror generated by the awareness that we are empty, powerless, dependent, contingent beings. . . . Idolatry therefore seeks something powerful enough to give us being, life, and worth, yet controllable enough so that it will be *our* being, life, and worth. . . . Where does the lie come in? It comes first in the denial of the one ultimate power that holds me in existence at every moment; it appears second in the pretension that anything created by that one power could replace it as a source of life and worth."[19]

Retracing our steps through this valley, we see that our false beliefs and misdirected affections may reveal themselves in idolatry, and like a mirror, idolatry exposes our deeply held longings and fears. When idolatry holds sway in our lives, we submit to its illusive promises and ultimately become like what we worship: deaf, dumb, empty, and confused. In conclusion, idolatry distorts our knowledge of God, ourselves, and others. Yet nothing can change the reality of our true condition: "all are naked and exposed to the eyes of [God] to whom we must give account" (Heb. 4:13 ESV).

The Valley of Denial

The biblical writers depict how difficult it can be for us to live with this truth: God is ultimate and we are not. Human beings are made in the image of God and to be in relationship with him, yet are separated by sin: "They show that the requirements of the law are written on their hearts, their consciences also bearing witness, and their thoughts now accusing" (Rom. 2:15). We suppress God's moral law that deep in our hearts we know exists and are held captive by our deceit: "the Scripture declares that the whole world is a prisoner of sin" (Gal. 3:22). But in his mercy "God made him who had no sin to be sin for us, so that in him we might become the righteousness of God" (2 Cor. 5:21). He clothes our naked, penitent souls with the robe of Christ's righteousness and turns our hearts to our truest desire: to know and to be known by our Creator, Redeemer, and Sustainer. And Psalm 84:5–7 offers a vivid promise to those who journey through life with God: "Blessed are those whose strength is in you, who have set their hearts on pilgrimage. As they pass through the Valley of Baca, they make it a place of springs. . . . They go from strength to strength, till each appears before God in Zion."

Still, we may guard our hearts from God, because before God alone our hearts are completely exposed. We long for relationship yet pull away from it as well. We might readily identify with Adam and Eve's sense of shame and regret over the loss of Paradise, but stumble over the totality of God's sovereignty and the false promises of sins that so easily enslave us. We may suppress his truth and cling to misdirected affections; we may ignore his ultimate claim upon our lives and elevate our own agendas and desires.

Here we will want to look at the technical terrain that we sometimes encounter in the valley of denial. Sigmund Freud observed the phenomenon of denial in his clinical study of defense. He witnessed individuals who unconsciously yet actively resisted becoming conscious of something that challenged their perception of the world and their sense of identity. Furthermore, they even resisted becoming aware of their own maneuvers to avoid what challenged their perception as well. Freud characterizes these various maneuvers as *defense mechanisms* and demonstrates how denial acts to keep at bay what we do not want to face.

For example, if we neither like the truth nor believe we are able to live with it, we may turn away from it. One feature of denial, then, is to *protect us from looking directly at the truth*, whether it involves our recurring fears, unrequited questions, or long-awaited hopes. Thus, if deep down I believe that God is inattentive to my prayers, I might shield myself from this belief by praying halfheartedly (after all, why bother if no one is really listening?) or skirt around whatever has led me to this conclusion. "There is often a protective cynicism that runs in the hearts of those who live in the reality of unanswered prayers," adds my colleague Jill Carattini.[20]

Just as in the valley of idolatry, we see here again how our wrong ideas about God eventually surface and expose our hearts. If we are unable to live with such a picture of God, we may avoid bringing it to mind or sidestep God altogether. Indeed, Dick Keyes contends that the Scriptures portray idolatry as essentially *God-avoidance.* He suggests, "The attempt to not face the face of God or face ourselves as we are begins the process of idolatry."[21] I have found this proverbial statement to be an accurate compass. When we are reticent to examine our deeply held, underlying assumptions about God, we will resist his Word and look for sustenance elsewhere. "The danger is not lest the soul should doubt whether there is any bread," cautions Simone Weil, "but lest, by a lie, it should persuade itself that it is not hungry. It can only persuade itself of this by lying."[22]

Furthermore, our emotions often disclose what we wish to suppress or fear to verbalize. If I am angry, I feel I have been hurt in some way or I need to protect myself from whatever or whomever elicited this feeling. Yet if I have been taught not to express anger—and especially toward God—I will find some way to deny or avoid this discordant feeling in order to maintain my view of self and of God that has been challenged. Again, we may circumvent these feelings even when we pray. However, we encounter a different approach in the prophets and psalmists who direct their emotional laments and prayers to God. As one biblical scholar says, "The Psalms help us understand that *every emotion is a theological statement.* . . . The psalmist disrupts our denial that we are angry or afraid. He disrupts our pretense that our anger and fear are not directed against God."[23]

THE VALLEY OF THE SHADOW OF DOUBT

Sometimes our denial takes an alternate form in a different valley. Here we find *doubt,* which is sometimes actually *denial in disguise,* acting as a defense mechanism protecting us against our difficult questions. These questions may be intellectual; often they are existential, surfacing through pain. In *God in the Dark: The Assurance of Faith Beyond a Shadow of a Doubt,* Os Guinness considers the disciples upon Jesus' resurrection. He likens their troubling experience to someone with an injury. The injured person—let us call him John—sees what he wants before him, but every time John grabs his tennis racket or bottle of water, he puts pressure upon this wound and so hesitates. Likewise, seeing Jesus in their midst, the disciples want desperately to believe that he has come back to life, but their wounds are still too fresh to touch. So Luke says they "disbelieved for joy" (Luke 24:41 ESV). This is an admittedly enigmatic idiom that still elicits some confusion and questions. Guinness comments, "[Jesus] stood before them, the sum of all they wanted. But for the sheer joy of what it would mean if true, they refused to believe in case it might not be. What they were saying in their doubt was that it was too good to be true, and this way they adroitly protected the wound and refused to risk reopening it. The one fact that they wanted became the one fact too much."[24]

Guinness illustrates the irony of this type of doubt. We *want* to trust that God is good and will never leave or forsake us, yet sometimes we dare not bank our lives on this for fear of disappointment. Cognitively we may have no trouble espousing this truth or judging it to be biblically accurate, but when we lose a loved one or relive a past hurt, we may doubt God's presence or, perhaps worse, question why he stood by and did nothing.

Guinness perceptively observes, "In almost every instance, the person is challenged to believe at the very point where he or she most needs and most wants to believe. This is not a coincidence. The psychological hurt of the doubt comes from the clash between the desire to believe and the fear to believe as they meet head-on right over the old wound. The doubter claims that the trouble with God's truth is that it is more desirable than credible. But neither the desirability nor the credibility of the matter are the problem. What matters to the doubter is that the wound remains covered and protected. So what would otherwise be eminently desirable and entirely credible must be dismissed."[25]

That's where I found myself one spring evening: in a parking lot, between the desire to believe and the fear to believe. I sat paralyzed and alone inside my car for three hours. I mistakenly sensed that God had closed a door. I wanted to believe he hadn't—yet I even feared the open door as well. Either way I felt I was at a dead-end and hope was lost. I was stricken, numbed by God's seeming abandonment. Dusk came and darkness fell upon my soul.

My experience and Guinness's depiction of doubt illustrate a powerful experience known as *ambivalence*. Psychologists define *ambivalence* as the experience of feeling two conflicting emotions simultaneously. Or, in Guinness's words, it is the clash between the desire to believe and the fear to believe. Such internal conflict can render us feeling powerless and angry if we continue to try to sidestep the fear and pain that has brought on our doubt. This then is another reminder of why we desperately need God's Word and companions along the way who will speak his hope and truth into our troubled souls. Thankfully, the night I sat in the parking lot, God met me there with both.

THE VALLEY OF DISSONANT VOICES

We noted that one function of denial is to protect us from looking directly at the truth. Of course, if we constantly strive to deny or suppress the truth, we will exhaust ourselves. Though our doubts and ambivalence may sometimes overwhelm us, they also help us ease our internal conflict by allowing us *to avoid commitment to a particular known truth.*

Similarly, two people may seek pleasure in an illicit relationship while their consciences persistently remind them of God's searing displeasure and their spouses at home. They must then find a way to reduce the painful dissonance between their conflicting emotions and the stark reality of the truth. Social scientists label the experience of attempting to hold two opposing views ("I know this is wrong but I want it") as *cognitive dissonance.* One endeavors to reduce the conflict by changing the conditions ("Did God really say?"), adding new conditions ("My spouse doesn't love me anyway"), or changing one's behavior. When the individual refuses to submit to the truth, an attempt is made to reconcile the internal conflict by rationalizing the behavior ("God understands my weakness") or by refusing to acknowledge the truth (avoidance).

In this valley we attempt to *internalize our dissonant voices in a way that allows us to alleviate our anxiety by avoiding commitment to a particular truth.* As we have seen in the case of ambivalence, this struggle is not always a moral dialogue between the voices of right and wrong; sometimes it is a desperate deliberation between hope and fear. This is especially true when one has endured a painful experience such as a debilitating illness or childhood trauma. Here, the doubting question is not "Did God really say?" but rather "Was God really there with me?" Moreover, whether one answers yes or no, the next question that inevitably surfaces is, "Can I really trust him?" This is where the sufferer may get stuck, for either way one's understanding of the goodness of God is severely tested. That is, if the answer is *"Yes,* God was there when I experienced this suffering," another voice may reply, "So why didn't he stop it?" If *"No,* God wasn't there," then, "How can I believe he is here with me now and will be in the future?" Therefore, in order for the sufferer to ease the anxiety felt, he or she will often avoid commitment to a particular known truth—*the Scriptures say God is trustworthy*—because the questions that challenge this very truth seem too painful to bear.

Guinness suggests that in such defining experiences we construct our picture of God. He writes, "Think back to some crisis. . . . What did your attitudes then show you of your real view of God? Or think back to some deep personal concern and the way you brought it to God in prayer. In situations like those, we see our real views of God. *What faith is asking always reveals what it is assuming.*"[26] Guinness poignantly observes the self-defeating nature of this doubt. "Afraid to believe what they want to believe, they fail to believe what they need to believe, and they alone are the losers. With some doubts, the issue rises at points that are not central to faith. . . . But this doubt is different. The issue raised does not lie on the circumference of life but at its very center. Whether it is solved is not a matter of indifference to faith but a matter of life and death."[27]

The Valley of Eshcol

I believe Os Guinness is absolutely right: this struggle is not peripheral to one's faith, but it is "a matter of life and death." If we avoid—or refuse—to settle certain questions, over time our doubts will erode our faith and our view of God. Once again, the Scriptures provide a striking illustration in the life of Israel.

In the opening chapter of Deuteronomy, the Israelites finally stand at the threshold of the Promised Land, and God tells them that they may take possession of it. Fearing the unknown, they send spies into the Valley of Eshcol, who in turn confirm God's word: "It is a good land that the LORD our God is giving us" (v. 25; see also Num. 13:23ff.). Yet the Israelites refuse to enter because they continue to waver with nagging fear and doubt. Moses recalls, "You grumbled in your tents and said, 'The LORD hates us; so he brought us out of Egypt to deliver us into the hands of the Amorites to destroy us'" (v. 27). So he assures them, "Do not be terrified; do not be afraid of them. The LORD your God, who is going before you, will fight for you, as he did in Egypt, before your very eyes, and in the desert. There you saw how the LORD your God carried you, as a father carries his son, all the way you went until you reached this place" (vv. 29–31). Moses likens God to a caring father tenderly picking up his weary child and carrying him home. It should be noted that this idea of the fatherhood of God radically separates the Israelites' faith from all the other nations', which saw God as distant, capricious, and beyond knowing. Instead, Moses reminds them, the LORD your God is compassionate, attentive, and trustworthy.

The next verse reveals, however, that the Israelites have not resolved their fear and doubts: *"In spite of this,* you did not trust in the LORD your God, who went ahead of you on your journey, in fire by night and in a cloud by day, to search out places for you to camp and to show you the way you should go" (vv. 32–33; emphasis added). Bible teacher Beth Moore underscores the significance of this introductory phrase as it appears in the King James Version: *"Yet in this thing* you did not believe the LORD your God." She proposes that we may have no trouble believing God in many areas of our lives, with the exception of "this thing." Yet leaving "this thing" unresolved will ultimately undermine our faith and trust in him because "this thing . . . corresponds with the deepest brokenness in your life."[28] Thus, "deep down in our psyche, we just know God is not going to be faithful to us here"—because God was seemingly unfaithful in our place of brokenness.[29]

If we have not wrestled with our heartaches before God and begun to experience some healing and restoration, nagging doubts and fears will undercut our faith not only here, but also eventually in other areas. Indeed, in the case of the Israelites, Scripture tells us that though they stood at the threshold of the Promised Land, "so we see that they were not able to enter, because of their unbelief" (Heb. 3:19). As Guinness concludes in his chapter aptly titled "Faith out of Focus," "If our picture of God is wrong, then our whole presupposition of what it is possible for God to be or do is correspondingly altered."[30]

THE STEEP DESCENT TO ATHEISM

Sometimes such disbelief becomes so powerful that one denies God's existence altogether. The doubter claims that because God is not observable in the valley of suffering, he does not exist. Such stories are sadly familiar and often heart-wrenching. Former media mogul Ted Turner readily admits his antagonism to God developed after his seventeen-year-old sister died of leukemia and his father committed suicide. One common feature, noticeably in the recent writings of atheists Sam Harris, Christopher Hitchens, and Richard Dawkins, is a stridency in disbelief. In his article "God's Dupes," Harris scoffs, "Everything of value that people get from religion can be had more honestly, without presuming anything on insufficient evidence. The rest is self-deception, set to music."[31] Ironically, such a defensive posture against the overwhelming majority of people who believe in God comes across as, in Harris's own words, *self-deception*. His remarks ultimately evoke the question, what are you *really* so angry about? That is, if you don't believe God exists, with *whom* are you angry? In his books and interviews, Harris retorts, "religious fundamentalists"—by whom he means anyone who believes in an objective moral law and moral lawgiver. Such people are "irrational," "deluded," and "deranged."[32]

Psychologist Paul Vitz provides perspective to this question in his poignant study of atheists Sigmund Freud, Frederic Nietzsche, Jean-Paul Sartre, and others in his book *Faith of the Fatherless*. Freud contended that "religious ideas have arisen from the . . . necessity of defending oneself against the crushing superior force of nature" and are therefore "illusions, fulfillments of the oldest, strongest and most urgent wishes of mankind . . . the benevolent rule of a divine Providence allays our fears of the dangers of life."[33] Yet Vitz shows how Freud and many notable atheists' early deprivation under absent and malevolent fathers gave birth to their lifelong hostility to God. (Conversely, many significant theists such as Blaise Pascal, G. K. Chesterton, and Dietrich Bonhoeffer had a positive and loving relationship with their father or a father figure.) They reasoned that if God were anything like their father, they *did not want* God to exist. Christian scholar Douglas Wilson notes this same ironic sentiment in a lengthy exchange with Christopher Hitchens, concluding that his angry arguments against a God he doesn't believe exists "reveal the two fundamental tenets of *true* atheism. One: There is no God. Two: I hate Him."[34]

Oxford zoologist Richard Dawkins ascribes his atheism to objective reason, yet his emotive metaphors speak otherwise; according to him, God is a "psychotic delinquent" and "a virus of the mind."[35] His Oxford colleague Alister McGrath (himself a former atheist) comments, "Like so many of my atheist friends, I simply cannot understand the astonishing hostility that he displays toward religion. Religion to Dawkins is like a red rag to a bull—evoking not merely an aggressive response, but one that throws normal scholarly conventions about scrupulous accuracy and fairness to the winds."[36] Dawkins looks to Freud's idea of "wish fulfillment" (the "most urgent wishes of mankind") to dismantle theism and support his athe-ism. But like Vitz, McGrath turns this argument upon its head, building upon Freud's own fundamental understanding of defense: that we subconsciously yet actively resist becoming conscious of something that challenges our perception of the world and our sense of identity. McGrath's argument is critical to understand-ing the way denial functions for the skeptic as well:

> Dawkins identifies "wish fulfillment" as a global feature of religion. Now there is a grain of truth in his analysis. The way that human beings perceive the world is indeed coloured by our agendas and expectations. "Cognitive bias" is a funda-mental characteristic of human psychology. Yet in general this unconscious bias is manifested not so much in our believing what we would like to be true, as in maintaining the status quo of our beliefs. The driving force is not wishful think-ing, but conservative thinking—thinking that conserves an existing worldview.
>
> For example, many people have a positive view of themselves, a sense that the universe is benevolent, and that other people like them. They maintain this view by attending to the data that fits this view, and minimizing that which does not. Others (such as depressed or traumatized people) see themselves as worthless, view the universe as malevolent, and . . . discount or minimize the significance of any data that does not fit in with this view.
>
> We thus have a built-in resistance to change our position—a resistance which is underpinned by "cognitive biases" which predispose us to fail to notice or to discount data that is inconsistent with our view. On the whole we do this because it is efficient—it is effortful and upsetting to have to change one's mind—even if the change is in a positive direction.[37]

THE VALLEY OF SELF-DECEPTION

Thus far we have seen that denial protects us from looking directly at the truth and that doubt may act as a defense mechanism shielding us from commitment to a particular truth. Additionally, we may also distort the truth through various *cogni-tive biases*—a general term used to describe the many ways we attempt to alter or disregard what we know to be true. One common bias McGrath notes above is "a built-in resistance to change our position." This resistance may act in tandem with what sociologist Herbert Fingarette describes as "knowing, intentional ignorance."[38] In his seminal work *Self-Deception*, Fingarette argues that such willful ignorance lies at "the deep paradox of self-deception." The self-deceived person "*persuades* himself to believe contrary to the evidence *in order to evade*, somehow, the unpleasant truth to which he has already seen that the evidence points."[39] You will recall earlier that F. F. Bruce uses the phrase "deliberate ignorance"—suppressing the truth that is accessible to us—which he characterizes as idolatry.

Fingarette employs the idiom "to spell out" to characterize how we make something explicit or become conscious of it. We understand what a person means, for example, when he or she says, "He let me know without actually spelling it out" or when one retorts, "You know perfectly well what I mean—do I have to spell it out for you?" To spell out "is to be explicitly aware of; to pay conscious attention to."[40] Fingarette goes on to describe "an individual's engagement in the world" as the way one perceives, feels, enjoys, or fears his or her environment. Building again upon Freud's analysis of defense, Fingarette thus characterizes self-deception or intentional ignorance as *a refusal to spell out an engagement*: "Self-deception . . . is the situation where there is an overriding reason *not* to spell-out some engagement. . . . We avoid becoming explicitly conscious of our engagement, and we avoid becoming explicitly conscious that we are avoiding it. . . . Thus the adoption of the policy of not spelling-out an engagement is a 'self-covering' policy. To adopt it, is perforce, never to make explicit, to 'hide' it."[41]

One way that we adopt a self-covering policy is to *construct an alternative story of our lives*, much like we saw the character Ruth do in glossing over her family trauma in the novel *Housekeeping*. Fingarette sees this as "the protective attempt on the part of the person to use elements of the skill he has developed in spelling-out as inventively as possible in order to fill in plausibly the gaps created by his self-covering policy. He will try to do this in a way which renders the 'story' as internally consistent and natural as possible, and as closely conforming as possible to the evident facts. Out of this protective tactic emerge the masks, disguises, rationalizations and superficialities of self-deception in all its forms."[42]

Tennessee Williams's powerful short story "Something by Tolstoi" vividly illustrates Fingarette's analysis in part. Jacob Brodzky is a shy, quiet Jewish son of a bookshop owner who longs only to marry his childhood friend Lila, an energetic and ambitious Gentile. He enters college upon his father's wishes, but when his father dies two months later, Jacob leaves college and marries Lila. Tennessee

Williams writes, "His love for her was the core of his life. There is a great danger to such a love. When the loved one is lost, the life is lost. It crumbles to pieces. This is what happened to the life of young Brodzky when his wife went away with the vaudeville company."[43]

After Lila announces her intentions, Jacob hands her the key to the door of the bookshop and says, "You will come back sometime, and I will be waiting." In agony, Jacob mourns her absence. However, he soon numbs himself by "reading as another man might have taken to drink or drugs." Nearly fifteen years pass and Lila decides to return home. She opens the door with the key she never let go of and says only, "Jacob." They stare at one another for a long time. "But the dullness, the total unrecognition in his eyes must have restrained her," says the narrator. " . . . Did she suppose that he was deliberately refusing to recognize her? Or did she imagine that the fifteen years had altered her beyond his knowing her?"

Jacob shows no sign of recognizing Lila and responds in a hollow voice, "Do you want a book?"

"I wanted a book, but I've forgotten the name of it," replies Lila. " . . . It is about a boy and a girl who had been constant companions since their childhood." And so at length she details their story, the facts he knew: his father's desire to send him to college; their marriage and bookshop apartment; her offer from vaudeville and departure; the key she could not relinquish. Still he shows no awareness.

"You remember it—you must remember it—the story of Lila and Jacob?" insists his wife.

"She was searching his face desperately," the narrator comments, "but there was nothing in it but bewilderment. He said at last, 'There is something familiar about the story. I think I have read it somewhere. It comes to me that it is something by Tolstoi."

Dropping the key, Lila runs in horror from the shop and Jacob "covered his face again with the large book and . . . resumed reading."

OUR UNFOLDING STORY

Tennessee Williams's heartbreaking story illustrates, in my reading, how deep the valleys of idolatry, denial, and self-deception may run, especially for a sojourner with seemingly no companions or sense of God's presence. (The story's narrator doesn't comment on Jacob's relationship with God.) An abandoned husband suppresses the memory of his wife, "the core of his life," to protect himself from the deep pain he experienced in her leaving. He adopts a self-covering policy that refuses to spell out what he wishes to avoid. When she steps into his life again, the narrative he has fabricated for himself has such power that he is unable—or unwilling—to recognize her and the love he once longed for. Even when she reminds him of the intimate details of their story, he is only able to recognize it as a sweeping tragedy that Tolstoi might have penned.

Perhaps this tale seems quite imaginary and farfetched, for how could Jacob *not* know? Yet at times I have stood in his shoes, and in a nearly mirror experience, Lila's as well. In hindsight I can attest, as Greg Bahnsen observes,

> not all of our beliefs are formed consciously, rationally, and with the giving of internal or external assent. To give assent to a proposition is explicitly to spell out (inwardly or outwardly) how one stands in respect to that proposition, thereby bringing one's belief to a conscious level of experience. . . . Holding a belief is not logically dependent upon a willingness or competence to express that belief verbally to oneself or others. . . . The cognitive and affective aspects of belief can sometimes be separated in a person and even be at odds with each other (e.g., hoping for what cannot be, fearing what you know does not hurt, failing to feel conviction in the face of strong proof). . . . *The fact that belief can be divorced from explicit assent shows us, then, that there can be beliefs held by a person of which he is not aware*—not consciously entertaining in his mind by introspection. A person can rely upon a proposition in his theoretical inferences and/or practical plans (e.g., "There is sufficient gas in the car's tank") without entertaining that proposition in mind; *the proposition may not come to mind until something goes wrong* (e.g., when he ends up stranded down the road).[44]

You may notice that here we have come nearly full circle: Bahnsen's observation is essentially what Michael Polanyi characterizes as "tacit knowledge." "We know more than we can tell," says Polanyi; or, as Bahnsen proposes, "Holding a belief is not logically dependent upon a willingness or competence to express that belief verbally to oneself or others." Again, we may have areas of unspoken or underdeveloped knowledge of ourselves and God. This is why we noted that it is not simply that we don't verbalize certain beliefs because we "suppress the truth in unrighteousness" or have "wrong ideas about God." Lila's puzzlement about Jacob's demeanor is a fitting metaphor for the complexity of our desires and actions: "Did she suppose that he was deliberately refusing to recognize her? Or did she imagine that the fifteen years had altered her beyond his knowing her?" We are left to ponder these questions in the light of our own understanding and relationships as well.

We have suggested that over time our knowledge of God and ourselves can deepen as we grow to see that we both know and are known and begin to flourish in the light of this awareness. In fact, the Scriptures reveal that God graciously discloses his truth *as we are able to receive it.* As such, before we conclude, it is critical to underscore that denial itself *is not the problem*, but rather its *overuse or underuse.* Denial is part of the fabric of our design as human beings, for it *allows us to function until we are able to receive and face the truth.*[45] That is, we are simply unable to take in at once everything we experience—whether joy, betrayal, or the consequences of our actions. Thus we may deny or sidestep the full extent of the experience and possible damage done. In fact, in circumstances such as trauma, our bodies quickly alert us to danger with a flood of adrenaline that stimulates a fight-or-flight response (defense mechanisms). If these two options are not available, we protect ourselves from the pain through emotional detachment or numbness. In extreme circumstances, the body may shut down and go into shock, when breathing and blood flow rapidly begin to slow and consciousness fades. Trauma can be so debilitating that one may not be able to begin to take in and process what was actually endured until months—or even years—later.

When we consider the whole of Scripture, we witness the biblical principle of *progressive and unfolding revelation.* That is, God makes himself and his purposes known to his people partially and sequentially. He gives Abraham a great promise—"I will make you into a great nation" (Gen. 12:2)—but does not tell him that this great nation would one day include every tribe and tongue redeemed through the crucified and risen Jesus. So we are introduced to the doctrines of redemption, consummation, and the Trinity in the Old Testament, but we are not able to comprehend their full expression until we come to the Gospels, the teachings of the apostles, and ultimately the *eschaton.*

When the Pharisees test Jesus and ask why the Mosaic law "commanded" divorce, Jesus tells them plainly, "Moses *permitted* you to divorce your wives because your hearts were hard. But it was not this way from the beginning" (Matthew 19:7; emphasis added). Jesus reveals that God, understanding the nature of the human heart, allowed for divorce in a number of circumstances for a season; but he grounds his argument for marriage in established teaching in Genesis 1–2, concluding that "what God has joined together, let man not separate" (v. 6). Likewise, the apostle Paul acknowledges to the Corinthians, "Brothers, I could not address you as spiritual but as worldly—mere infants in Christ. I gave you milk, not solid food, *for you were not yet ready for it. Indeed, you are still not ready*" (1 Cor. 3:1–2; emphasis added). Though many responded to his preaching, the gospel of unconditional love, repentance, and surrender to Christ's lordship was a radical paradigm shift for a city known for its sexual immorality and pagan temples devoted to Aphrodite.

Jesus' interaction with his disciples in John 14–16 is another instructive passage. On the eve of his arrest and crucifixion, Jesus comforts his disciples, saying, "Let not your hearts be troubled" (14:1 ESV). Then in a stunning revelation he declares, "And I will ask the Father, and he will give you another Counselor to be with you forever—the Spirit of truth. . . . He lives with you and will be in you. I will not leave you as orphans; I will come to you" (John 14:16–18). The disciples had walked closely with Jesus for three years. During that time, he spoke often of his impending death, and whenever this subject was broached, the disciples fought against it. Peter once cried, "Never, Lord! This shall never happen to you!" (Matt. 16:22–23), and Jesus rebuked him. Yet just hours before he will leave them, he introduces them to the Holy Spirit, for they will need the promise of his comfort and guidance in the traumatic hours to come. Jesus adds, "I still have many more things to say to you, *but you cannot bear them now*" (John 16:12 ESV; emphasis added). Jesus reveals his intimate relationship with the Spirit but does not disclose more because they are unable to receive this truth until the Spirit comes in fullness at the day of Pentecost. On this evening the Spirit appears no more to them than a mysterious promise; yet soon they will know him intimately as Advocate, Defender, Helper, Counselor, and Comforter.

THE VALLEY OF SOUL MAKING

Jacob Brodzky's tragic story is forged in the fire of idolatry and abandonment, dissolving him to ashes and dust in its flames. The narrator doesn't provide insight into Jacob's view of God, and the story leaves one wondering what could have brought this man recognition of the truth and restoration. Ironically, the narrator declares that if only Jacob's wife would return, he would find life again; thus he too is astounded when Jacob does not recognize his wife.

The biblical character Joseph's story is forged in the fire of idolatry and abandonment as well. His father Jacob "loved Joseph more than any of his other sons . . . . When his brothers saw that their father loved him more than any of them, they hated him and could not speak a kind word to him" (Gen. 37:3–4). So Joseph's brothers abandon him, throwing him into a well and selling him into slavery to a foreign country far beyond his home. Though God gives him favor in his captor's hands, he is unjustly accused of attempted rape, imprisoned for over two years, and forgotten by one he helps through interpreting his dream. Thirteen years after Joseph is sold into Egypt, he interprets Pharaoh's dream of coming famine and is made second-in-command under him. He marries and has two sons whom he names Manasseh "because God has made me forget all my trouble and all my father's household," and Ephraim "because God has made me fruitful in the land of my suffering" (Gen. 41:51–52). The names Joseph bestows upon his sons are verbal reminders of his thanksgiving to God for preserving and blessing him even in the desert of his abandonment.

We are not given insight into Joseph's soul in those initial painful and tender years when he first arrives in Egypt except that the author of Genesis repeatedly mentions, "*the LORD was with him;* he showed him kindness and granted him favor" (39:21; emphasis added; see also 39:2–5, 23). However, when his brothers come looking for food during the widespread famine, we are afforded an intimate view into his character. Like Lila before Jacob, we are told "Although Joseph recognized his brothers, they did not recognize him" (42:8). He was just a teenager when they deserted him, and more than twenty years have passed. So Joseph tests their trustworthiness by ordering one brother to remain in prison and the others to return home and bring their youngest brother, Benjamin. Not realizing that Joseph understands them, they announce, "Surely we are being punished because of our brother." Then we learn an anguishing detail about when they sold him into slavery: "We saw how distressed he was when he pleaded for his life, but we would not listen" (v. 21). Upon hearing their confession, Joseph "turned away from them and began to weep" (v. 24).

The brothers return home and bring back Benjamin, who also doesn't recognize Joseph. "As he looked about and saw his brother Benjamin, his own mother's son, he asked, 'Is this your youngest brother, the one you told me about?' And he said, 'God be gracious to you, my son.' Deeply moved at the sight of his brother, Joseph hurried out and looked for a place to weep. He went into his private room and wept there" (Gen. 43:29–30).

Joseph sends his brothers back home a second time and again tests their character by having his steward put his silver cup into Benjamin's sack. When the cup is discovered, will they abandon Benjamin to his fate or will they return to Joseph united as brothers on behalf of their youngest one's innocence? They return to Joseph, and now Judah (like Lila) spells outs the details of their story: their father is aged; the youngest son has a brother who is now dead; his father will die if his youngest does not return as promised. Judah then offers himself as a slave on behalf of Benjamin.

The many years of the brothers' self-covering and infighting culminates in their standing before, unbeknownst to them, the brother they abandoned, confessing their guilt and assuming responsibility. It is an amazing moment of transparency and transformation. The next chapter of Genesis begins,

> Then Joseph could no longer control himself before all his attendants, and he cried out, "Have everyone leave my presence!" So there was no one with Joseph when he made himself known to his brothers. And he wept so loudly that the Egyptians heard him, and Pharaoh's household heard about it. Joseph said to his brothers, "I am Joseph! Is my father still living?" But his brothers were not able to answer him, because they were terrified at his presence. . . . Then he threw his arms around his brother Benjamin and wept, and Benjamin embraced him, weeping. And he kissed all his brothers and wept over them. Afterward his brothers talked with him. (Gen. 45:1–3, 14–15)

This is the third time thus far we see Joseph weeping. He cries in response to his brothers' confessions and at the sight of his brother Benjamin, and each time his weeping becomes louder and unrestrained. Later when Joseph returns home and finally sees his father again, "he threw his arms around his father and wept for a long time" (46:29; see also 50:1). In five different scenes we witness Joseph weeping.

Joseph's brothers are terrified when he announces, "I am your brother Joseph, the one you sold into Egypt!" (45:4). But his words are not intended as a condemnation but rather an intimate revelation: I am *your brother*. Indeed, hearing his next observation, one can only wonder at what has been wrought in his tender heart. "And now, do not be distressed and do not be angry with yourselves for selling me here, because it was to save lives that God sent me ahead of you. . . . So then it was not you who sent me here, but God" (vv. 5, 8). He extends mercy and forgiveness to his brothers and assures them, "You intended to harm me, but God intended it for good to accomplish what is now being done, the saving of many lives" (50:20).

Joseph's story could have ended tragically like Jacob Brodzky's. Or he might have become scheming and fearful like his father, Jacob, whose deception prevented him for years from receiving the blessing God promised to give him. Instead, in his abandonment, enslavement, imprisonment, and success, Joseph entrusted himself to a kind and sovereign God whom he confidently believed would be with him. Where affliction might have born bitter fruit, we find instead tears of hope and reconciliation. "The vale of tears has proved to be the valley of soul making."[46] Joseph's brokenness and willingness to forgive becomes the door to healing and transformation—not only for him but also for his entire family.

HEARTS SET ON PILGRIMAGE

At the beginning of this chapter we suggested that our knowledge of God and ourselves is relational and reciprocal. It's not just that we know, but that *we are known and purpose to live in the light of this awareness*. Furthermore, the degree to which we are willing to entrust ourselves to whom he has revealed himself to be may limit or foster spiritual growth. If we have a false or inadequate understanding of God, we may protect ourselves from him or find counterfeit comfort in our imagined view, and thus not give ourselves to him fully. These are subtle valleys that challenge us along our spiritual journey.

We noted too that our relationship with God may be evidenced by the sentences we speak about our lives because they shape our understanding of what we believe and what we hope from him. We need other hearts set on pilgrimage through our valleys of joy and weeping (see Ps. 84:5–6, where "Baca" means "weeping" or "balsam"). We need the fellowship of those who love us and who are able to speak into our lives, gently setting before us what we cannot—or do not want to—see. Those who are able to sit with us when we weep, and work and wait with us through our doubts. Those who are able to speak the *whole* story to us, the gospel of God's truth and grace. When we begin to recognize and verbalize our struggles, we are then compelled to ask what we have done with them. That is, have we given voice and emotion to our doubts and unrequited hopes through hopelessness, unforgiveness, or resignation? Have these struggles over time eroded our trust in God's goodness and sovereignty in our lives? Or have these valleys shown us more of him, and given us hearts to reveal his compassion and faithfulness to others?

"Without knowledge of God there is no knowledge of self," writes Calvin. (You will recall earlier that Calvin says vice versa, "Without knowledge of self there is no knowledge of God.") He continues, "Again, it is certain that man never achieves a clear knowledge of himself unless he has first looked upon God's face, and then descends from contemplating him to scrutinizing himself. For we always seem to ourselves righteous and upright and wise and holy. . . . [yet it is] the Lord, who is the sole standard by which this judgment must be measured."[47]

This is why our souls so desperately need the mirror of God's Word, for ultimately it is the one true and trustworthy reflection of who we are and who we are becoming. Here we are exhorted and comforted, chastened and encouraged by the One who loves us and can speak into our lives like no other. We can "set our hearts at rest in his presence whenever our hearts condemn us. For God is greater than our hearts, and he knows everything" (1 John 3:19–20). We can bring our longings, fears, and questions before his throne of grace and let the light of Jesus' presence shine into every dark and confusing place in our lives. For God does not gloss over our stories, as the prayers of Scripture so readily reveal: "There are tears, anger, exaltation, thoughts of revenge, worship, tenderness, and confusion; all these are embraced in the life of prayer and praise. Far from being an expression of unreality, prayer draws us into the fully real; it draws us into the knowledge that we are human beings, men and women created in the image of God."[48]

And when we find ourselves at loss for words or wisdom, we can speak aloud his Word and ask him to pray on our behalf, even as he has promised: "For we do not know what to pray for as we ought, but the Spirit himself intercedes for us with groanings too deep for words" (Rom. 8:26 ESV). Then we can be assured that whatever valley and whatever companions are on our way, like Joseph and God's people through the ages, we are *never alone*.

PART THREE
Living Out the Answers

14

THE CHURCH'S ROLE IN APOLOGETICS AND THE DEVELOPMENT OF THE MIND

Ravi Zacharias

I have little doubt that the single greatest obstacle to the impact of the gospel has not been its inability to provide answers, but the failure on our part to live it out. I remember well in the early days of my Christian faith talking to a close Hindu friend. He was questioning the experience of conversion as being supernatural. He absolutely insisted that conversion was nothing more than a decision to lead a more ethical life and that, in most cases, it was not any different from other ethical religions. I had heard his argument before.

But then he said something I have never forgotten: "If this conversion is truly supernatural, why is it not more evident in the lives of so many Christians I know?" His question is a troublesome one. In fact, it is so deeply disturbing a question that I think of all the challenges to belief, this is the most difficult question of all. I have never struggled with my own personal faith as far as intellectual challenges to the gospel are concerned. But I have often had struggles of the soul in trying to figure out why the Christian faith is not more visible.

It occurred to me some time ago why the skeptic is so enraged by the professing Christian. These so-called skeptics live without worrying about absolutes. They just flow with the culture. When any moral issues come up, skeptics shrug their shoulders and say, "Well, to each his own." They give the same privilege to others that they give themselves—namely, that moral choices are personal and not absolute. But what angers them about the believer is that the believer is strong in his or her condemnation of someone else's immoral life while at the same time living a double standard. In other words, the Christian's private life is no different from that of the one who doesn't claim to be a believer. The only difference is the arrogance of condemnation in one and the acceptance of personal moral choices by the other. On the one hand, that charge of hypocrisy is the compliment vice pays to professed, albeit duplicitous, virtue. But sadly, that compliment distills down to rejection of the belief in the claims of the virtuous one.

After lecturing at a major American university, I was driven to the airport by the organizer of the event. I was quite jolted by what he told me. He said, "My wife brought our neighbor last night. She is a medical doctor and had not been to anything like this before. On their way home, my wife asked her what she thought of it all." He paused and then continued, "Do you know what she said?" Rather reluctantly, I shook my head. "She said, 'That was a very powerful evening. The arguments were very persuasive. I wonder what he is like in his private life.'"

As we have noted in this book, the ultimate calling upon the Christian is to live a life reflecting the person of Christ. This involves a threefold process. First, we cannot take seriously the skeptic's difficult questions until we ourselves have also worked through them. Second, when such answers are known, they must then be internalized (the process of spiritual transformation) so that, third, these answers will be lived out before a hurting and hungry world.

Because my Hindu friend had not witnessed spiritual transformation in the life of Christians, whatever answers he received were nullified. In the doctor's case, the answers were intellectually and existentially satisfying, but she still needed to know, did they really make a difference in the life of the one proclaiming them? The Irish evangelist Gypsy Smith once said, "There are five Gospels. Matthew, Mark, Luke, John, and the Christian, and some people will never read the first four." In other words, apologetics is seen before it is heard. For both the Hindu questioner and the American doctor, the answers to their questions were not enough; they depended upon the visible transformation of the one offering them.

FOR A START

First Peter 3:15 gives us the defining statement: "But in your hearts set apart Christ as Lord. Always be prepared to give an answer [*apologia*] to everyone who asks you to give the reason for the hope that you have. But do this with gentleness and respect." Notice that before the answer is given, the one giving the answer is called to a certain prerequisite. *The lordship of Christ over the life of the apologist is foundational to all answers given.* Peter, of all the disciples, knew well how to ask questions and also how fickle the human heart is. He knew the seductive power of the spectacular in momentary enthrallment. He knew what it was to betray someone and to fail. He knew what it was to try to explain the gospel—as he did at Pentecost. Peter's strong reminder of the heart of the apologist is the basis of all apologetic attempts. The spiritual condition and character of the apologist are of immense importance.

With character in mind, there follow two immediate imperatives: the quality of life lived and the clarity of answers given. The way the Christian's life is lived will determine the impact upon believers and skeptics alike. This is a defining line because the claim by the believer is unique. The claim is that of a "new birth." After all, no Buddhist or Hindu or Muslim claims his or her life of devotion to be supernatural, yet they often live a more consistent life. And how often does the so-called Christian, even while teaching some of the loftiest truths one could ever teach, live a life bereft of that beauty and character? In apologetics the question is often asked, "If there is only one way, how is it that there are few in all of creation who qualify?" That question is actually more potent than the questioner realizes. It should further be raised, "Out of the few who actually qualify, why are even fewer living it out?"

This call to a life reflecting the person of Christ is the ultimate call of everyone who wishes to do apologetics because of the snare of argument and its overriding appeal that suppresses the devotional side of truth. This applies especially to leadership within the church. If the shepherd is not living the way he should, how can the ones shepherded follow the right path? The skeptic is not slow to notice this disparity and, because of that, questions the whole gospel in its supernatural claim. What, then, is the Christian's claim?

A New Heart

The first effects of coming to know Jesus Christ are the new hungers and pursuits that are planted within the human will. I well recall the dramatic change in my own way of thinking. There were new longings, new hopes, new dreams, new fulfillments, but most noticeably a new will to do what was God's will.

This new affection of heart expels all other old seductions and attractions. This is where it all begins. You see, preaching and teaching and moralizing can come very easily for all of the wrong motives. Such hammering away at telling others to be good is easily the work of a power-driven person. The difference between one who has come to know Jesus Christ and one who merely prescribes what others should be doing comes down to the soul. In the one who castigates and condemns, the attitude is born out of a superior posture of mind—spiritual dominance. The one who comes to know Christ does his or her speaking knowing how impoverished is the heart and in need of constant submission to the will of the Lord—spiritual surrender.

There are several pictures of this in Jesus' evangelism. Let me just take one: the woman at the well (John 4:1–26). You recall how she raised one question after another as if that were really her problem. It would have been very easy for the Lord to call her bluff with some castigating words. Instead, like a gentle and nimble-handed goldsmith he rubbed away the markings of sin and pain in her life until she was amazed at how much true gold he brought out in her. He gave her hope, knowing all along who she was on the inside. The arrogance of condemnation within the church has to stop and take a second look at what our answers are all about. We cannot simply vanquish the person in an attempt to rescue the message. The value of the person is an essential part of the message.

This means the apologist's task begins with a godly walk. One ought to take time to reflect seriously upon the question, *Has God truly wrought a miracle in my life? Is my own heart proof of the supernatural intervention of God?* That is the apologist's first question. In the West we go through these seasons of new-fangled theologies. The whole question of "lordship" plagued our debates for some time as we asked, is there such a thing as a minimalist view of conversion? "We said the prayer and that's it." Yet how can there be a minimalist view of conversion when conversion itself is a *maximal* work of God's grace? "Old things are passed away; behold *all* things are become new" (2 Cor. 5:17 KJV).

If you were proposing marriage to someone, what would the one receiving the proposal say if you said, "I want you to know this proposal changes nothing about my allegiances and my behavior and my daily life; however, I do want you to know that should you accept my proposal, we shall theoretically be considered married. There will be no other changes in me on your behalf." In a strange way we have minimized every sacred commitment and made it the lowest common denominator. *What does my new birth mean to me?* That is a question we seldom ask. *Who was I before God's work in me, and who am I now?*

There was a Christian worker in India from Canada. His name was Mark Buntain. Mark worked for Christ in one of India's toughest cities, Calcutta. I met him first when I was a new believer and still in my teens. He invited me to speak at his large church when I was just nineteen years old. I remember meeting him before I spoke. As I stepped onto the platform, I was not even sure if it was in reality or in imagination. What did I have to say to a packed large audience in one of the city's largest churches with highly respected Christians on the platform? I struggled through that sermon, and when we were all together at lunch, Mark came over to me to thank me and then prayed with me that God would keep his hand on my life. About thirty years later I was preaching in his church again. I was once more and even more deeply overcome this time by the saintliness of the man. He beamed with the right kind of pride as he sat in the front pew and listened while I preached. He was looking at his own sunset years, celebrating the dawn of younger voices and an answered prayer for him.

I knew then and there why he was called Saint Mark. There was a gentleness and a depth to his inner peace; he spoke with a quiet and calm authority. He loved Christ, and that was his ultimate test. When he died, the Indian government made an exception to its laws. They did not as a rule permit foreign citizens to be buried in India. They changed that for Mark because they knew to have his body buried there was a fitting tribute to a man whose soul left its mark on the people. The interesting thing about Mark's ministry is that it took place in a city from whence came some of India's most sophisticated thinkers. Here in Calcutta, some of the most verbose and intricate discussions are held on Vedic and Buddhist writings. It was here that William Carey and Adoniram Judson came. It was here that the British first established their seat of power. In short, it was Athens and Rome wrapped up in one for the Hindu culture.

Today the impact of Mark Buntain lives on as a tribute to the message he lived with a pure heart. I am fully aware that we are all gifted with different personalities, but humility of spirit and the hallmark of conversion is to see one's own spiritual poverty. I have often reminded myself that it is not the presence of Mark Buntain that should make me nervous, but the presence of Christ on hand and within my heart that should make me tread carefully.

Arrogance and conceit ought to be inimical to the life of the believer.

Patience in the foibles of others is the hallmark of grace. A deep awareness of one's own new hungers and longings is a convincing force of God's grace within.

A NEW MIND

Included in the development of character is the discipline of study, particularly balanced study. This is the best resource for building intelligent and coherent answers. There is an exponential growth in knowledge in our time, and it is part of our Christian calling to work hard at understanding as much as we can the themes that must be addressed. I have to say candidly here what I have no doubt runs the risk of offense but needs to be said. Walk through any Christian bookstore today and take note of the books. The sections on miracles and gifts and self-help and soothing reading are plentiful. These books are needed to a point. Some of them are written by thoughtful writers. But you will scan the shelves in vain for the intellectual fodder that we desperately need.

The book of Romans in the Scriptures is possibly the one that has stirred more theological minds across the centuries than any other: Augustine, Luther, Melanchthon, Wesley, and the list goes on. Their lives were transformed by that one book. It is rich in doctrine and systematically presents the nature of faith and the thread of theological truth running from the beginning of creation. Yet ask the average young churchgoer to give you even a brief idea of what the book teaches, and you will be surprised at how little this one knows.

Life lived at a high pace exacts a greater cost than we realize. The ability to slow down and take time to study and pen thoughts is seen as a luxury when it should be seen as a necessity. The answer seems to be to study in small groups, which has immense value. But such studies are generally geared to the lowest common denominator and do not take the place of personal, disciplined growth. So what I speak of here goes beyond the small group approach.

A private regimented study of fine pieces of writing—literature, devotionals, books that will challenge and bless the intellect—all of these played a part in shaping my own depth of thinking and in shaping my response to people. All these are needed. When God spoke before he sent his Son and when God spoke after the ascension, it was through the written word. In the way he has fashioned us, we see the same value. The DNA difference between a chimpanzee and a human is very slight but the implications are monumental. The difference we have is the difference in the capacity to speak, write, and morally reason with truth and in abstract categories. Times are changing in the means by which we glean information, but whether it be on a computer screen or through a set of headphones, words and concepts are critical to building the way one thinks.

Here the key to good reading comes in two broad areas. First is the direct contact with the Word itself—I speak of the Holy Scriptures. The Lord reminds us that it is the Word that lasts forever (Isa. 40:8). He tells us that the Scriptures cannot be broken (John 10:35). David tells us that the Word hidden in the heart is an antidote to sin (Ps. 119:11). When Jesus was confronted by the enemy of our souls in the wilderness, every response Jesus made was from the written Word (Matt. 4:1–11). That is our Lord's estimate of his revelation.

If we do not win here, we may not win anywhere. But even here there is a subtle seduction. I know people who take pride in how much of the Word they know and use it as a sledgehammer to clobber others. That is not the purpose of study. The purpose of study is the shaping of the "wineskin," that is, in the way we think (Mark 2:22). The study that results in reproving and correcting is the fruit of living, not the root of it. The wisdom it gives is the fount from which all else flows.

The second area of study is supplemental and interactive reading, wrestling with the ideas that shape our lives. Whether we deal with narrative or metanarrative, we must know how the same story is told in different genres of literature. The mind is a powerful but fragile instrument. To neglect the mind is to stunt the gift of imagination. To overfeed the mind is to make mystery disappear, and the enchantingly subtle is tragically lost under the weight of explanation. I have known of apologists whose minds have played havoc with their own mental health in later years. Theirs was a costly lesson on the price of imbalance.

A NEW COMMUNITY

A short while ago, I was in Australia speaking at a conference on apologetics. One of the attendees told me about a man who had just met with a very unfortunate accident. He was hit by an elderly driver, and one of his legs needed to be amputated. The man was a believer and had read some of my books. "Russell would love to see you in the hospital," the conference attendee said. So after the meeting, I took a taxi and was taken to the hospital room. There lay this man in intensive care, leg removed, heavily medicated, with his wife by his side. He labored hard to speak to me. "So happy to see you, Ravi, and the good news is I'm seeing two of you." That let me know he was fighting hard to see the better side of this pain. But then he went on to say how troubled he was thinking of their children and not knowing how they were going to cope with this. As I prayed with him, he opened his eyes again and said this: "If it were not for the kingdom, I don't know how I would make it through." He was referring to the community of believers and how they had gathered around him.

That night I was mentioning his words to one of my hosts, and he made an interesting comment. "This is the easy time to come alongside when the injury is new and the courtesy is a hospital call. The test will come when his wife needs incredible emotional and logistical support in carrying the kids through their needs from day to day. Let's hope the kingdom is there for him then." He was right. The church as a community often rises to the need in the initial stages and in the momentary struggle. The long haul is hard for everyone but is the place where friendships that go beyond the surface help carry one through.

That recognized, however, the principal role of the church is that of teaching and instruction in righteousness both by description and prescription. This part is hard to do well, especially as our culture is immersed in a sea of distractions. Over the years, our training and our expectations have let up, and biblical exposition has become weak and insipid, with postmodern approaches dictating not just form but substance.

During my days in Cambridge, I sat under one of the finest expository preachers I had ever heard, and I asked him if he thought expository skill was a gift inherent or a skill imparted. He firmly believed it was a gift inherent—a gift from God. The more I think of it, the more I conclude that it is both: a gift from God and a gift that is polished by skill and discipline. If our teaching does not recover the high ground—and it must do this—the followers will be left as sheep without a shepherd. I may digress a bit here, but it is for a reason.

What is it that has held together the pantheistic religions of Hinduism and Buddhism? It is the glue of cultural attachment. It is the connectedness of family. These religions are unblushingly built on fear and superstition. But there is another side: the lore of mysticism that invades the soul without the intellectual rigor. To be sure, there is the systematizing side that intellectuals give that often has very little to do with the common understanding or practice. But by and large there is some kind of "peep behind the curtain" approach of exponents who play to the stands in the exploitation of their existential hungers. Deepak Chopra and writers of his genre have taken this mystical side and milked it for all its worth. Some of the substance is so pathetic that one wonders with what intellectual integrity such stuff is peddled.

But one has to grant them the intelligence of capitalizing on the cultural vacuum in the west. The West in recent times has built its culture on the pursuit of material gain and mass communication. What made those exploits possible was the spiritual capital of the Judeo-Christian worldview that had checks and balances built in to encourage the enterprising spirit while providing boundary lines within which to make those pursuits. But with the arrival of technology at its exponential best, the entertainment megamachine made sensuality the candy to be served, and the resulting bankruptcy left our culture unfettered and empty. Life became a combination of indulgent work and indulgent escape.

In came the Eastern gurus, having taught within their own culture first but having no great material gains, now teaching simplistic methods that never really worked in their own cultures. They came to the West sensing the vast gold rush there was to be had in mystical and meditative Eastern-speak. New terms came into vogue: *karma, chakra, tantra, yoga,* "may the force be with you," and so on. There was money in it. There was seduction in it. There was a serenity offered as escape from the rat race of material pursuit. So like the authors who wrote books on how to get rich and then became rich by telling that story (while not many of the readers got rich), the mystical religions told the high-paced materialists to slow down because money is not everything, while they themselves got rich on those very mantras. Retreats have been built by these masters of veneer who get the wealthy to fork out obscene sums of money for sessions that supposedly bring the bliss that money did not bring. It is a very polite way of exchanging bank accounts while promising to lighten their stress. The doublespeak is inescapable. What it exposed was that the human heart longs for something intangible called communion—communion that goes beyond the self and finds a resting place for freedom from care.

Where did this leave the church? Fighting fires of symptoms in the outer reaches of society and leaving the house of God undefended by the mind and unhinged from all mystery. Our entire generation of young people from the 1970s on were left untrained intellectually, unprepared to face a culture in turmoil while a flood of religions was in vogue. A new evangelicalism was now fashioned and defined by size and appeal of program, creating a subculture in which the methods of the decaying West were adopted, and the sensory appeal of religion was marketed. We have our own little retreats built with our own escape techniques.

Islam built its empire on hate and intimidation and fear and compulsion. The so-called radicals know that if they remove these threats the religion is finished. Pantheistic religions built it on inner peace and tranquility promised with techniques of breathing, stretching, and chanting. In effect it is ceremony, tradition, and superstition that holds it all together. The church came up with programs that engaged the imagination, and what has happened is that the skeptic stands back and sees the hollowness of it all. Culture at large is empty within, while huge mechanisms support that hollowness so that it doesn't implode.

Now, church community life becomes somewhat like a boxing ring where we come into the center for periods of time and then go back to our corners to get patched up at the end of the day. Is that harsh? I don't think so. I listen as I travel and hear story after story of broken lives and shattered optimism. Is there an answer here? Yes, I believe there is. Here I borrow from a metaphor used by a former Muslim. He described for me the two ways of looking at life and religious commitment. "In the West, if life is illustrated by a circle, then a small dot somewhere inside that circle is religion. Life is the ends; belief the means. For the Muslim, by contrast, religion is defined by the circle and a small dot somewhere in the middle is life. One's personal faith is the ends; life is the means." In other words, what defines what? What circumscribes what? Until we see reality ordered in the way God has designed it to be, we will always become imitators of the world with a pseudospirituality and a cosmetic faith.

THE TASK OF APOLOGETICS

The church in the West equates size with success and has lost the glimpse of the greater reality of what it means to be devoted to Christ. That is as bluntly stated as possible. The picture is bleak, and the road ahead seems uncertain. As a community we must have the strength to teach, care, nurture, and heal. The responsibility rests squarely on the shoulders of leaders who in turn train the younger ones how to be a part of the community.

A Clear Understanding

C. S. Lewis once stated that if you cannot explain a simple truth, chances are that you do not understand it yourself. In my own journey into apologetics, I recall spending many a morning run or walk asking myself if I trusted my own answers. How convincing were they to me? But then came a second question: do I really understand the depth of the questions that are being raised? That is what took me onto the long road of training.

My younger brother is a surgeon. I watched him over the years of study and preparation. It wasn't easy. But then after the basic degree came the years of specialization. The skill needed to do surgery on a part of the human body demanded that kind of understanding. Even at that, he had one advantage over the apologist. A heart surgeon does not need to know much about neurosurgery—that is a different specialization. He doesn't even have to know all the advancements made in other forms of surgery. But the apologist does not have the privilege of a single discipline. In the audience sit specialists from a variety of fields. They expect the one giving the answer to be trained in multiple disciplines. That's what makes it hard. It is all the more imperative that in answering we do not pretend to know, but answer what we do know with clarity.

The way culture has changed and the way familiar words lose their impact make it imperative that we not fall into the trap of repetition without engagement. Os Guinness tells the story of a young protégé of Francis Schaeffer who was sharing his faith with a French existentialist in a Parisian barroom. Unknown to the young Schaefferian, the Frenchman had read most of Schaeffer's books. With every answer the Christian gave, the atheist began to see the obvious, until finally, he broke his secret and said, "Excuse me, but do you write with a Schaeffer pen too?" That ended the discussion. Authenticity and genuine conviction are essential to dealing with truth questions. If the terms are parroted without understanding, the message is garbled.

Here it is important to point out a very common fallacy held by not only the common person but by the typical social critic or academic. The assumption is often made that somehow the Christian stands alone in a claim to uniqueness and exclusivity. The audacious nature of the Christian faith is constantly brought up in conversations: "How can you claim there is only one way?" The questioner is obviously not aware that every religion is exclusive at its core. Gautama Buddha was born a Hindu but rejected two of Hinduism's fundamental claims:

the caste system and the eternal authority of the Vedas. He would have roundly denounced the most popular of all Hindu writings, the *Bhagavad Gita* and the teaching of Krishna. Hinduism itself in its core teachings is exclusivist. Try criticizing Hinduism in India and you'll find out in a hurry how exclusive and "superior" the Hindu feels his religion is.

You see, truth by definition is exclusive. If truth were all-inclusive, nothing would be false. And if nothing were false, what would be the meaning of true? Furthermore, if nothing were false, would it be true to say that everything is false? It quickly becomes evident that nonsense would follow. What, therefore, has actually happened in popular thought is culture has been engineered to deal with truth issues. That is the nerve of the problem in communication. It is the sacred duty of a pastor to remind his people periodically of the very nature of truth, because if truth dies, even at the altar of cultural sensitivities, then so does the gospel in the listener's ears. The first and foremost task of the apologist, then, is to stand for the truth and to clarify the claims of the gospel.

An Eternal Truth

The Scriptures remind us that God's Word abides forever and can never be broken (Isa 40:8; John 10:35; 1 Peter 1:23). We are also reminded that faith comes by hearing and hearing by the Word of God (Rom. 10:17). Knowing the Word, staying in the Word, and defending the Word are all vital parts of apologetics.

A few years ago, I was in Albania, which by its own admission was the most atheistic country in the world. After I had the privilege of addressing the members of parliament, the curator of the local museum in the audience asked if I would come and be his guest that afternoon. I was reluctant to accept because of the demands on my time that day. But his continued insistence about something special he wanted to show me changed my mind, and I went. I little expected what I was going to see. Into the room where I was seated marched an armed escort. In a manner of a special dish being presented came two men with outstretched arms holding an ancient text in their hand. As they gently set it down before me, I was momentarily silenced and then the curator spoke. "This is the handwritten translation of the Gospel of Matthew done by St. Chrysostom. During the excavations of a church from the 900s, this was found buried deep under the ruins."

Chrysostom lived in the fourth century, and his translation, done in gold ink with perfectly justified columns, left me overwhelmed by the commitment and labor of a man who sought to preserve the earliest texts for us. Ironically, the page that was opened before me was the text of the woman with the alabaster ointment. The words of Jesus stating that wherever the gospel would be preached, there also would this story be told, was a remarkable tribute paid to a woman who was an outcast in her society.

Centuries of preservation of the sacred text demand of us that we do our part in presenting its message and defending its truth. Truth, very simply stated, boils down to two tests: statements made must correspond to reality, and the system of thought that is developed as a result must be coherent. The correspondence and coherence tests are applied by all of us in matters that affect us.[1]

In his own preaching, the pastor should be able to defuse most questions. If I may use terminology from the field of electricity, this is how I would word it. The pastor or leader who stands in the pulpit takes the two prongs of the heart and intellect within the seeker, and plugs them into the adaptor of his message, connecting it to the receptacle of God's power that energizes the soul of the recipient. When that happens, he has served as a conduit for meeting the need and apologetics has met its demand. That is the least one's preaching should do. In answering the questions, the pastor becomes the bearer of God's response.

If the subject is too technical for the pastor or leader to tackle, he must find resources or contacts who can help his people wade through their sincere questions. He himself does not have to have expertise in everything, but he must have the resources to which he can point people in their pursuit of answers. Even apologists must know their limitations and be able to refer a questioner to a suitable source. Never before has so much written material and, for that matter, video material been available to tackle the hard questions. Well-known exponents deal with issues that young minds grapple with, and in being cognizant of that material, church leaders demonstrate an awareness of the issues. I would go so far as to say that if we are unprepared to defend what we believe so that the defense is meaningful, we may as well give up on this generation.

A Removal of Barriers

Third, leaders are given the task to remove barriers in the path of the listener, so that he or she will get a direct look at the cross and the person of Christ. Unless we establish what the goal is, we often lead the listener to the wrong destination.

We are to be extremely careful that we do not so overphilosophize that in the end we lead people to a philosophizing faith with no devotional content to it.

This is what happened, incidentally, when the early church had its articulators and personalities that carried the message. Some boasted they were of Apollos, others of Paul. Some thought the "gods" had come in their midst. Human inclinations are terribly vulnerable to hero worship or ideational enchantment. The communicator with words should be careful to point beyond the articulation to the one the articulation points to.

Speakers fall into a huge trap when they are more concerned about how they say it than whom they are pointing to. C. S. Lewis mentions this in his book *The Great Divorce.* The Spirit tells the Ghost, a mortal from hell visiting heaven, "When you painted on earth—at least in your earlier days—it was because you caught glimpses of Heaven in the earthly landscape. The success of your painting was that it enabled others to see the glimpse too. But here you are having the thing itself. . . . That was not how you began. Light itself was your first love: you loved paint only as a means of telling about light."

"Oh, that was ages ago," replies the Ghost. "One grows out of that. Of course, you haven't seen my later works. One becomes more and more interested in paint for its own sake."

Then the Spirit warns, "Every poet and musician and artist, but for Grace, is drawn away from love of the things he tells, to love of the telling till, down in Deep Hell, they cannot be interested in God at all but only in what they say about Him. For it doesn't stop at being interested in paint, you know. They sink lower—become interested in their own personalities and then in nothing but their own reputations."[2]

Some years ago I was on a flight from Brisbane to Sydney in Australia. A young lady was sitting next to me, quiet and, in fact, somewhat troubled. I tried to make conversation but didn't succeed. She happened to ask me what I was doing in Sydney, and I told her I was there on a speaking trip. "On what?" she asked. "Answering life's deepest questions," I said. There was silence, and then she asked a question on death and its immediate aftermath. By the time we touched down in Sydney, we were deeply engaged in a fascinating conversation. "When will you be coming back to Brisbane?" I asked. It was not to be for another two months. She was visiting her boyfriend in San Francisco for that period. I gave her a telephone number of a missionary in Brisbane whom I thought she should contact on her return.

Two or three years went by, and I returned to Brisbane for some meetings. The missionary said to me, "I have a guest for dinner tonight who wants to see you." Wondering who it could be, I was utterly surprised to find out it was this young lady. She was now married to the gentleman from San Francisco, and they were both in seminary preparing to go as missionaries to India.

"What on earth happened?" I asked. Well, as it went, she got back from the United States and the first Wednesday she was in town she showed up in church, looking for the missionary I had asked her to meet. Her first encounter at church was a shock to her. *These people actually think they are talking to God when they pray!* she thought. But something kept tugging at her heart, telling her that she should keep attending. Two weeks later, the missionary was leaving on furlough and introduced her to the one taking his place. To make a long story short, in a few weeks she gave her life to the Lord, then introduced her fiancé to the Lord, and this is where they were now studying.

"What made you ask me about death when we were on that flight?" I asked her.

"I had just buried my father the previous week," she said, "and the question haunted me as to where he was." This is how God works in a person's questions and in the ensuing answers. If any one of us along her path had become the chief "answer bearer" to her, we would have lost her along the way. The task of the apologist is plainly and simply to remove the doubts and point people to the cross.

A Contextual Answer

Jesus illustrated profoundly how we are to answer questions effectively. Of course, he had the supreme advantage of seeing the very motives of the questioner, something we ourselves can never be absolutely certain about. But nevertheless, his method is instructive. Most often, whenever Jesus was questioned, he questioned the questioner, thereby enabling the questioner to articulate his or her own assumptions and test his or her own motives. Consider, for example, when a lawyer came to him and asked, "Good Master, what shall I do to attain eternal life?" Had that question been put to you or I, we would have force-fed the gospel instantly. Instead, Jesus asked the man, "Why do you call me good? There is none good but God" (Mark 10:17–18).

It's amazing, isn't it, what Jesus is doing here. He is asking the questioner if he believes Jesus is God, and if so, will he listen to him? If the lawyer doesn't believe Jesus is God, then why is he calling him good? For the lawyer, these concepts were now put to the test.

On another occasion, one came questioning Jesus as to why his disciples were not fasting when the disciples of John were fasting (see Mark 2:18–22; cf. Matt. 9:14–17). Jesus gave a twofold answer. The first was the immediate answer to the pointed question, but then came the answer to the question behind the question. Jesus reminded the questioner that one does not fast while the bridegroom is present. The time would come when his disciples would fast. But then came the real answer: "You do not put new wine into old wineskins" (Mark 2:22). What Jesus is saying is that to get them to fast would be to put fasting back into their legalistic mind-set, which is exactly what Jesus was trying to change. He was working on the "wineskins." He was reshaping their way of thinking before he gave them the thought to think about.

This is precisely the task of the apologist. Every questioner has a worldview. If you do not appeal to the legitimacy or the illegitimacy of the worldview, you will never give satisfactory answers to the skeptic.

In short, apologetics may begin in specifics but inevitably moves to the general, which then explains the specifics. Can we really appeal to the resurrection if the person does not even grant the miraculous? The stories of Jonah and Moses will be laughable to the skeptic who fails to concede that this is a moral and miraculous world in which we live. C. S. Lewis said that an egg that comes from no bird is no less miraculous than a bird that has existed from eternity.[3] Somewhere, somehow the possibility of the supernatural must be granted. The worldview of the Christian best explains the undeniable realities that we see around us.

Obviously the task is quite complex, especially on moral issues. For example, a teenager may ask her father at the dinner table one evening, "Dad, why is premarital sex wrong?" "Why do you ask?" the father may say. "Well, my social studies teacher told us today that sexuality is just a cultural thing and that we have no right to determine which culture is right and which one is wrong. Is that true?" Perhaps the father may say to her, "Tell your teacher that the Bible says that there are clear laws that God had put in place for what he intended sex to be." She may well hesitate and respond, "But my teacher does not believe the Bible."

The father is right in dealing with the problem for himself, but he puts his daughter in the untenable position of positing a conclusion without defending her source of authority. If the teacher were to grant the Bible as the authority, then the issue is made simpler. But if the Bible is denied that place, then the father has sent his daughter into the lion's den with nothing to defend her. That is why I am convinced that *the most effective defense of the faith and offense against falsehood must be based on an examination of worldviews.*

THE THREE LEVELS OF PHILOSOPHY

Over the years of thinking through this issue, I have formed an approach that many have been able to identify with, especially as far as preaching is concerned. I call it the Three Levels of Philosophy. I have presented this elsewhere in my writings, and because it has been my method over the years, I give it here. Many in the task of apologetics have responded that this has been very helpful for them as well. So if you are familiar with this from my other writings, please excuse the repetition.

Level One: Logic

Philosophy, as I see it in every life, comes to us at three levels. The first level is the foundation, the theoretical substructure of logic upon which inductions are made and deductions are postulated. Put plainly, it depends heavily upon the form and the force of an argument. Logic, to most minds, has never overflowed with romance and has seldom triggered excitement. Yet truth has a direct bearing on reality, and the laws of logic apply in every sphere of our lives.

Since the laws of logic apply to reality, it is imperative that these laws be understood if any argument is to stand its ground. There are really four laws of logic. (Beyond these there are formal and informal fallacies, but that will not be our task here.) The four are:

1. *The law of identity:* If A then not non-A.
2. *The law of noncontradiction:* Not both A and non-A.
3. *The law of rational inference:* If the premises are true and the argument valid, there is a rational deduction.
4. *The law of the excluded middle:* Just because two things have one thing in common does not mean they have everything in common.

It is impossible to get around these laws without establishing them as you are trying to get around them. So every time someone says, "Ah, that's all this logic stuff," they are playing word games to save face, and not admitting that they are assuming the very laws they are trying to deny.

The next question arises, how does one build a brief logical argument? Peter Kreeft, professor of philosophy at Boston College, has briefly addressed this issue of the importance of correct argumentation in his book *Three Philosophies of Life*. In a subsection entitled "Rules for Talking Back" he writes,

> There are three things that must go right with any argument:
> 1. The terms must be unambiguous
> 2. The premises must be true
> 3. The argument must be logical.[4]

In any argument, the application of this grid cannot be compromised if the conclusion is to be defended or refuted. Truth is indispensable to each statement, and validity is indispensable to each deduction. This dual combination is central to the persuasiveness of any argument, and if there is a flaw in either of the two, it fails.

This is level one in our philosophical approach, the theoretical realm where the laws of logic are applied to reality. To deny their application is futile and self-defeating because one must use reason to either sustain it or challenge it. In short, level one deals with why one believes what he believes and is sustained by the process of reasoning, incorporating truth and logic.

For example, I well recall an exchange I had once on the campus of the University of the Philippines in Manila. A student from the audience shouted out that everything in life was meaningless. I responded by saying, "You do not believe that." He promptly retorted, "Yes, I do," to which I automatically countered, "No, you don't." Exasperated, he said, "I most certainly do; who are you to tell me I don't?" "Then please repeat your statement for me," I requested. "Everything in life is meaningless," he stated again without qualification. I said to him, "Please remain standing; this will only take a moment. I assume that you believe your statement is meaningful. If your statement is meaningful, then everything is not meaningless. On the other hand, if everything is meaningless, then what you have just said is meaningless too. So in effect you have said nothing." The young man was startled for a moment and even as I left the auditorium, he was pacing the floor muttering, "If everything is meaningless, then . . . ." So it went!

Level Two: Imagination and Feeling

The second level of philosophy does not feel the constraint of reason or come under the binding strictures of argument. It finds its refuge in the imagination and feeling. Ways of thinking at this level may enter one's consciousness via a play or a novel, or touch the imagination through visual media, making belief-altering impact by capturing the emotions. It is immensely effective; literature, drama, and music have historically molded the soul of a nation far more than has solid reasoning. Level two is existential and fallaciously claims that it need not bow to the laws of logic.

However, many an individual who takes his emotions as a starting point for determining truth, in grabbing the finger of feeling thinks he has grabbed the fist of truth. By thinking exclusively at this level, he is driven, systematically, further inward, until his whole world revolves around his personal passion, with a dangerous self-absorption. He reshapes his worldview to a "better felt than tell't" perspective—if it feels good do it. Unfortunately, even many churches have given into thinking almost exclusively at this level, as evidenced in their worship and preaching. But we shortchange our audience when we divorce our preaching from serious engagement with difficult ideas and instead preach at the level of emotion.

Level Three: Prescription

The third level of philosophy is what I call "kitchen table conclusions." It is amazing how much of the moralizing and prescribing in life goes on during casual conversations. The settings can vary from sidewalk cafes, where frustrated philosophers pontificate on profound themes, to the kitchen table, where children interact with their parents on questions that deal with far-reaching issues. The question may be the nagging one of the day, or it could be a question raised in the classroom, such as the one raised above from the daughter to her father. This level of philosophizing escapes neither the child nor the academic dean of a prestigious school because "why?" is one of the earliest expressions of human life.

To summarize, level one concerns logic; the appeal is to reason. Level two addresses the imagination; the appeal is to the felt reality. And level three is where all is applied to the reality specific to the question. Putting it differently, level one states why one believes what he believes. Level two indicates why one lives the way he lives. And level three reveals why one legislates for others the way he does.

GETTING THROUGH AT THE RIGHT LEVEL

For every life that is lived at a reasonable level, these three questions must be answered. First, can I defend what I believe in keeping with the laws of logic? That is, is it tenable? Second, if everyone gave him- or herself the prerogatives of my philosophy, can there be harmony in existence? That is, is it livable? Third, do I have a right to make moral judgments in the daily matters of living? Is it transferable?

None of these levels can live in isolation. They must follow a proper sequence. Here is the key: one must argue from level one, illustrate from level two, and apply at level three. Life must move from truth, to experience, to prescription. If either the theist or atheist violates this procedure, he or she is not dealing with reality, but creating one of his or her own.

Remember the dinner table discussion between the father and his daughter regarding sexuality and culture? Notice that the father makes his argument at the third level—prescription—while the question comes at another level—are there absolutes? The father must instead establish at level one the reason for or reasonableness of his claim. He must show that an absolute by nature is not culturally determined. I realize that this is not easily done at any age, but it must be done when the mind is capable of engaging the argument.

On one occasion I ran up against this very question by a reporter. I had just finished lecturing at a university. She had very graciously stayed through the entire length of the lecture even though she had other pressing engagements. After the lecture was over, she was walking beside me and asked, "Can I ask you a question that really troubles me about Christians?" I was glad to oblige. "Why," she asked, "are Christians openly against racial discrimination but at the same time discriminate against certain types of sexual behavior?" (She was more specific about the types of behavior she felt we discriminated against.)

I said this to her: "We are against racial discrimination because one's ethnicity is sacred. You cannot violate the sacredness of one's race. For the same reason, we are against the altering of God's pattern and purpose for sexuality. Sex is sacred in the eyes of God and ought not to be violated. What you have to explain is why you treat race as sacred and desacralize sexuality. The question is really yours, not mine. In other words, our reasoning in both cases stems from the same foundational basis. You in effect switch the basis of reasoning, and that is why you are living in contradiction." There was silence and she said, "I have never thought of it in those terms." You see, when an argument is taken to the first level, it immediately finds a common point of reference. When it leaps only to the third level, it builds without a foundation.

This grid has been very helpful in evangelistic preaching as well: the argument (or proclamation), the illustration (or story), and the application (or invitation). The Scriptures provide the truth; the arts, literature, or current events provide the illustrations; and the application should go right to daily living and appeal to the will. This approach essentially underscores the three levels of philosophy and helps connect ideas with concrete reality.

A MASTER APOLOGIST AT WORK

When one looks at the Scriptures and studies the finest exponents of evangelistic preaching, the apostle Paul stands out as the quintessential example of how to cut across cultural lines and philosophical bents without compromising the message. This was brought home to me some time ago during a visit to Greece. To this day, at the base of Mars Hill is a huge bronze plaque with the words of Paul's address to Stoics and Epicureans, memorialized for us in Acts 17.

He began by saying, "Men of Athens! I see that in every way you are very religious. For as I walked around and looked carefully at your objects of worship, I even found an altar with this inscription: To an Unknown God. Now what you worship as something unknown I am going to proclaim to you" (Acts 17:22–23).

Paul's point of entry was where the Athenians were in their own thinking, and while his goal was to expose their intellectual failure, he began by affirming their spiritual hunger. Step by step, he proceeded from their need to the One who is omniscient—God as revealed in Christ. Paul was keenly aware of his context, and with compelling relevance he applied the truth of the gospel and won a hearing. Some influential men and women made their commitment to Christ that day, and the church was established on firm footing in Athens. In fact, one is quite taken aback to see the name of the main street that runs alongside Mars Hill—it is named after Dionysius the Areopagite, who made his commitment to

Christ at the end of Paul's message. Two thousand years later, the hill and the street stand as a tribute to a message and a recipient.

From Athens Paul moved on to Corinth, a setting that was quite dramatically different. William Barclay, the New Testament scholar, says of Corinth, "Above all, Corinth was a wicked city. The Greeks had a verb, 'to play the Corinthian,' which meant to live a life of lustful debauchery. The word *Corinthian* came into the English language to describe, in regency times, 'a reckless, roistering, regency buck.'"[5] Any reader of Paul's epistles to the Corinthians is familiar with the catalogue of vices that he lists, ending with the words, "As such were some of you." But one is immediately arrested by Paul's opening words to them: "I was with you . . . not with enticing words of man's wisdom, but in demonstration of the Holy Spirit and of power" (1 Cor. 2:3–4 KJV).

As I stood at Corinth, I was overwhelmed by Paul's message. There on a marble slab were etched those powerful words of 1 Corinthians 13, possibly the greatest exposition on love. How did Paul apply the truth of the gospel to a people so depraved? It is easy to see. Lofting over the ruins of ancient Corinth stand the remains of the temple of Aphrodite, the goddess of sensual love. This temple housed a thousand prostitutes who paraded their offerings each night before the insatiable Corinthians. Paul contrasted this vulgar expression of love with the purity and beauty of God's love, which rejoices with the truth and is eternal in nature. With what riveting force those words hold the reader captive today, disclosing the grandeur of love and overwhelming the imagination when read in the context of Corinth's greatest need.

As I reflected on Paul's approach, I could readily see the potency of truth when conveyed through the framework of one's thought and life. Paul would have made a horrendous mistake had he come to Corinth as he had to Athens, armed with logic and argument. In Athens it was a battle of the mind—philosophy. But in Corinth it was a battle for the body—sensuality. Yet there is a connection; indeed, an inextricable one. Both the minds and hearts of the hearers must be addressed such that they may be prepared to surrender to the gospel. But let us not miss the point. The way to the heart in each city had to be from a different starting point of the gospel, which culminated in a particular application. In other words, there is great danger in assuming that one approach fits all. Understanding and repentance are the fruit of expository preaching that is met with personal or even national application.

Some years ago, I was visiting a monastery in the Mediterranean region where a handful of monks for centuries have escaped into a secluded existence. Their lives are housed in caves and rocks, with prayer and solitude as their daily diet. As we walked through their library, we were shown that all the literature they were allowed to read was directly from Scripture or their saints. There was, however, a copy of one of Aristotle's books, but that had a danger attached to it. In medieval times, that genre of book was laced with arsenic on every page so that if perchance a monk took it up to read it, when he moistened his finger to turn the page, arsenic would make its way into his bloodstream and soon he would drop dead for having ingested worldly knowledge. As well meaning as these monks are, in attempting to speak to God about humanity, they have lost the ability to speak to humanity about God.

How different that was to the approach of the apostle Paul, who knew the ideas that shaped his audience and knew well how to harness those ideas to advantage for the cause of the gospel. It is vitally important for the pastor to know his audience. Thus I add to the injunction "Keep your finger on the text" this advice: "And your ear to the audience." To ignore the latter could well elicit the indictment, "Great sermon; wrong crowd." Identification is a critical first step.

From Speaking to Communicating

Paul well knew that he needed to bring his message down to their grasp—to translate the gospel from his worldview to theirs. Is it any different in our time? For example, even a magnificent word like *salvation* carries such a narrow idea to the one who does not understand the breadth that salvation brings. It is not just a "pie in the sky by and by when I die" message; its inheritance is immediate.

Jesus' message to the woman at the well was translated from her theological smokescreens, right down to where she lived. In his conversation, Jesus systematically moved her from her past to her present and from the proximate to the personal. She knew what he was talking about. Her ecstatic report to her own people was that he saw everything about her.

It was the same communication of the message that John used in the book of Revelation when addressing the churches. Communication requires words and concepts that do not create gaps but build bridges.

From Communicating to Convincing

Persuasion is the component that locks the listener in with inescapable interest, such that he or she begins to listen with felt need. Often times, this is the illustration or the story that draws the listener in with riveted attention. One can tell in any sermon when that moment comes. This persuasion ought not to be confused with the persuasion that only the Holy Spirit can bring. But I am convinced that in this step the Spirit of God takes the truth of what is said and lodges it into the heart of the listener to a point of contact with interest. Illustrations of this abound in virtually every listener who has responded at the end of the message.

From Convincing to Closure

The final step is that of justification—clarifying why what has been said is true and not false. Paul's reference to the resurrection is clearly that aspect in his message to the Athenians. That Jesus attested those claims by his dramatic defeat of death is the ultimate proof that he was who he claimed to be. This logically leads to the invitation toward repentance and trust in the offer of Christ's message of forgiveness and life.

The pastor has this privilege in public and in private to build the message systematically and relevantly. But it is here that the pastor's privilege builds beyond that of the evangelist. From preaching evangelistically, he is able to go to the next step.

A FINAL WORD—WORSHIP AS EVANGELISM

Finally, I present the whole community of God's people in worship as evangelism. Years ago, I read a definition of *worship* that to this day rings with clear and magnificent terms. The definition comes from the famed archbishop William Temple: "Worship is the submission of all of our nature to God. It is the quickening of the conscience by his holiness; the nourishment of mind with his truth; the purifying of imagination by his beauty; the opening of the heart to his love; the surrender of will to his purpose—all this gathered up in adoration, the most selfless emotion of which our nature is capable."[6]

The more I have reflected on that definition, the more I am convinced that if worship is practiced with integrity in the community of God's people, potentially, worship may be the most powerful evangel for our postmodern culture. It is imperative that in planning the worship services, the pastor and church leaders give careful attention to every element and make sure that worship retains both integrity and purpose. People come to church generally beaten down by the world of deceit, distraction, and demand. There is an extraction of emotional and spiritual energy that brings them "on empty" into the community. The minister's task is to so prepare during the week that he will be the instrument of replenishment and fresh energy of soul. Even being in the presence of fellow believers in worship is a restorer of spiritual hope. We so underestimate the power of a people in one mind and with one commitment. Even a prayer can so touch a hungry heart that it can rescue a sliding foot in a treacherous time.

A few years ago, two or three of my colleagues and I were in a country dominated for decades by Marxism. Before we began our meetings, we were invited to a dinner hosted by some common friends, all of whom were skeptics and, for all practical purposes, atheists. The evening was full of questions, posed principally by a notable theoretical physicist in the country. There were also others who represented different elements of power within that society. As the night wore on, we got the feeling that the questions had gone on long enough and that we were possibly going in circles.

At that point, I asked, if we could have a word of prayer with them, for them, and for the country before we bade them good-bye. There was a silence of consternation, an obvious hesitancy, and then one said, "Of course." We did just that—we prayed. In this large dining room of historic import to them, with all the memories of secular power plastered within those walls, the prayer brought a sobering silence that we were all in the presence of someone greater than us. When we finished, every eye was moist and nothing was said. They hugged us and thanked us, with emotion written all over their faces. The next day when we met them, one of them said to me, "We did not go back to our rooms last night till it was early morning. In fact, I stayed in my hotel lobby most of the night talking further. Then I went back to my room and gave my life to Jesus Christ."

I firmly believe that it was the prayer that gave them a hint of the taste of what worship is all about. Their hearts had never experienced it. Over the years I have discovered that praying with people can sometimes do more for them than preaching to them. Prayer draws the heart away from one's own dependence to leaning on the sovereign God. The burden is often lifted instantly. Prayer is only one aspect of worship, but one that is greatly neglected in the face of people who would be shocked to hear what prayer sounds like when the one praying knows how to touch the heart of God. To a person in need, pat answers don't change the mind; prayer does.

CONCLUSION

I know a young woman who is a hairdresser. The first time I went to her, halfway through my haircut, she asked, "Are you a Christian?" Rather surprised, I asked her why she asked. That went into a fascinating conversation. She was a Muslim from Iran. She told me her story. A couple of years earlier, she had a customer who she said kept looking at her through the mirror and she became quite uncomfortable. Then out of the blue, he said to her, "You look like a very troubled and unhappy person today. Are you all right?" That's all she needed to hear and the tears started to flow. "I have just come through a divorce; the papers have come through today," she said. "My heart inside is breaking." The gentleman kept very quiet and apologized for the pain she was feeling. As he was leaving, he went to his car, brought out a CD, and said, "You do not know me and you will probably not see me again. I am a missionary in Europe, and my family and I are leaving today for our field of service. I want you to listen to this CD today, and here is an address of an Iranian pastor not far from your shop. If you want to get some answers, phone him." With that, he left.

On her way home that evening, she put on that CD in her car. The hymns started to play. All of a sudden, "Amazing Grace" came on. The rest is history. She told me that as she listened to those hymns, one after another, some she understood, some she did not. She sat in her driveway with tears running down her face and just kept listening to the entire CD. Something within her said, *This is what I need.* The next day she called that Iranian pastor. He invited her to their church. She became a follower of Jesus Christ and, one by one, led her family to Christ. That missionary had no idea how the prompting of his heart met the need of one who was crying out within.

Intelligent answers, proclamation, music, and worship, in my estimation these are four profound means with which God communicates to the resistant heart. All this carries serious preparation of heart and mind. Many times building a relationship preconditions the heart because of a life observed. The pastor often carries the privilege of pulling it all together.

There is much more that one can say. The church as a unit gives occasion time and again, within the provision of its fellowship, to meet the needs of many a lonely heart. The pastor builds a congregation with that legitimate need in mind. But there are also many who have become so hardened to their own needs and so prejudiced in their own distortions of the gospel that one has to almost make the listener aware of the need before offering the hope.

It is one thing for a drowning victim who cries for help to be offered a lifeline. It is quite another for one to be swimming with strength into the deep, quite oblivious that the strength will fail and there will be none left to swim back. To underestimate the method required to reach such a one is to kill, not to rescue, because it is the need that is in effect. Or to change the metaphor, it is one thing for the wounded to feel the need for a hand of rescue; it is another for one to feel their own armor will never be pierced. For the latter, the weapons of God's warfare alone will suffice.

Conclusion

Apologetics for Today

Ravi Zacharias

The simplest and most effective outline I have ever seen on the Prodigal Son story is that presented by an old Scottish divine. He had three points to his sermon:

1. Sick o' home
2. Homesick
3. Home

In that outline the struggle for meaning, the escapades that reached a dead end, and the final arrival back to where it all began is the storyline. In many ways, that is the path of an apologist. Why doesn't life add up? Why doesn't the pursuit of pleasure add up? And finally, where is it all meant to add up? Our approach to apologetics at a popular level aims to answer just such questions.

But before I say anything further in defense of that approach, I should say a word about the great impact of apologists and the rigorous discipline that is at its core. I will ever personally be indebted to my teachers and instructors. Without them, I would have abandoned this discipline long ago. I think of the impact of professors like Norman Geisler, John Warwick Montgomery, John Gerstner, and numerous others. There were those in the biblical studies departments like Walter Kaiser, Gleason Archer, John Stott, I. Howard Marshall, J. I. Packer, and others who gave me a love for the Word of God. That balance between the love of the Scriptures and the rigorous argumentation of why this is God's Word gave me the imperatives I needed to preach and teach, especially in areas of great resistance.

When one looks back across the landscape of apologetics over the last century, C. S. Lewis in the United Kingdom and Francis Schaeffer in the United States (and his L'Abri fellowship based in Switzerland) are two of the most commonly referred-to exponents whose names are writ large in this field. We will not be able to fully appreciate the role they played until we are in the very presence of God and recognize how these choice servants stood in the gap. As we look at the role and place of apologetics and the key names in the discipline, we must not forget that some by design were highly academic as they needed to be, while others touched the reader in the imagination or moral intuition.

We must understand the method as various apologists reflect different approaches to persuasive content. Norman Geisler, deeply committed to the right use of the classical arguments, has been brilliant in using them. His depth is often needed to blunt the hard-nosed attacks. C. S. Lewis, on the other hand, appealed to the moral imagination in a way that no other has done in recent memory. His style of argument and his brilliance in the field of literature make him highly readable and in many ways capture you in Narnia without your knowing that's where he wanted to speak to you. Francis Schaeffer saw the West in the early days of its spiritual demise and was almost prophetic in the warnings he sounded. As volatile issues such as abortion and sexual orientation became hot topics in the public sphere, Schaeffer sounded the warning sirens of a foundationless culture. He was truly a culturally directed apologist. No real comprehension of Christian apologetics is possible without reading these scholars.

Having said all that, we come to the hard question of approaches and methods. In many ways there have been powerful apologists of a completely different sort whose writings in the public square made for moral argumentation at a journalistic level. I refer to popular writers like G. K. Chesterton, Malcolm Muggeridge, George MacDonald, and others. The landscape has been rich in different voices, all basically arguing for a moral framework, which they considered defensible only if there were a God to justify it.

So as we bring this volume to a close, we once again stress a few basics. First, do not ever depend on one knockout method that will bring about the desired result. Go back across the last few centuries and revisit the kind of relevance it would have taken. In the 1500s and 1600s, rationalism reigned as the deciding epistemology—meaning that only mathematical certainty could determine truth or falsehood. Man was seen as a rational being. In the 1700s and 1800s, empiricism and the scientific worldview made certainty the private stronghold of the sciences. Man was seen as an investigative being. In the 1900s, existentialism became the way of thinking in meaningful categories. Man was seen as a self-defining being. By the end of the twentieth century, postmodernism was rising as the prevalent worldview. Man was seen as a linguistic being, constructing his or her own meaning out of words.

You remember how Isaiah talked about a woodsman hewing down the timber and then cutting it down to smaller sizes till he carved his idol and then fell down and worshiped it (Isa. 44:13–18)? Well, postmodernists have done that with language. They have taken their craft of linguistic skill, fashioning a world of reality just by words, deconstructing it to his or her own image and worshiping at that altar. What you will notice in all of these "-isms" is that somehow, in some way, man becomes the measure.

What we have sought to accomplish as a team in writing this book is to reinforce time and again that apologetics is not to be a single-lane approach. Rather, just as a human being is a composite, so also should the approach be to that person. There is a sense in which the rational is the basis, but then issues of meaning, investigation, language, emotion—all of these come to play at some point. I have very little doubt that the prodigal son ultimately did not come because of some incredibly designed argument; instead, his memory of home and all he had lost in a relationship began his homeward trek.

So if there is one term that captures the apologetic approach we have used, it would be the relational-reality model. All reality is ultimately defined by the Holy Trinity, God who is a Being in relationship. All relationships have to be based on the recognition of truth. God is the truth. Truth is that which corresponds to reality as it is, not necessarily as we construct it to be. Pointers to the truth come to us in language and experience. Truth is ultimately a characteristic of propositions. That is why, "In the beginning was the Word" (John 1:1).

As we yearn for meaning, we look for that which is not just enchanting but that which is perpetually so without the high cost of ecstasy. "I have come that they may have life, and have it to the full." Those are the words of Jesus in John 10:10. The apologist does not, therefore, depend on one knockout argument but in the response to the real for which we all ultimately search.

The second important facet is to know how the Holy Spirit works in convicting the listener. Here, I take the classic message of Paul to Felix, as he confronted one who had the power of a king but the mind of a slave. When you analyze the message, you see some simple truths. Paul spoke to him of righteousness, of self-control, and of judgment. I see these three connections as a point of reference, a point of relevance, and a point of disturbance. People either justify themselves or judge one another. What is the basis? Some measuring point of righteousness. Every person fails to measure up to even his or her own standards. Self-control is the rarest form of virtue. Every person wants the balances to be set straight, especially when he or she is on the receiving end of imbalance. So this great apostle deals with realities he knew his listener either assumed or recognized.

But, I think, there is more. Righteousness is the struggle met by the grace of the Son of God's provision for us. Self-control is the power given to us by the indwelling of the Holy Spirit. Judgment is the prerogative and power of the Father. There is clearly a trinitarian component to Paul's presentation. Righteousness deals with the past of my life that is now covered. Self-control deals with the present of my life as I face each day. Judgment deals with the future setting when I shall stand before God. This approach deals with the tenses of life: past, present, and future. And finally, in this approach of Paul, I see this fascinating reality. Paul deals with the very issues about which Jesus said the Holy Spirit would bring to conviction to the world: sin, righteousness, and judgment (John 16:8). Whatever approach we use, we must not violate the very role of God's Holy Spirit, who alone can bring true conviction.

The third important facet is to remember that the role of the apologist is to win the person, not the argument. That happens when the real questions surface and the real value of the questioner is upheld. Don't get baited into personal attacks.

During the Second World War, the Nazis had taken hold of some old Norman homes, heavily walled and protected. From those small structures, they set up their big guns and, as the enemy would storm the land, from these little homes the firepower unleashed would take a heavy toll on the Allies. At one point, a commanding officer commissioned small platoons to take these strongholds so that this deadly force could be neutralized when reinforcements arrived. On three different occasions one platoon leader was found to be rather bewildered and hard-pressed to know what to do. The commanding officer came close to him and asked why he had not yet made his move. "I don't know how to overpower a small home like that," he said. "I'll show you once," replied the commander, "and then you're on your own."

How did one get into a position of leadership without knowing how to neutralize a small stronghold? That's what happens when the training is rushed and the danger is large. In many ways this is what we now face in the church today. We have basically an "untrained" membership with the danger quite large. To add to the challenge, we cannot simply "take strongholds." We must do so while preserving the life of the one using that stronghold. Tossing a verbal grenade down the chimney chute will not do.

WITH GRATITUDE

I want to add some personal words as I end this book. As usually happens in the linear landscape between an author with an idea and a finished book, a publisher stands. In this case, a warm and casual lunch meeting with Byron Williamson and Joey Paul several years ago in Birmingham, Alabama, was when the idea for this book was born. Straightway out of that meeting, the format of the book and the contribution of each person was discussed in specific and measurable terms. From this discussion, and the enthusiasm and resolve of Byron and Joey, *Beyond Opinion* came to be. I'm thankful to them. My literary agent, Robert Wolgemuth, and his team have as always been friends and advisors as the book has unfolded. I also appreciate Matt Baugher and Thom Chittom of Thomas Nelson, and Margaret Manning, an associate writer with RZIM, who came alongside Danielle DuRant as the project neared completion.

Words cannot express the gratitude I have for my colleagues, alongside whom I have worked for so many years. You will notice that the RZIM writing team for this book is broadly based internationally. My Oxford colleagues have played a very special role in our worldwide mission. Some years ago, RZIM officially was linked with Wycliffe Hall, Oxford, in bringing to birth The Oxford Center for Christian Apologetics. We team teach courses there, and the program has drawn students from all over the world. One look at their credentials and you will know this team was put together by the grace of God, because each is uniquely gifted but has chosen to work with this team.

Amy Orr-Ewing is one of the most sought-after speakers in Europe today. She and her husband, in a daring mission to the Taliban years ago, took the gospel right into the living quarters of the tyrannical. Her academic achievements at Oxford met new benchmarks.

Alister McGrath is a prolific writer and eminently qualified to respond to the strident and hate-ridden atheism of our time. His softer touch and brilliant mind bring a much-needed counterweight to the Sam Harrises and Richard Dawkinses of our day.

American born, Indian (of parentage from India, that is) Alison Thomas is fast becoming a beloved name in apologetics to high school students. She is innovative, creative, and courageous. I believe she is one special young woman, gifted for a very demanding task.

Sam Soloman hails from an Islamic nation and has faced very tough situations in his life. There are very few in our world today so immersed in an understanding of the Qur'an and so passionate in his love for the gospel. I have seen him speak at highly charged situations and shine the light of Christ with splendor. You will learn much from his chapter.

L. T. Jeyachandran was a highly placed engineer in Indian Civil Service and has worked with our ministry for well over a decade now. I am always amazed at the insights he brings and the practicality of what he teaches. His understanding of Eastern thought is native to his thinking with highly relevant biblical counterperspective.

John Lennox is a huggable scholar who is an expert in his discipline of mathematics and a devout student of the Scriptures. I tease him when I refer to his professorial designation as Instructor in Pure Mathematics, asking him if there was really any such thing because it caused me untold harm in my own college grades. The only unfortunate thing about reading Professor Lennox's chapter is that you cannot glimpse his cherubic face.

It is a pity that you will only read Michael Ramsden in this volume and not gain the power of his humor in conversational apologetics. I always kid him that the archangel asked for a name-change in heaven when Michael Ramsden was named on earth. Michael is the finest example of what he writes—conversational apologetics.

Joe Boot, when this book began, was RZIM's Canadian director. He is now in an adjunct role with us and has entered a church-planting ministry in Toronto. Joe is a deep thinker, and so it was an even greater challenge to him to resist the urge and keep the content at a "lower shelf." His reach is far and his mind sharp.

I'Ching Thomas hails from Malaysia while based in Singapore for RZIM. She has already made extraordinary inroads in some very unique settings.

Stuart McAlister hails from Scotland and started off his early days as a barroom bouncer. One look at his physique, and you will know why he was selected for the job! On a serious note, Stuart has served time in prison in Eastern Europe for smuggling in Bibles during the frigid days of the Cold War and the reign of demagogues. He is as brilliant as he is devout in what he does for the Lord.

I have purposely saved the last for the most important: Danielle DuRant, the managing editor of this book. This volume would never have reached publication without her. She has worked with RZIM for more than fifteen years, and I keep reminding her she has a "no-trade" clause in her "contract" with us. Danielle's hard work, keen mind, informed intellect, disciplined memory, loyal support, and tender heart have made her an invaluable asset in my own speaking and writing. Normally such words are saved for acknowledgments, but most never read that portion. So I have left it for these closing words. I have deeply valued all that she does for me personally and now this work for a worldwide readership.

Each one of these writers joins me in wishing the reader both blessing and impetus in doing the task of the apologist well, for the glory of God. It is my sincere prayer that this book will help train the one who wants to overpower strongholds while preserving the lives within by giving them the message of hope and peace.

One of my favorite hymns is that written by Charles Wesley:

> O Thou Who camest from above,
> The pure celestial fire to impart,
> Kindle a flame of sacred love
> Upon the mean altar of my heart.
>
> There let it for Thy glory burn
> With inextinguishable blaze,
> And trembling to its source return,
> In humble prayer and fervent praise.
> Jesus, confirm my heart's desire
> To work and speak and think for Thee;
> Still let me guard the holy fire,
> And still stir up Thy gift in me.

Ready for all Thy perfect will,
My acts of faith and love repeat,
Till death Thy endless mercies seal,
And make my sacrifice complete.

Such passion can only be carried out when it goes beyond opinion to conviction of the mind and soul.

ABOUT THE CONTRIBUTORS

Joe Boot is an RZIM adjunct associate and former director of RZIM in Canada. He obtained a diploma in theology from Birmingham Bible Institute in Great Britain followed by a year of study and vocational training at a school for Christian leadership in Nottingham. A widely respected communicator and educator, he has spoken in more than twenty countries and addressed audiences at Eton College, Oxford University, London School of Theology, University of Toronto, Waterloo University, and Forman University College in Pakistan. Boot is the author of *Why I Still Believe* and *Searching for Truth*, published both in Europe and North America.

Danielle DuRant is director of research and writing at RZIM and research assistant to Ravi Zacharias. She received her MDiv from Gordon-Conwell Theological Seminary. DuRant oversees a variety of writing projects and is the editor and a featured writer for RZIM's publication *Just Thinking*. She is the general editor of the four-volume *RZIM Critical Questions Discussion Guides* and the managing editor of *Beyond Opinion* as well as *Is Your Church Ready?* and *Who Made God?*, edited by Norman Geisler and Ravi Zacharias.

L. T. Jeyachandran is executive director of RZIM (Asia-Pacific) Limited in Singapore. He received a master of technology in structural engineering from the prestigious Indian Institute of Technology in Chennai and worked in India for twenty-eight years as a senior civil engineer with the federal government. He took early retirement to join RZIM in India and functioned as director of ministries until moving to Singapore. A keen student of theology, biblical languages, and comparative religions, Jeyachandran is well-known as a Bible expositor. He is a frequent lecturer at the Oxford Centre for Christian Apologetics and speaks worldwide in churches and universities.

John Lennox is reader in mathematics at Oxford University, fellow in mathematics and the philosophy of science at Green College, Oxford, and joint director of the Oxford Centre for Christian Apologetics. He holds the degrees of MA and PhD from Cambridge and was reader in pure mathematics at the University of Wales where he was awarded a DSc degree. He also has an MA in bioethics. Lennox has lectured and written widely on the interface of science, philosophy, and theology and engaged in an open forum with Richard Dawkins. His books include *God's Undertaker: Has Science Buried God?* and *Christianity: Opium or Truth?* (coauthored with David Gooding).

Stuart McAllister is director of training at RZIM and speaks worldwide on global issues such as pluralism, postmodernism, and consumerism that face the church. Born in Scotland, McAllister served with Operation Mobilization for twenty years in Austria. During that time, he was imprisoned on several occasions for distributing Christian literature and preaching the gospel in communist countries. He served as general secretary of the European Evangelical Alliance and developed an evangelistic mobilization called "Love Europe" that sent several thousand team members across Europe with the message of the gospel.

Alister McGrath is professor of historical theology at Oxford University, senior research fellow at Harris Manchester College, Oxford, and president of the Oxford Centre for Christian Apologetics. He holds first class honors degrees in both chemistry and theology from Oxford University and was awarded an Oxford DPhil for his research in the natural sciences. McGrath has written a number of important works on Reformation history, theology, and evangelicalism. He has a special interest in atheism, evident in his books *Dawkins' God, The Twilight of Atheism,* and *The Dawkins Delusion?* He has formally debated Christopher Hitchens and other prominent atheists.

Amy Orr-Ewing is training director of RZIM Zacharias Trust in the UK and director of programs for the Oxford Centre for Christian Apologetics. She gained a first class degree in theology at Christ Church, Oxford University, before receiving a master's degree in theology at King's College, London. Orr-Ewing has coauthored *Holy Warriors: A Fresh Look at the Face of Extreme Islam* and has contributed to *God and the Generations* and *Worth Knowing: Wisdom for Women*. She has also written *Is the Bible Intolerant?* (shortlisted for the 2006 UK Christian Book Awards) and *But Is It Real?* Orr-Ewing speaks and lectures globally on apologetics.

Michael Ramsden is director of RZIM Zacharias Trust in the UK, joint director of the Oxford Centre for Christian Apologetics, and lecturer in Christian apologetics at Wycliffe Hall, Oxford. While doing research at Sheffield University, he taught moral philosophy and lectured for the International Seminar on Jurisprudence and Human Rights in Strasbourg. Ramsden speaks to audiences worldwide and is involved in a number of initiatives to equip and train emerging leaders and evangelists throughout Europe. He has contributed to the book *Preach the Word!* and has written a series of articles for *Idea* magazine, giving an evangelical response to some of today's most challenging issues.

Sam Soloman is an RZIM adjunct associate and head of the Islamics department at Elam Ministries, a mission on the frontline of ministry to the Muslim world. He is a formidable authority on Islamic issues and has special expertise in Sharia law. From a Middle Eastern background, Soloman lectures extensively and teaches postgraduate courses for nationals from Muslim countries and missionaries working in the Muslim world. As a human rights activist, he is much in demand and has represented persecuted Christians in a number of countries. Soloman has been called to brief US Congressmen, European Parliamentarians at Brussels, and the British Parliament at Westminster.

Alison Thomas is an itinerant apologist with RZIM. She received a master's degree in classical apologetics from Southern Evangelical Seminary where she was mentored by Norman Geisler. By invitation, Thomas travels globally to defend the beauty and credibility of the gospel. Her conversational style creatively couples theology and philosophy to equip the believer and engage the skeptic. She speaks mainly to students and young professionals in diverse settings such as a women's conference in Dubai, Focus on the Family, Calvary Chapel, and the Oxford Inter-Collegiate Christian Union.

I'Ching Thomas is associate director of training at RZIM (Asia-Pacific) Limited in Singapore. She graduated with honors with a BA in communications from Universiti Sains Malaysia and later received an MA in Christian apologetics from Biola University. Thomas worked for seven years as a marketing and communications consultant for various multinational companies in Malaysia and then with Operation Mobilization as a missionary in a Middle Eastern country. There she served as the director of short-term missions and steered the program in a new direction by spearheading efforts in reaching the most unreached part of the field.

Ravi Zacharias is founder and president of RZIM and senior research fellow at Wycliffe Hall, Oxford. He received his MDiv from Trinity International University and has been conferred a Doctor of Divinity degree from both Houghton College and Tyndale College and Seminary, Toronto, and a Doctor of Laws degree from Asbury College, Kentucky. Zacharias has spoken in over fifty countries and in numerous universities, notably Harvard, Princeton, and Cambridge. He has addressed writers of the peace accord in South Africa, the president's cabinet and parliament in Peru, and military officers at the Lenin Military Academy and the Center for Geopolitical Strategy in Moscow. He has been privileged to give the main address at the National Day of Prayer in Washington DC and twice at the Annual Prayer Breakfast at the United Nations in New York. His many books include *The Grand Weaver, Jesus Among Other Gods,* and the Gold Medallion winner *Can Man Live Without God?*

NOTES

INTRODUCTION: AN APOLOGETIC FOR APOLOGETICS—RAVI ZACHARIAS

1. Robert M. Pirsig, *Zen and the Art of Motorcycle Maintenance: An Inquiry into Values* (New York: HarperTorch, 2006).

CHAPTER 1: POSTMODERN CHALLENGES TO THE BIBLE—AMY ORR-EWING

1. "Postmodernist Anthropology, Subjectivity, and Science: A Modernist Critique," Melford E. Spiro, *Comparative Studies in Society and History*, 38, no. 4 (October 1996), 759–80.

2. According to footnote 1,128 in *The Starr Report*.

3. Roland Barthes, "The Death of the Author," in *Image-Music-Text* (New York: Hill and Wang, 1978), 417.

4. Jean-François Lyotard, *The Postmodern Condition: A Report on Knowledge*, trans. Geoff Benington and Brian Massumi (Minneapolis: University of Minnesota Press, 1984), 82.

5. Ibid.

6. Michel Foucault, "The Archaeology of Knowledge" and "The Order of Discourse" in *Untying the Text: A Post-Structuralist Reader*, Young, Robert, ed. (London: Routledge, 1981); Michel Foucault, *Discipline and Punish: The Birth of the Prison*, trans. Alan Sheridan, (New York: Vintage Books, 1977), 27.

7. Jacques Derrida, *Of Grammatology*, trans. Gayatri Chakravorty (Baltimore: Johns Hopkins University Press, 1998), 49.

8. E. P. Sanders, "But Did It Happen?" *The Spectator* Vol. 276 (6 April 1996).

9. Foucault, "Nietzsche, Genealogy, History" in Stanley J. Grenz, *A Primer of Postmodernism* (Grand Rapids: Eerdmans, 1996), 162.

10. Rowan Williams, "Doubtful Mysteries Blind Us to Real Faith," *Mail on Sunday*, April 16, 2006.

11. Dan Brown, *The Da Vinci Code* (New York: Doubleday, 2003).

12. See, e.g., Michael Green, *The Books the Church Suppressed: Fiction and Truth in The Da Vinci Code* (Toronto: Monarch, 2005).

13. F. F. Bruce, *The Books and Parchments: How We Got Our English Bible* (Basingstoke: Pickering and Inglis, 1984), 113.

14. Comment in *Matt. Ap. Euseb. H.E.* 6. 25. In this catalog he omits James and Jude but includes them in his 13th Homily on Genesis and lists the whole Canon in his 7th Homily on the book of Joshua.

15. John Barton, *How the Bible Came to Be* (Louisville, KY: Westminster John Knox Press, 1998), 85.

16. For more regarding the rules of warfare and God's mercy, see the chapter "How Could a Loving God Command Genocide?"in Paul Copan's *That's Just Your Interpretation* (Grand Rapids: Baker, 2001).

17. See, e.g., Peter Craigie, *The Problem of War in the Old Testament* (Grand Rapids: Eerdmans, 1978); Susan Niditch, *War in the Hebrew Bible: A Study in the Ethics of Violence* (New York: Orbis Press, 1993); Gerhard Von Rad, *Holy War in Ancient Israel* (Grand Rapids: Eerdmans, 1991).

18. For further study on this see Stanley N. Gundry, ed., *Show Them No Mercy: 4 Views on God and the Canaanite Genocide* (Grand Rapids: Zondervan, 2003).

19. Most Christians today fall into the middle two positions.

20. Robin Gill, *A Textbook of Christian Ethics,* 3rd ed. (London: T & T Clark, 2006), 257ff.
21. Aquinas systematizes this theory in the thirteenth century, and Francisco de Vitari develops it in the sixteenth century.
22. For a further study of Christian just war theory, see Gill, *A Textbook of Christian Ethics.*

CHAPTER 2: CHALLENGES FROM ATHEISM—ALISTER MCGRATH

1. Alister E. McGrath, *The Twilight of Atheism* (New York: Doubleday, 2004).
2. Dirk Obbink, "The Atheism of Epicurus" in *Greek Roman and Byzantine Studies* 30 (1989): 187–223. For an analysis of these Olympian disputes, see Jenny Strauss Clay, *The Politics of Olympus: Form and Meaning in the Major Homeric Hymns* (Princeton, NJ: Princeton University Press, 1989).
3. For the intellectual background of the French Revolution, see Alan Charles Kors, *Atheism in France, 1650–1729* (Princeton, NJ: Princeton University Press, 1990).
4. The best study of atheism in the German Democratic Republic is in German: Hans Gerhard Koch, *Neue Erde ohne Himmel: Der Kampf des Atheismus gegen das Christentum in der DDR: Modell einer weltweiten Auseinandersetzung* (Stuttgart: Quell-Verlag, 1963).
5. See the analysis in David C. Lewis, *After Atheism: Religion and Ethnicity in Russia and Central Asia* (New York: St. Martin's Press, 1999).
6. Stéphane Courtois, *The Black Book of Communism: Crimes, Terror, Repression* (Cambridge, MA: Harvard University Press, 1999).
7. There is a great wealth of literature on this subject. For a useful survey and introduction, see Harold G. Koenig and Harvey J. Cohen, *The Link Between Religion and Health: Psychoneuroimmunology and the Faith Factor* (Oxford: Oxford University Press, 2002).
8. This point emerges from scholarly studies such as Jennifer Michael Hecht, *The End of the Soul: Scientific Modernity, Atheism, and Anthropology in France* (New York: Columbia University Press, 2003); Michael Hunter and David Wootton, *Atheism from the Reformation to the Enlightenment* (Oxford: Clarendon Press, 1992).
9. Those interested in a detailed cultural analysis will find much to reflect on in Vattimo's pioneering analysis of the situation: Gianni Vattimo, *The End of Modernity: Nihilism and Hermeneutics in Postmodern Culture* (Baltimore, MD: Johns Hopkins University Press, 1988).
10. Sam Harris, *The End of Faith: Religion, Terror, and the Future of Reason* (New York: Norton, 2004); Daniel C. Dennett, *Breaking the Spell: Religion as a Natural Phenomenon* (New York: Viking, 2006); Richard Dawkins, *The God Delusion* (Boston: Houghton Mifflin, 2006). For a response to Dawkins's latest book, see Alister E. McGrath and Joanna Collicutt McGrath, *The Dawkins Delusion?: Atheist Fundamentalism and the Denial of the Divine* (Downers Grove, IL: InterVarsity, 2007).
11. See the use made of the 9/11 event in Sam Harris, *Letter to a Christian Nation* (New York: Knopf, 2006).
12. See the careful and thorough accounts in Robert A. Pape, *Dying to Win: The Strategic Logic of Suicide Terrorism* (New York: Random House, 2005); Diego Gambetta, ed., *Making Sense of Suicide Missions* (Oxford: Oxford University Press, 2005).
13. For a well-informed riposte, see David Martin, *Does Christianity Cause War?* (Oxford: Clarendon Press, 1997). Another book of importance at this point is Rodney Stark, *For the Glory of God: How Monotheism Led to Reformations, Science, Witch-Hunts, and the End of Slavery* (Princeton, NJ: Princeton University Press, 2003). For atheist appeals to this issue, see Harris, *The End of Faith,* and Dawkins, *The God Delusion.*
14. See Arno J. Mayer, *The Furies: Violence and Terror in the French and Russian Revolutions* (Princeton, NJ: Princeton University Press, 2002).
15. Dimitry V. Pospielovsky, *A History of Marxist-Leninist Atheism and Soviet Anti-Religious Policies* (New York: St Martin's Press, 1987).
16. See Delos Banning McKown, *The Classical Marxist Critiques of Religion: Marx, Engels, Lenin, Kautsky* (The Hague: Martinus Nijhoff, 1975).
17. For a good analysis, see William Lloyd Newell, *The Secular Magi: Marx, Freud, and Nietzsche on Religion* (New York: Pilgrim Press, 1986). For recent severe criticisms of Freud, see Frederick C. Crews, *Unauthorized Freud: Doubters Confront a Legend* (New York: Viking, 1998).
18. Czeslaw Milosz, "The Discreet Charm of Nihilism" in *New York Times Review of Books* (19 November 1998), 17–18.

19. An additional point here is grounded in Christian theology: perhaps we have been made to long for God. As Augustine of Hippo once put it in a prayer: "You have made us for yourself, and our hearts are restless until they find their rest in you."A similar theme, of course, is found in C. S. Lewis' autobiography, *Surprised by Joy.*

20. See most recently Richard Dawkins, *The God Delusion* (Boston: Houghton Mifflin, 2006). For a detailed analysis and rebuttal of Dawkins's attitudes to faith, see Alister McGrath, *Dawkins' God: Genes, Memes, and the Meaning of Life* (Oxford: Blackwell, 2004). Similar attitudes are found in Daniel C. Dennett, *Breaking the Spell: Religion as a Natural Phenomenon* (New York: Viking Penguin, 2006).

21. Richard Dawkins, *The Selfish Gene* (Oxford: Oxford University Press, 1976), 198.

22. Richard Dawkins, "Lecture from the Nullifidian," December 1994, available at http://richarddawkins.net/ article, 89, Lecture-from-The-Nullifidian-Dec-94,Richard-Dawkins, accessed 12 August 2007.

23. See, for example, Victor Reppert, *C. S. Lewis's Dangerous Idea: In Defense of the Argument from Reason* (Downers Grove, IL: InterVarsity, 2003).

24. Francis S. Collins, *The Language of God: A Scientist Presents Evidence for Belief* (New York: Free Press, 2006).

25. This idea is set out most fully in Richard Dawkins, *A Devil's Chaplain: Selected Writings* (London: Weidenfield & Nicholson, 2003).

26. Stephen Jay Gould, "Impeaching a Self-Appointed Judge" in *Scientific American* 267, no. 1 (1992), 118–21.

27. See Peter B. Medawar's significantly titled book *The Limits of Science* (New York: Harper & Row, 1984).

28. For the original article, see Gilbert Harman, "The Inference to the Best Explanation"in *Philosophical Review* 74 (1965), 88–95. The best recent study is Peter Lipton, *Inference to the Best Explanation* (London: Routledge, 2004).

29. Readers might like to follow up this point by looking at Thomas Dixon, "Scientific Atheism as a Faith Tradition" in *Studies in History and Philosophy of Biological and Biomedical Sciences* 33 (2002), 337–59.

30. In recent years, Ravi Zacharias has used dialogical conversations with great effect in his ministry. Two books illustrate his approach especially well: *The Lotus and the Cross: Jesus Talks with Buddha* (Sisters, OR: Multnomah, 2001) and *Sense and Sensuality: Jesus Talks with Oscar Wilde on the Pursuit of Pleasure* (Sisters, OR: Multnomah, 2002).

31. Kai Nielsen, *Reason and Practice* (New York: Harper & Row, 1971), 143–44. For Nielsen's interaction with a leading Christian apologist, see James P. Moreland and Kai Nielsen, *Does God Exist?: The Debate Between Theists & Atheists* (Buffalo, NY: Prometheus Books, 1993). A point that is often not appreciated here is that atheists have doubts, just like Christians. They cannot prove their position, so they are open to the same anxieties about whether they are right. This is extremely important in helping Christians set their own doubts in perspective and in opening up some important apologetic conversations. I explore this point in detail in Alister McGrath, *Doubting: Growing through the Uncertainties of Faith* (Downers Grove, IL: InterVarsity, 2006).

32. C. S. Lewis, "Is Theology Poetry?"*Essay Collection* (London: HarperCollins, 2000), 21.

33. There are many resources of importance here. Two classic resources are C. S. Lewis, *Mere Christianity* (London: Collins, 1952); C. S. Lewis, *Surprised by Joy* (London: Collins, 1959). Some of the most interesting works to appear more recently include: Corbin Scott Carnell, *Bright Shadow of Reality: Spiritual Longing in C. S. Lewis* (Grand Rapids: Eerdmans, 1999); Art Lindsley, *True Truth: Defending Absolute Truth in a Relativistic Age* (Downers Grove, IL: InterVarsity, 2004); Ravi K. Zacharias and Norman L. Geisler, *Who Made God: And Answers to Over 100 Other Tough Questions of Faith* (Grand Rapids: Zondervan, 2003). These works are saturated with arguments and thinking that confute simplistic atheist definitions of faith.

34. See, for example, Michael J. Buckley, *At the Origins of Modern Atheism* (New Haven, CT: Yale University Press, 1987); Louis Dupré, "On the Intellectual Sources of Modern Atheism" in *International Journal for Philosophy of Religion* 45, no. 1 (1999), 1–11. Those who read German will benefit here from Winfried Schröder, *Ursprünge des Atheismus: Untersuchungen zur Metaphysik—und Religionskritik des 17. und 18. Jahrhunderts* (Stuttgart-Bad Cannstatt: Frommann-Holzboog, 1998).

35. For a fascinating analysis of the situation in Russia, with much wider implications, see Mikhail Epshtein, "Post-Atheism: From Apophatic Theology to 'Minimal Religion'"in *Russian Postmodernism: New*

Perspectives on Post-Soviet Culture, eds. Mikhail Epshtein, Slobodanka Vladiv-Glover, and Aleksandr Genis, (Oxford: Berghahn, 1999), 345–93.

36. There is a vast literature on the topic of postmodernism. A good place to start is James W. Sire, *The Universe Next Door: A Basic Worldview Catalogue*, 4th ed. (Downers Grove, IL: InterVarsity, 2004).

37. For an excellent book that does precisely this, see Ravi Zacharias, *Jesus Among Other Gods: The Absolute Claims of the Christian Message* (Nashville: Word Publishing Group, 2000).

38. For some excellent comments, see Ravi Zacharias, ed. *The Real Face of Atheism* (Grand Rapids: Baker, 2004).

CHAPTER 3: CHALLENGES FROM YOUTH—ALISON THOMAS

1. J. Budziszewski, *How to Stay Christian in College* (Colorado: NavPress, 2004), 15.
2. Alister McGrath, "Understanding and Responding to Moral Pluralism." Lecture given at the Center for Applied Christian Ethics, Wheaton College, Wheaton, IL, 1994.
3. Daniel Dennett, *Breaking the Spell: Religion as a Natural Phenomenon* (New York: Viking, 2006), 53.
4. Richard Howe, "Colleges Think Left, Students Think That's Right" *American Family Association Journal*, (August 2006), http://www.afajournal.org/2006/august/0806colleges.html.
5. Richard Howe, "Campus Largely Leaning Left, But Why? Insights from a Christian Philosophy Professor" *American Family Association Journal*, (September 2006), http://www.afajournal.org/2006/september/0906colleges.asp.
6. April Shenandoah, "History of America's Education, Part III: Universities, Textbooks, & America's Founders." *The Progressive Conservative*, 14, no. 40 (14 April 2002); Tim LaHaye, *Faith of Our Founding Fathers* (Green Forest: Master Books, 1990), 78.
7. Gary DeMar, *America's Christian History: The Untold Story* (Atlanta: American Vision, 1993), 99.
8. Ellwood P. Cubberly, *Public Education in the United States* (New York: Houghton Mifflin, 1919), 43–44; DeMar, 100.
9. See the thorough accounts in David Limbaugh, *Persecution: How Liberals Are Waging War Against Christianity* (New York: Regnery, 2003).
10. *Reuters*, "Court Bars Religious Tiles from Columbine," 27 June 2002.
11. *Charisma News Service*, "Parents Fight School Christmas Ban," 23 December, 2002.
12. Jon Dougherty, "School Sued for Barring Bible Club," *Worldnetdaily.com*, 7 January, 2003. worldnetdaily.com/news/article.asp?ARTICLE.ID=30348.
13. Jessica Cantelon, "Parents of Second Grader Sue School for Religious Discrimination," *CNSNews.com*, 1 August, 2002.
14. Gary Lyle Railsback, "An Exploratory Study of the Religiosity and Related Outcomes Among College Students," Doctoral dissertation, University of California at Los Angeles, 1994 (PhD).
15. Nancy Pearcey, *Total Truth: Liberating Christianity from Its Cultural Captivity* (Wheaton: Crossway, 2005), 19.
16. Dallas Willard, *Renovation of the Heart: Putting on the Character of Christ* (Colorado Springs: NavPress, 2002), 105.
17. George Barna, "Teens Change Their Tune Regarding Self and Church," *The Barna Update*, April 2002, www.barna.org/FlexPage.aspx?Page=BarnaUpdate&BarnaUpdateID=111.
18. Christian Smith and Melinda Denton, *Soul Searching: The Religious and Spiritual Lives of American Teenagers* (New York: Oxford University Press, 2005), 269.
19. Charles Potter, *Humanism: A New Religion* (New York: Simon and Schuster, 1930), 128.
20. Pearcey, *Total Truth*, 19.
21. Smith and Denton, *Soul Searching*, 187.
22. George Barna, "A Biblical Worldview Has a Radical Effect on a Person's Life," *The Barna Update*, December 2003. www.barna.org/FlexPage.aspx?Page=BarnaUpdate&BarnaUpdateID=154.
23. See, e.g., Gary Habermas and Mike Licona, *The Case for the Resurrection of Jesus* (Grand Rapids: Kregel Publications), 2004.
24. Os Guinness, *Unspeakable: Facing Up to Evil in an Age of Genocide and Terror* (San Francisco: HarperOne, 2005), 40.

25. Ravi Zacharias, "The Pastor as an Apologist," in Ravi Zacharias and Norman Geisler, *Is Your Church Ready? Motivating Leaders to Live an Apologetic Life* (Grand Rapids: Zondervan, 2003), 22.
26. Ronald Sider, *The Scandal of the Evangelical Conscience* (Grand Rapids: Baker, 2005).
27. Ibid.,128.
28. Pearcey, *Total Truth*, 378.
29. H. G. Wells, *Experiment in Autobiography* (New York: Macmillan, 1934), 52–53. Quoted in Paul Vitz, *Faith of the Fatherless: The Psychology of Atheism* (Dallas: Spence, 1999), 51.
30. Vitz, *Faith of the Fatherless*, 140.
31. Edward Erwin, "The Faith of Our Founding Fathers," *Words for the Walk*, 1998 quoted in David Limbaugh, *Persecution: How Liberals Are Waging War Against Christianity* (New York: Harper, 2004), 9.

CHAPTER 4: CHALLENGES FROM ISLAM—SAM SOLOMAN

1. "And I tell you that you are Peter, and on this rock I will build my church, and the gates of Hades will not overcome it"(Matt. 16:18).
2. "And he will send his angels with a loud trumpet call, and they will gather his elect from the four winds, from one end of the heavens to the other"(Matt. 24:31).
3. See Mark 13:28–29 (parable of the fig tree) and Matthew 16:1–4 (signs of the times).
4. See, for instance, Al-Bukhari 6413:

ال رسول الله أمرت أن أقاتل الناس حتى يقولوا لا إله إلا الله فمن قالها فقد عصم مني ماله
ونفسه إلا بحقه وحسابه على الله فقال والله لأقاتلن من فرق بين الصلاة والزكاة فان الزكاة حق
عمر فوالله ما هو المال والله لو منعوني عناقا كانوا يؤدونها إلى رسول الله لقاتلتهم على منعها قال
6413; البخاري 1312 البخاري -إلا أن قد شرح الله صدر أبي بكر فعرفت أنه الحق

Al-Bukhari 379:

ول الله أمرت أن أقاتل الناس حتى يقولوا لا إله إلا الله فإذا قالوا وصلوا صلاتنا
تقبيلوا قبلتنا وذبحوا ذبيحتنا فقد حرمت علينا دماؤهم وأموالهم إلا بحقها وحسابهم على الله
البخاري

Al-Bukhari 6413:

قال رسول الله أمرت أن أقاتل الناس حتى يقولوا لا إله إلا الله عصم مني ماله ونفسه إلا بحقه وحسابه :
على الله فقال والله لأقاتلن من فرق بين الصلاة والزكاة فان الزكاة حق المال والله لو منعوني
و إلا أن شرح الله عناقا كانوا يؤدونها إلى رسول الله لقاتلتهم على منعها قال عمر فوالله ما ه
6413. البخاري 1312 البخاري صدر أبي بكر فعرفت أنه الحق

5. Sura 85:21–22 "this is a Glorious Qur'an, 22 (Inscribed) in a Tablet Preserved!"
6. Sura 3:54 ". . . and Allah too deceived, and the best of deceivers is Allah."
7. Sura 9:5 ". . . then fight and slay the Pagans wherever ye find them . . . "
8. Sura 5:51 "O ye who believe! take not the Jews and the Christians for your friends and protectors . . ." Also 60:1 and 98:6.
9. Sura 9:28 "O you who believe Verily, the pagans are Najasun (impure, profane)"
10. Sura 22:78 ". . . It is He (Allâh) Who has named you Muslims both before and in this (the Qur'ân), that the Messenger (Muhammad) may be a witness over you. . . ."
11. Sura 9:1 "Freedom from (all) obligations (is declared) from Allâh and His Messenger to those of the pagans."
12. Sura 64:16 "So keep your duty to Allâh and fear Him as much as you can . . ." and 2:284 "Allâh burdens not a person beyond his scope (or ability) . . . "
13. Sura 56:8-60
14. Sura 2:207 "And of mankind is he who would sell himself, seeking the Pleasure of Allâh. And Allâh is full of Kindness to (His) slaves" and 3:92 "By no means shall ye attain righteousness unless ye give (freely) of that which ye love . . . ."

15. This was validated by Qur'anic injunctions, such as

Sura 68:4 "You O (Muhammad) are the most exalted standard of character."

Sura 53:2–5 "Your companion is neither gone astray nor misled, nor does he say anything of his own desire, it is all an inspiration sent down to him. He was taught by one mighty in power."

Sura 33:21 "You have indeed in the Messenger of Allah a beautiful pattern of conduct for anyone whose hope is in Allah and the last day, and who engages much in the praise of Allah."

Sura 4:80 "He who obeys the Apostle has already obeyed Allah."

Sura 48:8–10 "We have truly sent you (Muhammad) as a witness as a bringer of glad tidings and as a warner. In order that you (people) may believe in Allah and His Messenger, that you assist him and celebrate his praises morning and evening. Verily those who pledge their fealty (absolute loyalty) do no less than pledge their fealty to Allah."

Sura 59:7 "And whatsoever the Messenger (Muhammad) gives you, take it, and whatsoever he forbids you, abstain (from it), and fear Allah. Verily, Allah is Severe in punishment."

16.

لله الف اسم ولمحمد ايضا الف اسمها يخفى أن جميع أسمائه صلى الله عليه وسلم مشتقة من

صفات قامت به توجب له المدح والكمال فله من كل وصف اسم قال وكما أن لله عز وجل الف إسم

للنبي صلى الله عليه وسلم ألف إسم

128، صفحة السيرة الحلبية، الجزء لكتاب ا

وروى البخاري ومسلم والترمذي وغيرهم عن جبير بن مُطْعِم أنه قال: سمعت رسول الله صلى الله

عليه وسلم يقول : "إن لي أسماء: أنا محمد، وأنا أحمد، وأنا الماحي الذي يمحو الله بي الكفر، وأنا

الـعاقب' الذي ليس بـعده أحدالحاشرُ الذي يحشر الناس على قدمي، وأن ".

كان محمد نورا بنين يدي الله قبل ان يخلق الله ادم بـارب عة عشر ألف عام

كنت نورا بيـين يدي ربـي عز وجل قبـل ان روى علي بن الرحسن عن أبيه عن جده قال: قال رسول الله:

عامي خلق آدم بـارب عة عشر ألف

17. This is based on Sura 3:19: "Truly the religion with Allah is Islam," that goes on to say that "Islam declares that it and it alone is the sole religion of Allah," and in Sura 3:85 "whoever seeks a religion other than Islam, it will never be accepted of him, and in the Hereafter he will be one of the losers."

18. See, for example:

Sura 57:28 "O you who believe [in Mûsa (Moses) (i.e. Jews) and "Iesa (Jesus) (i.e. Christians)]! Fear Allah, and believe too in His Messenger (Muhammad), He will give you a double portion of His Mercy, and He will give you a light by which you shall walk (straight), and He will forgive you. And Allah is Oft-Forgiving, Most Merciful."

Sura 21:107 "And We have sent you (O Muhammad) not but as a mercy for the 'Alamîn (mankind, jinns and all that exists)."

Sura 9:128 "Verily, there has come unto you a Messenger (Muhammad) from amongst yourselves (i.e. whom you know well). It grieves him that you should receive any injury or difficulty. He (Muhammad) is anxious over you (to be rightly guided, to repent to Allah, and beg Him to pardon and forgive your sins, in order that you may enter Paradise and be saved from the punishment of the Hell-fire), for the believers (he is) full of pity, kind, and merciful."

19. To understand why the "no compulsion" reference is quoted so often despite its being abrogated, please see the section on Takkiya.

20. The following Qur'anic verses and others like it have abrogated that often-quoted phrase "no compulsion in religion":

Sura 9:5 "When the forbidden months are past then fight and kill the unbelievers wherever you find them, and seize them, beleaguer them and lie in wait for them, in every stratagem of war, but if they repent (meaning accept Islam) and establish regular prayers, and practice regular charity . . . then they are your brethren in religion (Islam)."

Sura 9:11 "But if they repent, perform As-Salât (Iqâmat-as-Salât) and give Zakât, then they are your brethren in religion. (In this way) we explain the Ayât (proofs, evidences, verses, lessons, signs, revelations, etc.) in detail for a people who know."

Sura 8:38–39 "Say to the unbelievers, if they desist from unbelief their past will be forgiven them, but if they persist the punishment of those before them is already a warning to them. And fight and kill them, until there is no more tumult or dissention and that everywhere religion will be unto Allah."

21. See Suras 58:22; 60:1, 4; 5:51; 9:29.

22. This verse was given to Muhammad when one of his followers in Mecca, Ammar bin Yasir, was made to worship the Qurayshi idols and listen to the denigration of Muhammad, yet his heart was at ease. So according to Qur'anic expositors, this verse was revealed to put Yasir's conscience at ease and rest, with its application to every Muslim. See also Sura 3:28: "Let not the believers take for friends unbelievers rather than believers. If any do that, in nothing will there be help from Allah; except by way of precaution that ye may guard yourselves from them But Allah cautions you Himself." The word "guard" in the phrase "guard yourselves from them" is known as Takkiya. In addition to allowing the denial of faith in case of need, the Qur'anic injunctions make it both a permitted alleviation as well as an obligation as per Sura 3:28, cited above.

This obligation legitimizes all activities in words and deeds contrary to what one might hold within: for example, to display love outwardly but inwardly to hate, or to evince loyalty outwardly but inwardly to feel enmity—all for the cause of Allah.

So, for instance, Al Zamakhshari, one of the most notable Islamic scholars and Qur'anic expositors, explains how one could outwardly display loyalty and friendship while the heart inwardly would remain full of hate and enmity until either the obstructing factors are removed or the Islamic community is so securely strong to launch an open attack.

Fakharadin A'razi states that if a Muslim fears those unbelievers among whom he may be because of their excessive power and strength, then he needs to pledge loyalty and love outwardly on condition that he inwardly would object to what he himself is saying; in other words, he would be saying the opposite to all that he inwardly believed.

As an addition to Takkiya, Muhammad sanctioned lying by saying that Allah will not hold a Muslim accountable when he lies in these three situations: (a) when in war, espionage, concealment, or in weakness, (b) with his wife, or a wife with her husband, and (c) when reconciling or maintaining peace. Muhammad went on to say, "War is deception." This deception can be practiced at a personal level as well as at a community level through its leaders and institutions.

Takkiya is practiced by all Muslims, Sunni and Shiites alike, and all other Islamic sects, but because it's more vocalized by the Shiites in their teachings than the others, some think that it is exclusively a Shiite doctrine. It has been reported that Ali, the fourth Khalifa, said that "it is a mark of belief to prefer justice if it injures you, and injustice if it is of use to you."

Takkiya can be practiced if it is necessary, even when under oath. Sura 2:225: "Allah will not call you to account for thoughtlessness in your oaths, but for the intention in your hearts." Sura 5:89: "Allah will not call you to account for what is futile in your oaths but He will call you to account for your deliberate oaths. For expiation, feed ten indigent persons, on the scale of the average for the fools of your families, or clothe them, or give a slave his freedom. If that is beyond your means fast for three days: that is the expiation for the oaths you have sworn, but keep to your oaths . . . "

23. For instance, in Pakistan, numerous Muslims, backed by mosques, have under oath accused innocent Christians, Hindus, and others of blaspheming Muhammad. Others, having burned or torn pages of the Qur'an, then presented it as evidence of blasphemy, as though committed by those non-Muslims, namely Christians, either for personal gain or jihad against that community. Many of these victims have spent years in horrible conditions behind bars, while families became outcasts, losing their jobs and livelihoods. Almost all had to go in hiding and move from where they originally lived.

In the recent crisis of the Danish cartoons, some Muslims themselves added more cartoons to those that they were rioting about, which showed Muhammad in a worse light. They then showed these to fellow Muslims in order to whip up frenzy and violence against Europeans. Many were killed in a number of Islamic countries, and many others lost their livelihood as their businesses were burnt down by Muslims.

How can a Muslim do that? There is a Fatwa—an Islamic juristic decree—endorsing the insult of Muhammad if done in the state of Takkiya. This was issued in India and it can be found in: Fatwas of Kadikhan al fur ghani al hanafi 489, the Indian Fatwas published in Beirut by Dar al A'hiya a'turath al

Arabi. "Takkiya permits Muslims to bow before an idol in a state of Takkiya": the compilation of the Qur'anic injunction by Kartabi, Section 10:180.

24. Following are some of the operative Qur'anic injunctions in support of the doctrine of biblical corruption:

Sura 2:75 "Do you (faithful believers) covet that they will believe in your religion in spite of the fact that a party of them (Jewish rabbis) used to hear the Word of Allah [the Taurat (Torah)], then they used to change it knowingly after they understood it?"

Sura 2:77 "Know they (Jews) not that Allah knows what they conceal and what they reveal?"

Sura 2:79 "Then woe to those who write the Book with their own hands and then say, 'This is from Allah,' to purchase with it a little price! Woe to them for what their hands have written and woe to them for that they earn thereby."

Sura 7:157 "Those who follow the Messenger, the Prophet who can neither read nor write (i.e. Muhammad) whom they find written with them in the Taurât (Torah) and the Injeel (Gospel)."

25. Sura 2:216 "Fighting is prescribed for you, and you dislike it. But it is possible that you dislike a thing which is good for you, and that you love a thing which is bad for you. . . . "

CHAPTER 5: CHALLENGES FROM EASTERN RELIGIONS—L. T. JEYACHANDRAN

1. It is important to note that the word *Hinduism* is of comparatively recent coinage and cannot be traced back earlier than the eighteenth century. Dayanand Bharati, *Understanding Hinduism* (New Delhi, India: Munshiram Manoharlal, 2005), 3, 13. However, the word will be used throughout this chapter as a convenient referent.

2. Michael C. Brannigan, *The Pulse of Wisdom*, 2nd ed. (Belmont, CA: Wadsworth/Thomson Learning, 2000), 360–361.

3. N. T. Wright, *New Testament and the People of God* (London: Society for the Promotion of Christian Knowledge, 1996), 47–80.

4. Kevin Vanhoozer, *The Drama of Doctrine* (Louisville, KY: Westminster John Knox Press, 2005), 15–25.

5. Curtis Chang has very ably demonstrated this in the very different contexts of Augustine and Thomas Aquinas. See Curtis Chang, *Engaging Unbelief* (Downers Grove, IL: InterVarsity, 2000), 26.

6. James W. Sire, *The Universe Next Door*, 3rd ed. (Downers Grove, IL: InterVarsity, 1997).

7. James W. Sire, *Naming the Elephant* (Downers Grove, IL: InterVarsity, 2004), 22.

8. Bharati, *Understanding Hinduism*, 100–101.

9. Swami Dayanand Bharati, *Living Water and Indian Bowl*, rev.ed. (Pasadena, CA: William Carey Library, 2004) 68–69. He would prefer to be called a *bhakta* (devotee) of Christ rather than a Christian, as the latter word has unfortunate connotations in certain parts of India. After ten years of service with a conventional missionary society in India, he has now chosen to live as a *swami* (holy man), and he disciples seekers from higher castes.

10. A. J. Appasamy. "A. J. Appasamy Speaks to the Indian Church," *Pilgrim Magazine*, 2, no. 4 (1943). Rev. Appasamy was a pastor in the Church of South India when liberalism and syncretism were rampant among some of the church's more influential theologians. He faithfully stood by the exclusivity of Christ while emphasizing the need to identify the longing of the Hindu devotee so that Christ could be presented as the answer to that need. I still remember an hour spent with him in 1963. I was a new Christian and just completing my undergraduate degree in engineering. Appasamy was a bishop in the church at that time and retired some time thereafter.

11. Elizabeth J. Harris, *What Buddhists Believe* (Oxford, UK: Oneworld Publications, 1998), 42–44.

12. Brannigan, *The Pulse of Wisdom*, 67.

13. Ibid., 360.

14. Ibid., 328.

15. Ravi Zacharias, *The Lotus and the Cross* (Sisters, OR: Multnomah, 2001), 82–83. The book records an imagined three-way conversation with the Buddha, Jesus, and Priya, a Thai girl racked by AIDS as a result of a life of prostitution. The Buddha is unable to offer the ultimate hope of forgiveness that is the prime aspect of Jesus' ministry.

16. Deepak Chopra, *How to Know God* (New York: Harmony Books, 2000) 288–97.

17. Vishal Mangalwadi, *When the New Age Gets Old* (Downers Grove, IL: InterVarsity, 1992), 7. I owe a great deal to this book for the material on New Age. I consider this volume very significant because it uniquely

combines both Western and Eastern contributions to this movement. I also value the author's friendship, scholarship, and the hours we have discussed New Age in India since we first met in 1970. Much of the material quoted in the eight important expressions of New Age is taken from this book.

18. Shirley MacLaine, quoted in Mangalwadi, 7.
19. Francis A. Schaeffer, *The Complete Works: Vol. I, A Christian View of Philosophy and Culture* (Wheaton, IL: Crossway Books, 1982), 113.
20. Fritjof Capra, *The Tao of Physics*, 4th ed. (Boston: Shambhala, 2000).
21. Mangalwadi, *When the New Age Gets Old*, 117.
22. Ibid., 127.
23. Ibid., 131.
24. Ibid., 159.
25. Chopra, *How to Know God*, 270–271. These are examples of which the whole book abounds!
26. Swami Ranganathananda, *The Message of the Upanishads* (Bombay, India: Bharatiya Vidya Bhavan, 1993), 145. Upanishads are the scriptures of Hinduism that belong to the end of the Vedic period (c. 700 B.C.). See Brannigan, *Wisdom*, 4–5.
27. George Grimm, *The Doctrine of the Buddha* (Delhi, India: Motilal Banarsidass, 1995), 381.
28. Brannigan, *Wisdom*, 193–95, 200.
29. This is not different from the use of negative adjectives employed by Christian theology in describing God and his truth: *absolute, infinite, immortal, invisible, immutable, impassible*. For more on this point, see the opening pages of my other chapter in this book, "A Trinitarian Paradigm for Apologetics and Spiritual Transformation."
30. Brannigan, *Wisdom*, 227.
31. The section on negative critique is drawn from the excellent analysis under *Pantheism* in Norman Geisler's *Christian Apologetics* (Grand Rapids: Baker, 1976), 187–91.
32. We Christians in India also have to remember that in fighting against oppressive caste and class systems, we do not have to be anti-Brahmin in order to be pro-Shudra nor be anti-rich in order to be pro-poor!

CHAPTER 6: CHALLENGES FROM SCIENCE—JOHN LENNOX

1. It should hardly need to be said that this does not mean apologizing for Christianity in the sense of making an excuse for it! It carries the sense of explanation and elucidation, dealing with misunderstandings and objections raised.
2. The terms *materialism* and *naturalism* are often used almost interchangeably, although there is a difference. According to the *Oxford Companion to Philosophy*, naturalism is "most obviously akin to materialism but it does not have to be materialistic. What it insists on is that the world of nature should consist of a single sphere without incursions from outside by souls or spirits, divine or human . . . but it need not reject the phenomena of consciousness, nor even identify them somehow with material phenomena as the materialist must." The important thing here is that both materialism and naturalism are inherently atheistic.
3. As in Hinduism and certain forms of Buddhism, for example.
4. Richard Dawkins, *The Blind Watchmaker: Why the Evidence of Evolution Reveals a Universe Without Design* (New York: Norton, 1996), 6.
5. There is some justifiable complaint about the addition of the adjective *intelligent* to *design*, since *design* usually implies intelligent activity.
6. See also the comments on Galileo below.
7. Peter Atkins, "The Limitless Power of Science," in *Nature's Imagination*, John Cornwell, ed. (Oxford: Oxford University Press, 1995), 132.
8. Survey by Edward J. Larsen and Larry Withan, "Scientists are still Keeping the Faith," *Nature* 386 (April 1997), 435–6.
9. Edward O. Wilson, "Intelligent Evolution," *Harvard Magazine* 108, no. 2 (2005), 33.
10. Melvin Calvin, *Chemical Evolution* (Oxford: Clarendon Press, 1969), 258.
11. Alfred North Whitehead, *Science and the Modern World* (London: Macmillan, 1925), 19.
12. C. S. Lewis, *Miracles* (London: Collins, 1947), 110.
13. Johannes Kepler's widely cited quote is found in his work *Astronomia Nova De Motibus*.
14. Joseph Needham observes that the idea of natural law is absent in Chinese culture. See his book *The Great Titration: Science and Society in East and West* (London: Allen and Unwin, 1969).

15. In his famous *Letter to the Grand Duchess Christina* (1615) Galileo claims that it was the academic professors who were so opposed to him. They were trying to influence the church authorities to speak out against him. The issue at stake for the professors was clear: Galileo's scientific arguments were threatening the all-pervading Aristotelianism of the academy.

16. Galileo also stirred up trouble for himself by putting the arguments of the then pope, his former friend, into the mouth of a character Simplicio—the fool!—in his book *Dialogue on the Tides.*

17. See Colin Russell, "The Conflict Metaphor and Its Social Origins," *Science and Christian Belief* 1, no. 1 (April 1989), 3–26.

18. Michael Ruse, *Darwinism Defended* (Reading, MA: Addison-Wesley, 1982), 322.

19. Their suggestions have resulted in the so-called Science Wars.

20. Atkins, *Nature's Imagination,* 125.

21. Bertrand Russell and Michael Ruse, *Religion and Science* (Oxford: Oxford University Press, 1970), 243.

22. "Why" questions connected with function, as distinct from "why" questions associated with purpose, are usually regarded as within the provenance of science.

23. Peter Medawar, *Advice to a Young Scientist* (London: Harper and Row, 1979), 31. See also his book *The Limits of Science* (Oxford: Oxford University Press, 1984), 66.

24. Atkins, *Nature's Imagination,* 127–28.

25. Richard Dawkins, "Growing Up in the Universe" (lecture, Royal Institution Christmas lectures, London, 1991).

26. Francis Crick, *The Astonishing Hypothesis: The Scientific Search for the Soul* (London: Simon and Schuster, 1994), 3.

27. John Polkinghorne, *Reason and Reality: The Relationship between Science and Theology* (London: S.P.C.K., 1991), 76.

28. E. Tryton, "Is the Universe a Vacuum Fluctuation?" *Nature* 246 (1973), 396.

29. Keith Ward, *God, Chance and Necessity* (Oxford: One World Publications, 1996), 23.

30. Peter W. Atkins, *Creation Revisited: The Origin of Space, Time and the Universe* (Harmondsworth, England: Penguin, 1994), 143.

31. Ibid., 49.

32. Paul Davies, quoted in Clive Cookson, "Scientists Who Glimpsed God," *Financial Times* (29 April 1995): 20.

33. Eugene Wigner, "The Unreasonable Effectiveness of Mathematics," *Communications in Pure and Applied Mathematics,* 13 (1960): 1–14.

34. Polkinghorne, *Reason and Reality,* 76.

35. Ward, *God, Chance and Necessity,* 1.

36. Although considerable effort is being made by Hawking and others to remove the idea of such a "singularity."

37. Sir John Maddox, "Down with the Big Bang," *Nature,* 340 (10 August 1989): 425.

38. Malcolm Browne, "Clues to the Universe's Origin Expected," *The New York Times* (12 March 1978), 1. At the time of writing, Neil Turok of Cambridge is challenging the standard Big-Bang model by suggesting that our universe was not a unique event but is likely to have been one of many such events in an eternal space-time. Watch this space!

39. Paul Davies, *God and the New Physics* (London: J. M. Dent and Sons), 1983.

40. Roger Pinrose and Martin Gardner, *The Emperor's New Mind* (Oxford: Oxford University Press, 1989), 344.

41. Ibid.

42. Arno Penzias, "Creation Is Supported by All the Data So Far," *Cosmos, Bios and Theos,* eds. Henry Margenau and Roy Varghese, (La Salle, IL: Open Court, 1992), 83.

43. Martin Rees, *Just Six Numbers* (London: Weidenfeld and Nicholson, 1999).

44. E. Harrison, *Masks of the Universe* (New York: Macmillan, 1985), 252, 263.

45. Arno Penzias, quoted in Denis Brian, *Genius Talk* (New York: Plenum, 1995), 164.

46. Richard Dawkins, *The Blind Watchmaker* (London: Longmans, 1986), 1.

47. Ibid., 14.

48. See, for example, *Intelligent Design Creationism and Its Critics,* ed. Robert T. Pennock (Cambridge, MA: MIT Press, 2001).

Notes

49. John Houghton, *The Search for God: Can Science Help?* (Oxford: Lion Publishing PLC, 1995), 54.

50. See David N. Livingstone, *Darwin's Forgotten Defenders* (Edinburgh: Scottish Academic Press, 1987).

51. Daniel Dennett, *Darwin's Dangerous Idea: Evolution and the Meaning of Life* (New York: Simon and Schuster, 1995), 22–23.

52. This means, of course, that Richard Dawkins's dichotomy of "God or evolution, but not both" is far too simplistic. Microevolutionary processes are agreed to occur by all sides, and so, from a theistic perspective, the world God created is a world in which natural selection processes have a role.

53. T. Dobzhansky, *The Origins of Prebiological Systems and of Their Molecular Matrices*, ed. S. W. Fox (New York: Academic Press, 1965), 310.

54. For example, the major university text on *Evolution* by Peter Skelton, ed., (Harlow, England: Addison Wesley, 1993), 854.

55. Michael Behe, *Darwin's Black Box* (New York: Simon and Schuster, 1996).

56. Charles Darwin, *Origin of Species*, 6th ed. (New York: New York University Press, 1988), 154.

57. Dawkins, *The Blind Watchmaker*, 91. It should be noted that some people have claimed that Darwin's theory is unfalsifiable (using Karl Popper's analysis). Darwin's concept of irreducible complexity shows otherwise.

58. Bill Gates, *The Road Ahead*, (New York: Blue Penguin, 1996), 228.

59. Léon Brillouin, *Science and Information Theory*, 2nd ed. (New York: Academic Press, 1962), 269.

60. Peter Medawar, *Limits of Science*, 79.

61. Kurt Gödel, quoted in Hao Wang, "On Physicalism and Algorithmism: Can Machines Think?" *Nature's Imagination: The Frontiers of Scientific Vision*, ed. John Cornwell (Oxford: Oxford University Press, 1995), 173.

62. Ibid.

63. Ilya Prigogine and Isabelle Stengers, *Order out of Chaos* (London: Fontana, 1985).

64. Stephen Meyer, *The Return of the God Hypothesis* (Seattle: Discovery Institute Center for the Renewal of Science and Culture, 1998), 37.

65. See, for example, Michael Behe, *Darwin's Black Box* and references there.

66. Meyer, *The Return of the God Hypothesis*, 23.

67. Francis Collins, public statement, 26 June 2000. For one of many news sources, see http://news.bbc.co.uk/1/hi/sci/tech/805803.stm.

68. Alvin Plantinga, "Should Methodological Naturalism Constrain Science?" in *Christian Perspectives for the New Millennium*, eds., Scott B. Luley, Paul Copan, and Stan W. Wallace, eds. (Addison, TX: CLM/RZIM Publications, 2003).

69. As we have said earlier, when we are investigating the laws and mechanisms of the universe, for the most part it makes little difference whether we suppose that there is real design or assume only apparent design.

70. It is to be observed that even the Genesis account limits the number of such special events. Furthermore, the creation sequence ends with the Sabbath on which God ceases from the direct activities involved in the process of creation (see Gen. 1).

71. John Polkinghorne, "The Laws of Nature and the Laws of Physics" in *Quantum Cosmology and the Laws of Nature: Scientific Perspectives on Divine Action*, 2nd ed., eds. Robert John Russell, Nancey Murphy and C. J. Isham (Vatican City and Berkeley: The Vatican Observatory and The Center for Theology and Natural Sciences, 1999), 438.

72. Dawkins, *The Blind Watchmaker*, 141.

73. Recall, too, that it was faith in the Creator that led to the meteoric rise of science.

74. We note that, if they came to superstitiously believe that Mr. Ford *was* the engine, that would stop their science dead. There is a great difference between a God who is the Creator and a god who is the universe.

75. Arthur Schawlow, "One Must Ask Why and Not Just How," in *Cosmos, Bios, Theos*, eds. Henry Margenau and Roy Varghese (La Salle, IL: Open Court, 1992), 107.

Chapter 7: Conversational Apologetics—Michael Ramsden

1. Richard Dawkins, *The Selfish Gene*, 2nd ed. (Oxford, England: Oxford University Press, 1989), 198.

2. Again, Richard Dawkins leads the atheist charge on this front with the publication of his book *The God Delusion* (London. Bantam, 2006). For an excellent counter-response by a contributor to this book, see Alister McGrath's *The Dawkins Delusion* (London: SPCK, 2007).

3. I would suggest reading the relevant articles on faith in *The New International Dictionary of New Testament Theology* and *The New International Dictionary of Old Testament Theology* (Grand Rapids: Zondervan, 1986), edited by Colin Brown, as a good starting point.

4. Some people think that this verse stands in tension with Hebrews 11:1. However, this is far from the case. Hebrews 11:1 says that "Faith is the substance [*upostasiz*, literally " 'the reality' "] of things hoped for, the evidence [*elegcoz*, literally "the proof"] of things not seen" KJV. Hebrews 11:1 does not introduce either a speculative element or a 'blind" element to faith, both of which are alien to the concept of faith in both the New and Old Testaments, as we shall see.

5. This is the force of meaning, for example, in John 3:19–21.

6. Jonathan Edwards, "A Divine and Supernatural Light," Sermons and Discourses, 1730–1733, in *The Works of Jonathan Edwards, vol.17*, Mark Valeri, ed., quoted by John Piper, *God Is the Gospel: Meditations on God's Love as the Gift of Himself* (Wheaton, IL: Crossway Books, 2005), 64; emphasis in original.

7. Piper, *God Is the Gospel*, 84.

8. See Dennis Potter in his introduction to *Brimstone and Treacle: A Play* (London: Methuca, 1978).

9. D. Z. Philips, *From Fantasy to Faith: Morality, Religion and Twentieth Century Literature*, 2nd ed. (London: SCM Press, 2006), 35.

10. Alister McGrath, *Dawkins' God: Genes, Memes and the Meaning of Life* (London: Blackwell, 2005), 84.

11. Paul actually stresses in all of his writing both what is called the *indicative* (if you are a Christian, then these things *will* follow) and the *imperative* (if you are a Christian, then you *will make every effort* to live this way.) There is no contradiction here. It is because of the new life we receive in Christ, when we put our faith in him, that we are then in position to live it out.

12. Jesus was also asked this question earlier in Luke's Gospel in 10:25, and there he gives a different but connected reply. The version of this event in Mark 10:18 is identical with Luke (*ti me legeiz agaqon oudeiz agaqoz ei mh eiz o qeoz*—"Why do you call me good? No one is good but God alone.") In Matthew 19:16, the question is raised in a slightly different form (*ti me erwtaz peri tou agaQou*—"Why do you speak to me about the good?") and the reply is also slightly different (*eiz estin o agaqoz*—"only one is good"). Some argue that the response in Luke should be read in conformity with the reply in Matthew (Don Carson's expository commentary on Matthew, for instance). However, I think that given the reply in Matthew, Mark, and Luke contain the response that only one—that is God—is good, the question can be rightly understood not just to be asking about what is "the good," but also *who* is good. Certainly Luke and Mark are very clear, and given that Matthew has a personal response too—there is only one who is good, i.e., God—I think we can understand both the question and answer in light of this.

13. For an excellent survey of Paul's argument here, together with an overview of the dating question, I would recommend F. F. Bruce's *The Epistle to the Galatians: The New International Greek Testament Commentary* (Grand Rapids: Eerdmans, 1988). His exegetical argument on this point runs throughout the length of the book, and so is hard to refer to just a few pages, although chapters IV, V, and VI contain the bulk of his exposition on this matter.

14. The phrasing of verse 6 seems to strengthen this point, by the use of two different words for "another." The chain of reason is as follows: They have been called by grace, but they are now moving to another (*eteron*) gospel, i.e., a gospel that is not about grace (*eteroz* normally means another of a different kind). The point is then reinforced when he says that this other gospel is *not* another (*alloz*) of the same kind, that is, the gospel of grace that they once had and first responded to. See F. F. Bruce, 81.

15. John R. W. Stott, *The Cross of Christ* (Downers Grove, IL: InterVarsity, 1989), 90.

16. Isaiah Berlin, "My Philosophy," *The History of Ideas* (Oxford, England: Oxford University Press, 2005). Available online at http://www.cs.utexas.edu/users/vl/notes/berlin.html.

17. Jane Austen, *Pride and Prejudice* (London: Peerage Books, 1991), 113.

18. Ibid., 114.

19. Ibid., 113.

CHAPTER 8: BROADER CULTURAL AND PHILOSOPHICAL CHALLENGES—JOE BOOT

1. Peter Kreeft, *Christianity for Modern Pagans* (San Francisco: Ignatius, 1993), 26.

2. James K. A. Smith, *Introducing Radical Orthodoxy* (Grand Rapids: Baker, 2004), 89; Smith suggests that

even what often masquerades as postmodern thinking is only modern thinking in a new outfit with some new terminology.

3. Hans Küng, *Does God Exist?* (New York: Doubleday, 1978), 15.

4. Kreeft, *Christianity for Modern Pagans*, 115.

5. Hans Küng, *Does God Exist?*, 17.

6. This usually rests in a misunderstanding about the nature and project of biblical apologetics; it is not optional but a scriptural command to the church. The biblical call to "give a defense" and "persuade others" need not be party to the Cartesian project. Rather, it can take an Augustinian, Trinitarian, presuppositional direction as exemplified in Van Til, Dooyewerd, and Frame. Furthermore, a narrative-based apologetic that seeks to capture the heart and mind with the epic of salvation culminating in the Incarnation and resurrection can be effectively employed.

7. I have borrowed this apt phrase from Curtis Chang in his insightful book *Engaging Unbelief: A Captivating Strategy from Augustine & Aquinas* (Downers Grove, IL: InterVarsity Press, 2000).

8. C. S. Lewis, *Mere Christianity* (New York: Macmillan, 1952), 190; emphasis added.

9. Smith, *Introducing Radical Orthodoxy*, 46–47.

10. Küng, *Does God Exist?*, 20.

11. Alvin Plantinga, "Augustinian Christian Philosophy," in *The Augustinian Tradition*, ed. Gareth B. Matthews (Berkley: University of California Press, 1999), 20–21.

12. Ibid., 20.

13. Küng, *Does God Exist?*, 66–67.

14. Ibid., 68, emphasis added.

15. Merrill Callaway, "Does Logic Need Faith?" *Journal of Creation* 20, no. 2 (2006): 126–27. For a full account of this remarkable mathematical proof of "incompleteness" showing the incapacity of a system to prove all its own axioms, see also pp. 123–27.

16. Albert Wells, *Pascal's Recovery of Man's Wholeness* (Richmond, VA: John Knox Press, 1965), 152.

17. Cornelius Van Til is one good example of this in many respects; in particular, the centerpiece of his apologetic, the Trinity, as the solution to the ancient problem of the one and the many. His brilliant solution shows how the doctrine of the equal ultimacy of the persons in the Trinity provides the necessary preconditions for knowledge of any kind to begin. I offer a popular introduction to this line of thought in my book *Why I Still Believe* (Grand Rapids: Baker, 2006). He is anticipated by Augustine in both *On the Trinity* and the *Confessions* (see especially, Book 13, Chapter 11, the final paragraph). Augustine repeatedly identifies the illumination of Christ as a precondition for knowledge and intellection.

18. Kreeft, *Christianity for Modern Pagans*, 40, quoting Søren Kierkegaard.

19. C. S. Lewis, *Poems* (New York: Fount Paperbacks, 1994), 143.

20. Benford, Gregory, "Gregory Benford," in *What We Believe but Cannot Prove*, ed. John Brockman (New York: Harper Perennial, 2006), 225.

21. C. S. Lewis, *Miracles* (New York: Fount Paperbacks, 1974), 97–98.

22. Kreeft, *Christianity for Modern Pagans*, 217.

23. Ibid., 107.

24. Ibid., 111.

25. Michael Robinson, *God Does Exist* (Bloomington, IN: AuthorHouse, 2006), 45.

26. Augustine, "The Advantage of Believing," in *On Christian Belief*, Augustine for the Twenty-First Century, trans. Ray Kearney, ed. Boniface Ramsey (New York: New City Press, 2005), 140.

27. Smith, *Introducing Radical Orthodoxy*, 181–82, emphasis added.

28. Augustine, "The Advantage of Believing," 143–44.

29. Ibid., 144.

30. Ibid., 146.

CHAPTER 9: EXISTENTIAL CHALLENGES OF EVIL AND SUFFERING—RAVI ZACHARIAS

1. Justin Hayward, "Question," © copyright 1970 Tyler Music Ltd., London, England. Essex Music International, Inc. New York.

2. Gabriel Marcel, *The Philosophy of Existentialism*, Manyan Harari, trans. (New York: Carol Publishing Group, 1995), 19.

3. Peter Kreeft, *Making Sense Out of Suffering*, (Ann Arbor, MI: Servant, 1986), 51.

4. David Hume, *Dialogues Concerning Natural Religion, Part 10*, ed., Henry D. Aiken (New York: Hafner, 1963), 64.

5. Sam Harris, *Letter to a Christian Nation* (New York: Knopf, 2006), 48.

6. Ibid., 50–52, 54.

7. Bertrand Russell makes this argument in a BBC debate on the existence of God with Father Frederick Copleston in 1948. This debate can be found in *Bertrand Russell on God and Religion*, ed. Al Seckel (Buffalo, NO: Prometheus Books, 1986); see pages 138–139 for the relevant discussion. A transcript of this debate is also available online through several sources, such as http://www.bringyou.to/apologetics/p20.htm; this conversation appears under the subtitle "The Moral Argument."

8. J. L. Mackie, quoted by J. P. Moreland, "Reflections on Meaning in Life without God," *The Trinity Journal*, 9NS (1984): 14.

9. Kai Nielsen, "Why Should I Be Moral?" *American Philosophical Quarterly* 21 (1984): 90.

10. Bertrand Russell, "Letter to *The Observer*," 6 October 1957.

11. See Alvin Plantinga, *Warrant and Proper Function* (New York: Oxford University Press, 1993) and his essay "Naturalism Defeated," available at http://www.homestead.com/philofreligion/files/alspaper.htm

12. Jean-Paul Sartre, *Being and Nothingness* (New York: Pocket Books, 1984), 478.

13. David Hume as cited by James Stuart Stewart, *The Gates of New Life* (New York: Charles Scribner & Sons, 1938), 4.

14. Richard Dawkins, *Out of Eden* (New York: Basic Books, 1992), 133.

15. Richard Dawkins, "Viruses of the Mind," *1992 Voltaire Lecture* (London: British Humanist Association, 1993), 9.

16. G. K. Chesterton, *Orthodoxy* (Garden City, NY: Doubleday, 1959), 41.

17. C. S. Lewis, quote cited in *The Quotable Lewis*, eds., Wayne Martindale and Jerry Root (Wheaton, IL: Tyndale, 1989), 270.

18. To gain an understanding of the Trinity, see L. T. Jeyachandran's chapter in this volume.

19. In his interview with Peter Singer, Marvin Olasky records, "He also reaffirmed that it would be ethically OK to kill 1-year-olds with physical or mental disabilities, as soon as possible after birth.'" See "Blue-State Philosopher," *World* magazine, Vol. 19, No. 46 (November 27, 2004). Available online at http://www.worldmag.com/articles/9987.

20. Douglas Coupland, *Life After God* (New York: Scribner, 2002), 359.

21. Philip Hallie, *Lest Innocent Blood Be Shed* (Philadelphia: Harper & Row, 1979), 2, cited by Eleonore Stump in her essay "The Mirror of Evil," Thomas V. Morris, ed., *God and the Philosophers* (New York: Oxford University Press, 1994), 244.

22. Ibid., 241–42.

23. Stump, "The Mirror of Evil," 240, 242.

24. Malcolm Muggeridge, *A Twentieth Century Testimony* (Nashville: Thomas Nelson, 1978), 72.

25. Hayward, "Question."

CHAPTER 10: CROSS-CULTURAL CHALLENGES—I'CHING THOMAS

1. Harold A Netland, *Encountering Religious Pluralism: The Challenge to Christian Faith and Mission* (Downers Grove, IL: InterVarsity, 2001), 250.

2. This is a lengthy subject that we cannot explore here, but a helpful discussion of it can be found in James Sire's book *Naming the Elephant: Worldview as a Concept* (Downers Grove, IL: InterVarsity, 2004).

3. Lit-Sen Chang, *Asia's Religions: Christianity's Momentous Encounter with Paganism* (New Jersey: China Horizon/Horizon Ministries Canada, 1999), 53. For more on this subject within Islam and Buddhism/Confucianism, see Norman L. Geisler and Abdul Saleeb, *Answering Islam: The Crescent in the Light of the Cross* (Grand Rapids: Baker, 1993) and Michael C. Brannigan, *The Pulse of Wisdom: The Philosophies of India, China and Japan*, 2nd ed. (Belmont, CA.: Wadsworth, 2000).

4. "Hell," Walter A. Elwell, ed., *Baker Theological Dictionary of the Bible* (Grand Rapids: Baker, 1996), 338.

5. Lesslie Newbigin, *The Gospel in a Pluralist Society* (Grand Rapids: Eerdmans, 1989), 4.

6. Netland, *Encountering Religious Pluralism*, 282.

7. Ibid., 280–81.

8. The Hungry Ghost Festival is an annual event celebrated by traditional Chinese to venerate the dead.

9. Daniel Tong, *A Biblical Approach to Chinese Traditions and Beliefs* (Singapore: Genesis Books, 2003), 60–77.

10. While Taoism and Confucianism are often perceived as opposing schools of thought, they are also generally accepted as two complementary sides of human nature. For example, Taoism stresses a human's relationship with nature and highlights our intuitive faculties, whereas Confucianism emphasizes reason and a human's relationship with others in pursuit of communal harmony. Basically, these two philosophies, when held together, seek to maintain the harmony of man's various relationships—with oneself, with nature, and with fellow man. See Michael C. Brannigan, *The Pulse of Wisdom: The Philosophies of India, China and Japan*, 2nd ed. (Belmont, CA.: Wadsworth, 2000), 23–24.

11. I was informed that subsequently this lady resolved her dilemma by trusting the fate of her mother in the loving hands of God and took the step of faith to become a Christian.

12. Chang, *Asia's Religions*, 55.

13. Ou Yang Hsiu, as quoted in Chang, *Asia's Religions*, 55.

14. Chang, *Asia's Religions*, 55.

15. Netland, *Encountering Religious Pluralism*, 282.

16. Harold A Netland, *Dissonant Voices: Religious Pluralism and the Question of Truth* (Grand Rapids: Eerdmans, 1991), 152–53.

17. Netland, *Encountering Religious Pluralism*, 12.

18. Ibid.

19. Netland, *Dissonant Voices*, 151–52.

20. Malaysia, for example, has legal restrictions on proselytizing among Muslims stated in its Federal Constitution (Article 11, Clause 4).

21. Netland, *Dissonant Voices*, 154.

22. Saying that a religion "works" raises all sorts of difficult and interesting questions that we cannot pursue here. What does it mean to say that a religion "works"? How do we know that it's *true* that it works instead of merely *seeming* to work, or is that question itself insignificant if the *belief* that the religion works *works* for the believer? Does the "work" that the belief accomplishes come with a *warranty*? How long is it guaranteed to work? A month? Five years? Your lifetime? Forever?

23. Os Guinness, *Time for Truth* (Leicester, England: InterVarsity, 2000), 83–84.

24. In the context of Christianity, to say that the gospel works means that God's plan to redeem mankind through the work of Christ will be accomplished. The vision of redeemed humanity in Revelation 7 is the Christian's certain hope. Those who put their trust in Christ will be part of that great throng before the throne. Regardless of what happens in this life (and Jesus promises hardship), putting one's faith in Jesus is efficacious—in other words, it works—to save the believer—and that's guaranteed forever (2 Tim. 1:12).

25. Netland, *Encountering Religious Pluralism*, 282.

26. Ibid., 247–48.

27. Ibid., 13.

28. I highly recommend D. A. Carson's *The Gagging of God: Christianity Confronts Pluralism* (Grand Rapids: Zondervan, 1996) for an instructive discussion on this passage in relation to cross-cultural evangelism.

29. James W Sire, *Why Good Arguments Fail: Making a More Persuasive Case for Christ* (Downers Grove, IL: InterVarsity, 2006), 140.

30. See Don Richardson, *Peace Child* (Ventura, CA: Regal, 1990).

31. Newbigin, *The Gospel in a Pluralist Society*, 13.

32. Netland, *Dissonant Voices*, 286.

33. Michael Green, *Asian Tigers for Christ* (London: Society for Promoting Christian Knowledge, 2001), 36.

34. Carson, *The Gagging of God*, 510.

35. Netland, *Encountering Religious Pluralism*, 251.

CHAPTER 11: THE TRINITY AS A PARADIGM FOR SPIRITUAL TRANSFORMATION—L. T. JEYACHANDRAN

1. Colin E. Gunton, *Act and Being* (London: SCM Press, 2002). The total thrust of his book is that whatever we know of God's being is through his activity in creation and history. Because of his perfection in

every aspect of life, there is no dichotomy between what he is and what he does. Description of God's attributes in abstract and negative terms does injustice to God's concrete, direct action in history.

2. Karl Rahner, quoted in Robert Letham, *The Holy Trinity* (Phillipsburg, NJ: R&R Publishing Co., 2004), 4.

3. See, for example, Roger E. Olson and Christopher A. Hall, *The Trinity* (Grand Rapids: Eerdmans, 2002), 95–115.

4. Bruce A. Ware, *Father, Son and Holy Spirit: Relationship, Roles & Relevance* (Wheaton, IL: Crossway, 2005), 16; emphasis in original.

5. Letham, *The Holy Trinity*, 25.

6. Title of one of Dr. Ravi Zacharias's audio CDs.

7. It is not possible, philosophically, to conceive of more than one independent, infinite entity. In polytheisms, this problem is actually seen as each of the many gods has to be finite and limited in power and jurisdiction.

8. Letham, *The Holy Trinity*, 17–85.

9. Olson and Hall, *The Trinity*, 13–79; Letham, *The Holy Trinity*, 87–268.

10. The seed thoughts on these aspects are briefly but ably treated by Francis Schaeffer in *He Is There and He Is Not Silent* (first published in 1972) and is now part of *The Complete Works of Francis Schaeffer: A Christian Worldview, Volume 1, A Christian View of Philosophy and Culture* (Wheaton, IL: Crossway, 1982), 277–344.

11. See Stanley J. Grenz, *The Social God and the Relational Self* (Louisville, KY: John Knox Press, 2001), 4. I would, however, hold that relationality and substantiality have both to be emphasized in God as well as human beings and not the former at the expense of the latter. Only in that way can we see the mutual importance of *both* the individual *and* the community.

12. For an eloquent treatment of this subject and its application to the significance of human beings, see Colin E. Gunton, *The One, the Three and the Many* (Cambridge, UK: Cambridge University Press, 1993), chapter 7.

13. Colin E. Gunton, *Becoming and Being* (London: SCM Press, 2001), 35–55. This volume is Gunton's rebuttal of the fatal flaws that result from the process theology of Charles Hartshorne.

14. Gunton, *The One, the Three and the Many*, 6, 16–21.

15. Further, it is so common for people to espouse a moral value without being able to provide a basis for it!

16. *The God Who Is There* is the title of Francis Schaeffer's first of three books; the others are *He Is There and He Is Not Silent*, and *Escape from Reason*. They are often referred to as a trilogy of his apologetics.

17. Michael Polanyi, *Personal Knowledge* (Chicago: The University of Chicago Press, 1974).

18. Bernhardt S. Ingemann (1826), "Through the Night of Doubt and Sorrow," trans. by Sabine Baring-Gould in *The People's Hymnal*, 1867.

19. Guillermo Gonzalez and Jay Richards, *The Privileged Planet: How Our Place in the Cosmos Is Designed for Discovery* (Washington, DC: Regnery, 2004). A DVD of the same title is also available. I find the title fascinating and disturbing at the same time because it says something about my responsibility for this amazing planet! Gonzalez and Richards are part of the Intelligent Design movement and make a strong plea that belief in an intelligent Designer actually promotes the growth of knowledge by providing a valid incentive for research. Atheists such as the late astronomer Carl Sagan of Cornell and biologist Richard Dawkins of Oxford have averred that belief in an intelligent, knowledgeable God will stunt the progress of true science.

20. Alister McGrath, *A Passion for Truth: The Intellectual Coherence of Evangelicalism* (Downers Grove, IL: InterVarsity, 1996), 91.

21. Gene Edward Veith Jr., *Postmodern Times* (Wheaton, IL: Crossway, 1994), 144.

CHAPTER 12: THE ROLE OF DOUBT AND PERSECUTION IN SPIRITUAL TRANSFORMATION—STUART McALLISTER

1. Dietrich Bonhoeffer, *Letters*, 17, 370, quoted in Roger Lundin, *From Nature to Experience: The American Search for Cultural Authority* (Lanham, MD: Rowman & Littlefield, 2005), 40.

2. C. S. Lewis quoted in Richard Purtill, *C. S. Lewis's Case for the Christian Faith* (San Francisco, Ignatius Press, 2004), 53.

Notes

3. Alister E. McGrath, *The Mystery of the Cross* (Grand Rapids: Zondervan, 1988), 102.
4. McGrath, *The Mystery of the Cross,* 104.
5. Leslie Stevenson and David L. Heberman, *Ten Theories of Human Nature* rev. ed. (Oxford University Press, 1998).
6. Ibid, 8.
7. Ibid.
8. C. S. Lewis, *The Lion, the Witch, and the Wardrobe* (New York: HarperCollins, 2005), 81.
9. Ibid, 30.
10. Ibid, 126.

CHAPTER 13: IDOLATRY, DENIAL, AND SELF-DECEPTION: HEARTS ON PILGRIMAGE THROUGH THE VALLEYS—DANIELLE DURANT

1. Esther Lightcap Meek, *Longing to Know: The Philosophy of Knowledge for Ordinary People* (Grand Rapids: Brazos Press, 2003), 99.
2. John Calvin, *Institutes of Christian Religion, The Library of Christian Classics,* vol. XX, ed., John T. McNeill (Philadelphia: The Westminster Press, 1960), 35.
3. Greg Bahnsen, "The Crucial Concept of Self-Deception in Presuppositional Apologetics" in *Westminster Theological Journal* LVII (1995): 1–31. Available online at http://www.cmfnow.com/articles/pa207.htm).
4. Marilynne Robinson, *Housekeeping* (New York: Picador, 2004), 3; emphasis added. Readers of *Just Thinking* may recall that a portion of this introductory material appeared in a similar form in my article "Praying with Our Eyes Closed," Spring/Summer 2005.
5. Ibid., 194.
6. Ibid., 116.
7. Meek, *Longing to Know,* 99.
8. Catherine Marshall, *Adventures in Prayer* (Grand Rapids: Chosen Books, 1996), chapter 1.
9. Ibid., 17.
10. F. F. Bruce, *Romans: Tyndale New Testament Commentaries* (Grand Rapids: Eerdmans, 1985), 77; emphasis added.
11. Michael Polanyi, *The Tacit Dimension* (Garden City, NY: Doubleday, 1969), 172.
12. Bruce, *Romans,* 77–78; emphasis added.
13. Luke Timothy Johnson, *Faith's Freedom: A Classic Spirituality for Contemporary Christians* (Minneapolis: Augsburg Fortress, 1990), 61. I am indebted to my former colleague Bill Smith for introducing me to Johnson's work on idolatry; see Smith's article "The Dynamic of Idolatry: The Work of Luke T. Johnson with Implications for Psychotherapy," *Journal of Psychology and Christianity* 15, no. 1 (1996): 5–16.
14. Dick Keyes, "The Idol Factory," in *No God but God: Breaking with the Idols of Our Age,* edited by Os Guinness and John Seel (Chicago: Moody, 1992), 32.
15. Ibid., 45, 31–32.
16. Johnson, *Faith's Freedom,* 61.
17. I am indebted to a wise mentor for making this observation.
18. Johnson, *Faith's Freedom,* 65.
19. Ibid., 62.
20. Jill Carattini, "Questioning Gabriel," *A Slice of Infinity,* http://www.rzim.org/slice/slicetran.php?sliceid=1307.
21. Keyes, 48
22. Simone Weil, *Waiting on God* (London: Routledge & K. Paul, 1952), 139.
23. Dan B. Allender and Tremper Longman III, *The Cry of the Soul: How Our Emotions Reveal Our Deepest Questions About God* (Colorado Springs: NavPress, 1994), 34, 35.
24. Os Guinness, *God in the Dark: The Assurance of Faith Beyond a Shadow of a Doubt* (Wheaton, IL: Crossway Books), 149.
25. Ibid., 150.
26. Ibid., 70.
27. Ibid., 151.

28. Beth Moore, "Who Do You Trust?" part 2 (video lecture), available at http://www.lifetoday.org/site/DocServer/2-21-07.doc?docID=686.

29. Ibid.

30. Guinness, *God in the Dark,* 69; emphasis added.

31. Sam Harris, "God's Dupes," *The Los Angeles Times* (15 March 2007), available at http://www.samharris.org/site/full_text/gods-dupes1/.

32. In a *Los Angeles Times* interview with Sam Harris, *Times* staff writer Gina Piccalo observes, "In the world of ideas, Harris is valued as much for insulting both the delicate 'we are one' sensibilities of the liberal left and the Christian tenets of the conservative right. He argues with equal fervor against multiculturalism, religious tolerance, the piety of Christian missionaries (whom he considers 'genocidal'), and the 'moral intuitions' of Mother Teresa (which he calls 'deranged')." See "Oh, Dear God It's Him Again," *The Los Angeles Times* (2 October 2006).

33. Sigmund Freud, *Civilization and Its Discontents,* ed. and trans. J. Strachey (New York: Norton, 1961), 30, quoted in Paul Copan, "Is Atheism a Psychological Crutch?" unpublished paper.

34. "Is Christianity Good for the World?" Christopher Hitchens and Douglas Wilson debate, part 5, http://www.christianitytoday.com/ct/2007/mayweb-only/121-52.0.html.

35. Richard Dawkins quoted in Alister McGrath (with Joanna Collicutt McGrath), *The Dawkins Delusion: Atheist Fundamentalism and the Denial of the Divine* (London: SPCK, 2007), 1, 40.

36. Ibid., xi.

37. Ibid., 34–35.

38. Herbert Fingarette, *Self-Deception: With a New Chapter* (Berkeley: University of California Press, 2000), 29.

39. Ibid., 28.

40. Ibid., 44.

41. Ibid., 42, 48.

42. Ibid., 48-49.

43. Tennessee Williams, "Something by Tolstoi," *Collected Stories* (New York: New Directions Books, 1985), 17–25.

44. Bahnsen, "The Crucial Concept of Self-Deception in Presuppositional Apologetics," emphasis added.

45. I am again indebted to a wise mentor for this important observation.

46. Gordon Wenham, *Genesis 16–50,* WBC 2 (Dallas: Word, 1994), 399.

47. Calvin, *Institutes of Christian Religion, The Library of Christian Classics,* vol. XX, 37.

48. Viv Thomas, *Second Choice: Embracing Life As It Is* (Milton Keynes, UK: Paternoster Press, 2000), 64.

CHAPTER 14: THE CHURCH'S ROLE IN APOLOGETICS AND THE DEVELOPMENT OF THE MIND—RAVI ZACHARIAS

1. An important fine-tuning of this has been done by Norman L. Geisler in his book *Christian Apologetics* (Grand Rapids: Baker, 1988). See his chapter 8, "Formulating Adequate Tests for Truth."

2. C. S. Lewis, *The Great Divorce* (New York: Collier Books, 1946), 80–81.

3. C. S. Lewis, *God in the Dock: Essays on Theology and Ethics* (Grand Rapids: Eerdmans, 1994), 210.

4. Peter Kreeft, *Three Philosophies of Life* (San Francisco: Ignatius Press, 1989), 54.

5. William Barclay, *The Letters to the Corinthians,* Daily Bible Study Series, rev. ed. (Philadelphia: Westminster, 1975), 2.

6. William Temple, *Readings in St. John's Gospel* (London: Macmillan, 1940), 68.

JESUS AMONG OTHER GODS
978-0-8499-4327-0

In a world with so many religions, why Jesus?

We are living in a time when you can believe anything, as long as you do not claim it to be true. Each chapter of the unique book, Zachrias considers a unique claim that Jesus made and then contrasts the truth of Jesus with the founders of Islam, Hinduism, and Buddhism with compelling insight and passionate conviction.

Also Available: Jesus Among Other Gods Youth Edition ISBN: 978-08499-4217-4

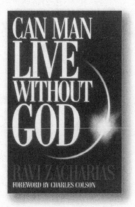

CAN MAN LIVE WITHOUT GOD
978-0-8499-4528-1

In this brilliant apologetic defense of the Christian faith—the likes of which we haven't seen since C.S. Lewis—Ravi Zacharias exposes the emptiness of life without God, discussing subjects including antitheism, the meaning of life, and the person of Jesus.

CRIES OF THE HEART
978-0-8499-4387-4

One of the greatest thinkers of our time covers new ground by exploring the deepest cries of the human heart. Through moving stories and relevant questions, Ravi Zacharias invites readers to join him in finding answers to the question: How can things be right when they feel so wrong?

DELIVER US FROM EVIL
978-0-8499-3950-1

In this compelling volume, Ravi Zacharias examines the mystery of evil. This brilliant writer and gifted teacher traces how secularization has led to a loss of shame, pluralization has lead to a loss of reason, and privatization has lead to a loss of meaning.